Early Reviews of
Treasure Island: The Untold Story

"John Amrhein's *Treasure Island: The Untold Story* is a superlative example of historical fact being well balanced through the use of fictional narrative in order to create a dialogue animating the truth behind Robert Louis Stevenson's *Treasure Island*. Above and beyond the intensive research that Amrhein conducted to develop the entire story, as well as his uncanny ability to connect events and people through time, this work is also a genuine contribution to the scholarly field of knowledge about maritime history during the 18th century. Ultimately, Amhrein's work serves as a compendium of historical fact and events surrounding a story that has captured the imaginations of both young and old for nearly a century and a half."

—James Perry, Archivist & Historian, Monterey County Historical Society

"Tales about Ocracoke Island, Hyde Co., North Carolina have always been of interest to us. This one is fascinating. Not only does this story bring *Treasure Island* alive in an exciting new way but documents Ocracoke's contribution to one of the greatest adventure stories of all time. It is a privilege and a pleasure to recommend this intriguing book."

—Isabelle Homes, President, Hyde County Historical & Genealogy Society

"Anyone interested in piracy and Stevenson's *Treasure Island* will enjoy it and find new material and a fresh perspective."

—Dr. Patrick Scott, Director, Irvin Department of Rare Books & Special Collections (includes the Robert Louis Stevenson Collection) and Distinguished Professor of English, Emeritus, University of South Carolina

"The story would have been known to Stevenson's ancestors who lived in St. Kitts. The narratives that would have entered family oral tradition may have inspired a great deal of the fiction that Stevenson created in *Treasure Island*. *Treasure Island: the Untold Story* is another page in the island's mostly unknown history."

—Victoria O'Flaherty, Director, The National Archives of St. Kitts

"*Treasure Island: The Untold Story* is a well written, thoroughly researched, unbiased tale of intrigue, treachery, passion, love, and real-life decisions. The history is well presented and the accompanying photographs, documents, and prints let the reader go back to the past and relive this great sea adventure. I can truly say that this the best book I have ever read about pirates! Read it and you will relive it!"

—Charles George, *Wreck Diving Magazine*

"What an adventure! The author's thorough research and meticulous attention to detail is skillfully woven with humanizing snippets of information that bring his historical characters to life. The reader, with any interest in harsh maritime life on the high seas on the Caribbean and Atlantic seaboards in the mid 18th century, gets a tantalizing glimpse into how challenging it must have been. The real joy to any St. Christophile is, of course, the fascinating "behind the scenes" tour of the making of Robert Louis Stevenson's *Treasure Island*. The links to the Caines Plantation, Dieppe Bay, and downtown Basseterre all bring Mr. Stevenson's story to life in a way not imagined by the author but much appreciated by anyone with an interest in the history of the island."

—Daisy Mottram, Honorary Secretary, St. Christopher (St. Kitts) National Trust

This Book Belongs To:
ALBERT J. MEYER, JR

TREASURE ISLAND

TREASURE ISLAND
The Untold Story

By John Amhrein, Jr.

New Maritima Press, LLC

Copyright 2012 by John Amhrein. No portion of this book may be reproduced in any form whatsoever without written permission from the publisher.

LCCN 2010915642

ISBN-10 0983084300

ISBN-13 9780983084303

New Maritima Press, LLC
P.O. Box 1918
Kitty Hawk, North Carolina 27949
www.newmaritimapress.com

Table of Contents

List of Illustrations Part One	viii
Acknowledgements	xi
The Piece of Eight	xiii
Introduction	xv
Part One: Treasure Island	
Chapter One: Owen Lloyd, Privateer	1
Chapter Two: Pieces of Eight	11
Chapter Three: Ocracoke: Pirate's Lair	27
Chapter Four: Blackbeard's Last Prize	35
Chapter Five: The Voyage	61
Chapter Six: Treasure Island	67
Chapter Seven: The Unfortunate Spaniard	93
Chapter Eight: The Empty Gallows	105
Chapter Nine: The Governors' Greed	111
Chapter Ten: Silver and the Embassies	139
Part Two: Return to Treasure Island	
Chapter Eleven: Return to Treasure Island	167
Chapter Twelve: Stevenson's Last Book	205
Chapter Thirteen: The Hunt for Lloyd	233
Epilogue: And Last	310
Bibliography	312
End Notes	323

List of Illustrations
Part One

Credits for Images, Chapters One through Ten

Chapter One: Adapted from *A map of the most inhabited part of Virginia containing the whole province of Maryland with part of Pennsylvania, New Jersey and North Carolina. Drawn by Joshua Fry & Peter Jefferson in 1751.* Courtesy of the Library of Congress.

Chapter Two: Plan of Vera Cruz, *London Magazine*, July 1762.

Chapter Three: LEFT: *A New and Accurate Map of the Province of North and South Carolina, Georgia, etc, Emanuel Bowen, 1747*, courtesy of the North Carolina State Archives, Raleigh.
RIGHT: *A New and Correct Map of the Province of North Carolina by Edward Moseley, late surveyor general of the said province 1733*, Moseley Map (#MC0017), with permission the Special Collections Department, J. Y. Joyner Library, East Carolina University, Greenville, North Carolina, USA.

Chapter Four: Capture of the Pirate, Blackbeard, 1718 depicting the battle between Blackbeard the Pirate and Lieutenant Maynard in Ocracoke Bay. Jean Leon Gerome Ferris, 1920.

Chapter Five: Frank R. Stockton, *Buccaneers and Pirates of Our Coasts.* The MacMillan Company, Ltd., London, 1919.

Chapter Six: Adapted from Thomas Jefferys', *West India Atlas* of 1775, courtesy of the Library of Congress.

Chapter Seven: *Wreck of the Nuestra Señora de los Remedios (alias La Ninfa)* a Prize to the Royal Family Privateers taken 5 February 1746 and Lost in November following near Beach Head on the Coast of Sussex engraved by John Boydell, 1753. With permission and copyright, Greenwich Maritime Museum.

Chapter Eight: View of St. Eustatius courtesy of the Nationaal Archief, The Netherlands. Invr. 310.

Chapter Nine: View of Basseterre, St. Kitts from Thomas Coke, *History of the West Indies…*, Volume III.

Chapter Ten: Londinum [sic] - Urbs Praecipua Regni Angliae: 18th century, Anonymous. With permission and copyright, the Museum of London.

For Delphine.

The World owes you for this one.

Acknowledgements

There are many who have contributed along the way to make this an unforgettable story. Without my wife Delphine, this would not have been possible with her intuition, critical commentary, and her love and support. My children, Shane and Madeline, added an important dimension, and my daughter-in-law, Liv Cook, made an important contribution. My researchers worked diligently to bring this international event to print. Thanks again to Victoria Stapells who has been with me for thirty years in scouring the archives of Spain as well as her assistants, Genoveva Enriquez Macias, Esther Gonzáles Pérez, and Guadalupe Fernández Morente. In England, Tim Hughes, Simon Niziol, Peter Galagher, and Dianne Strang probed the archives and libraries of London. Maggi Blythin, Lona Jones and Gill Winstanley searched the archives and libraries of Wales while Bronwyn Curnow at the Powys County Registrar and Catherine Richards of the Powys County Archives made their own contributions. Alan McLeod followed Stevenson's trail in Scotland and Laurence Harvey provided photographs. Victoria O'Flaherty opened fragile documents for me at the archives of St. Kitts and was always available to answer my questions. Lindon Williams formerly of the St. Christopher's Heritage Society provided research assistance and Carla Astaphan provided pictures of Shadwell. Also, thanks to Yvette Caines who shared her family history. Dr. Marion Blair of the Antigua and Barbuda National Archives readily answered my questions. In Denmark, Peter Phister made some truly remarkable finds and Dr. Birgit Christensen supplied the end game with valuable translations and more document finds. Erik Gøbel of the Danish National Archives provided guidance and Henriette Gavnholdt Jakobsen, archivist at the Danish Maritime Museum, supplied the eighteenth century engraving of St. Croix. Spencer and Jeanie Oliver also helped with some translations. Nicole Brandt and Victor van den Bergh of the National Archives of the Netherlands made some extremely valuable and unexpected finds while Anne Lee of europeantranslation.net translated, not only the Dutch documents, but French as well. John Flora handled California and the Stevenson connection there. "Joyce Cox investigated the Nevada connection." Carol Carine travelled the windy roads at the Isle of Man. To Pam Coronado, my psychic investigator, who never ceases to amaze me. Others who volunteered: The Joyner Library East Carolina University, Adrienne Bell, Etherington Conservation Services, The Museum of London, the Greenwich Maritime Museum, Verna Penn Moll answered my questions about the records in Tortola, Catherine and Donald Mahew, Addison Richardson and Don Mitchell of Anguilla, and Gray Curtis of the Scituate Historical Society. Ken and Beth Wynne helped me with the genealogical collections of the Mormon Church. Special thanks to Captain Dave DeCuir of *Antiquity* who took me and my family on many great adventures at Treasure Island. To my editors, I owe a great deal: Connie Buchanan, Ann Buskirk, Buddy Hullet, Pam Banks, and Marilyn Wyscarver. To Robert Pruett and his great staff at Brandylane Publishers. Thanks to Andrea White of sykesvilledesign.com for the website. To Jim Breashears who made some good suggestions and for his enthusiasm for the story. There would have been no treasure buried at Treasure Island without the miraculous intervention of Father Junípero Serra and St. Barbara who saved the galleon. And most importantly, to the One who wrote this story as I am only the messenger.

For the many sources used in this book, please consult the Notes and Bibliography at the end.

The Piece of Eight

arried in galleons from the New World to Spain, the Spanish piece of eight was a coin recognized throughout the world in the Colonial Period for its beauty and consistency in silver content. The early versions of the coin were made by cutting pieces off of a flattened bar of silver, weighed, then stamped with the coat of arms of the ruling Spanish monarch. These coins were called cobs, derived from "cut of the bar." The big drawback of this type of coinage was that because of their irregular shape, people would cut or chisel off pieces of the coin and still attempt to pass them off at full value. The term "chiseler" is still used today to describe a cheater or a swindler. Merchants and many individuals had their own money scales during this period to protect themselves from chiseled or counterfeit coins.

In 1732, the problem was solved by manufacturing or milling coins with machinery, producing uniform coins similar in quality to those of today. The coins were perfectly round and had a patterned edge. One side of the coin featured the Spanish Coat of Arms, on the other twin globes flanked by the Pillars of Hercules along with the year of minting. The coins also came to be known as "Pillar Dollars." The peso, piastre, or the piece of eight, would become the model for the American dollar. The term "bits" replaced "reales." Two bits would become the quarter, and four bits a fifty cent piece.

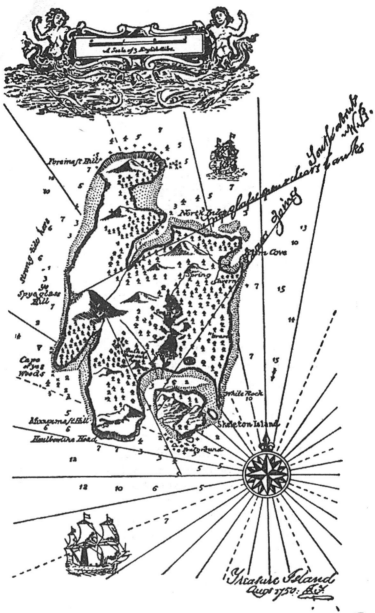

Introduction

It happened in 1750. It was the year that Western civilization started its recovery from a conflict, commonly known as King George's War, between the great powers of England and Spain that had lasted nine years and left many in physical, psychological or financial ruin. It was also in this year that a wealthy Spanish captain named Juan Manuel Bonilla and two Englishmen, Owen Lloyd and his one-legged brother, John, would chance to meet at sea. These former enemies were diverted from their respective courses by a fearful West Indian hurricane. A huge treasure would soon change hands—involuntarily.

The incredible chain of events that began to unfold in the aftermath of this fateful encounter would lead to the burial of Spanish treasure on an uninhabited Caribbean island, and the electrifying aftermath would be remembered for many years to come. The most famous treasure map in the world, dated August 1750, would become the inspiration for a tale that would entertain millions of youngsters and adults alike for the next century. The map would also propel a struggling unknown writer to the limelight, making his name one of the most recognized in literary history: Robert Louis Stevenson.

Part One

Treasure Island

There is a tide in the affairs of men, which, taken at the flood, leads to fortune.

— William Shakespeare

Chapter One
Owen Lloyd, Privateer

Norfolk, Virginia, June 1746

"Until death do us part," repeated Owen Lloyd as he gazed into the joyful eyes of his bride, Christian. When Reverend Smith declared them man and wife, applause echoed from the pews of the Borough Church as the newlyweds turned to make their exit. Owen was beaming while Christian smiled tearfully at the friends and family who extended their hands as the couple walked by. In attendance were many merchants and sea captains who were friends of Lloyd, as he too was a ship owner and merchant. Behind them was Charles Caines, Christian's brother, who had come in from St. Christopher's, an island in the Caribbean, to give his sister in marriage. Their father had passed away nine years before. Charles was followed by Owen's best man, his older brother, John, who hobbled along on his wooden leg, an uncomfortable replacement for the one he had recently lost in an engagement with a Spanish ship. At that moment, the American Colonies were at war, often subjected to attacks and ship seizures from French and Spanish privateers who not only patrolled the coast, but also ventured inside the Chesapeake Bay to pillage and terrify the inhabitants. This war that had been waged for the past seven years between England, Spain, France and other European nations would become known as King George's War. Even in the comfort of a house of God, the parishioners were mindful of this constant threat.

The hazard of the Spanish and French privateers was of little concern to Owen. He not only dodged the enemy ships as he routinely traded between Virginia and St. Christopher's, more commonly known as St. Kitts, bringing back rum, sugar, and molasses, but he had made a daring capture as a privateer the year before.

Lloyd was captain of the sloop, *Elizabeth*, owned by Nicholas Gibbons, plantation owner at Dieppe Bay, a small village located on the north end of

St. Kitts. Lloyd began his employment with Gibbons by making trading runs between Boston and Ocracoke Inlet, North Carolina, and St. Kitts. In July 1744, he arrived at Boston from St. Kitts to find that war had been declared by England against France. Spain and England had been at war since 1739. With France in the war, the English settlements in the Leeward Islands were at risk because of the neighboring French islands of Martinique, St. Martin's, and St. Bartholomew's. Lloyd remained in Boston until late September, having to secure a cargo destined for Gibbons' plantation. As he idled in Boston, he kept abreast of the news and the actions of the Spanish privateers on the American coast. He also read with great interest the many accounts of Spanish treasure being seized by English and American privateers. In his daydreams, he captured many treasure-laden Spanish galleons.

When Lloyd arrived at St. Kitts, he found that a proclamation had been issued at Antigua for privateers to combat the hostilities of the French now being perpetrated on the English in the Leeward Islands. Gibbons and Lloyd planned a cruise, hoping to encounter the enemy and capture a valuable prize. The *Elizabeth* was not a large vessel, only sixty tons, armed with eight cannon and carrying a twelve-man crew. While off the coast of Martinique in April 1745, Lloyd spotted a lone vessel flying French colors. As he approached from the leeward, he recognized the stench of human cargo–it was a French slave ship from Angola. He ordered his crew to stations and fired a broadside at the slaver. Although the Frenchman was a much larger ship and a superior force, they dropped their colors and then their sails. When Captain Lloyd boarded, he found that, besides 362 slaves, she was loaded with gold dust, dry goods, and elephant tusks. She proved to be a very valuable prize.

When he returned to Gibbons' plantation, he was welcomed as a hero as he had greatly enriched the already prosperous sugar planter. There was great celebration and Lloyd had earned enough from that seizure to buy the *Elizabeth*. Gibbons' neighbor, Charles Caines, who maintained his own plantation on the opposite side of the village, was there to help celebrate. With him was his recently widowed sister, Christian. Christian was taken with Lloyd from the very beginning. He was thirty at the time and quite handsome. She admired his courage and devoured every word as he related his adventures.

Owen Lloyd was equally attracted to her. He was also attracted to the Caines plantation, where he saw opportunity. The plantation had been run by Christian's twenty-year-old brother Charles and their mother Frances since her father died. The Caines family was politically prominent and well known on the island. On the plantation were a great house, servants' quarters, boiling house, stable, windmill, and a warehouse that stored the sugar, molasses, and rum that would be shipped to the American Colonies. Before long, Owen and Charles had struck a mutually beneficial business relationship. Owen would ship the rum, molasses, and sugar from the plantation to Virginia and return with peas, corn, and other food crops as well as barrel staves, hoops, and heads to be used in the storage and shipment of rum.

Owen transferred his business interests to Norfolk, where his brother John lived, and registered the *Elizabeth* under Owen Lloyd & Co. of Virginia with the naval officer at Hampton. When Owen returned to St. Kitts in late February of 1746, he found that his status as the local hero had diminished, as another privateer had recently brought in a Spanish snow with 36,000 pieces of eight on board. Before Owen left in June, he witnessed a Spanish galleon brought in by the British warship, HMS *Woolwich*. She was carrying treasure and other cargo worth over one million pieces of eight.

But Owen Lloyd was forced to put the dangers of privateering behind him as he set out for Virginia with Christian, her brother Charles, their slaves, mahogany furniture, and his remaining share of the French Guineaman. He was now a family man and neither Christian nor her brother Charles would approve of his returning to his dangerous pastime.

Owen and John Lloyd were Welshmen born not far from the coast in the town of Rhuddlan in Flint County in northern Wales. They were fortunate enough to come from a well-to-do family. John, six years older than his brother, entered the British Navy in 1720 at the age of eleven when he volunteered as a servant aboard HMS *Adventure* where he saw the Caribbean for the first time. He was following in the footsteps of his uncle, James Lloyd, who had entered the Royal Navy at the same age in 1706. Unfortunately, the year after John went to sea his father became ill and it was believed that he did not have long to live. Owen became the man of the house at age six. Besides his mother, Owen had a sister, Elizabeth, a year older than he, and a younger brother, Vincent, born two years behind him, to look after. Before his father died in 1724, two more sisters were born. Owen thought enviously of the adventures that John was experiencing on British warships and longed for the day when he too could go to sea.

3

John served aboard a number of Royal Navy ships, some of them with his uncle when he was just a second lieutenant. In November, John Lloyd arrived at Jamaica with his uncle, now a first lieutenant, on HMS *Lyon*. The *Lyon* had left Spithead in June and had made port calls at Madeira and Barbados before her arrival. John was promoted to midshipman when he transferred to HMS *Seaford* where he only served a short time. Uncle James had been promoted to captain and took charge of the sloop-of-war, *Happy*, at Port Royal where John joined him as a midshipman. For the next year, John Lloyd and his uncle were on surveying duty around Jamaica, Cuba, and South Carolina. John left his uncle and the *Happy* at Charleston in March of 1731. His last duty was as a midshipman on HMS *Royal Oak*, a third rate man-of war of seventy-guns on station in Portsmouth, England, where he served until he left the navy in October of 1732.

Earlier that year, Owen decided that it was his turn to join the navy. His family could now fend for themselves. His sister, Elizabeth, was eighteen and his brother, Vincent, was now fifteen. On June 2, 1732, at the age of seventeen, Owen joined his uncle as a midshipman aboard the *Happy* and served until July of 1735. He spent most of his duty in Charleston and then left the *Happy* upon her return to Deptford when he transferred to HMS *Alborough*, serving until his discharge at Whitebooths Bay on the east coast of England in late October of 1735.

Owen and John were serving in the merchant trade when war broke out in 1739. Trading vessels were armed and many captains and ship owners received commissions as privateers to hunt the enemy at will. The Lloyd brothers were not only too old to return to the king's navy as midshipman but they found running their own sloops to be more profitable. It was during this time that John Lloyd lost his left leg as a result of a Spanish cannonball. John's physical wounds healed and he was later fitted with a wooden leg, but John's health, both physical and mental, began to deteriorate.

When Owen arrived in Virginia with his new bride and a promising career as a merchant captain, John was quite envious. It always seemed like his little brother led a charmed life. John was a thirty-eight-year old cripple with no constant companion other than his wooden leg. John and Owen were often at odds with each other.

Owen Lloyd's financial horizon looked bright at first. He had the *Elizabeth*, guaranteed contracts with St. Kitts, and twenty-four slaves that he could sell or lease out. After the wedding, Owen and Christian settled down to a life as routine as could be expected during a war. Owen managed to avoid the Spanish and French privateers patrolling the coast and the islands in the West Indies. He felt lucky. On the other hand, he fretted over his brother John. Since losing his leg, John was having trouble finding suitable work.

Owen was well known in Norfolk as well as in Hampton across the river. He frequented the taverns around the waterfront, drank rum, and regaled the other sailors with tales of his high seas adventures, especially his capture of the French Guineaman. He saw himself in some ways equal to Blackbeard and Black Sam Bellamy, who had both captured French slave ships in 1717, making them their flagships. They too had started out as privateersmen, but Lloyd stopped his fantasy short of ever becoming a pirate. Lloyd, however, missed the thrill of hunting enemy prizes. He was regarded by many as somewhat of a rascal, while others held Owen Lloyd in high regard. He had the ability to lead and persuade. Men and women alike found him to be quite charming.

Owen tended to embellish his stories, even though it usually wasn't necessary and he seemed to always find himself in the middle of some drama. He was known not only as a storyteller but also as a competent mariner. Captain John Hutchings, ship owner, former mayor and councilman for the Borough of Norfolk, was a very successful merchant. He also owned a number of houses and stores on Main Street near the wharf. He hired Owen to captain his ship, the *Rawleigh*, to trade with the West Indies importing rum and sugar from Jamaica and Barbados. This arrangement freed up the *Elizabeth* so that Owen could get John working again. Owen contracted with Alexander MacKenzie, a merchant of Hampton, to send the *Elizabeth* to the Portuguese island of Madeira with a load of wheat in return for a cargo of Madeira wine. John would captain the sloop. MacKenzie insisted that the voyage be as profitable as possible and take on as much of the highly prized wine as the *Elizabeth* could hold. To allow for the extra weight, it was decided to remove the guns from the *Elizabeth*. This was a risky move in the time of war. On March 4, 1747, John Lloyd and the *Elizabeth* cleared customs and arrived weeks later at Madeira, where he traded his cargo for a sloop full of wine. John Lloyd soon departed for his return to Virginia.

The *Elizabeth* traversed the Atlantic without incident, but when she arrived off the Virginia coast, John Lloyd was captured by the notorious Spanish privateer, Don Pedro de Garaicochea. From April to November 1747, over thirty-five English vessels had been captured and carried into Havana. Garaicochea was credited with eleven, which included the *Elizabeth*. John Lloyd was taken to Havana and thrown in the damp dungeon in the coral stone cellars of the Governor's Castle or the Royal Fuerza. The *Elizabeth* was condemned as spoils of war.

Back in Norfolk, Owen Lloyd found out that, not only was his brother not coming home, but his sloop was gone for good. Faced with financial ruin, Owen cooked up a plan. He would try to ransom John out of his Havana prison. To scrape together the needed money, he and Christian mortgaged his slaves to his boss, Captain Hutchings. Soon enough, Owen set sail for Jamaica on the *Rawleigh*.

From Jamaica, Owen sailed with a flag of truce to Havana along with the cash. Governor Francisco Cagigal de la Vega found the money more desirable than a one-legged cripple unfit for physical labor. John was released from prison, leaving behind healthier but less fortunate Englishmen who would labor in mines or crew Spain's shorthanded galleons. Owen Lloyd saw the notorious Garaicochea at work refitting his fleet of privateers, planning his next foray off the Virginia Capes.

In mid-November, Owen departed Kingston, Jamaica, but did not make for Norfolk as planned. Instead, he went to St. Kitts to get medical care for John, who had been ill fed and was weak from his prison stay. Leaving his brother behind, Owen returned to Norfolk in February of 1748. He informed the other captains in Hampton that Garaicochea was planning another attack on English shipping off the Virginia coast.

Without a vessel of his own, Owen Lloyd had to seek positions on other vessels, and there weren't many openings. Hutchings had other vessels in his merchant fleet but there were few vacancies. The *Rawleigh* was sold, leaving Lloyd unemployed. Jobless at the young age of thirty-two, Owen languished in Norfolk. Christian, pampered most of her life at the family plantation on St. Kitts, was forced to mortgage her treasured mahogany furniture to John Hutchings and take up seamstress work. It was a matter of survival.

Life in Virginia was hard on Christian. She still loved Owen, but the promise of a comfortable life had evaporated. The winters were harsh. The Spanish and French privateers still menaced the trade, boldly entering the Chesapeake Bay. British warships had been ordered to the Virginia station as a deterrent, but the privateers continued their harassments nearly at will. The warships HMS *Hector* and HMS *Otter* were now patrolling the Virginia Capes and the Chesapeake Bay and were successful in capturing some of the privateers. The townspeople of Hampton saw hundreds of Spanish prisoners landed and then shipped out to Havana in exchange for Englishmen.

Owen was off to the West Indies that summer in a sloop belonging to Hutchings to bring back rum and sugar. On his return, almost within sight of Hampton, he was captured by a Spanish privateer, along with another vessel belonging to Hutchings. On July 26, while they were at anchor inside Cape Henry, the *Otter*, which had just captured two French privateers and was returning to Hampton with them, came upon the Spanish schooner with the two vessels, which included Owen Lloyd, and fired a broadside. The schooner weighed anchor and fled. Outside the capes, Captain Sam Maisterson, on board HMS *Hector*, heard the cannon firing, which lasted until sunup. He went in pursuit of the schooner and made the capture. Lloyd was free to proceed home.

By August of 1748 word was reaching America about a cessation of hostilities between England, France, Spain, and the Netherlands. There was a lot of celebration on both sides of the Atlantic, but it changed little for the inhabitants of Norfolk and Hampton. Spanish privateers were still threatening their coastal trade. But gradually the cessation was generally honored and the peace treaty at Aix-La-Chapelle was signed on October 18, 1748. Everyone's future looked brighter.

Meanwhile at St. Kitts, John Lloyd regained his strength and was hired to captain the snow, *Polly*, from St. Eustatius, a Dutch island nine miles away from the Caines plantation. He arrived in Philadelphia on the *Polly* on October 31 and then found passage back to Hampton.

In Norfolk, the two brothers got into trouble often, carousing and brawling around the boisterous waterfront taverns. John still resented his younger brother. Despite all of Owen's setbacks, John knew that Owen would overcome and come out on top of things as usual.

That May, Owen scraped together enough money to purchase a house in Hampton. This was a logical location as it was the designated port for customs and ship registration for the lower James River and included the town of Norfolk across Hampton Roads. Hampton was established in 1610 on the site of a former Indian fort. It bordered Hampton River and was laid out on two principle streets. Queen Street ran from the town gate east to the river and ferry landing that would take people, including their horses and carriages, across Hampton Roads to the borough of Norfolk six miles away. King Street ran north to south, intersecting

Queen Street in the center of town where the community well was located. King Street ended at the county wharf at its south end, and along this street were numerous inns and taverns that catered to the mariners, merchants, and common seadogs who arrived from Europe, the West Indies, and other American ports.

The new home of the Lloyd family was located on the north side of Queen Street about a hundred yards from the parish church and the town gate. Christian liked the location because it was removed from the taverns on King Street and was a short walk to the Sunday services of Reverend William Fyfe. Their neighbors were other mariners, merchants, and harbor pilots. It was a peaceful existence, but they were still struggling from financial setbacks heaped on them from the war. On October 19, 1749, they suffered more misfortune. A devastating hurricane struck Virginia and much of the eastern seaboard. In Hampton, houses, warehouses, and piers floated away. Whole trees were ripped out by the roots. Scores of people drowned. The streets of Hampton merged with the river, covered with four feet of water. Dead animals floated amongst the storm debris. In some places, small craft were found a mile from shore. Christian found herself nearly swimming inside their house as the flood waters set to ruining the rest of her possessions. It was the worst storm in the memory of Hampton's oldest residents.

The floodwaters receded and soon Hampton returned to normal. Owen tried once again to persuade his wife that things would get better, but he had no vessel and no meaningful employment. The bills mounted.

In May of 1750, Owen was charged with petty larceny, arrested, and put into the Hampton jail located across the courthouse lawn from his back yard. There were other writs against him and he was sued by Mary Brodie, the daughter of a prominent physician. As a defense, or possibly a bargaining chip, Owen filed his own suit against the doctor's son for trespass and battery.

Owen gained his release through the assistance of his former boss, Captain Hutchings. Hutchings had grown weary of Lloyd but still found him a captivating fellow. Hutchings posted bail and intervened with Sheriff Armistead, who didn't care much for Lloyd in spite of his popularity among the other mariners.

After Owen arrived home from jail, Christian declared that she had had enough. What were once endearing qualities seen in his bravado and charm, she now saw as restlessness and irresponsibility.

She left for St. Kitts on May 23, 1750, aboard the schooner *Peggy*, which was owned by Norfolk's mayor, Durham Hall. She also carried her Negro slave,

Arabella, and her children, and returned to the comfort of the family plantation. Owen was devastated. On the surface, he appeared to be a very independent person, but Christian was, in the language of his trade, the stabilizing ballast in his life. He realized that it was time to leave Virginia and go to St. Kitts and start over there. It was his affection for John that had brought him to Virginia.

Owen tried to persuade John to go with him and start a new business venture, but John was quite hesitant to leave his new bride. In early March of 1750, he had married Elizabeth Hall of Norfolk, where they resided in a tenement on the west side of Church Street not far from the Borough Church. John's marriage brought new happiness, easing his depression and lessening his dependence on Owen. Looking toward his future as a merchant captain, John bought 150 acres of land on a point on the east side of the Pasquotank River in northeastern North Carolina, about forty-five miles away. This region was beginning to prosper and offered a new opportunity for trade.

On August 14, the *Peggy* returned from St. Kitts. Lloyd learned from Captain Ivy that Christian had been delivered safe. Owen began his plans to get to St. Kitts and plead his case with her. He also needed to get out of town because of the pending lawsuit and because he was out of money. He suggested to John that now was the time to get out of Hampton and head for St. Kitts. Despite John's newfound happiness from his recent marriage, he succumbed to Owen's persuasions. He would not take his wife as she and Christian had nothing in common. Christian was educated while Elizabeth could not even sign her own name. John figured he could return soon enough to Norfolk to be with her, so he bought into his brother's schemes one more time.

September 3, 1750

It was hot and the air was heavy with humidity. John and Owen had just left the tavern and headed south for the docks at the end of King Street in the hopes of catching a breeze wafting off the Chesapeake Bay. However, the air was uncommonly still. Even the ever-chattering sea gulls had disappeared. To the south, dark clouds were billowing. The brothers watched. Perhaps a little rain would cool things down. It looked like a thunderstorm, but what was headed their way was a wind that would change their lives forever.

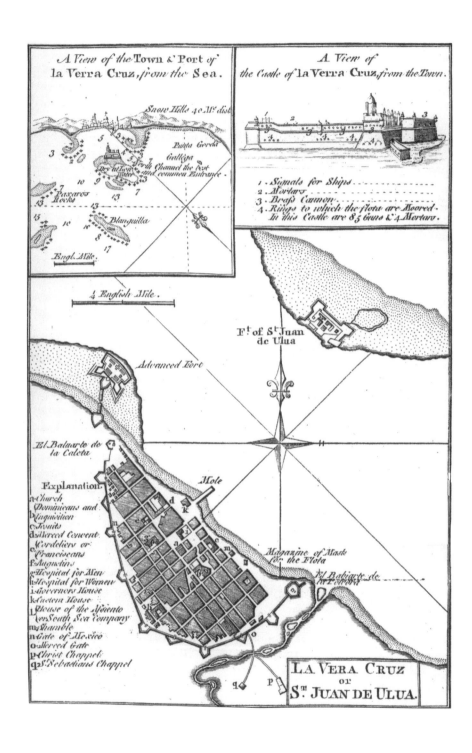

Chapter Two
Pieces of Eight

Vera Cruz, Mexico, May 29, 1750

The tired mule strained at the overloaded wagon, his quivering flanks lathered with sweat as he struggled to pull the load of heavy chests filled with silver coins, popularly called pieces of eight. There were other wagons in front as well as behind him that had been arriving from the mint at Mexico City and from the surrounding regions. Whips cracked and shouts rose above the din as drivers vied for the easiest spot to unload. Goods and supplies of all kinds were being shipped to the galleons moored in the harbor of Vera Cruz. Once again, the treasure train that stretched a half-mile back through town towards the gate in the rear of the city came to a halt. Then, the black muleteer in the lead wagon urged the donkeys forward to position his load of silver for transfer to the waiting treasure ships tied to the stone wharf, known as the mole. Vera Cruz was alive with activity; ships were loading and unloading, others rode at anchor or were moored to the bronze rings embedded in the fortress wall across the harbor. On the merchant galleons and warships of King Ferdinand VI, sailors attended to long overdue repairs to the towering masts, yardarms, and rigging that overshadowed the ships' crowded decks.

Work was slow. The midday sun bore down on the mostly black and shirtless slaves and on the galleon crew as they guided each 200-pound chest into the ship's steamy cargo hold. Grim-faced treasury officials carefully inspected the chests as they were loaded aboard to guarantee that there was no smuggling to avoid the king's taxes. Captains and crews looked for the opportunity to ship cargo that was not registered. Sometimes they took advantage when the officials were distracted or were paid to look the other way. This scene had been played out for centuries. The greedy Spaniards routinely extracted thousands of tons of treasure from the mines manned by overworked Indian and African slaves.

About the streets of Vera Cruz roamed Spanish aristocrats and soldiers, Italian, French, and Irish opportunists, and brown-skinned Indians, remnant of a nearly forgotten Aztec civilization. This city, the gateway to New Spain, or Mexico, as it was now known, was the oldest and richest city on the continent of North America. It had been the major hub of commerce since it was founded by Hernando Cortes in 1519. Through Vera Cruz a steady stream of European goods and slaves flowed and as did nearly all of the mercury needed for the refining of silver. In contrast to these secular excesses, thousands of priests and nuns destined for the churches and monasteries across Mexico began their journey at the docks of Vera Cruz in their mission to convert a heathen population. From this treasure-laden city, not only was all of the gold and silver production of Mexico sent, but also silks, spices, and porcelain ware; and other Far Eastern curiosities from the Philippines were shipped twice a year to Acapulco on the west coast of Mexico and carted over land to Vera Cruz. There was another product that equaled silver in value and was unique to Mexico: a valuable red dye known as cochineal, derived from dried insects that thrived on cactus plants. It was produced in the Oaxaca region west of Vera Cruz. Among its other uses, this popular export gave the British army their brilliant "redcoats."

The approach to Vera Cruz was guarded by La Gallega, a coral reef that lay a half-mile offshore. But the reef was insufficient on its own to protect the valuable treasures stockpiled for shipment to Spain. In the first half of the sixteenth century, the conquistadors realized the need for more armed fortifications. In 1565, tens of thousands of slaves cut huge blocks of brain coral and laid them upon the western edge of the reef. More stone, brick, and coral were added to build what became a fort named San Juan de Ulúa. From this fort, guns were trained seaward as well as back toward the city across the harbor, thus discouraging any direct attack on Vera Cruz by enemy ships. Attached to the base of the exterior walls were large bronze mooring rings for the galleons to moor. It was from here that the largest shipments of treasure left the New World for Spain.

In 1683, the Dutch pirate, Lorencilo, with 800 desperate men, landed and took the city, plundering and terrorizing the inhabitants while locking them inside the churches. He left with valuables worth nearly seven million pieces of eight. Later that year, construction began on a stone wall around the city. The treasure shipments continued.

One galleon now lying at the mole, or wharf, was the *Nuestra Señora de Guadalupe*. Her owner was a Spanish merchant named Juan Manuel Bonilla, who had been waiting for his cargo of treasure and other goods to arrive at the docks since he had entered the harbor the previous December. Bonilla had now been in Vera Cruz months longer than he had anticipated.

At fifty-one years of age, Bonilla was pudgy and had a ruddy complexion influenced by rich food and excessive alcohol consumption. He dressed the part as an aristocratic and prosperous merchant wearing velvet coats over lacy blouses and shiny black leather shoes. His arrogance and elitism made him unpopular with his new crew. Bonilla had hired an able boatswain named Pedro Rodriguez to oversee the men and manage the ship. Rodriguez was dark complected and of Moorish descent, as were most of the crew. It was easy for him to gain the respect of these men as they were of his class—lowly, dark-skinned Moors that were shunned by the fair-skinned Castilians who ruled Spain and monopolized trade.

Bonilla was pacing at the waterfront while observing the final loading of his galleon. He knew that he was running out of time. He still had to stop in Havana, Cuba, before he could begin his journey home. The hurricane season was now upon them, putting his ship and treasure at even greater risk. Frustrated and hot, Bonilla wiped his brow and tucked his handkerchief into his lace-trimmed sleeve. He nodded to Tomás Andrinos y Carriedo, his supercargo and brother-in-law, and walked through the main gate of the city in search of some shade and the company of someone of equal pedigree.

Cádiz, Spain, The Year Before

It was February 1749. There was a great deal of excitement at the docks opposite the plaza of San Juan de Dios, the central plaza of this ancient port city. Juan Manuel Bonilla had recently purchased from Jacob Westerman, a German merchant residing in Cádiz, the frigate called the *Nuestra Señora de Guadalupe*, alias *La Augusta Celi*, for 28,000 pesos. She carried twenty-eight iron cannon on a single deck and was nearly 102 feet long and twenty-six feet wide. At her bow was the figurehead of the mythical nymph. Bonilla was standing with his brother-in-law, Tomás Carriedo, admiring his new ship. They were making plans to load cargo for Vera Cruz.

Bonilla's "new" ship was not new at all, however. She had to undergo an extensive overhaul. The hull, sides, and decks needed caulking, and repairs were required in the masts and rigging. Even the launch that came with the ship needed to be careened. As required by the Crown, an inspection was performed by Ciprian Autran, a high-ranking official in the Real Armada. Autran was charged with determining the vessel's size and dimensions to compute her cargo capacity so that the proper taxes could be levied and to safeguard against the smuggling of undeclared cargo that was rampant among the Spanish merchants. Autran was accompanied by a lawyer and a notary who made the final determination that, including the steerage area, the *Guadalupe* could carry a little over 342 *toneladas*, a measurement of space or volume. With this calculation duly recorded, Carlos Valenciano, the *Contador Mayor* with the House of Trade in Seville, imposed taxes of 55,134 pesos against the ship to be paid into the government bank, the *Depositaria de Indias*.

As if this was not enough, the multi-layered Spanish bureaucracy ordered an additional 685 pesos for the *almirantazgo* tax to be paid. The Spanish king had his heavy hand in every transaction.

Bonilla's voyage to Vera Cruz and subsequent return to Spain with treasure and merchandise was to be his financial salvation. For the past thirty years, Bonilla had traded European goods for treasure in this heavily guarded city. But it had been four years since he had last been to Vera Cruz. His last voyage, in 1747, ended days after his departure from Cádiz, when he was intercepted by English privateers. His current treasure voyage was being undertaken to replenish his bank account and reinstate him into the good graces of his partner in the lost galleon venture. Her name was Angela de Prado y Sarmiento of Seville, Spain; she was Bonilla's mother-in-law.

In spite of the ongoing war between Spain and England, Bonilla and his mother-in-law planned a bold voyage to Vera Cruz loaded with 110 tons of mercury for the silver mines in Mexico on behalf of the Royal Treasury. Their ship was the thirty-six gun *Nuestra Señora de los Remedios*, more commonly know by her alias, *La Ninfa*.

Bonilla and four other merchants were ready to sail in February 1747, but got wind that English privateers, salivating over the rich galleons, were lying in wait for them. Bonilla and the other merchants retired to their homes, or those of friends in and around Cádiz, to wait it out. Commodore George Walker of the *Prince Edward*, informed by a spy in Spain, was aware of their moves. Walker hatched a clever plan. He took his fleet of five privateers, the so-called *Royal Family* of privateers, to Lisbon, Portugal. Each vessel was named after an English prince. Here he pretended to refit and repair his ships by striking his top masts and lowering their yards. He knew that news of this would soon reach Cádiz by way of the Spanish ambassador or merchants in Lisbon with interests in Cádiz. Bonilla took the bait. On February 14, 1747, *La Ninfa*, crewed with 260 men, raised anchor and set sail for Vera Cruz with the four other ships. Bonilla was not in command of his ship, but rather Bernardo del Alamo, who had been hired by Bonilla's mother-in-law on previous voyages to Vera Cruz.

Back in Lisbon, Walker had carefully calculated the time for the news of his pretended refit to reach Cádiz. On the same morning that he estimated the return of Bonilla and the others to their anchored ships in the harbor of Cádiz, he ordered the *Royal Family* to get underway.

On the evening of February 20, Bonilla found Walker's fleet sailing toward them and they were quickly surrounded. Walker fitted out a tender and a barge from the *Prince Edward* and rowed after *La Ninfa*. Bonilla saw no other choice but to surrender. Not a shot was fired.

Bonilla's ship was quickly taken and English guards were placed on board. The captain, crew, and ship were then escorted to Lisbon and the ship's officers interrogated. When news of the capture reached Cádiz, rumors circulated that two prominent English merchants in Cádiz, William Mauman and Anthony Butler, were suspected as the informants to Commodore Walker.

Some of Walker's officers observed that several of the Spanish gentlemen and their ladies traveling as passengers had been aboard another Spanish merchant captured only weeks before. One of the Spaniards remarked to his captor, "O good Señor Englishman! It is very comical indeed. You make as much haste to take us as we make haste to be taken!"

On March 2, *La Ninfa* entered the harbor of Lisbon escorted by her English captors. Lisbon was a neutral port, welcoming both Spanish and English alike. Once there, the Spanish were free to go but many lingered and held a "musick and a ball," inviting the English privateersmen as guests. Dressed in their finest clothes and jewels, they sent a flaunting message to Commodore Walker still out on cruise: their private jewels had escaped him.

On March 25, 1747, Bonilla and Tomás Carriedo left for Cádiz. Bonilla was now in a dilemma. Though his life was not in danger, his future was. He was caught between the merchants who had shipped with him, his English captors with whom he was trying to negotiate a ransom payment for the ship and her cargo, the King of Spain's minister, the Marqués de Ensenada, and his mother-in-law. Bonilla offered 380,000 pieces of eight for the cargo and 20,000 for his ship, which was rejected by the English who had seen his register that listed cargo valued at over one million pesos. After much give and take, the English agreed to return the ship and cargo, exclusive of the king's mercury, for 450,000 pieces of eight. Bonilla failed to close the deal and left Lisbon much to the frustration of the king and some of the merchants. The merchants in Lisbon wanted to buy the cargo directly from the English but they saw the opportunity to squeeze Bonilla into a more lucrative settlement. Bonilla was now telling the *Consulado* in Cádiz that he was about to settle the deal for 300,000 pieces of eight.

Months later, HMS *Bedford*, Captain Townsend, was escorting *La Ninfa* and two other prizes, *Mountfort* and *Agatha*, to Portsmouth, England, when on December 10, they encountered a great storm that cast Bonilla's ship onto the rocks at Beachy Head on the south coast of England. Many of the locals in the area flocked to the wreck. Most of her valuables were saved, but the ship was lost. Bonilla, who was insured, later recovered some of his losses but his profiteering ventures with Vera Cruz were postponed. He did, however, manage to ship goods on other merchant ships in return for chests of silver sent home on Spanish warships.

If it had not been for Bonilla's mother-in-law, with her money and influence, and the help of some investors in Cádiz, Bonilla would not have had the *Guadalupe* for his current voyage to Mexico. He did not let his previous loss discourage him, but he did have difficulty getting merchants to ship with him and finding competent crew. It would be almost a month before anyone took the risk of consigning goods onto the *Guadalupe*. His plan was to get to Vera Cruz as soon as possible so as to return under the guard of the returning Spanish warships. He also wanted to avoid the West Indian hurricanes that posed the greatest threat to his ship now that the war was over.

Bonilla turned the present chore of supervising the loading of cargo over to Carriedo. All that was available at the moment was the cargo of Bonilla's mother-in-law. She registered 60,000 pounds of iron stored in 1,141 barrels on her own account. This dense and heavy cargo made the *Guadalupe* settle too low in the water. He had room for a great deal more cargo so he needed to lighten the ship. Bonilla ordered eight cannon removed, which left him with eight six-pound and twelve four-pound iron cannon to defend his ship. Though his decreased armament was of some concern, the war that raged nine years had finally ended.

Cargo consignments trickled in from March through August: iron manufactures, spices, textiles, wine and spirits, paper, olive oil, vinegar, and other European commodities packed in bales, barrels, and chests, were loaded. Besides the cargo, Bonilla was to carry twenty Franciscan priests destined for the missions of Mexico. The *Guadalupe* was nearly ready to sail.

On August 31, 1749, Bonilla bid farewell to Maria, his wife of fifteen years, and his five children. His youngest and namesake was only fifteen months old. Bonilla owned part of a building in Cádiz where he centered his business interests, but Maria resided in their home in Puerto de Santa Maria across the Bay of Cádiz. After a teary goodbye, he ferried across to his waiting ship. Here he found Carriedo sharing his last moments with his wife Juana, Bonilla's sister.

Bonilla was anxious to get underway and urged Carriedo to finish his goodbyes. Visions of treasure to be loaded at Vera Cruz had already displaced those of the family he had just left. The *Nuestra Señora de Guadalupe* was towed clear of the wharf, hoisted sails, and passed the fort of Santa Catalina, which guarded the harbor mouth of Cádiz. The ship buzzed with excitement. The Franciscan priests, dressed in sandals and full-length habits of brown cloth cinched at the waist with double-knotted ropes, chatted excitedly as they pointed out landmarks and marveled at the sailors as they scampered effortlessly up and down the rigging. Most had never before been to sea. The reality of their voyage began to set in. The *Guadalupe* crew were dressed more comfortably on this summer day. Many were shirtless and barefoot, scurrying about the deck tightening rigging as the sails filled with the Mediterranean breeze. Bonilla strode the quarterdeck in anticipation. It had been two long and difficult years. Everyone on board shared the same vision that lay far away over the blue horizon. They were destined for the Vera Cruz, the oldest and richest city in the New World.

The *Guadalupe* sailed past the Canary Islands that lie 150 miles west of Cape Cantin on the west coast of Africa to pick up the trade winds that would propel them across the Atlantic. Despite some bad weather, they succeeded in crossing the ocean, and on October 18 made a scheduled stop at San Juan, Puerto Rico, to take on water and supplies. On the 31st they departed for Vera Cruz.

Thirty-six days later, on December 1, 1749, the *Guadalupe* was lumbering before the wind when the lookout spotted the mountain behind Vera Cruz, then smoke from the lime kilns south of the city. Hearing the lookout's cry, those not already on deck rushed to get their first glimpse of the fabled city. Soon, the spires of the cathedral and the Convent of San Francisco came into view, followed by the fortress of San Juan de Ulúa and the stone walls that fortified the city. Suddenly, a storm blew in from the north forcing Bonilla to fall off the wind and head for Campeche. Before reaching the safety of that port, the *Guadalupe* was caught in yet another storm on December 3. For two days, the ship was dashed about by towering waves. It was so horrific that, on the following day, the crew mutinied and demanded that Bonilla run the ship ashore to save themselves. The pumps could no longer keep up with the water and everyone despaired except one thirty-six-year-old, short, swarthy priest with black eyes and a scarce beard named Father Junípero Serra. He had remained calm throughout the storms. The priests decided to pick a patron saint to ask for deliverance. It being December 4, they chose St. Barbara, as it was her feast day. In unison they prayed, "Long live Santa Barbara." The storm ceased immediately, the winds and seas calmed, and two days later, the *Guadalupe* arrived safely in the harbor of Vera Cruz.

With great relief, Bonilla ordered Rodriguez to signal the fort and prepare for a mooring. The ship's boat was readied while the crew began to furl the sails, bringing the ship into the lee of the fort. From the rampart, the *Guadalupe's* signal was acknowledged and men poured from the gate onto the landing to receive the cables from the bow of the *Guadalupe*. The boat was lowered and the cable ends were placed on board, the men rowed to the landing, handed the cable end to fortress personnel, who then fed the lines through the bronze mooring rings anchored in the stone walls. This done, the cables were passed back to the bow of the galleon and secured.

Bonilla entered the fort and informed the officials of his intention to unload. Then he was rowed across the harbor to the mole. Alongside was the seventy-gun warship, *La Reyna,* loading supplies, cargo, and treasure. After disembarking from the launch, the confident captain strode through the gate opposite the mole and entered the *aduana*, or customs house. Here he made arrangements to bring the *Guadalupe* over to unload.

Once secured to the mole, the long-awaited cargo was quickly unloaded and distributed to eager merchants who would, in turn, convert their shipments into tidy profits. The *Guadalupe's* passengers, which included the Franciscan priests, entered the gated city.

The priests walked to the Convento de San Francisco just inside the gate across the street from the customs house where they would rest before their overland journey to Mexico City. In order to fulfill their vows to St. Barbara made days before, Father Serra held a solemn celebration in her honor. He preached and gave everyone a detailed account of the voyage and their miraculous deliverance.

Departure day marked the beginning of a historic journey for Father Serra. He shunned the use of a horse for his travel. He instead chose to walk the 180 miles with another priest to the shrine of Our Lady of Guadalupe. This was the start of the journey for Father Serra who, in 1769, would establish the Spanish mission churches along the California coast, which included San Diego and San Francisco.

After meeting with the treasury officials, Bonilla walked to the plaza, the center of city life. Situated two blocks from the mole, it was bordered by the governor's house on the east, on the south by the cathedral, also known as the *Iglesia Mayor*, and on the other two sides by arcaded shops, markets, boardinghouses, and a new hotel that was about to begin construction. The spire of the cathedral stood above all of the other rooftops. The governor's house was a two-story baroque-style building that covered an entire block and shared space with the *cabildo*, the town council. The governor's house had its own courtyard and watchtower, which enabled the governor to keep an eye on the galleons in the harbor. It had a flat roof and whitewashed stone and stucco exterior, as did most buildings in Vera Cruz. The roof provided a clear view of the harbor and often a refreshing breeze. Like the shops, it was fashioned with archways and covered porches on both floors surrounding the entire building. This allowed for cooling in the tropical sun and kept the rain from the doors and windows.

Vera Cruz had as many hospitals as churches because of the ever-present tropical diseases. There was the Hospital Real, called San Juan de Montesclaros, run by the priests of San Hipolito, and hospitals run by the Bethlemites and the Order of San Juan de Dios.

Vera Cruz's new governor, Don Diego de Peñalosa, had taken office only months before, on August 13, 1749. Bonilla was intent on meeting him and purchasing a few favors.

Governor Peñalosa delivered some dire news: during the previous summer there had been an epidemic of the *vomito negro*, or yellow fever, that had ravaged the city, killing many. Buzzards could still be seen perched on rooftops standing vigil, hoping to capture the smell of death. Foreigners were particularly susceptible to this disease as evidenced by the devastation aboard the warship *Reyna* under the Conde de la Gomera that had been in the harbor since July 29. The epidemic had invaded the city, so the horrified crew remained aboard waiting for the anticipated treasure shipments. In spite of their best precautions, some of the men became infected, spewing black vomit that spread the disease throughout the crew and they were forced ashore into crowded and understaffed hospitals. By the time the epidemic ended in September, nearly all of the crew had died. The *Reyna* had to remain in port waiting for crew replacements and treasure shipments.

The treasure storerooms in Vera Cruz had been emptied just prior to the arrival of the *Reyna* by the warships *La Galga* and *El Fuerte*, under the command of Don Daniel Huony, and other ships that had arrived earlier with Admiral Don Juan de Eques' mercury fleet. Nearly six million in silver pieces of eight and other valuables had already been shipped out, roughly half of 1749's output of the mint at Mexico City.

In late December, *La Reyna* set sail with cargo valued at nearly four million pieces of eight. Some last items put on board were two gifts for the Queen in Madrid. One was a portrait of the Our Lady of Guadalupe in a gold frame with emeralds and rubies. The other was a figure in the shape of a pelican with gold incrustations. It was only after *La Reyna* had sailed that Bonilla could make arrangements to receive any treasure on the *Guadalupe*.

The departure of *La Reyna* did little to alleviate the demand for silver. There were other ships at Vera Cruz, and more on their way. The *Nuestra Señora de los Godos*, Captain Pedro Pumarejo, arrived shortly after *La Reyna's* departure. Bonilla had last seen him in Cádiz just before he left. Don Joseph de Respaldiza was originally to sail back to Spain on his ship the *San Antonio de Padua y Nuestra Señora del Rosario* alias *La Bella Sara*. This ship sank in a storm on January 19, 1750, at the lime kilns just south of Vera Cruz, and Respaldiza was forced to buy another ship for the return journey. He purchased the brig, *Nuestra Señora de Soledad y San Francisco Javier*, which had arrived in Mexico from Maracaibo, Venezuela, with a cargo of cacao. Respaldiza was also in line for treasure. With the competition for silver heating up, Bonilla was grateful that he had left Spain ahead of the others.

Governor Peñalosa went on to tell Bonilla that he should expect delays loading his return cargo of silver and cochineal because there had been a drought earlier in the year, followed by storms and hurricanes and then an earthquake in Guadalajara. Peñalosa also complained that smuggling was still rampant and hard to control, but he had his port officials watching the coast. Smuggling was not just a game for small-time harbor rats. Galleon captains tested the king's tax collectors as well. When unregistered cargo was discovered, a weak excuse would be made, the taxes collected, and the captain was free to go. But if the captain was successful in concealing his booty, he would reap the financial reward of some fifteen percent in avoided taxes.

Juan Manuel Bonilla soon found himself in the same situation as the *Reyna* crew. In January, he fell ill and was confined to bed in town. He delegated authority to his brother-in-law. He would occasionally look from his window to glimpse the activity of the city where he would often see a vulture or two wheeling overhead. He prayed to St. Francis for the return of his health and tried to blot from memory the vision of the hungry raptors.

Winter turned to spring, bringing the tropical heat and humidity, which would not only jeopardize the health of his crew but also his cargo of cochineal. Before long, it would rot in the sacks that were stored in the damp hold of the *Guadalupe*. The dye alone was worth nearly a quarter million pieces of eight.

By the end of May, the *Guadalupe* was loaded and ready to depart, riding at her moor at the fort. Bonilla, still weak and on the mend, was rowed back across the harbor to the mole where he disembarked and passed through the gate. Two blocks away, he approached the guard at the entrance to the governor's house and after being granted an audience, he learned from Governor Peñalosa that the treasury officials had released his ship and that he could leave in the morning, assuming a favorable wind. Bonilla thanked him for his hospitality during his extended stay. Peñalosa was glad to see the pompous merchant go.

After an uneventful voyage, Bonilla entered the harbor at Havana in early June. Other ships were arriving from Mexico and the Spanish Main. One was *El Salvador*, Captain Don Juan Cruañes, loaded with cocoa, sixteen chests of silver and four chests of gold coins valued at 140,000 pesos. Another ship, *San Pedro*, a Portuguese vessel licensed to sail with the Spanish under Captain John Kelly, had also arrived carrying silver coins, doubloons, silverware, jewelry, two gold bars and thirteen silver bars. Both had come from Cartagena, Columbia. The *Nuestra Señora de los Godos* arrived from Vera Cruz with nearly 600,000 pieces of eight.

Havana was a city that prospered from the galleon trade and tobacco grown in the surrounding countryside. By 1750, there were nearly 4,000 houses within its stone walls. Leprosy and other diseases were rampant and the harbor waters smelled of human and animal waste.

As soon as Bonilla had arrived, he called on his good friend, Governor Francisco Cagigal de la Vega. Many years before, he witnessed Bonilla's marriage to María Agustina de Utrera in Cádiz.

In the harbor, Bonilla noticed the warship *La Galga* making ready to sail for Spain. Bonilla's original plan had been to load at Vera Cruz in time to return with a well-armed man-of-war, but his delays in Mexico cost him that opportunity. He saw the protection he needed in the fifty-six gun *La Galga*. She had been left behind the previous November when the treasure fleet of General Benito Spinola cleared for Spain. Bonilla made his wishes known to the other captains destined for Spain, and together they made a direct request to Don Daniel Huony, captain of *La Galga*, and Lorenzo Montalvo, the port minister, to have *La Galga* and the *Nuestra Señora de Mercedes*, a schooner belonging to King Ferdinand, to escort them back to Spain. It was agreed that since the readiness of *La Galga* and the *Mercedes* coincided with their departure they would act as escort.

La Galga's departure had been delayed because Captain Huony had orders to ship various tobacco products, some of which had not arrived at the warehouse of the *Real Compañia*. Bonilla loaded an additional cargo during the wait: 329 chests of sugar, 240 hides, and 26 sacks of cacao. Other shippers registered additional sugar and vanilla.

On July 30, Captain Huony wrote to Lorenzo Montalvo, the port minister, complaining about the crown's request to load tons of astilla on his ship. The astilla consisted of lightweight tobacco stems and leftovers packed loosely in bags. Huony pointed out that this bulky lightweight cargo was dangerous for him to carry, as he did not have much in the way of heavy cargo to ballast his ship. The mahogany planks he was carrying were his heaviest freight. Montalvo agreed and advised Governor Cajigal de la Vega on August 2 to hold the astilla for another ship. Having no immediate answer from Bonilla's old friend, the governor, Huony pleaded his case directly to him on August 5. His departure date was moved back.

Bonilla became extremely impatient. He was growing more and more concerned about hurricanes. His brush with death in the storms off of Vera Cruz the previous December was still vivid in his mind. Huony was equally concerned and was contemplating shortening his masts to accommodate the unsafe load.

Bonilla, seeking to expedite the matter, agreed to take on twenty-nine tons of the astilla, thus settling the dispute between Huony and the *Real Compañia*. On August 13, the governor advised the crown that the tobacco had been loaded, although the *Real Compañia* had exceeded its authority in the matter. *La Galga* had not finished packing her holds. By August 16, the register for the *Guadalupe* was closed. Bonilla was ready for departure, but Huony was not. Huony had other problems, as he had been trying to find suitable crew. To supplement his Mexican recruits, nearly fifty English prisoners were hauled out of the Havana dungeons and put on board.

An English prisoner named Captain Thomas Wright, who routinely traded with the Spanish, had been charged with the theft of some tobacco and was taken on board the *Guadalupe* to face a court back in Spain.

The next day, *La Galga's* register was closed. Bonilla began to relax. Four more ships had now joined Bo*nilla: the Nuestra Señora de los Godos*, the *San Pedro, El Salvador,* and the *Nuestra Señora de Soledad*. The fleet would be getting underway in the morning.

On August 18, the fleet cleared the harbor entrance at Morro Castle and with little difficulty entered the Straits of Florida, known as the Bahama Channel to the Spanish. The *Guadalupe* and the other ships in the convoy were experiencing a northerly headwind. Unbeknownst to them, that northerly breeze came from the western edges of a severe storm system and it was headed straight for them.

At dawn on August 25, the fleet was northeast of Cape Canaveral, Florida: the northerly winds increased, signaling an approaching storm. As the skies darkened, Bonilla ordered his topsails taken in, his main reefed, and shrouds tightened in preparation for what was coming. By 4 p.m., the wind abruptly changed from north to west and then from the south and by 9 p.m., the southeast. He now realized that they were in a full hurricane. The fleet struggled to stay together and as they fell off the wind, the distance between them increased. The eye of the storm having passed north of them, the fleet was now locked in place on the northeastern edge of the storm, driving with the wind and the northbound currents.

Bonilla's tormented face mirrored the angry sea. This was an important voyage. It was his first shipment of treasure that he was able to transport since he lost *Nuestra Señora de los Remedios* to the English privateers in 1747. But then if he was dead, losing his treasure would be of no consequence. He prayed to St. Francis and the Virgin Mary for deliverance, reminded of St. Barbara's intervention on her feast day when he was blown off Vera Cruz the year before. On this trip, however, he wasn't carrying a flock of Franciscan priests.

As the southeast winds and Gulf Stream currents continued propelling them north toward the Carolina coast, the distance between the ships increased.

Bonilla huddled in his cabin and barked out orders to his boatswain, Pedro Rodriguez. The pumps were constantly manned. As great waves washed over the decks, several crewmen were swept away.

La Galga and the *Mercedes* were now north and east of him. The *Guadalupe's* mizzen mast broke on the 26th, which allowed her to ride easier in the following seas.

The wind had already ripped away all of her topmasts. She continued in this state until the 28th, when Bonilla sighted a ship northwest of him. He recognized her as *Los Godos*. Bonilla signaled a change in course and the two ships turned southwest as he knew he was being driven towards the shoals of Cape Hatteras, North Carolina. *Los Godos* soon vanished in the darkness.

As the eye of the storm passed close by, the winds increased and shifted easterly, pushing the wallowing galleon closer to land. To slow the ship down, Bonilla ordered the main top mast cut down. No sooner was that done, than a huge following sea slammed her stern and broke the rudder. She was now totally out of control. Soundings were taken to measure the approach of the coastline. Bonilla's only hope was to get some anchors over in shallower water, but the timing of this maneuver was critical. If anything went wrong now, his ship was guaranteed to be driven into the deadly shoals of Cape Hatteras and all would be lost.

Miraculously, *La Galga*, *Los Godos*, the *Mercedes*, and the *San Pedro* cleared Cape Hatteras Shoals and continued northward. But the fate of the *Nuestra Señora de Soledad* and *El Salvador* was sealed. The night before, on August 29, they were both thrown against Cape Lookout.

At dawn, August 30, Bonilla sounded twenty brazas of water and realized that the coast was nearby. He was unaware of the fate of the *Soledad* and *El Salvador*. All day, the winds continued to drive him toward shore. At 6 p.m., Bonilla dropped his two largest anchors three miles off the shore of Core Banks, south of Ocracoke Inlet, North Carolina. The pilot estimated that they were at latitude 35°. He knew that he was in the vicinity of Cape Hatteras and in English territory.

The *Guadalupe* was in a shattered condition; the only timber standing was the base of her fore and main masts. The men were at all four pumps desperately trying to keep her afloat. The ship strained at her anchor cables; they were all that kept them between safety and disaster.

During this time, *Los Godos* and *San Pedro* met up with each other off Cape Henry, Virginia, and encountered a third vessel, *La Marianna*, a Spanish sloop sailing from Campeche to Santo Domingo that had been swept out of the Caribbean. The three of them arrived safely at Hampton, Virginia, and anchored off the mouth of Hampton River on September 5. That same day, *La Galga*, which had missed the entrance to Chesapeake Bay, drove ashore on Assateague Island at the border between Maryland and Virginia. The *Mercedes* ran aground six leagues north of Cape Charles, Virginia, the northern cape at the entrance to Chesapeake Bay.

The crew of the *Guadalupe* had endured five days of terror as they were driven from their intended course. Although Bonilla had lost several men overboard in the storm, his ship and treasure were safe for the moment.

With no rudder and no masts, the *Guadalupe* rode hard at her two anchors and waited for the wind to die down. Bonilla retired to his cabin with Carriedo and Pedro Manuel de Ortega, his pilot.

Meanwhile, in Hampton, Virginia, a sloop was preparing to depart for the West Indies. On board would be two brothers who would soon be welcomed as saviors by Bonilla. That warm welcome would become a gesture he would later regret.

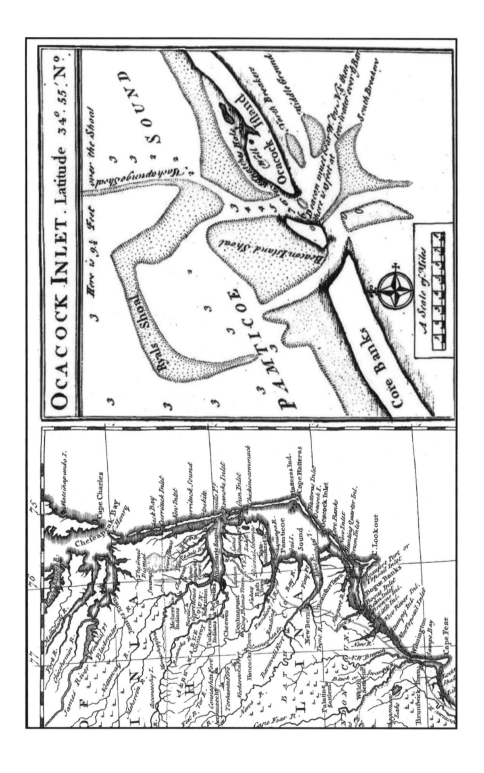

Chapter Three

Ocracoke: Pirate's Lair

Mother Hawkins' Tavern, Hampton, Virginia

It was the evening of September 8 and there was much drinking and rowdy celebration at the popular tavern owned by the widow Ann Hawkins. The tavern, located on King Street a block from the wharf, was a large brick building with wooden floors and a high ceiling with exposed beams. It could accommodate a goodly crowd. It was here that the news of the day was discussed over a meal or a measure of wine, beer, or liquor. There was a backgammon table, cards and dice, and sometimes music or a cock fight for entertainment. The proprietor, Ann Hawkins, had lost her husband eight years before and was left with two sons and three daughters to raise. She had taken over the popular tavern when her brother–in-law passed away. The tavern was her only means of survival.

Dining at Mother Hawkins' that evening was Major Wilson Cary, the naval officer, and the county sheriff, Robert Armistead. Cary, adorned in his wig and fine waistcoat, was the most powerful man in the county wielding control over all maritime commerce at Hampton and at Norfolk across Hampton Roads. As for Sheriff Armistead, he was a well-respected man who had little patience for those who would break the law or disturb the peace. He never hesitated to use the county jail on the northwest end of town. But unlike Major Cary, Armistead was a man of the people. The residents of Hampton liked him, especially Ann Hawkins. Armistead always called on her in the late hours to make sure that she was safe and her sometimes-boisterous clientele were behaving. Mrs. Hawkins needed little help: she knew how to handle the rowdy seamen and could drink and swear with the best of them. But it wasn't easy being a tavern keeper and a mother of five. Her tavern was no place for her children, who out of necessity assisted their mother serving meals and liquor. The townspeople frowned but such was the life of an eighteenth century widow. The court had recently ordered guardians for the children.

This particular evening there was a different kind of celebration under way at the tavern. It had been about twenty-four hours since the hurricane had moved on, but before it left, it had driven three Spanish ships to seek the safety of Hampton Roads. *Nuestra Señora de los Godos*, *San Pedro*, and *La Marianna* came to anchor off the mouth of Hampton River, as directed by the bay pilot who had escorted them from outside the Virginia Capes. Captain Pumarejo of the *Los Godos* and officers from *San Pedro* and *La Marianna* had rowed ashore and landed at the wharf while their crews still worked relentlessly at the pumps, keeping their ships afloat. Between *Los Godos* and *San Pedro*, there was cargo and treasure valued at nearly a million pieces of eight. They had been greeted with stares and scowls from the surly seamen who loitered at the docks and quickly realized the Spanish ships were in danger. Captain Pumarejo, directed to the office of Major Wilson Cary, asked permission to unload their treasure and get protection. Fearing an uprising by the locals and foreign seaman alike, Sheriff Armistead counseled Cary against it.

Wilson Cary, although somewhat sympathetic to the plight of the Spaniards, opted to enforce the king's customs laws in the strictest sense. He declared that the cargo could not be unloaded without permission from Thomas Lee, president of the council and acting governor of Virginia. Cary then turned the distressed Spaniards away, forcing them to travel across the river to Norfolk where there was a safe anchorage in the Elizabeth River. To get to Williamsburg thirty miles west of Hampton to meet with Thomas Lee, the Spaniards would now have to first ferry from Norfolk to Hampton.

In the dimly lit tavern, thick with tobacco smoke from clay pipes and Mrs. Hawkins' cigar, tankards and glasses were raised honoring Major Cary for his decision to deny the hated Spaniards entrance to the town. Almost all the tavern patrons had suffered during the late war with Spain. Nearly a hundred vessels had been taken by privateers off of the Virginia coast. The sight of the *Nuesta Señora de los Godos* had ripped the scab off the old wound. She was known to many, especially John Hunter, Hampton's wealthiest merchant, as the English ship, *Harrington*. John Hunter, former captain of the *Harrington*, had sailed her into Hampton in 1747. The following year, she was captured by none other than Don Daniel Huony. Huony, it will be recalled, was now in command of the warship *La Galga*, that had been driven ashore on Assateague Island on Virginia's coast just days before.

Major Cary stood to recognize the toast and made his own. "God save the King," he bellowed, which was followed with glasses raised by all. "God save the King."

The toasts soon switched. George Ware, a notorious imbiber of spirits, rose to offer an oath against the detestable Spaniards: "Since those Spanish devils still seize our vessels and make prisoners of honest Englishmen, I say let's take their treasure and send them home to that papist nitwit Ferdinand without a single piece of eight!"

"Hear! Hear!" chanted the chorus while raising their tankards and glasses. Mrs. Hawkins followed suit. Seated at the pinewood table in front of the great stone hearth, now idle this late summer evening, were John and Owen Lloyd. Everyone's eyes turned toward them as John Lloyd hammered his peg leg against the worn wooden floor. The tavern patrons knew that he had lost his leg during a wartime engagement with the Spanish. This was their last night in Hampton; they were departing the next morning for the West Indies. Seated at the table with them was Captain Benjamin Tucker of the *Hannah*, destined for the island of Montserrat in the Leeward chain. He was going to drop Owen and John off at St. Kitts en route to Montserrat. The *Hannah* was the first vessel they found that could take them to St. Kitts. She was a small sloop whose loading was delayed by the recent hurricane. Captain Tucker informed the Lloyds that after Major Cary released the *Hannah* in the morning they would be underway.

The next morning the Lloyd brothers departed Owen's house and made their way east down Queen Street and then south on King Street past Mother Hawkins' tavern to the *Hannah* making ready at the wharf. Owen followed John as he thumped up the gangway on his wooden leg. Captain Tucker ordered the lines cast off and the *Hannah* was towed out of Hampton River past Blackbeard Point. It was here, thirty-two years before, that the severed head of that nefarious pirate was put on a pole after he was killed at Ocracoke.

It was a beautiful sunny day and they were finally underway. The *Hannah* heeled a little more to port as her sails tightened against the balmy southeast breeze. They cleared Cape Henry at the mouth of Chesapeake Bay and set a course for the Caribbean.

Captain Tucker was thankful that he had not been at sea when the recent hurricane swept the Virginia coast. He was also thankful that his little sloop survived the pounding it took riding at anchor off of Hampton. John and Owen

Lloyd made themselves comfortable near the helm and contemplated their future. Owen thought mostly of Christian and of his new opportunity at St. Kitts. He was well known and respected on the island, and once there, he could collect money that was due him from various merchants and planters. Once again, John put his faith in his enterprising little brother. Owen had convinced him that they would soon reverse the string of misfortunes that had befallen them.

September 10, 1750, off North Carolina

As the *Hannah* rounded the shoals of Cape Hatteras, she encountered some unusual swells generated from the conflict of the northbound Gulf Stream with the southbound Labrador current. Oddly, under a bright sunny sky, the *Hannah's* hull pounded through the contrary seas. Soon, her planking, which had been tested during the hurricane at Hampton, began to loosen. A seam opened and seawater began to gurgle into the hold. Captain Tucker ordered the pump manned. There was now deep concern on everyone's faces. The beautiful sunny sky contradicted the real danger presently at hand. Owen remained calm and encouraged Captain Tucker to make for Ocracoke Inlet. After Owen told Tucker that he was very familiar with the shoals around the inlet, Tucker gave command to him.

The pumping continued, and Owen skillfully maneuvered the sinking sloop through the inlet. The dinghy was made ready and Lloyd steered for shallow water. Once the boat was lowered alongside, Captain Tucker, his crew, and the Lloyd brothers scrambled into the crowded boat and paddled the short distance to the beach inside the inlet, watching as the *Hannah* settled to the bottom.

Owen gestured to the pilot's house off in the distance, telling them they could find help there. The men began their march along the beach that skirted the inside of the inlet and trended toward the house of John Oliver, the harbor pilot. Owen dropped back to keep his peg-legged brother company. Walking in the soft sand was difficult for John. As they approached Oliver's house, they could see a number of men idling about. There were tarps and makeshift tents strung from bent limbs of the live oaks. Smoke from the cooking fire carried off with the ocean breeze. Last week's hurricane had stranded other crews on this remote barrier island that lay twenty miles out into the Atlantic. Owen Lloyd was familiar with Ocracoke Inlet and its active commerce. He was certain that he and John would soon be on their way to the West Indies.

Thirty-Two Years Before

The smell of burning oak and roasting beef permeated the air. Men walked about, others paired off in intense conversation and there were a handful tending the cooking fire. These were desperate men, adventurers, social misfits, and rebels. They were a band of pirates who had plundered ships from the Gulf of Mexico, to the Caribbean and the eastern seaboard of America. They had chosen Ocracoke Inlet as their refuge. There was William Howard, Edward Salter, Israel Hands, and about twenty-two others. One stood out above all the rest. A tall, lanky man with a jet-black beard named Edward Teach, lately known as Blackbeard, the pirate. His ship, the *Revenge*, lay at anchor off the point formed by the creek that separated this part of the island from the sea beach. Piled around their campsite were hogsheads of sugar, bags of cocoa, a bale of cotton and indigo, and their daily staple, rum. This was not early September 1750 but 1718, thirty-two years before.

Edward Teach was a brute of a man, wild eyed, with a long black beard that grew up to his eyes. He would twist it into small tails bound with ribbon. In battle, he wore three brace of pistols besides his cutlass and knives. He stuck lighted matches under his hat, which smoldered and smoked, making him look like a fury from hell.

Blackbeard had only begun pirating two years before aboard another pirate vessel owned by Captain Benjamin Hornigold. In 1717, Blackbeard assumed the command of a French Guineaman that Hornigold had captured. He renamed it the *Queen Anne's Revenge*, which mounted forty guns. With his new command, Blackbeard set off to plunder all the shipping he could find. While he hunted for Spanish treasure ships, he only scored cargoes of wine, rum, sugar, dry goods, and small amounts of gold and silver belonging to the captains and their crews. He never had the opportunity to raid a treasure galleon. His last act of terror was to blockade the harbor of Charleston, South Carolina. And then it was not treasure that he sought but medicines for himself and crew.

Blackbeard and his men had come to Ocracoke Island to seek refuge and a pardon, which he obtained from Charles Eden, North Carolina's self-serving governor. Blackbeard had promised earlier in the year to abandon his criminal ways, but temptation had driven him that August to take a French ship carrying chiefly a cargo of sugar. He returned to Ocracoke expecting help from the governor.

Ocracoke is part of a chain of sandy barrier islands that stretch 200 miles along the coast of North Carolina and twenty miles from the mainland of southeastern North Carolina. If it were not for the inlet of the same name through which most of the plantation trade flowed, there would be little human activity around these desolate sand banks. It was a perfect pirate refuge.

After leaving Charleston, Blackbeard lost the *Queen Ann's Revenge* at Topsail Inlet, some seventy miles southwest of Ocracoke. His crew went aboard the *Revenge*, a sloop that was consort to his flagship, and made for Ocracoke. After he arrived, Blackbeard called on Governor Eden at the little town of Bath, forty miles up the Pamlico Sound from Ocracoke. Here, he signed an affidavit that he had found the French ship derelict at sea. Eden went along with this and received sixty hogsheads of sugar; another twenty went to Tobias Knight, the customs collector.

Law-abiding residents became alarmed at Blackbeard's presence as he roamed at will and threatened the local inhabitants. Governor Eden did nothing. Because of this, some concerned citizens made a plea to Governor Alexander Spotswood in Virginia for help. Spotswood knew that something had to be done and that he would have to take the initiative since Governor Eden was not inclined to do anything. While in Bath, Blackbeard got wind of a plan at Hampton that a sloop was being sent to Ocracoke to capture him so he returned to his ship riding at anchor inside the inlet.

On November 17, 1718, Governor Spotswood ordered Lt. Robert Maynard of HMS *Pearl*, anchored off Hampton, to Ocracoke. Maynard took two shallow-draft sloops down the coast and entered Roanoke Inlet, fifty miles north of Ocracoke. Here he hired a pilot and they made their way down Pamlico Sound for the eight-gun *Revenge* anchored in the inlet. It was hoped that they would catch Blackbeard off guard while he was watching for ships coming in from the sea. Maynard's plan was to storm the pirate ship and go at it hand to hand. He arrived on the 22nd and pretended to be a trading vessel as he had no cannon and he kept his men below deck.

As Maynard drew closer, he thought he was looking at the devil himself. Blackbeard stood taller than any of his men. His eyes were menacing, like open gun ports.

Blackbeard took up a bowl of liquor and bellowed out for all to hear that there would be "damnation to anyone who that should give or ask for quarter." Maynard replied that he expected no quarter nor would he give any. Blackbeard then let loose with a broadside of partridge shot sweeping the deck and wounding twenty of Maynard's men. Lt. Maynard and his men stood fast while their sloop continued toward the pirates, his remaining men still below deck. Maynard came along side Blackbeard's sloop, whereupon the rest of his crew rushed up from the hold and swarmed onto the *Revenge*. They were met with hand grenades, pistol shots, and slashing cutlasses. Maynard wounded Blackbeard with his pistol, but the fierce monster stood firm and prepared to deliver a cutlass blow in return. Before he delivered that potentially lethal blow, one of Maynard's men slashed Blackbeard's neck and throat. The fearless pirate fought on and was shot five times and cut in nearly twenty places. The water around the sloops turned red with blood.

One of Maynard's men swung his cutlass hard against Blackbeard's neck. His head flopped over onto his shoulder, dangling by a few uncut ligaments. The scourge of the Atlantic seaboard fell dead and his crew soon surrendered. Maynard ceremoniously finished cutting the head from Blackbeard's body. This would not only be his trophy but proof to Governor Spotswood that the pirate had been killed and that Maynard deserved the bounty. The dead pirates were taken ashore with Maynard's casualties and buried in shallow unmarked graves. Later, Maynard attached the grisly trophy to his sloop's bowsprit and sailed victoriously back to Hampton where the head was put on a pole and planted at the entrance to Hampton River for all to see. Two of Blackbeard's crew were later hanged there. From 1718 on, Blackbeard's final anchorage would be remembered as Teach's Hole and he would be memorialized as one of the most notorious pirates in history. A number of his crew were pardoned and returned to productive lives.

Blackbeard's master, Israel Hands, who was at Bath when his captain was taken, would live on in history serving as coxswain to another notorious pirate, a one-legged brigand called Long John Silver. Silver, however, was only a fictional character invented by Robert Louis Stevenson for his classic, *Treasure Island*. Blackbeard and his pirate crew rested beneath the wet sands of Ocracoke. For thirty-two years they waited, hoping, that on their horizon someday, there would be another prize, *a Spanish prize*.

Blackbeard captured and killed at Ocracoke Inlet, November 22, 1718

Chapter Four

Blackbeard's Last Prize

Five Leagues Southwest of Ocracoke Inlet, August 31, 1750

It was dawn and the galleon, *Nuestra Señora de Guadalupe*, was riding hard at her double anchors as she rose and fell with the ocean swells. The weather had eased but the seas continued to run high. While Captain Juan Manuel Bonilla rested in his cabin, some of the crew had set a new sail on a yard and were going to fasten it to what was left of the main mast pole. The boatswain, Pedro Rodriguez, was directing others to cut down the stoppers from the remaining yards and were throwing everything they could overboard. Captain Bonilla, hearing the commotion, stepped outside his cabin and found Rodriguez and some of his men dismantling the foresail. It was evident that Rodriguez and the storm-weary crew were planning to run the *Guadalupe* ashore. They had seen several of their shipmates washed overboard only days before, for which they now blamed Bonilla because of his incompetence. Once shipwrecked, the sailors could abandon their bungling captain and plunder his cargo of treasure. They knew that there was no Spanish authority on shore, and they probably assumed that the English would be of no assistance to Bonilla. If the *Guadalupe's* anchors didn't hold, Bonilla's treasure was doomed.

The *Nuestra Señora de Soledad* had wrecked at Drum Inlet, thirty miles southwest of Ocracoke Inlet. She had lost all of her masts and Captain Molviedo had thrown all of her cannon overboard in an attempt to save the ship. The *Soledad* lay heeled over on her side in the breaking surf. Fortunately, everyone survived. When the *Soledad's* owner and master, Don Joseph Respaldiza, came ashore, he found a hut inhabited by a herdsman. Here he learned that civilization was some sixty miles away at New Bern, where the governor of North Carolina could be found.

Five leagues to the southwest of the *Soledad*, *El Salvador* was totally lost on

Cape Lookout. Her hull had been torn open, spilling men, treasure, and cargo into the sea. The only survivors were three men and a boy; Captain Cruañes perished.

The *Guadalupe* strained at her anchor cables as the southeast wind threatened to condemn the ship to the same fate as the *Soledad* and *El Salvador*. If Bonilla had continued on his northerly course, he would most assuredly have foundered on the shoals of Cape Hatteras. And if he had been in closer proximity to the *Soledad* and *El Salvador*, he would most likely have met their same fate. He was a lucky man, so it seemed.

Captain Bonilla warned his crew that, according to royal decrees, severe punishment awaited them when they returned to Spain if they continued their disobedience. He reminded them of their obligations to King Ferdinand. Some of the crew laughed and others ignored him. Bonilla was assuming that they wanted to return to Spain. Desperate, Bonilla "promised in the name of all principles" to pay them double wages as long as they got the ship and treasure to safety. The mutinous crew relented.

The following day, the first of September, the seas being much calmer, Bonilla ordered Rodriguez to haul the ship's boat down, which the crew did, but they chopped it into pieces, hoping that Bonilla would be forced to run the ship onto the beach. The next morning, he got the pinnace into the water and tied it alongside. Some of the crew boarded and rowed toward the unfamiliar shore. They soon returned and reported that they had seen cattle tracks on the beach.

Bonilla convened a meeting in his cabin with his pilot and his brother-in-law, Tomás Carriedo, and it was suggested that he take Thomas Wright, the English prisoner, ashore to find help. Wright was from Charleston, South Carolina, a port town 180 miles to the south. Wright had been the captain of the schooner *Little Betsey* based in Charleston, which he used to trade with the Spaniards at Havana. Wright knew the Spanish language so he was a valuable asset to Bonilla. Now, he volunteered to go ashore.

The pinnace returned to the beach and Wright bade Bonilla farewell while giving his word that he would come back with help. Wright headed north among the sand dunes and marshes, finding more cattle tracks and a few herdsmen's huts. He reached Ocracoke Inlet fifteen miles north of the *Guadalupe's* anchorage. Here he met John Oliver, a pilot, who was skilled in bringing vessels into the harbor. Wright returned and reported to Bonilla where they were. Encouraged by the news, he made plans to get his disabled galleon and fortune in silver to the safety of the inlet while Wright returned to the inlet.

Bonilla's galleon remained anchored off the beach waiting for the pilot to arrive. John Oliver soon returned with Wright. Oliver told Bonilla that it looked as if his ship could get into the inlet but it would be very risky towing his ship in because of the strong currents and a winding channel that was flanked with sandbars and extremely shallow water. Bonilla decided to offload the treasure and put it on the beach opposite his anchorage. Some of the Bankers, a name for the residents of the neighboring sand banks, had come out in canoes. Bonilla hired them to assist the *Guadalupe's* pinnace in ferrying the treasure chests ashore and storing them under guard on the beach. This maneuver was hazardous as the boat could easily broach in the breaking surf, spilling treasure chests. The hospitable natives happily agreed to oblige Bonilla, charging him over 1,700 pesos for their assistance. While the treasure was being landed, Bonilla turned his attention to the condition of his ship. She was still leaking and probably unable to survive another storm anchored in the open ocean. Bonilla boarded Oliver's pilot boat; with anxiety and fear, he headed north for Ocracoke.

September 10, 1750

Not long after their sloop sank, John and Owen Lloyd arrived at Oliver's house and found out from a restless crowd that the storm had dismasted a Spanish galleon, which was now anchored down the coast. News spread that plans were being made to tow the ship into Ocracoke. Having recently witnessed the arrival of other Spanish ships at Hampton, the Lloyds were intrigued. But they would be leaving soon as they had already found passage on the *Roanoke*, the snow belonging to Captain Samuel Dalling, which was bound for the West Indies.

The Lloyd brothers rested with the other distressed seamen around the campfire and listened to the speculation about the Spanish galleon. It seemed that no one was interested in seeing the Spaniards rescued.

A boat soon pulled ashore piloted by Oliver. All eyes watched as a somewhat portly man dressed in fine clothes, a wig, and a sword came ashore. It was Captain Bonilla. With him was Thomas Wright. Oliver, with Wright interpreting, was seen introducing Bonilla to a Captain Dalling. Bonilla began negotiating with Dalling to tow the *Guadalupe* into Ocracoke Inlet from her anchorage fifteen miles to the south. Dalling refused, saying it was too dangerous and he did not want to take responsibility. The truth was that Dalling cared little to help the Spanish. After a handshake and Bonilla's promise to pay Dalling 3,755 pieces of eight, Bonilla became the owner of the *Roanoke*. Dalling then nodded toward the Lloyd brothers and told him that Owen was experienced in navigating the inlet and that he should negotiate with him to act as pilot.

Dalling introduced the Lloyd brothers to Bonilla and explained to Owen that he had just sold the *Roanoke* and that he would not be able to take him to St. Kitts. Owen was disappointed but rebounded when he was given the opportunity to tow the *Guadalupe* into the inlet for a sum of 500 pieces of eight.

Owen and John boarded the *Roanoke* with Bonilla, some Spanish crew, and John Oliver, who carried a rudder that he hoped would fit the stern of the *Guadalupe*. They set sail for the galleon, and the Englishmen at Ocracoke eagerly awaited the arrival of the treasure ship.

Back at the *Guadalupe*, the Spanish crew had grown weary of transporting the treasure to the beach. They had only ferried fifty chests in two days. Now, Rodriguez encouraged them to abandon the *Guadalupe* and take up arms.

When the *Roanoke* arrived, the Lloyds marveled at the disabled galleon. They watched as Bonilla ferried over to her and climbed on board. Minutes later, he was seen to be very agitated. His crew had presented their latest demands. Lloyd found out that the crew had abandoned the pumps after Rodriguez had announced that the voyage was over and there was enough silver on the beach to satisfy their wages. Bonilla was desperate for help.

Oliver unloaded the rudder he had brought from the inlet onto the *Guadalupe*. Towing would be much easier if the galleon could steer her own way through the channels in the inlet. It turned out the rudder wouldn't fit. They prepared the *Guadalupe* for towing but they had to wait for a favorable wind from the south.

Bonilla tried to negotiate with his disobedient crew, offering them paper money and written promises, but they refused. Any further delay would result in the *Guadalupe* sinking with her remaining treasure and cargo, forcing Bonilla to give in to their demands. Ultimately, he paid fifty-seven men 100 pesos each and they agreed to finish carrying the silver and cochineal onto the beach. Owen and John watched from the *Roanoke* as the silver was conveyed and about a third of the cochineal. On board the *Guadalupe*, some of the crew started ransacking cabins. They took axes to the trunks of several passengers and began draping themselves with the jewels they found. Bonilla pleaded with the crew to return the jewels without result. The abused passengers were no longer inclined to help Bonilla with his predicament.

Pedro Rodriguez, Bonilla's unruly boatswain and the instigator in the whole affair, treated the *Guadalupe* as if she were already a wreck. Rodriguez and some of the crew moved to the bow and threatened to cut the anchor cables and let the *Guadalupe* drive ashore. Bonilla would later describe Rodriguez as "a man lost forever," for whom turning back was not an option. It was a clear case of mutiny but Bonilla was not in a position to press the charge. He would have to deal with him later. For now, he had a ship and a million-dollar cargo he needed to protect.

Bonilla went ashore to guard the treasure chests stacked on the beach. Seeing this as his last opportunity to run the ship ashore, Rodriguez cut both anchor cables instead of weighing them up as he'd been ordered. The other officers and crew were taken aback by this act of desperation but managed to maintain control of the ship.

When winds finally shifted to the southeast, a thick cable from the bow of the *Guadalupe* was hauled over and fastened to the stern of the *Roanoke*. Without a rudder on the *Guadalupe*, the towline would have to be shortened so that the galleon would follow behind. Bonilla ordered some armed guards on board and gave command of the vessel to Owen Lloyd.

Now Lloyd found himself towing a disabled Spanish galleon still laden with a valuable cargo of cochineal and other cargo. Two years earlier, with Spain and England at war, things certainly would have been different. He wished it were two years ago. If only the boys at Mother Hawkins' could see him now. He gave his brother John a nervous smile. They both looked back at the shattered *Guadalupe* and the treasure chests piled up on the beach. They could not believe what they were doing considering the losses they both had suffered from the Spanish just a few years before. Owen smelled opportunity, but he wasn't quite sure what it was.

There was little wind and it took three days to tow the *Guadalupe* the fifteen miles to the inlet. By September 14, they were safely inside the estuary and anchored in Teach's Hole. But the ship grounded on a sandbar so the Spaniards abandoned her and went ashore. Owen Lloyd disengaged the *Roanoke* and went to his own anchorage. For the next two nights, the *Guadalupe* was left unattended.

Bonilla was in the process of transporting the treasure chests from the beach to the pilot's house with the hired canoes. This was a tedious task; the treasure had to be carted over the beach and marsh to the sound, then loaded onto the canoes and carried to the inlet. While he was occupied with this, another snow that was in the harbor briefly tied up alongside the *Guadalupe* and stole some items from her cabins.

On September 17, Bonilla penned a letter to the Marqués de Ensenada, the minister of the navy, and Don Francisco de Varas y Valdes, president of the House of Trade in Seville, in which he related his misfortunes, including the condition of his ship and his mutinous crew. He reported that "even the letters of the merchants have been opened in case any gold was included as well as other irreverences to the cargo which was loaded under the deck. Nothing has been safe from looting." Bonilla demanded an investigation be made into the "atrocities of the crew" when they returned to Spain. While drafting his letter, he received reports about the loss of *La Galga* on the Virginia coast. Unknown to Bonilla, Captain Huony and most of his crew were safe and sailing down Chesapeake Bay on their way to Norfolk, and *Los Godos* and *San Pedro* were at anchor in the Elizabeth River, opposite the town. Bonilla feared that Captain Pumarejo and his crew may have been lost. He had received reports that the boat that belonged to the *Los Godos* had been sighted adrift near Ocracoke and that unidentified corpses had been found along the coast.

John and Owen Lloyd spent a lot of time ashore at the camp listening to the talk among the Bankers. Lloyd was convinced that they would soon move against the Spaniards and seize the treasure. News had come from down the coast that some treasure had been taken from *El Salvador* by a Bermuda sloop, and that Respaldiza was hastily salvaging the *Nuestra Señora de Soledad*.

Since the earliest days, the Bankers were rugged and independent, bordering on lawlessness, thanks in part to the remoteness of Ocracoke and neighboring islands. There was the legitimate business of raising cattle in the marshes that insulated the backside of the islands and there was the illegitimate business of plundering shipwrecks and their helpless victims on the oceanfront. These Bankers were known to the authorities on the mainland as a wild and ungovernable set of "indigent, desperate Outlaws or Vagabonds." The Bankers had a deep hatred for the Spanish, thanks to their activities along these islands during the late war.

During the summer of 1747, Spaniards from St. Augustine came ashore between Ocracoke and Cape Fear and killed all of the inhabitants' cattle and hogs, burned vessels, and even killed several of the Bankers. And in July 1741, Pedro Estrada had set up base at Ocracoke. John Oliver was one of the harbor pilots at the time. He had left his house to render assistance to the sloop *Guarnsey*, loaded with naval stores bound for Boston, which had run aground on the Horse Shoe Shoal five miles inside the inlet. The *Guarnsey* had run afoul of her own anchor and sank in nine and a half feet of water. Captain Carkett and his crew, with Oliver's help, managed to rescue the cargo and put it onto the beach at Ocracoke. When they returned to the sunken sloop, Estrada's men came up to them and drove them off. Upon returning to the inlet, they saw that the cargo stored on the beach was burning and much to their distress, they observed the Spaniards firing shots into Oliver's house. Oliver's elderly wife could be heard screaming in fear. The Spaniards packed up and left soon afterwards.

Most recently, on September 15, 1748, two Spanish privateers from Havana, Vicente López and Joseph León Muñoz, had gone up the Cape Fear River, landed at Brunswick Town, and plundered it. This would have been expected the month prior to the news of the ceasefire, but now such conduct, although consistent with Spanish behavior, was contrary to the mutually intended peace.

They remained three or four days wreaking havoc, forcing all of the inhabitants to flee into the woods. The smallest of their sloops then proceeded four miles farther up the river and took possession of a ship lying at anchor. They also took several other vessels at and near Brunswick and were proceeding to load them full of plunder.

Captain Day, a gentleman from Brunswick, with as many of the inhabitants as he could possibly muster, surprised the privateers as they were loading the vessels. Captain Day with about fourteen others gave them a full volley of small arms, killing some and taking others prisoner. Two Spaniards escaped by swimming out to their sloops. The enraged Spanish crews fell to cannonading the town, but the people ashore put up a stout resistance for several hours. At length, the largest of the Spanish sloops blew up, killing a total of eighty Spaniards including their commodore and twenty English sailors who were being held prisoner on board. Thirty-seven more were taken prisoners. The other sloop thought it proper to make her escape, carrying with her only one small vessel loaded with naval stores.

The damage done by the Spanish was later assessed at £5,233, a costly sum for the time.

Captain Juan Manuel Bonilla had landed not only with a mutinous crew, but in a hotbed of Spanish resentment. Having suffered in the war as well, his self-centered thinking blinded him to the local perspective. In his mind, the war was over, and he expected cooperation from all of the English-speaking natives. He did not immediately grasp the fact that the Bankers derived their living in part from shipwrecks. Nor did he know that the Bankers were still emotionally at war. Making matters worse, it was now known to everyone at Ocracoke that *La Galga* had a large number of English prisoners on board and one of them had drowned trying to escape from his Spanish captors after she drove ashore. The locals there were having a free-for-all on the wreck. With this news came some editorial comment. The editor of the *New York Gazette* suggested that all of the Spaniards in Bonilla's fleet be seized until Spain restored every vessel taken illegally since the peace treaty was signed. The Bankers couldn't have agreed more. They wanted revenge.

Owen Lloyd had heard the rumblings among the Bankers about seizing Bonilla's ship. He had observed firsthand the mutinous behavior of the Spanish boatswain who still had control of Bonilla's crew. Lloyd was convinced that somebody was going to steal the treasure. But who?

The Spanish crew, talking among themselves, realized that Bonilla and the *Guadalupe* would probably be there for a long time. They approached Bonilla "in a most tumultuous manner" and "through violence" threatened to abandon him and forced him to pay their wages. Bonilla was in a dilemma: if he paid the crew the wages, they might leave him on his own, but if he didn't, then their departure seemed all but guaranteed.

Having already given his men a hundred dollars apiece to transfer the treasure to the beach at Core Banks, Bonilla now offered them nine dollars a month to remain, which they refused. They demanded twelve and Bonilla saw no other recourse but to submit. John Oliver agreed to let him store the treasure in his house, the only one in the area, but only after receipt of 166 pesos. This deal was made just in time.

The *Guadalupe* was anchored near the creek leading to the landing for Oliver's house, her fifteen remaining cannon ready to repel any attack. Bonilla had divided his crew between the ship and Oliver's house. That night, some Bankers rushed into the guard's room at the house and seized some firearms, but they met with enough resistance at the house and from the ship that their plans were foiled. Owen Lloyd knew that they would try again.

Afterwards, Bonilla paid the crew what they demanded, and as he'd feared, many promptly boarded a snow with some of the passengers and left without even securing the *Guadalupe* in the harbor. Bonilla now realized that to protect the treasure and discourage further attacks from the Bankers, he would have to load the treasure back on board, consolidate his few remaining guards, and better utilize his remaining cannon.

Meanwhile, Ocracoke Harbor was becoming congested with other vessels, some arriving in their regular course of trade, others to witness the disabled treasure galleon which was now being talked about up and down the East Coast. All eyes were on the treasure ship. The air was thick with tension. Captain Bonilla had flashbacks of the vultures that had hovered outside his window at Vera Cruz. He was unsure which way to turn. Thomas Wright, his former prisoner, was encouraging him to take his treasure to Charleston, but Norfolk was closer. He needed to hire another vessel to transport his treasure and he needed to do it soon. That vessel was on its way.

Boston, Massachusetts, August 26, 1750

Thirty-three-year-old Captain Zebulon Wade and his sloop, *Seaflower,* entered customs at Boston, Massachusetts. It was another routine trip from Ocracoke, the same trip he had been making since the early days of the war. He would carry American and European goods to Ocracoke, which would be bartered for naval stores and produce from North Carolina plantations. Captain Wade loved the sea but wished he could be home more often. His career had come more by legacy than choice. He came from a seafaring family; his father and brother were both mariners. Now he was headed home to Scituate where his family lived, a small seacoast village about fifteen miles south of Boston.

Wade's wife, Mercy, had grown accustomed to his trips since their marriage six years ago. Once more, she was grateful that her husband had survived the dangers of the war as he dodged the Spanish and French privateers lurking along the American coast. Zebulon greeted his three children with hugs—his twins, Zeb and Barney, not yet two years old; and Anna, who was just born that summer. While he was gone, she had been baptized.

Regretfully, Captain Wade told his wife that his two partners had arranged another trip to North Carolina and that he would have to return to Boston in a few days to load the *Seaflower*. Wade was under a lot of pressure because his finances were in jeopardy. In January, he had left for Ocracoke but was unable to return for four months. The great hurricane that had wracked the eastern seaboard the previous October had disrupted the North Carolina plantation commerce, forcing Wade to have to wait for cargo. The contract with his shipping partners had a stiff penalty for the delay.

After his brief visit, Captain Wade hitched a ride up to Boston where he supervised the loading of his sloop. Among his crew were two sailors, Jonathan Deacon, aged twenty-seven, and Isaac Ray, aged seventeen, both of Massachusetts. There were also two apprentice seamen from North Carolina. Abraham Pritchett, a gangly teenager of nineteen, was from New Bern. His father had died the year before so he had set off to make his own fortune. And there was Thomas Hobson, a fourteen-year-old ship's boy.

On September 1, Wade notified the customs officer of his intention to clear port. Before leaving, he heard of a hurricane that had struck the coast of North Carolina and Virginia. By the 9th, he was underway and expected to make Ocracoke in four or five days.

Back home, Wade's wife, Mercy, fearing that Zebulon had sailed head on into the hurricane, consulted the Boston newspaper for more news and found that the *Seaflower* had not cleared until after the storm. With great relief, she settled down and waited for his return. Then news came in about some Spanish treasure ships loaded with millions of pieces of eight that had been lost on the North Carolina coast. This rare event captured her interest as it did with many who lived in the American colonies. She could barely wait for Zebulon's return; she wanted to hear all about it.

On Board the *Seaflower*, Ocracoke Inlet Bearing Southwest by West

Ship's boy, Thomas Hobson, was busy scrambling about the deck performing his duties when he heard Abraham Pritchett calling out from the helm as Ocracoke

Inlet was coming into view. All eyes on deck turned to the inlet while Captain Wade gazed through his glass and spied the familiar opening in the sand banks, looking for any movement and studying the condition of the breakers at the outer bar. The bar projected from the north end of the Core Banks that lay to the south of the inlet and extended across two-thirds the mouth of the inlet. It was a dog-leg approach, one that could only be accomplished with the right wind and an incoming tide.

The *Seaflower* came to anchor outside the bar. While waiting for the tide to change, the crew began readying the sloop for final anchorage. As they cleared the bar, Thomas Hobson was grinning. They had entered Teach's Hole, a location that delighted his youthful fantasies. Being raised in North Carolina, he had heard many times of the story of Edward Teach, notoriously known as Blackbeard, who met his demise at this very location. Some stories were told by old salts who claimed to have witnessed that dramatic event. His mentor, Abraham Pritchett, grew up across the Pamlico River from the family home of William Howard, Blackbeard's quartermaster. Howard had been captured in Virginia when Lt. Maynard took Blackbeard at Ocracoke but had the remarkable good fortune to receive a last minute pardon from Governor Spotswood, avoiding the hangman's noose. He was still alive and in the area. Hobson had left home to seek adventure and escape the tedium of the family farm located near the Albemarle Sound. He looked forward to the day that he could take the helm.

Pritchett, pointing in the direction of the *Guadalupe*, said he had never seen a vessel of this size inside the inlet before. They studied the battered ship with her masts down and much of her rigging removed. On deck, bedraggled, dark-haired seamen scrambled over her decks and rigging. Wade came to the conclusion that this ship had survived the recent hurricane.

The crew of the *Seaflower* observed a crowd on shore and makeshift tents of sailcloth. There were boats ferrying to and from the *Guadalupe*. Other small local vessels were anchored idly nearby. Hobson joined the other *Seaflower* crew in the dinghy. Hearts pounding in their chests, they rowed toward shore and entered the small creek that sheltered other boats belonging to vessels in the harbor. They joined the crowd that consisted mostly of seamen, some from the traders anchored in Teach's Hole, and others who had lost their vessels in the storm. And then there were the Bankers, the rough-looking characters who lived in the area.

While Captain Wade consulted with the pilot, Thomas Hobson remained close by Pritchett's side. The two of them heard some men talking about the *Guadalupe*, saying that she was carrying treasure and cargo worth over a million dollars. Hobson could not grasp the enormity of that number. There was talk about other Spanish treasure ships dashed to pieces on the sand banks of Cape Lookout.

Ocracoke was becoming more and more intriguing to Hobson. There was much excitement among the men accompanied by drinking and singing. Some were cursing the Spaniards; others talked in hushed tones as they stared at the shattered hulk of the *Guadalupe*.

From the crowd emerged Owen Lloyd. He recognized Zebulon Wade, as Lloyd had run trading sloops out of Boston to Ocracoke seven years before.

The two men clasped hands as Wade asked his old acquaintance what he was doing there. Lloyd filled him in on his business in Virginia and his marriage to Christian four years before. Wade learned that the Lloyd brothers had been shipwrecked recently at the inlet while headed for St. Kitts and then lost their passage to St. Kitts when Bonilla purchased Dalling's vessel. Wade could see that Owen and his brother were a bit worn out from their ordeal so he invited them aboard the *Seaflower* for dinner. Owen and John returned to Wade's sloop, which was anchored not far from Bonilla's galleon and after boarding were introduced all around to the other crew. As dinner was prepared in the great roasting pan, the two captains shared their recent years.

Owen related how he had met his wife after he captured the French Guineaman near Martinique and carried her into St. Kitts. As always, he took the opportunity to embellish his tale. Pritchett, Hobson, and the others gathered around, listening intently. Owen told of his experiences at Virginia and the loss of his sloop, *Elizabeth*, to the Spanish, John's imprisonment at Havana, and his subsequent financial ruin.

Wade praised God the war was over and said as soon as they could get a cargo they would be on their way. However, that might take some time as the hurricane had devastated the region's commerce. Before exchanging cargo, they would have to wait for the arrival of the shallow-draft vessels from high up the sounds.

On September 20, Bonilla sent his chief pilot, Felipe García, to Virginia with a letter hoping to find Captain Daniel Huony of *La Galga*.

Norfolk, Virginia

After a difficult overland journey to Norfolk, the roads thick with mud from the recent rains, Felipe García found Captain Huony who had arrived on the 19th. García informed him that Bonilla was in dire straits. Huony, still suffering from exhaustion after his ordeal at sea and at Assateague, could do little. He ordered his chaplain, Father Juan Martin, to accompany García to Williamsburg and act as interpreter while García requested licenses from Virginia's acting governor, Thomas Lee, for ships to carry their cargo and crews back to Spain. He made the request for not only the *Guadalupe* but for the crews of *La Galga* and the three other Spanish ships at Norfolk. García requested shallow-draft vessels and sailors to help unload the ship at Ocracoke as many of Bonilla's crew had deserted. Huony found two vessels to hire at six hundred pesos each, which belonged to Owen Lloyd's former boss, Captain John Hutchings of Norfolk. This was a truly exorbitant fee but the Spaniards had no choice but to pay it. Red tape, however, delayed their hoped-for departure. The Spaniards discovered that they needed "permits" from the customs officials first. In late September, Huony wrote to Bonilla about the steps that he was taking in Norfolk on his behalf but the letter never arrived.

Edenton, North Carolina

Gabriel Johnston, the governor of North Carolina, had first heard of the Spanish shipwrecks when Don Joseph Respaldiza, the master of the *Nuestra Señora de Soledad*, called on him in early September at his home across the Chowan River from Edenton.

Gabriel Johnston was born in Scotland in 1699, educated in medicine at St. Andrews, and distinguished himself in London in letters and politics. He had emigrated to North Carolina around 1730 and was appointed governor in 1734 through his connections with the Earl of Wilmington. He was an ambitious governor but was hampered by a shortage of cash. He married Penelope Eden, the stepdaughter of the former governor, Charles Eden, who had famously cavorted with Blackbeard. When Charles Eden died, Johnston took up residence at his Eden House plantation across the river from the town of Edenton, both settlements owing Governor Eden for their names.

Johnston listened intently as Respaldiza reported through his interpreter the fate of the Spanish fleet. He had not yet learned that *La Galga* and the *Mercedes* were beached on the Eastern Shore of Virginia or that the other ships had made it safely into Norfolk. Respaldiza had departed the coast before receiving any good intelligence on the rest of the fleet except for Bonilla, who by that time had towed the *Guadalupe* into Ocracoke. The governor was told that Bonilla was carrying 400,000 pieces of eight and a fortune in red dye. Respaldiza also reported that immediately after the storm had passed, a Bermuda sloop owned by Thomas and Ephraim Gilbert had come ashore and had taken sails and rigging from *El Salvador* and it was also believed some chests of treasure as well. Other locals were threatening the *Soledad*, now laying over in the surf. Johnston issued orders for Gilbert's sloop to be apprehended and then set off for New Bern in company of Respaldiza. He also sent word into the countryside for members of His Majesty's Council to convene as soon as possible. Upon arrival at New Bern, he received further information about the wrecks and then sent reports of the disaster to the Duke of Bedford and to James Abercromby, the agent for North Carolina in London. Johnston complained that Bonilla had been in North Carolina for almost a month without asking for protection or any assistance, which Johnston told the officials in London that he was ready to provide. But until that time, he would take "no manner of Notice of them." Johnston reminded the Duke that his salary was now £12,000 in arrears and any other governor so situated would have felt justified in seizing the treasure under the laws of trade. To himself, Johnston took great notice. Thoughts of a million-dollar cargo in his jurisdiction, brought in by a former enemy, kept him awake at night.

New Bern was the present capital of the colony and center of trade for the Pamlico and Albemarle Sounds and located on the Neuse River about sixty-five miles from Ocracoke Inlet. While waiting for the council to arrive, Governor Johnston heard that Bonilla had been unloading and reloading the *Guadalupe* as well as bartering with the locals with goods and money from the ship, even after being warned against it. His actions were deemed "contrary to all Treaties and Usages" and subjected the ship to confiscation. Customs officers applied to Governor Johnston asking permission to make the seizure. Johnston refused saying it might jeopardize the peacetime relationship that was supposed to be developing between England and Spain. Seeking some legal means to go after the treasure, the customs officers turned to Peter Randolph in Virginia, surveyor general of customs in North America, for permission to seize the ship. Randolph readily agreed.

Word had gotten out that Thomas Wright had encouraged Bonilla to carry his cargo to Charleston, South Carolina. This would not only have infuriated Governor Johnston but would have been certain demise of his treasure. Since Bonilla had made no formal protest to protect his insurances, Governor Johnston knew he would be dealing with "a very wrong headed man."

Johnston became angry and frustrated over the conduct of the Spaniards. Respaldiza had already pushed the governor too hard for assistance. Upon his arrival in New Bern, Respaldiza wrote to Bonilla warning him that the Englishmen were nothing but "brutes" and that Johnston had no sympathy for their misfortunes because he saw "a wickedness only observed among the Spaniards and not in any other nation…"

Once Bonilla found out that Respaldiza was in New Bern, he sent a message and requested that some of his crew be sent down to Ocracoke as most of his men had now deserted. Respaldiza outfitted a sloop and promised the sailors extra pay if they would accompany him, but half way down the Neuse River, they rose against him, forcing him to turn back to New Bern. The local authorities threw the rebellious sailors in jail. Respaldiza incurred additional expenses to free them and Bonilla remained stranded, desperately in need of help.

Meanwhile, the Bankers plundered what they could out of the remains of the *Soledad* and *El Salvador*. The local officials stood by and watched. Governor Johnston realized that the *Guadalupe* was in serious danger as he heard of a "villainous confederacy" among the Bankers who were plotting to seize the galleon. He could not call out the local militia because many of them were reported to be involved in the scheme themselves. Even though he lacked sympathy for the Spaniards, he needed to maintain law and order in his colony or answer to the king.

Johnston realized that he needed a strong force at Ocracoke, one that he could control. At his disposal was the North Carolina station ship, HMS *Scorpion*, the twenty-gun sloop-of-war headquartered at Charleston, South Carolina. He dispatched an express rider to Charleston with orders for the *Scorpion* to proceed immediately to Ocracoke.

On October 5, Johnston reported to the council on the Spanish ships, in particular the *Guadalupe*. The council agreed to send to Ocracoke fellow councilman, Colonel James Innes, who lived on a plantation along the Cape Fear River. In 1740, Innes had served in the British army against the Spaniards at the fort of Boca Chica at Cartagena, Columbia. He understood the Spanish language and Spanish methods of trading and was well known for his judgment and cool conduct. His instructions were to assess the situation and find out what had to be done to protect the *Guadalupe*. Before leaving New Bern, Johnston also gave Innes secret instructions to infiltrate the Bankers and make false promises and spread misinformation to "amuse and delay them." He needed to buy some time for the *Scorpion* to get to Ocracoke.

Colonel Innes had to wait for the weather to clear before leaving. At Ocracoke, a gale raged, keeping Captain Bonilla pinned in his cabin. For over two days winds lashed the harbor, whipping up waves that rocked the *Guadalupe*. The ship, now fully loaded again, was hammering the bottom at high tide and was full aground as the tide ran out. The pounding could cause the stern post or some main frames or planking to give way and flood his ship, probably condemning her forever. Bonilla fretted over his ship and treasure. When the gale finally subsided, Oliver and some other Englishmen helped Bonilla move the ship higher up the inlet in deeper water, but he was still exposed to the weather. Soon, Bonilla discovered that the *Guadalupe* needed extensive repairs and would not be of any service in the transportation and rescue of his treasure. He would have to hire some English vessels to transport his cargo to the nearest safe harbor. That was Norfolk, Virginia, where a British warship, HMS *Triton*, was on station. The number of English seamen continued to increase at Ocracoke.

Four days before the gale, a sloop captained by William Blackstock arrived from Rhode Island. With him was his son-in-law, James Moorehouse from Connecticut, and sailors James McMahon and Enoch Collins. The gale had battered his sloop, rendering it useless. Blackstock was a short, powerfully built Scotsman who resided in Pasquotank County, North Carolina. He had lost an eye and insisted on wearing a primitive glass replacement; this had become discolored, making his handicap even more noticeable. His gruff, bombastic personality endeared him to no one. Blackstock needed only one eye to appreciate the opportunity that lay before him.

Just before the gale, a sloop called the *Mary*, owned and operated by Captain Samuel Fitz-Randolph of Woodbridge, New Jersey, joined the increasing number of waiting vessels that were filling the anchorage. Fitz-Randolph had left the port of Perth Amboy, New Jersey, on September 30 with his two sons, Sam Jr. and Kinsey. The other crewmen were the captain's son-in-law, William Waller, Thomas Edwards, Benjamin Moore, Joseph Jackson, and Silas Walker. Fitz-Randolph regularly traded with Virginia and the West Indies from his New Jersey home.

Bonilla, seeing "danger on all sides," realized that he needed to act quickly. He studied the *Seaflower* and the *Mary*. They looked like what he needed to get the most valuable cargo out of harm's way. Once again, he enlisted the aid of Thomas Wright as interpreter and sent him over to the *Seaflower* with Pedro Rodriguez. They negotiated with Wade to load as much cargo and treasure as he could onto the sloop for transport to Norfolk. Wade agreed after Bonilla offered 570 pieces of eight as prepayment. He could take the Lloyd brothers to Hampton, unload Bonilla's treasure and cargo, and find a new load for Boston, thus reaping an additional profit. This voyage would enable him to recoup his losses from his trip to Ocracoke in January. Rodriguez conveyed the same offer to Captain Fitz-Randolph using his crewman, William Waller, as interpreter. The *Seaflower* and *Mary* moved into position alongside the *Guadalupe* and on October 11 the loading began.

John and Owen Lloyd shuttled to and from their camp on shore to the sloops and the *Guadalupe* while befriending the crews. The Spaniards paid them no mind as the brothers had been their rescuers. Lloyd could see that the loading process was nearly complete and it looked like Bonilla was going to get his treasure to Norfolk. He had lost count of the treasure chests being loaded on the sloops. There were numerous bales of cochineal and tobacco being loaded as well.

Lloyd had been observing Pedro Rodriguez from the beginning. He saw the influence he had over the *Guadalupe* crew and Rodriguez's lack of respect for Bonilla. While many of the Spaniards had left, Rodriguez and others had remained. Owen discussed this with his older brother. They came to the conclusion that if the Bankers didn't seize the treasure it was likely that Rodriguez and his followers would. With the treasure and arms consolidated it looked like any attempt on the treasure would end up with bodily harm. Owen thought he saw a window of opportunity for himself.

James McMahon and Enoch Collins, two of Blackstock's crew, anxious to return to the north, applied for a position on the *Seaflower*. Wade told them they could get a ride to Norfolk but they would be working for free.

That evening, McMahon and Collins shared supper with Wade and his crew and the Lloyd brothers. Owen dropped suggestions, seemingly in jest, about what would happen if they were to sail away with the treasure. Captain Wade pretended not to hear. McMahon and Collins looked at each other in disbelief but said nothing. Wade's young crewmen began to dream of being rich. Never again, they whispered among themselves, would they ever see so much money in one place. These daydreams were interrupted when someone stated the obvious: that it was piracy and they could hang for it. Lloyd exploited their natural hatred and prejudice against the Spaniards. He reminded them that most of the English could care less if the Spaniards lost their money. Wade, seeing the look in his crewmen's eyes, tried to counter Lloyd's solicitations by relating stories of the pirate hangings in Boston twenty-four years before. He also reminded them that just stealing a horse was a hanging offense.

Lloyd dismissed the idea of hanging, telling Wade and the rest that they can't hang unless they were caught first. He pointed to the inlet three and a half miles away and offered that, once at sea, there was no one who could catch them. They could go to some West Indian island where they could live rich and unmolested for the rest of their lives.

Captain Wade reflected on his financial situation and the many months of the year he was away at sea separated from his family. He did not respond to Lloyd's last enticement.

Lloyd already knew that for any plan to work it would have to include Zebulon Wade. He offered him a way in and a way out. He told Wade that he could lock himself in his cabin and pretend he had nothing to do with it. If they got caught, Lloyd said he would take the blame and testify to that fact. The others smiled approvingly. Wade went to his cabin and said nothing. The seduction of Zebulon Wade had begun.

Just down the inlet at another camp, other plans were being hatched. The one-eyed Blackstock had been watching the Lloyd brothers shuttling between the sloops, the galleon, and shore. With Blackstock was a merchant named William Dames from the Eastern Shore of Maryland and an old man named Charles McClair. Dames knew the Lloyd brothers well. He had recently been sued by John Lloyd in Norfolk and lost a judgment of £80. Dames told Blackstock that the brothers were troublemakers and were up to something. Blackstock's former crewmen, Enoch Collins and James McMahan, began reporting back to him on what Lloyd had been saying on board the *Seaflower*. Blackstock began to develop a plan of his own.

The *Seaflower* was nearly full, loaded with fifty chests of silver pieces of eight, two chests of worked silver, 136 bales of cochineal, bales of tobacco stems, some indigo and hides. On board the *Mary* were fifty chests of silver, a chest of jewels, cochineal, and other valuables.

On October 16, Colonel Innes arrived from New Bern and boarded the *Guadalupe*. Observing that the sloops could easily make off with the treasure, he informed Bonilla that he was now in a "dangerous predicament." Innes told Bonilla to halt any further loading of the sloops until the *Scorpion* arrived. Unbeknownst to them was that she had left Charleston only the day before. Pointing out that it was foolish for Bonilla to place so much confidence in men who were strangers to him, Innes offered to oversee the transporting of the cargo to New Bern, a safe haven for the treasure. Bonilla agreed, but not Pedro Rodriguez, and he had all the crew on his side. In the end, it was decided not to unload the cargo from the sloops or change the destination to New Bern.

Colonel Innes's arrival stymied the plans of the local customs officers to use Randolph's authority in Virginia to effect a seizure. If they acted contrary to the governor's orders, they would have to answer to King George.

The *Seaflower* and the *Mary* separated from the *Guadalupe* and anchored close by. Bonilla and Colonel Innes were now ready to leave for New Bern. Bonilla ordered that ten armed Spanish guards be placed on board each sloop. Ten guards would clearly outnumber the English crew on each sloop. Bonilla also ordered that the sails be removed and put on shore, disabling the sloops and preventing their premature departure. These orders, signed by both Bonilla and Colonel Innes, were given in writing to Pedro Rodriguez. Either Bonilla thought that his boatswain would now obey an English official or Bonilla was too afraid or embarrassed to admit that he had no ranking officer whom he could really trust. His brother-in-law had no authority.

Pedro Rodriguez padlocked the cargo holds of the sloops and took the keys. As the sloops assumed anchorages close to the guns of the *Guadalupe,* Bonilla figured that the treasure was safe and the proximity of the *Mary* and *Seaflower* to his ship would keep the Englishmen from mischief.

Bonilla told his brother-in-law, Tomás Carriedo, that he would return as soon as he'd met with Governor Johnston. He was feeling a lot better about his situation as he departed for New Bern.

The next day, Owen and John rowed out to the *Seaflower*, boarded, and asked to see Captain Wade. Asking for some privacy, they retired to his cabin. The Spanish guards paid no attention to them.

Owen looked at Wade with a grave expression and told him that he had a serious problem. Wade, quite perplexed, asked for an explanation. Owen said that he thought he was in danger of losing his sloop and possibly his life. Wade frowned and looked confused. He told Owen that he had Rodriguez and his armed men guarding the treasure and the sloop and that they would be going with him to Norfolk. He even reminded Owen that he'd been paid 570 dollars. Owen laid out his case that Rodriguez couldn't be trusted and that Bonilla's orders meant nothing to him. He reminded Wade that Rodriguez had tried to run the galleon ashore before coming into the inlet. Owen told Wade that once the *Seaflower* was at sea that he and his crew would probably be shot and thrown overboard.

Wade slumped into his chair. The color drained from his face. He had not considered this possibility. What Lloyd had said made sense. Even if Rodriguez did not attempt such a thing, the Bankers might be planning an attack. He weighed his options. He told Owen he'd just give back their money and transfer the treasure back on board the *Guadalupe*.

Owen told him that it was too late for that. Once that demand was made it was certain that Rodriguez or the Bankers would make their move.

Wade was bent over with his face in his hands, massaging his brow. He had considered days before of succumbing to Lloyd's overtures but was pulled back by thoughts of his family. Now Zebulon Wade listened as Lloyd laid out his final plan.

Owen estimated that the next few days would be their window of opportunity. That same window applied to the others who had been plotting and planning. He explained that, based on his observations of the tides, the Spaniards would be having their lunch aboard the *Guadalupe* midday as usual and the tide would be going out. All they needed was a favorable wind.

Owen Lloyd realized that if he sailed away in the *Seaflower*, the Spaniards might pursue them in the *Mary*. After his meeting with Wade, Owen and John called on Captain Fitz-Randolph. They didn't realize that Fitz-Randolph and his crew already had acquired a lust for Spanish pieces of eight themselves.

When Colonel Innes and Captain Bonilla had departed for New Bern, Thomas Edwards and Kinsey Fitz-Randolph had gone below to their cabin in the *Mary* and cut a hole in the bulkhead separating the cargo hold from the cabin. They crawled inside and broke the seals on four treasure chests and removed a bag of coins from each chest. The four bags totaled 4,000 pieces of eight and were divided up between the captain, his two sons and several of the other crew.

The Lloyds explained their plan to Fitz-Randolph. They pointed out that the Spanish guards only stayed aboard the sloops at night then in the morning, they would leave for the *Guadalupe*. That could change any time, they argued, and Rodriguez could easily take off with the sloops when the armed guards were on board. His vessel and possibly their lives were at risk and it was going to happen soon. The *Scorpion* was on her way and Bonilla would be returning in a few days. On shore, the surly Bankers had the sloops under constant surveillance. When the Spanish guards were on the *Guadalupe*, they paid little attention to the sloops and would not be able to act quickly if both vessels acted in tandem. To succeed, they would have to sail out together, thus denying the Spaniards any ready vessel for pursuit. Fitz-Randolph welcomed the plan and John Lloyd came on board.

In the harbor, the changing tides would first point the vessels to the west away from the inlet's mouth as the tide ran out. As the tide ran in they would point towards the sea and the mouth of the inlet. The vessels would point seaward but the flow of water was against the escape route to the sea. For two days, Owen Lloyd had watched the tide changes. Every twelve and a half hours there was a high tide, the high tide peaking a half hour later each day. Every afternoon, the winds would generally come out of the southwest—a direction that was favorable for sailing out.

Contrary to Bonilla's order, the sails of the *Seaflower* and the *Mary* had not been removed. They could be raised at any moment. Moreover, there were only seven guards on each sloop, not the ten that Bonilla had ordered. Lloyd focused his attention on Rodriguez. He had clearly disobeyed his orders. *When will he make his move?* Owen wondered.

Hampton, Virginia, October 18

The two vessels hired by Captain Huony at the request of Felipe García were the brig *Letitia*, Captain Matthew Delany, and the schooner *Molly*, Captain John Pitton. They were loaded with biscuit, salted pork, a large barrel of aguardiente, and a smaller one of wine. There were ten sailors, six soldiers, and a sergeant on board. With favorable winds, they could reach Ocracoke in a day and a half. They had just received clearances from Major Wilson Cary in Hampton but departure was delayed. Unfortunately, Felipe García became ill and was confined to bed. Captain Huony appointed *La Galga's* Lt. Manuel de Echanis to go in his stead. They would not depart until October 21.

At the same time that García fell ill, HMS *Scorpion* came to anchor off Bald Head at Cape Fear, a two-day sail south of Ocracoke.

In Scituate, Massachusetts, Mercy Wade was wondering why Zebulon had not returned. Their wedding anniversary had been several weeks ago. Having missed the great hurricane, he should have been home for the celebration. She read in the Boston papers more accounts of ship losses at Ocracoke and of the Spanish fleet but no mention of the *Seaflower*. It looked like her husband might be facing more financial penalties on his late return.

Ocracoke Inlet

The mosquitoes lifted from the marsh in search of human prey as the sun set on this early fall evening. John Lloyd was complaining. He was anxious to leave and get to sea. Owen agreed.

Owen's plan was no different than what Rodriguez appeared to have in mind, but the safety of the sloops' crews were at least guaranteed. If they were caught, Owen was to take the blame and Captains Wade and Fitz-Randolph could disavow their involvement, saying that they were in their cabins and did not know of the conspiracy. It was a good plan, but thanks to the spies on board the *Seaflower*, it was no longer a secret.

William Blackstock was growing uneasy. He too wanted the treasure, but he also knew that the Bankers were looking for an opportunity and that the Spanish boatswain was up to something. HMS *Scorpion* could arrive at any moment. And now it looked like the Lloyd brothers had taken control of the situation. Blackstock's single eye darted between the loaded sloops and the *Guadalupe*. He turned and saw Enoch Collins headed his way.

"Tomorrow," said Collins. "It's going to happen tomorrow." Collins then returned to the *Seaflower*. Blackstock instructed William Dames, his son-in-law, and Charles McClair to get ready.

At dawn on October 19, Thomas Wright, the former prisoner on the *Guadalupe*, told people publicly that he was leaving for Charleston in a small boat with a Spaniard named Isidro Gonzáles, alias *Churribillu*. But instead of leaving right away, they remained in the vicinity out of sight.

Later that day, the *Scorpion* entered the Cape Fear River. Her captain, Thomas Randall, who had just taken command the month before, was oblivious to events 140 miles away at Ocracoke. The ship had taken on 850 gallons of beer and other supplies just before leaving Charleston on October 15. The *Scorpion* was en route to Johnston's Fort on the Cape Fear River to celebrate the anniversary of the coronation of King George on the 23rd. The express rider dispatched by Governor Johnston had arrived at Charleston too late.

October 20, 1750

Captain Blackstock watched Owen and John Lloyd board their skiff and pull for the *Seaflower*. Owen climbed aboard and John rowed over to the *Mary*, tied up the skiff, and joined Captain Fitz-Randolph on deck. The vessels, pointed eastward to the mouth of the inlet, tugging at their anchor cables. Because the tide was coming in, the time was not yet right. Blackstock watched impatiently from shore.

On board the *Guadalupe*, Thomas Carriedo was relaxing with his fellow Spaniards, hardly noticing the activity on the sloops. He was comforted knowing that Felipe García would return from Norfolk at any hour with armed guards and supplies from Captain Huony.

By 2 p.m., the Spanish guards were finishing lunch aboard the *Guadalupe*. The wind started to freshen from the southwest and the tide, as predicted, started running out. The *Guadalupe* swung around on her anchor cable as did the *Seaflower* and the *Mary*. From shore, a dinghy pushed off with Blackstock and his crew. On board the *Mary*, Captain Fitz-Randolph remained in his cabin. On deck, John Lloyd occasionally glanced at the *Seaflower*. In the bow of the *Seaflower*, Enoch Collins lounged at the anchor bit watching the quarterdeck and the skiff coming up from the rear against the current. Owen Lloyd was on the quarterdeck with Jonathan Deacon and Isaac Ray making a kerf for the anchor and James McMahon was idling, pretending not to notice the approaching skiff.

Below the quarterdeck in his cabin, Zebulon Wade lay in his bunk agonizing over what he had gotten himself into, nearly incapacitated with fear over what was about to take place. Owen Lloyd had seduced all of his crew and he'd been forced to go along. He stared at the cabin ceiling, listening to his crew shuffling about and their muffled conversations coming from above. When the tide changed, he felt the sloop pull tight on the anchor cable. He knew that this would be their last tide change at Ocracoke. Suddenly, his thoughts were interrupted. Something struck the hull of the *Seaflower* and he heard the scraping sound of oars pulled through their locks. He sat bolt upright, his heart pounding. He feared the Spaniards had returned. Something was wrong.

Indeed it was. Blackstock and his crew were swarming on board the *Seaflower*. They fanned out across the deck. Some went forward, slipping one anchor cable and weighing the second one up. The others proceeded to raise the sails while Blackstock took the helm.

From his bunk, Wade heard Owen Lloyd shout out, "In God's name, don't!"

Then there was a voice that he didn't recognize. "Shut up or I'll bash your brains in with this handspike!" It was Blackstock threatening Lloyd. Wade's heart sank deeper. There was a stranger onboard and there was a great commotion.

The *Seaflower* was now underway. Blackstock, still brandishing the handspike, had no idea that the helm pin was missing. The wind filled the sails as the sloop fell before the wind, scudding out of control. Unable to steer, they almost ran into a snow lying at anchor between the *Guadalupe* and the inlet and just cleared the broadside guns of the galleon.

Seeing all this from the *Mary*, John Lloyd alerted the crew and attempted to cut her anchor cable while the sails were being raised. The *Mary* veered into shallow water and ran aground, creating complete pandemonium. From the decks of the other vessels anchored nearby and along the shore of Ocracoke Island, reactions ranged from total disbelief and shock, to outright cheering. Many just smiled and watched, wishing the Lloyd brothers well. The Bankers scowled with disappointment.

"Recognizing the vileness of the two sloops leaving at the same time and for the same reason," the Spanish officials armed themselves and jumped from the *Guadalupe* into the ship's dingy and rowed after the *Seaflower*. They pleaded with Lloyd and his gang to stop.

Feeling the bow of his sloop rise on an ocean swell, Captain Wade knew they had cleared the treacherous sandbar outside the inlet. He rose from his bunk, looked out the stern windows, saw the Spaniards turn back and, with some relief, collapsed back into bed listening to the loud shouts and celebration overhead. His thoughts turned soon enough to his predicament. He was now a pirate, at least in the legal sense. His father had often talked about the pirate trials in Boston and the imprisonment of Captain Kidd at the Boston jail fifty years ago. What would Joseph and Ruth Wade think of him now?

On deck, Owen Lloyd was relieved to be clear of the inlet but distraught over the fact that his brother hadn't made it. His plans appeared to have been compromised. Owen now had to gain control of a situation he hadn't planned for. Fourteen-year-old Thomas Hobson could not believe what had just gone down. Not only was there a bold robbery of Spanish treasure but there had been a last-minute double cross. *If only Blackbeard were here!*

Chapter Five

The Voyage

After seeing Blackstock's crew weigh the second anchor and move for the helm, Owen Lloyd quickly regained his balance. This was no time for onboard conflict. He immediately barked out orders to Abraham Pritchett, Jonathan Deacon, and the other *Seaflower* crew to assist in setting the sails. Having accepted Lloyd as their new leader, they didn't hesitate to comply.

Lloyd only looked back to the inlet during the brief moments that permitted him. In his mind, he visualized the plight of his brother. But he had a fortune in treasure, greater than any single haul of Blackbeard, that was his to lose if he did not maintain control of the sloop's crew. As the sun was setting, he took one last look at Ocracoke Inlet as it disappeared from view. The *Seaflower* steered well off the coast in order to avoid the shoals of Cape Lookout. That night, they passed not only the wrecks of *El Salvador* and *Nuestra Señora de Soledad*, but the sunken hulk of Blackbeard's former flagship, the *Queen Anne's Revenge*.

Lloyd entered Wade's cabin and found him distraught, so he encouraged him to come on deck. He reminded him that he was a rich man and the worst was behind him. Lloyd needed Wade to show solidarity with him because he needed the loyalty of the crew if he were to marginalize Blackstock and his friends.

Wade paid little attention to Lloyd's request and demanded to know who the strangers were. Lloyd explained that they appeared to be friends of the crew that Wade had hired and insisted again that he come on deck.

Although unable to fully cope with his anxiety, Wade nonetheless agreed. He expressed his unity with Lloyd by proclaiming him master of the sloop, thus keeping Blackstock at bay. Lloyd declared that they were headed to the French Island of St. Bartholomew's that lay southeast of St. Martin and nearly in sight of St. Kitts, his ultimate destination. Wade returned to his cabin. Lloyd steered eastward for the edge of the north-flowing Gulf Stream on the assumption that HMS *Scorpion* was near shore and headed toward Ocracoke. Once they passed Charleston, they would be home free. Everyone kept an eye on the southern horizon looking for the approaching warship and across the stern to make sure they weren't being followed.

Unknown to Lloyd, the *Scorpion* had the day before detoured into the Cape Fear River and anchored just off Brunswick Town at Johnston's Fort—hardly a fort at all but a primitive affair of mounded sand for gun emplacements and a barracks building. It was named after the current governor, Gabriel Johnston, and was only two years old.

In the early morning of October 21, the express rider, who missed the *Scorpion* at Charleston, arrived at Cape Fear with news of the disabled Spanish galleon at Ocracoke. Captain Randall immediately hoisted a signal flag alerting all hands on shore and on board that the *Scorpion* was preparing to get underway. Unknown to Captain Randall, the treasure that he was ordered to protect had just sailed past him the day before.

Randall had only prepared for a short journey from Charleston to Cape Fear. As his crew were reboarding, fresh beef was loaded as well as firewood and water. By the time they were ready to sail, rain driven by gale-force winds had set in. It would not be until the morning of the 25th that the *Scorpion* could sail. Captain Randall remained to celebrate King George's coronation ceremony on the 23rd in spite of the foul weather. A fifteen-gun salute returned by the fort finished the event.

While the *Seaflower* was passing Cape Fear, the southwest winds had increased to a moderate gale with some driving rain. The overloaded sloop rolled in the swells and her bowsprit plunged into the seas, the leeward scuppers occasionally filling with water. Owen Lloyd was at the helm squinting at the horizon looking for the outline of other ships.

Though aware that this was King George's anniversary, the crew was oblivious to the celebration going on at Johnston's Fort. They were having their own party, and it was not in recognition of Britain's King George, but rather their windfall delivered to them by an incompetent Spanish galleon captain, subject of King Ferdinand.

Some crewmen, anxious to determine their share, began asking about it. Blackstock, wanting as much as possible for himself, suggested a paltry share of only fifty or one hundred pieces of eight to certain crewmen.

Lloyd seized the opportunity to solidify his authority. "Everyone, including the ship's boy, will get an equal share once we arrive at the island," he vowed.

Blackstock realized that he had to go along with Lloyd. The pecking order had been firmly established. Wade, as part owner of the *Seaflower* and captain, had passed his command to Lloyd.

The crewmen delighted in Lloyd's promise of an equal division. Each one of them dreamed of the comfortable future he would have. They each had money to buy his own plantation, including slaves, or to purchase his own vessel and hire crew. These thoughts blinded them to the reality that they were wanted men.

It was apparent from the start that there was not enough food to go around. The *Seaflower's* voyage had been planned for only eight men; now there were twelve. To avoid fighting, the food was shared and resulted in little open argument.

Captain Wade, physically ill, remained mostly in his cabin. The reality of the situation had set in and Zebulon Wade was worrying about seeing his family again. Hobson would, as he always liked, spend his free time out on the bowsprit, watching the dolphins ride the bow wave. The others, except for Blackstock and his cohorts, bonded, unified by dreams of wealth and shared adventure.

Aware that there would soon be people looking for the *Seaflower*, Lloyd chose to change the name to the *Elizabeth*, the name of his former sloop taken three years before by the infamous Spanish privateer, Don Pedro Garaicochea. Lloyd now had his revenge.

Lloyd's thoughts turned soon enough to his beloved wife Christian and St. Kitts. Once the treasure was divided he would return to his wife a rich man. She would soon forget all of his shortcomings and the hardship she had suffered in Virginia. During the voyage, Lloyd routinely turned the helm over to Blackstock and Abraham Pritchett while he reveled with the other crew.

St. Kitts, properly called St. Christopher's, is part of the Leewards, a chain of small islands which, combined with the Windward Islands, are collectively known as the Lesser Antilles.

In 1750, the English seat of government was Antigua, where the captain general of the Caribbean Islands presided. Antigua and St. Kitts were not just the centers of government but also the hubs of English civilization and trade. These islands, settled by the English, had many fine plantations that grew sugar cane, cotton, and tobacco.

The other islands, including Anguilla, Montserrat, and the Virgins, were "outposts" and were inhabited by a hardy and independent type with little respect for law and order. These people had seen the likes of Blackbeard, Stede Bonnet, and William Bellemy, pirates of the first order, come and go, and fearing for their lives, openly traded with them.

Shipping in the islands was often threatened by Spanish and French privateers. The islanders would sometimes avenge themselves. Should a vessel of another nation wreck in the Virgins, it was considered fair game and became legal plunder for those who lived at Tortola and Spanish Town, also known as Virgin Gorda, a former Spanish possession now occupied by the English.

One such incident occurred in 1734 when a Spanish ship wrecked on Anegada, a low-lying island north of Tortola and Spanish Town, which has a large coral reef that is almost impossible to see until you are upon it. Governor Matthew, Captain General of the Leewards, wrote to the Board of Trade in England about the incident: "I know not what to Do with the Inhabitants of Anguilla, Spanish Town and Tortola. They Live Like so many Banditts in Open Defiance to the Laws of God and Man. Whilst I was in England they Pyrated upon a Spanish Ship Wreck'd on the Angedoa as they always Do on Such Occasion and Did such things to Men of Distinction and their Ladys on Board as I cannot without Blushing Recollect to Myself, much less Repeat to Your Lords."

It did not take Lloyd long after the *Seaflower* struck out for the West Indies to realize that the hull of the sloop had become foul after her long anchorage in the warm waters of Ocracoke Inlet. She was a dull sailer as the growth of barnacles and moss created extra drag. After ten days, they had only made it in the latitude of the Bahamas. To the west, they passed Abaco, Eluethra, Rum Cay, and the Caicos. Lloyd steered well clear of them to avoid vessels trafficking with the Spanish islands of Hispaniola and Puerto Rico.

On or about November 11, Lloyd sighted the green mountains or rather large hills of Spanish Town. Realizing he was near the dangerous shoals of Anegada, he turned south for the open sea. Lloyd decided to put into Coral Bay at the southeast end of the Danish island called St. John's, which lay near the British Virgin Islands and forty miles north of St. Croix. He did not want to land in a more traveled port like St. Croix or St. Thomas carrying such a valuable, not to mention, illegal cargo. There was a small trading post inside Coral Bay where he could take on fresh water and supplies. Here he picked up some hogs, turkeys, chickens and some flour. It was common knowledge that the Danes bartered with English malcontents and pirates. It was in the neighboring island of St. Thomas that earlier Danish governors had given numbers of pirates protection.

James Moorehouse had allied himself with Lloyd, but his father-in-law, Blackstock, had not, and one of Lloyd's top priorities was getting rid of Blackstock and his two friends, Dames and McClair. To do so, he would have to propose an immediate division of the treasure. On November 12, before the *Seaflower* left St. John's, Lloyd informed the crew that they would be anchoring at a neighboring island and the treasure would be equally divided. Each would have the opportunity to either bury their share or risk keeping it.

The *Seaflower*, now the so-called *Elizabeth*, tacked out of Coral Bay and made for Norman's, a deserted island four miles east of them. The verdant peaks of the island were in plain view as they headed for the mouth of a large bay. Everyone was on deck, including Zebulon Wade. Shortly, it would be the moment that they all had been waiting for—the division of the Spanish treasure.

Chapter Six

Treasure Island

The *Seaflower* had arrived off the west end of Norman's Island on November 12, 1750. Before them was the mouth of a great bay flanked on each side with rocky and precipitous shores. The entrance was guarded by a nearby pointed rock jutting out of the water and resembling a giant Indian's head. The treasure-laden sloop dropped anchor behind some rocky cliffs that rose directly out of the sparkling turquoise sea. There were several partially flooded caves in the base of the cliff. Some of the crew thought that they might be a good place to hide their loot. On second thought, they decided that it would be safer for each man to bury his treasure in locations of their own choosing. Norman's Island had several high hills providing a commanding view of the sea at all approaches. They were in plain sight of Tortola and Road Town seven miles away that was the center of British government in the Virgin Island chain. But at that distance it was impossible to detect what they were doing.

This was the moment they had been waiting for. For twenty days they had tried to figure out exactly what was in the hold. There were many chests of coins, but they were mostly covered by the bags of cochineal and the bales of tobacco and hides. As soon as the hatch cover was raised and set aside, several excited sailors jumped down into the hold and started tossing bags of cochineal onto the deck. Then came the treasure chests—and the exclamations of sheer joy. They were all rich! The rum bottle was passed around. There was backslapping and celebration. Owen was a little more somber. He wished his brother were there. He also knew that he needed to maintain order as the division was made.

As the cargo was heaped on deck they could see that many of the chests and bales were marked with "B," Bonilla's initials. This brought out more unsympathetic laughter. In total they found:

50 chests of Spanish pieces of eight, marked with letter "B," each chest containing three bags of coins with one thousand per bag.
2 chests of wrought silver plate marked with "MB."
118 bags of cochineal containing two hundred pounds in each bag, marked with the letter "B."
10 more bags of cochineal with various owners' marks.
7 serons of indigo with different marks.
3 chests of vanilla.
86 tanned hides.
371 raw hides.
140 bags of tobacco stalks.

The total value of their theft was worth nearly a quarter of a million pieces of eight. Lloyd and his crew were euphoric. The last thing on their mind was the effect it would have on Juan Manuel Bonilla, that arrogant and bungling Spaniard.

It was agreed that the silver would be divided thus: each of the twelve men got four chests, including Thomas Hobson, the ship's boy. That left two remaining chests of coins that the crew voted to give to Captain Wade and Lloyd as a "present." The remaining two chests of worked silver, cochineal, indigo, vanilla, and hides were to be equally divided. That day, Thomas Hobson became one of the richest fourteen-year-old boys in the world.

On the 13th, the first of the treasure went ashore. Two-hundred-and-fifty-pound treasure chests were carefully lowered over the side into the bobbing dinghy and then rowed to shore. Lloyd pretended to be disinterested in where everyone was headed but secretly recorded in his mind where he thought the treasure was being buried. Lloyd then took his turn with Wade. Each man chose to keep various amounts of silver on board and their shares of the cochineal and tobacco were returned to the hold.

After everyone, including Lloyd and Wade, had buried their shares it was now Blackstock's turn. The next day, Blackstock, Dames, and McClair were put on shore with their shares of the treasure as well as their share of the cochineal, indigo, and tobacco. Blackstock's son-in-law, James Moorehouse, chose to remain aboard with his share.

No sooner than everyone's treasure was safely hidden, the *Seaflower* crew observed from across the sun-dappled waters a small boat coming from the direction of Tortola. When Lloyd realized that the boat was headed for them, he ordered all treasure and cargo still on deck to be stowed below. They watched and waited as the resolute craft closed in on them. Thomas Wallis, in his tiny coble, had been observing the *Seaflower* anchored off the uninhabited island for the last two days and decided to go over and investigate. After pulling alongside, he came aboard and inquired as to what they were doing and why they had they not come into the road of Tortola. Lloyd was quick to answer saying that they had stopped to fix a leak and would soon be on their way. Wallis seemed to accept Lloyd's explanation and rowed off. Lloyd wasted no time getting the anchor up and sailed for St. Thomas. Blackstock, Dames, and McClair were marooned with no food or water.

After the *Seaflower* was on her way, Thomas Wallis unexpectedly turned around and rowed back into the bay, discovering Blackstock on shore alone. Blackstock accepted his offer to go to Tortola but being concerned about what kind of trouble lay ahead, he gave the assumed name of William Davidson. Being in need of help, he confided in Wallis that they had salvaged some valuables from a wreck in North Carolina. Wallis took him to the house of Abraham Chalwell, the president of the council at Tortola. The lieutenant governor, James Purcell, was away in England to confer with members of the Board of Trade. Blackstock related his tale to Chalwell who took his deposition, but Blackstock still maintained that he was William Davidson. He admitted to leaving at Norman's cochineal, indigo, and some tobacco stems, which he said were worthless. Chalwell went over the next day to see for himself. He found the tobacco and then traveled to another part of the bay where, in addition to more cochineal, he happened upon Charles McClair and several others searching for treasure. Chalwell, quite excited about discovering some treasure of his own, confronted McClair with the threat, "old man if you have any money, bring it out, I will take care of it for you or these people will take your life for it." McClair brought out six bags of coins and reluctantly gave them to Chalwell, who stayed up all night guarding the treasure and then carried it over to Tortola the next morning.

On November 15, a shallop belonging to a Captain Purser of St. Kitts arrived at Norman's. McClair, who was still on the island, came upon three more bags as well as some loose coins scattered on the ground. They loaded this on Purser's shallop. By this time William Dames had appeared and, with him on board, they carried the money and cochineal to Chalwell's house at Tortola for safekeeping. Dames persuaded some of the looters to pay him some of what they found. He had convinced them that doing so would give them clear title to the money.

Others swarmed over from Tortola to "rob the robbers," as it was later described. They decided it was best to work as partners or in gangs to more effectively comb the island and cut down on what could be a dangerous competition. One such group, led by John Haynes, found three bags of silver, while another group led by John Collins and his gang found only one. They decided to join forces with others on the island and that each man would share alike, except the owners of the vessels that brought them to the island, who would reap an extra share. Things became more complicated when another group, headed by Christopher Hodge and Thomas Stephens, two other Tortola residents, came upon a large cache, prompting Haynes and Collins to demand a share of it.

All of the booty was taken to John Haynes' house on Tortola for storage and later division. William Dames followed them there to claim what more he could.

St. Thomas

Just as Norman's Island was fading from view, Lloyd could see the harbor of St. Thomas over the *Seaflower's* starboard bow. He and the others were greatly relieved to be rid of Blackstock. But the rules of the game had changed. Lloyd had been certain that after his getaway from Ocracoke it would take a while for the news of the robbery to reach the West Indies, giving him time to return to his wife and get safely situated. He had no idea that the treasure had already been discovered. The *Seaflower* came to anchor in the harbor of the West India Company at Charlotte Amalie, St. Thomas. The sloop's hull was totally fouled and she was too slow to be of any further use. She would have to be careened before they could proceed to St. Kitts. Still on board were a number of chests of treasure, and a great deal of cochineal, indigo, vanilla, and hides. Lloyd felt safe here because of the reputation the island had for welcoming refugees, thieves, and even pirates. After leaving Abraham Pritchett in charge of the *Seaflower*, Lloyd and Wade set off to find Governor Christian Suhm and make application for citizenship. Wade was a nervous wreck, leaving Lloyd to do all of the talking. Suhm, the thirty-one-year-old governor, took to Lloyd's charms and told him that he would be welcome to the island but he would have to get his wife. That would prove his intention to become a permanent resident. But Lloyd was smart enough not to divulge that he had stolen the treasure or that he still had a quantity on board the *Seaflower* in the harbor. Lloyd now needed to get to St. Kitts as soon as possible, so he chartered a schooner and departed for St. Croix with Wade, Thomas Hobson, Jonathan Deacon, Isaac Raye, and James Moorehouse with their share of the remaining treasure. Pritchett was to remain and finish the overhaul with the other crew.

After they departed, word reached St. Thomas about the free-for-all going on at Norman's and Blackstock being questioned by the authorities at Tortola. Gert Sprewart de Wint, a merchant of the island, noticed the unregistered sloop in the harbor and sent notice to Governor Suhm. Cannons from Fort Christian were fired, alerting everyone to be on the lookout. Pritchett knew that he needed to get away as soon as possible. He and James McMahon also chartered a schooner and loaded aboard their shares of the treasure that they still had on board the *Seaflower*. The captain of the schooner became concerned when he saw the chests and insisted that they inform the governor. But he was paid well and agreed to take Pritchett and McMahon to St. Eustatius, a Dutch Island near St. Kitts, where they promised that they would notify the governor. Enoch Collins was detained in town for five days while he was questioned. He later fled on his own to neighboring St. John's.

Sheriff Ditlev Wildhagens ordered a search of the abandoned sloop and prepared an inventory of everything, including the pigs and chickens. The animals were immediately put to auction while Governor Suhm took possession of the rest. After arriving at St. Croix, Lloyd and Wade bought a sloop from someone named Jan Wats for 3,000 pieces of eight and proceeded to St. Kitts.

Ocracoke

Having learned that the *Seaflower* and Zebulon Wade were from New England, Bonilla dispatched one of his officers to Rhode Island and Boston to go look for Wade on the chance that he had returned home. He brought news of the event, which was reported in the *Boston News-Letter* of November 19. The paper said that the *Seaflower* got away with 150,000 dollars in chests of silver and 100,000 dollars worth in cochineal after twelve men had repelled the Spaniards with the threat of gunfire. Zebulon and his crew could be in the area by this time, the article surmised, but that apprehending him might be difficult as "a man with such a number of dollars about him, may be said to have powerful friends."

The *New York Gazette* of November 23 had reported their concern over the incident:

> It is much feared that the master and mariners will meet with condign punishment, besides bringing lasting infamy on the British nation, for their treachery to people in distress…and give the Spaniards a plea for using poor Englishmen ill, that may have the misfortune to fall into their hands: They will doubtless think they ought to have justice come them; notwithstanding if any of our vessels from the Bay happen to be lost on their coast, or put their ports in distress, they will not only seize the vessel and cargo, but make the men prisoners; although they have in nature no more right to the wood in the Bay, than the English have to the mines in Mexico. Their depredations and captures on the high seas by their Guarda Costas, is a piece of Villany, little inferior to this robbery; tho' tamely suffered by us, who are near becoming dupes of all nations.

Mercy Wade found all of this impossible to believe. She had to tell her children that she did not know when their father would be coming home. As for Zebulon's parents, they were dumbfounded.

Norman's Island

Wallis took Blackstock back over to Norman's to search for more treasure. Having no luck, they heard that everything had now been taken away by the plantation owners of Tortola. It was said that President Chalwell's son had twenty bags, John Haynes had thirty bags, and that Mrs. Adrianna Jeff had made off from the island with "two canoe loads of money, jewels and plate." Among others, a man named O'Neal came over from Virgin Gorda to join in on the plunder as had Rebecca Purcell, the sister-in-law of Governor Purcell who was still away in England.

On November 21, a council meeting was held at President Chalwell's house at

Sea Cow Bay, Tortola. Before they could get to the issue of the treasure, Chalwell's father delivered up a Negro woman named Monimia, who had allegedly killed a slave that belonged to him. Monimia confessed, whereupon the council convicted her of murder and sentenced her to be hanged by the neck until she was dead.

Moving on to new business, President Chalwell informed the board that Blackstock (aka William Davidson), William Dames, and Charles McClair (now going under the alias of Charles Livingston) had landed at Norman's Island with some money, cochineal, and indigo, which they removed from a Spanish wreck on the Carolina coast. Chalwell produced the deposition of Blackstock. Major James Young, councilman and coroner for Tortola, thought that perhaps they should be detained. Then he reconsidered, and after a vote it was decided by four to two that the anxious three could leave with the money and effects then in Chalwell's possession.

This being decided, the money and cochineal—worth nearly 9,500 pieces of eight—was divided up among Blackstock, Dames and McClair, and the officials of Tortola. Blackstock kept one bag of indigo and the remaining cochineal was sold for cash.

Dames gave President Chalwell a "present" of five pieces of silver plate for his wife and then convinced Christopher Hodge, John Collins, and the others, when they arrived with more money, to give him 1,180 pieces of eight in return for a receipt stating the silver still in their possession was legally theirs.

Anxious to leave Tortola before anyone changed his mind, Dames and Blackstock bought Captain Purser's shallop for 1,000 pieces of eight. At first, Chalwell refused to clear them but after a discussion, the council agreed that they could leave without cargo for North Carolina. Dames and McClair decided to separate from Blackstock. Dames purchased his own sloop, the *Rebecca*, and paid to have the vessel registered to him as of December 1, 1749, instead of 1750, hopefully providing him additional cover as he was going to flee to Bermuda. He arrived there on February 10, 1751, and promptly sold his interest in the sloop. She was then renamed the *True Blue*. Three days later, he sailed for Madeira and from there, proceeded to Ireland. McClair remained behind and married a "young woman" from President Chalwell's family.

At Sea, November 24, 1750

Owen Lloyd could see Mt. Misery, the extinct volcanic mountain that crowned the northern end of St. Kitts, coming into view. The ever-present grey cloud necklaced its peak. The trade winds carried a mixture of the sweet scent of the cane fields, the pungent odor of the manure used in the new plantings, and the acrid smoke from the fires beneath the steaming coppers of cane juice. Wade, Hobson, Deacon, Moorehouse, and Raye were anxious to see this beautiful island that Lloyd had so often described. Lloyd was envisioning a grand reception, much like the one he had five years earlier when he brought in the French Guineaman.

They arrived at Dieppe Bay, a small village at the north end of St. Kitts that lay in the shadow of Mt. Misery, and anchored inshore of the Hogsties reef. This was directly opposite the plantation of Charles Caines, Owen Lloyd's twenty-five-year old brother-in-law. That same day, Blackstock, with Captain Purser, Dr. Thomas Young of Tortola, and an unidentified old man as crew, left Tortola for St. Eustatius, which lay only nine miles northwest of the Caines plantation.

When the sloop anchored, Lloyd rowed ashore, bringing along his newfound friends and some of his treasure. From up the hill at the main house, Charles and Christian, who saw the sloop come to anchor, strolled down to the beach to investigate. Lloyd recognized them and began laughing and then waved to let them know it was he. Once the boat touched the black sand beach, Owen jumped out of the boat and rushed to greet his anxious wife.

"We're rich! We're rich!" exclaimed Lloyd. "Our problems are over!" Christian failed to react, but hung her head as Charles stepped forward and told Lloyd that they knew what he had done and that he was in big trouble. He told Lloyd that the whole Caribbean was looking for him.

Lloyd was surprised that this news had preceded him. He immediately thought about his brother John back in Ocracoke. Had the officials there been able to make him talk? Was he a prisoner of the Spaniards—of the English?

Charles interrupted that thought, suggesting somewhat forcefully that he'd better leave as soon as possible. The Caines family was well known on the island. Charles could not afford the scandal.

Lloyd protested, claiming that Lt. Governor Burt could be convinced to let him stay. But things had changed at St. Kitts. There were new governors in office. Lt. General Gilbert Fleming was now acting governor of the Leeward Islands and had just installed Ralph Payne as deputy governor for St. Kitts, replacing the incompetent and crooked William Burt. Lloyd was told that Fleming was on the island and at his plantation so he needed to leave right away for everyone's sake.

Christian sat on a volcanic rock that resembled a small, low-backed chair that protruded from the lawn while Owen tried to console her. He explained to Christian that he had been offered asylum at St. Thomas, but only if she would return with him. Unfortunately, Christian was not prepared to go. Lloyd looked across the sea to the neighboring island of St. Eustatius. The island was a principal Caribbean trading center and an open port owned by the Dutch. Lloyd felt comfortable going there as the Dutch had no use for the Spanish and they would certainly find no disfavor of his actions at Ocracoke. Lloyd pointed to Mt. Mazinga, which towered over the small island making St. Eustatius seem closer than the nine miles it really was. "I will be right over there," he assured Christian.

Lloyd promised that he would return for her once she was ready to leave for St. Thomas. Before he beat a hasty retreat, Lloyd turned over to his brother-in-law more than 5,000 pieces of eight as well as a silver basin, a silver cup, a serving dish, plates, cutlery, a salt shaker and other items of worked silver that had belonged to Bonilla.

St. Eustatius

On November 26, Lloyd and his crew sailed casually into the harbor and moored opposite the lower part of town just off the warehouses and shops. The other ships swinging at their anchors paid them no mind. James Moorehouse, Jonathan Deacon, and Isaac Raye went ashore to find a tavern, leaving Lloyd, Wade, and Hobson on board.

Unbeknownst to all of them, Governor Johannes Heyliger had just received notice of the piracy from Governor Johnston in North Carolina. He was informed that Owen Lloyd and Zebulon Wade were headed for the West Indies. Word quickly spread around the island and to the ships in the harbor that a fantastic theft had occurred. The *Seaflower* was to be apprehended along with her crew. Heyliger had not yet heard the Lloyd had abandoned her at St. Thomas.

As Moorehouse, Deacon, and Raye were celebrating in the tavern, offering up pieces of eight without asking for the return change for their food and drink, the presence of Lloyd's schooner was brought to the attention of Governor Heyliger.

Soldiers were dispatched to the vessel to investigate, and after boarding, demanded that Lloyd and Wade show their registration papers. Lloyd led them to believe that Wade was in charge. Wade, identifying himself as Jacob Gerard, admitted that he had no registration for the schooner. Upon inspection of the vessel, the Dutch authorities found 5,702 pesos, a silver button, and three silver spoons. Heyliger ordered them arrested and taken to the fortress above town. Alerted by the commotion, Moorehouse, Raye, and Deacon left the tavern and watched the soldiers escort their three shipmates up the hill and through the gate of the fort. The prisoners were then locked in a barracks building. Not tarrying a moment longer, the other three turned on their heels and fled the island.

Blackstock arrived at St. Eustatius soon after, but when he found out what happened to Lloyd, he and his crew fled to the island of Anguilla, about a day's sail to the north. After landing, Blackstock resumed his charade as Davidson. Here he met a Daniel Smith and loaded his silver, cochineal, and indigo on board Smith's vessel. Blackstock had told him of the piracy and that he needed to escape the Caribbean. Governor Benjamin Gumbs of Anguilla, who had also just received Governor Johnston's proclamation, grew suspicious of the new arrivals. Accompanied by guards, he marched down to the beach and ordered Blackstock and his vessel seized. After questioning Blackstock about the cochineal and indigo, Gumbs put guards on Blackstock's shallop and Smith's sloop as well. During the commotion, however, Smith was able to get the silver ashore and hide it before the guard came on board. Gumbs then sailed over to St. Kitts and called on Governor Payne to report on his discovery.

At 1 p.m. on the same day that Lloyd left St. Kitts for St. Eustatius, Lt. General Gilbert Fleming and his wife had left their hillside home outside Bassaterre, St. Kitts, and boarded HMS *Shark*. After a routine salute of thirteen guns from the fort, the warship departed for St. John's, Antigua, the capitol of the British Leeward Islands. The Duke of Bedford had ordered him to assume temporary governorship of the Leewards while the captain general, William Matthew, was in England. Fleming told the island officials that he would probably be away for several months attending to chancery business and a scheduled visit to Montserrat.

Flemings' appointment of Ralph Payne as Deputy Governor of St. Kitts in the place of William Burt had been well received on the island. When Fleming had informed Payne that he was leaving, he knew nothing of Lloyd's landing days before at the north end of the island.

St. Thomas

No sooner had Owen Lloyd left St. Thomas than Governor Suhm made his move on the valuable cochineal and indigo discovered aboard the abandoned *Seaflower*. On November 28, 1750, he sent two officials from St. Thomas, Mathias Hyldloft, secretary, and Stephen Desbroses, counselor, to Puerto Rico to meet with the newly installed Spanish governor, Agustin de Pareja. Their mission was to discuss the issue of Negro slaves escaping to Puerto Rico and gaining protection there by "embracing the Christian religion." Upon their arrival they presented a flattering greeting from Governor Suhm:

> I also knew the rare qualities which are yours, particularly your integrity and feelings for justice which deserve all attention. Therefore I cannot wait to present to your Highness my congratulations and I wish with all my heart that the desires of your Highness may always be fulfilled and that the government may give you many opportunities for clearly illustrating your noble merits and for furthermore taking the profit of them.

Governor Suhm had made no mention of the *Seaflower* sitting in his harbor loaded with Spanish goods, although Pareja already knew that they were there from reports coming in from Spanish crews who had left the wrecks in North Carolina and made it to Puerto Rico. In an unexpected move, Desbroses took it upon himself to file a written report about Owen Lloyd's arrival at St. Thomas and the discovery of Spanish treasure at Norman's Island. He was there at the beginning when Lloyd had arrived and had even purchased two turkeys from the sheriff's sale of livestock aboard the *Seaflower*. Desbroses told Pareja that Lloyd had fled to St. Croix and bought a sloop and it was said he intended to fetch his wife from St. Kitts and then return to St. Thomas.

Governor Pareja drafted a response to Suhm. He told Suhm that he knew of Lloyd's theft, that he was certain that the Spanish cargo belonged to Spain, and that he expected it to be safeguarded until it could be picked up. As for Lloyd, "Captain Owen Lloyd is certainly malicious and the suspicion held of his person is fundamental with regard to this event." Pareja also said he was writing to Lt. General Fleming at Antigua to inform him of the affair.

St. Eustatius

On November 28, Governor Heyliger called a meeting of the council and ordered the interrogation of the prisoners. In his deposition, Wade readily admitted his true identity and gave them his age of thirty-three and his birthplace, Scituate, Massachusetts. They questioned him further as a Dutch scribe recorded their testimony:

The council: "Captain Wade, why did you use the name Jacob Gerard?"

Wade: "Because I was captain of a vessel that had made a mistake and I knew that this would be known very soon around."

The council: "And what mistake is that?"

Wade: "Having carried away cash, cochineal, indigo, hides and tobacco from North Carolina taken from a Spanish ship there."

They asked him to identify those who had accompanied him and to explain how the treasure had been divided.

Wade: "At Norman's Island everyone hid and buried his share to his own liking and after the division there were two chests with money left, one of which had been given to him [Wade] as a present because he was the captain and joint owner of the vessel. The other one had been given as a present to Owen Lloyd."

Wade went on to explain that St. Thomas was their ultimate destination and that they had not formulated any plans after that.

The council: "Don't you know that this is punishable by death?"

Wade: "Yes, many out of foolishness have been urged to do so."

The council: "Who persuaded you to do this"?

Wade: "William Blackstock, William Dames, Charles McClair and James Moorehouse—Owen Lloyd already being on board—came on board and whilst I was in my cabin they locked me in and immediately I heard that the ship was unmoored."

The council: "Did you make any noise or cry for help as you noticed this?"

Wade: "No, because that wouldn't have helped."

The council: "After you took off with the money did the Spaniards pursue you or shoot at you?"

Wade: "They did not shoot, but lowered a boat that could not catch up with us."

When they were done with Wade, the council had Owen Lloyd brought in.

After some preliminary questioning in which Lloyd explained that he was born in Wales and last lived in Virginia, they asked about Wade:

The council: "Why does he call himself Jacob Gerard when you call him Zebulon Wade?"

Lloyd: "I can't help it when someone takes a false name."

The council: "Why are you here in the fortress?"

Lloyd: "I was ordered by the Governor to sit in here."

The council members, exasperated with his evasions, asked, "Didn't you realize you could be thrown in jail for this?

Lloyd: "No, on the contrary. It was our intention to go to St. Christopher's after coming from North Carolina and there I would have disclosed everything, but the captain and crew changed course at night and I had been only a passenger. They had first arrived at St. John, where they had bought some provisions and from there to Norman's Island."

The council: "When you arrived at St. Christopher's, what would you have disclosed there?"

Lloyd: "If we had sailed to St. Christopher's, I would have gone immediately to the attorney John Baker and tell him how I had been a passenger in a vessel that was carrying very much cash and would have advised him."

Lloyd, portraying himself as an innocent passenger, gave his account of the division of treasure at Norman's and described Blackstock and Dames as the chief "instigators of the whole enterprise." They were the ones, according to Lloyd, who had demanded in vain that they all sign and swear to "articles" to keep everything secret.

The council: "When you were at St. Christopher's did you tell anyone about the money and where you buried it at Norman's?"

Lloyd: "I told my wife, nowadays being there, and my brother-in-law, Charles Caines, and to some other people on the plantation. But because my brother-in-law said that he believed that I had committed something bad, I had become numbed and had been terrified into such a state that I did not know what to do and in that state I had come here."

The council: "We understand that the people of Tortola have uncovered a lot of money. It is said that they have fifty-two chests full of money. Could there be any left?"

Lloyd: "I'm willing to die if I would not find another part, because it was almost impossible that all the money could be found, without being discovered by me, Captain Wade or the three sailors who had come here with me."

The council: "Do you know the whereabouts of the three sailors you left at St. Thomas?"

Lloyd: "No, I have not seen them since."

Next they called in Thomas Hobson, the ship's boy. After being asked the same questions and offered nothing new, he was let go and the council, presided over by Governor Heyliger, began deliberations.

Lloyd had convinced them during his testimony and afterwards that he could lead them to the remaining treasure buried at Norman's Island. Governor Heyliger wanted some of the loot for himself as he had a personal grievance against the Spanish. He claimed they owed him 3,800 pesos for a boat and for four valuable slaves who had escaped the year before to Puerto Rico. The Spaniards had informed him that they were not liable for anything, as the slaves had left the "heretics" of St. Eustatius to convert to Christianity. Heyliger and the council agreed to Lloyd's proposal. He was escorted onto the bark, *Don Phillip*, bound hand and foot in chains. Next came Commandant Andres Ravene and a unit of soldiers. On November 28, at 7:30 that evening, Captain Jan Farrow weighed anchor and the *Don Philip* sailed for Norman's Island. Ravene was also carrying a letter to be delivered to the governor of St. Thomas that demanded possession of the *Seaflower* and Lloyd's accomplices, Pritchett, McMahon, and Collins. But Ravene would not need that letter. After leaving St. Thomas, Pritchett and James McMahon sailed on to St. Croix in their rented schooner but found that Lloyd had left already for St. Kitts. By November 24, Pritchett and crew were again underway and making for St. Eustatius. After recognizing the extinct volcanic peaks of St. Eustatius and Saba jutting from the sea, the young adventurers decided to go ashore at Saba and have some fun.

St. Kitts

Governor Ralph Payne was anxious to report to his superiors his account of the capture of Blackstock and his stolen cargo. Without losing time, he penned a letter on November 30 to Gilbert Fleming, who was en route to Antigua. Payne knew that Fleming would be impressed with his assumption of responsibility. He informed Fleming about the discovery of the stolen treasure at Norman's Island, adding that the chief pirate was Owen Lloyd, husband to Christian Caines of St. Kitts. Her deceased father, of course, was well known to Fleming, as Charles Caines was one of the original subscribers to land in Cabosterre, the former French section of St. Kitts. Fleming was the commissioner for that land subscription in 1725. Payne told Fleming that "he thought it his duty to acquaint your Honor of this most flagrant piece of wickedness." And for the people of Tortola, he added that it would be difficult to "wrest it (the treasure) out of the hands of such people." Payne informed him that President Chalwell, although doing his utmost to secure the stolen treasure, was "a considerable sharer of the spoils." Payne heard from reliable sources that Lloyd had sent "two barrels of dollars" to his wife, so he directed Richard Wilson, Chief Judge of the Court of the King's Bench, to issue a warrant for the seizure of the treasure at the Caines plantation.

In the afternoon of November 30, after a tedious three-day sail from St. Kitts, HMS *Shark,* with Gilbert Fleming aboard, arrived at St. John's, Antigua, to a thirteen-gun salute from the garrisons at James Fort and Rat Island. The next day, there was a grand reception attended by most of the distinguished gentlemen and ladies of the island. Three days later, Fleming received Governor Payne's letter about the treasure being discovered at Tortola, and promptly, but very discreetly, assembled an armed guard. He gave orders to find transportation to Tortola as soon as possible. He was preparing to go on a treasure hunt in the name of King George of England.

As luck would have it, HMS *Shark* had just sailed the day before for Carlisle Bay, Barbados, to rendezvous with HMS *Tavistock, Glasgow,* and *Rose.* The sloop *Christian* and a shallop were hired and manned with nearly seventy troops from Lt. General Philips's regiment. Also on board were Fleming's servants.

On the morning of December 3, Lt. General Fleming hastily wrote to the Duke of Bedford to express his concerns that President Chalwell of Tortola was "failing in his duty and even sharing in the cash" and while referring to the inhabitants of Tortola as "banditti," he said that "few of them have better principles." William Matthew, the captain general of the Leeward Islands, had appointed Captain James Purcell as the lieutenant governor of Tortola. He needed a strong leader who was upright and had the courage and fortitude to govern the ungovernable. Purcell was the man for the job, as he had distinguished himself as a brave privateersman in the late war. Purcell also maintained a plantation at St. Kitts.

After disparaging the people of Tortola for their evil ways, Fleming praised the new deputy governor of St. Kitts while condemning William Burt, whom he had just replaced. "It is very probable that if I had left the Command to Mr. Burt, the best thing that would have happened would have been his silence until all of the money had vanished".

Before departing, Fleming honored his previous commitment to attend a joint session of Antigua's assembly and council at the new courthouse. Fleming was warmly received. He proclaimed his loyalty to King George II and reassured the house members that he was a "sincere friend" of Antigua. After he spoke, Colonel Samuel Martin, the speaker, rose, and thanked Fleming for his willingness to assume command of the Leeward Islands, demonstrated by his prompt arrival from St. Kitts. He pledged the loyalty and obedience of his fellow Antiguans to Fleming and the king. It was a flowery ovation, but Fleming heard none of it. He could barely keep focused on the officials assembled before him. His thoughts were of buried treasure.

Fleming made no public statement about the theft of the treasure or his imminent departure. The last thing he needed was to incite those people of Antigua who might want to join the free-for-all at Norman's Island. The preparations and ultimate departure of Gilbert Fleming were reported the next day in the *Antigua Gazette*, leaving the residents to wonder what kind of situation demanded such secrecy and haste as well as such a large contingent of soldiers.

On the morning of December 4, Fleming boarded the *Christian*. Before heading for Tortola, he stopped for intelligence at St. Kitts and to post his proclamation for apprehending Owen Lloyd and the others. Copies were going to be sent to Nevis and Montserrat.

The proclamation only named Owen Lloyd as one of the pirates, as Fleming had not yet learned the names of his confederates. He commanded the officers of justice in the Leeward Islands to do all in their power to apprehend Lloyd and his associates and recover as much of the treasure as possible so that it could be restored to the Spanish. And to the citizens in general:

> I do hereby require and Charge all Persons whatsoever at their Perils not to be any way aiding or assisting or to harbor or Conceal the said Pirates and Felons or any of them and that all and every person and persons whatsoever within my said Government do forthwith deliver up to me the said Lieu^t

General or Lieu^t Governor or Deputy Governors being upon the respective Islands within my Government all and every part of the treasure come to their hand, possession, or power upon pain of being prosecuted as Law Directs as parties or Accessories to the same Piracy and Felony....

That night, the *Christian* anchored in Basseterre Harbor, St. Kitts, near Governor Payne's plantation and barely a mile from Shadwell, Fleming's own residence. Governor Payne and Governor Gumbs, who was still there, came out to speak with him about Davidson (Blackstock), his shallop with the cochineal, and his accomplices being held at Anguilla.

Fleming and Governor Gumbs departed and headed for Anguilla to interrogate the prisoners. Upon arrival, Fleming questioned everyone and realized that Blackstock had indeed been involved in the North Carolina incident. As for Daniel Smith, Fleming found him "so hardened in his villany that I could not bring him to a confession." He ordered everyone released but Smith and Blackstock, who had agreed to a make a full confession. Fleming took Blackstock's deposition en route to Tortola, where he confessed that his real name was in fact William Blackstock, not Davidson. As the *Christian* continued on to Tortola, Fleming was given a full account of Blackstock's version of events as they had unfolded in North Carolina and at Norman's Island, and his dealings with President Chalwell and the other officials at Tortola. Blackstock also insisted that Owen and John Lloyd were the instigators of the piracy and, "having been ill-used by Lloyd," he decided it best to remain at Norman's Island with Dames and the old man, Charles McClair, though Blackstock was still calling him Charles Livingston.

Fleming, although not surprised by the conduct of the officials at Tortola, realized that their actions would complicate the recovery of the Spanish treasure. He was still suspicious of Blackstock and later, when he related his confession to the Duke of Bedford, he revealed that Blackstock "seemed as ingenuous as if he had only a regard for the truth." Fleming, with the soldiers on board to back him up, was relishing the idea of bringing some law and order to the Virgin Islands. He also harbored his own fantasies about the buried treasure and the capture of Owen Lloyd. Before arriving, Fleming had drafted a new proclamation to be posted at Tortola and to be distributed throughout the islands.

On November 30, while Fleming was departing St. Kitts for Antigua, Owen

Lloyd was on the *Don Phillip* making an unscheduled return to Norman's Island with his Dutch guards. At four that morning, they were drifting in a windless sea toward the island of Saba. Captain Farrow informed the guards that he needed to go ashore and purchase an anchor that would be needed at Norman's. While he was ashore, the wind picked up and the crew was able to bring the bark into the harbor. By now it was ten in the morning. Captain Farrow rowed back to the *Don Phillip* and reported to Ravene that he'd just seen two suspicious-looking seamen ashore who had just arrived in a schooner rented at St. Croix. They appeared to have a lot of money because they were buying things while offering more than what they were worth.

After ordering the soldiers to guard Lloyd and keep an eye out in case they were needed, Commandant Ravene went back with Captain Farrow to pay a little visit to the schooner and ask some questions. Ravene told the soldiers to keep their distance so as not to raise any alarm. When they boarded the schooner, they found two men and a black boy. Ravene asked the men where they had come from, who the captain was, and where they intended to go. The two men cooperated, saying that one of them was a passenger, and the other crew, and that the two who had hired the boat were ashore with the captain and another passenger.

Presently, Abraham Pritchett and James McMahon came back to the schooner and found Ravene and Farrow on board. Ravene asked them what they were doing there and they said that they had merely hired the schooner to go to St. Eustatius with some friends. Ravene wrote down their names, then sent Captain Farrow over to the *Don Phili*p to ask Owen Lloyd the names of his accomplices. Lloyd gladly complied.

Meanwhile, Ravene took the opportunity to question the black boy about these passengers. Did they have any money? he asked, "hard pieces of eight?"

"Yes," the boy replied, "There were pieces of eight on board."

Farrow returned from his visit with Lloyd and with the names that were given to him. Ravene compared the two lists and found that they did not correspond. He gave orders to have Lloyd brought on board. Pritchett and McMahon, more frightened than agitated, demanded to know by what authority he had seized control of the schooner. "You will know very soon!" Ravene snapped.

In due course, Lloyd came on board, shuffling along in clanking chains. His fellow conspirators took one look at him and their faces fell. There was no way out. Lloyd, who was asked if he knew them, readily acknowledged their identities.

Ravene ordered them arrested and demanded to know if there was any money on board. Yes, they admitted, there was some money and silver plate stored below. Ravene found a chest and two barrels of treasure in the hold. Every coin and piece of silver was counted and the final total recorded—11,167½ pieces of eight and 478 ounces of old worked silver. The two prisoners were sent ashore in handcuffs and placed in the custody of the commander of Saba. Later, Ravene gave orders to have Pritchett and McMahon sent along with the treasure to Heyliger at St. Eustatius. Lloyd was hauled back aboard the *Don Philip*, chains dragging.

Commandant Ravene proceeded to Norman's Island, where he arrived on December 4. He took Lloyd ashore at the places Lloyd had previously described as locations of buried treasure. All that was found were twenty-one pieces of eight strewn about the sand, overlooked somehow by whoever had beat them to it. For Lloyd, there was some measure of relief because it showed he was telling the truth, but he had not lived up to his end of the bargain and had to face Governor Heyliger again.

Fleming and his entourage arrived at Tortola on December 6, and moved into the houses of Captain John Purcell, the brother of Governor James Purcell, and a Mrs. White. He was informed that Governor Heyliger, without permission from the British government of Tortola, had sent soldiers to Norman's Island to search for treasure. Fleming was incensed and later wrote to the Duke of Bedford that had he caught them there, he would have seized their vessel. If he had, Lloyd would have been taken as well, who was with them already bound in chains.

Fleming summoned a meeting with President Chalwell and some of the other prominent residents. He found that they were not disposed to admit to possessing any treasure even after being shown evidence to the contrary from Blackstock's deposition. Things became more complicated when the islanders started acting as if the silver was rightfully theirs while exchanging their pieces of eight for goods. After mulling over the situation, Fleming came up with a plan. Fleming knew that these were a "resolute people" and would flee if they thought that the money would be taken from them forcibly. He decided to mix a little "mildness with resoluteness" of his own to gain their confidence. Armed with Blackstock's deposition, he started with Chalwell, who was being kept in custody. Chalwell was no fool; he wanted to negotiate. He suggested that as a reward for declaring the money, each finder might be allowed to keep a third. Though Fleming was disposed to first consult with the Duke of Bedford on this matter, he realized that would take too much time and that this was probably the best way to reclaim some of the money. The next day, Fleming called a council meeting at the home of Mrs. White. He launched into a speech about the "heinousness and fatal consequences of piracy" and the punishment that would be dealt those who intended to conceal the recovered treasure. He praised the people of Tortola for their industry and hard work, as they had created a thriving commerce valuable to England. To participate in the looting would ruin their newfound reputations as law-abiding citizens. With that, he drafted a proclamation that was read and affixed in the most public place on the island.

Fleming's proclamation admonished all of his lieutenant and deputy governors throughout the Leeward Islands to do everything in their power to recover all treasure and apprehend any of the "pirates" who may still be on the run. He also gave the citizens of Tortola a deadline of December 22 to turn over any money or effects that they had, or information as to where more may be concealed. In return, he offered one fifth of the booty recovered as a reward. Anyone caught after the deadline would be prosecuted as an accessory to piracy.

Fleming's "gentle threats" apparently produced results. By December 19, at the next council meeting, a number of people stepped forward and surrendered their treasure. At the meeting, Fleming announced the suspension from the council of President Chalwell and Thomas Stephens because of their involvement with the stolen money. Robert Phipps of St. Kitts, one of the owners of Norman's Island, was named to the council in their place. But in the process of punishing the guilty, some innocent people were treated badly. The council members were blaming the "negroes," claiming that they had the greatest part of the loot. Fleming encouraged them to make a diligent search and to find and punish the guilty ones.

Fleming was farsighted. He might make these people behave while he was there and had a sloop full of soldiers, but he knew that after he left they would revert to their old ways. Hoping to instill in them some rectitude, he proposed to the council that they needed to build a church. There was no excuse for them not to have one; after all, there were over 400 families living on Tortola and the other islands. He also recommended that they build a courthouse and jail. The council wholeheartedly concurred. They would find a preacher and encourage the citizens to support a new church.

After the meeting, Fleming sent the shallop with a detachment of soldiers over to Norman's Island to look for money and to bring back any others who were found with it. Afterwards, he called a council meeting. The members conferred among themselves about what he had told them at the last meeting and agreed to individually declare all they knew about the treasure from Norman's Island and all of those who were in possession of it.

On December 12, Fleming had dispatched Captain Fraser of the Antigua Regiment in the shallop to St. Thomas. He carried a letter from him addressed to Governor Suhm and a copy of Blackstock's deposition. Fleming asked him to turn over the *Seaflower* and all of her lading so that Fleming could make a full accounting to the Spanish government. The English were now going overboard to create goodwill between themselves and Spain. Safe commerce depended on good relations with Spain.

In his return letter, Governor Suhm informed Fleming that Lloyd and his crew had fled "before their crime was known, otherwise I should have secured them." He denied Fleming's request for Lloyd's sloop or the goods it contained. Suhm said that he had orders from his sovereign to "keep a good understanding with all the adjacent Governments," therefore he was obliged to deal with the Spaniards directly and not through him. Additionally, Suhm wasn't convinced that the sloop was Spanish property. He told Fleming that he would give the Spaniards two months to make their claim. After that, the goods would be put to "public sale" and he would secure the proceeds until the owners came for it. The sloop would be sold if necessary to help cover the "damages of His Catholick Majesty." Furthermore, as far as Suhm knew, none of the culprits were within Fleming's jurisdiction. If they were, then of course they would be "directly delivered." Governor Suhm did, however, furnish Fleming with an inventory of the Spanish goods found in Lloyd's sloop.

Captain Fraser took Suhm's letter and departed for St. John's to look for any of Lloyd's confederates thought to have fled there. Enoch Collins had but was not apprehended. Fraser's effort was in vain so he returned to Tortola and reported to Fleming.

Scituate, Massachusetts

The Wade family was in shock. Zebulon's mother, father, and his wife, Mercy, could not believe what was being reported in the newspapers. By mid-December, news had reached Newport, Rhode Island, by a vessel that had come in from St.

Thomas, that most of the men from the *Seaflower* had been captured and were in custody for the theft of treasure from a Spanish galleon. On December 31, this news was printed in the *Boston Weekly News-Letter*. Although Zebulon was not mentioned by name, everyone who had been following the story and knew the Wade family realized that Mercy's husband was now in prison. Mercy could not fathom what would make her husband do such a dangerous and unnecessary act. Mercy did not know Owen Lloyd.

St. Eustatius

After being apprehended at Saba, Abraham Pritchett and James McMahon arrived at St. Eustatius on December 7 and were ushered into the fortress and separated. The council was convened for the purpose of interrogating them about the stolen treasure. Governor Heyliger looked on as the council began with James McMahon.

McMahon, who called himself James Matthews, said he had been born on St. Eustatius. He swore that it was his intention to deliver the money to the authorities and that was why he'd been headed to St. Eustatius. When asked about his fellow conspirators, Blackstock, Dames, Moorehouse, and McClair, he did not hesitate to blame Blackstock as the chief instigator of the plot: "It was 2 o'clock. As soon as they had come aboard, Blackstock had let the cable slip, while Dames, Charles, and Moorehouse hoisted the sails. Blackstock looked for the helm pin, the boat started to turn and it nearly hit an English boat."

The council: "What about Lloyd and Wade? Did they object?"

McMahon: "I heard Lloyd call out, 'For God's sake, don't raise the sails!' and I saw Blackstock pick up a handspike, he was cursing and swearing."

The council: "Where was Captain Wade?"

McMahon: "In his cabin."

The council: "Did you not know that such acts of theft are serious offences and punishable with the death penalty?"

McMahon: "Yes, but I got into it in a naive and innocent way. I did not know about their intentions in advance. That is why I took my share given to me on Norman's Island with me to hand it over to the government."

McMahon was dismissed and nineteen-year-old Abraham Pritchett was escorted in by his guards. He confirmed McMahon's testimony and explained that he'd buried his share at Norman's, all but one hundred pieces of eight. The council thought back on Lloyd's statement that Blackstock and Dames demanded that everyone sign a document that they would keep everything secret. Pritchett said that he had not heard anything about this. He did confirm that Blackstock threatened to "beat Lloyd's brains in" with a handspike. There were more questions:

The council: "Were there any arguments or fights during the journey about the sloop taking off?"

Pritchett: "No, none, except one afternoon, but I did not know anything about it, and on Norman's Island they had argued over whether there were more chests with money on board, because they had heard an English officer in North Carolina say so."

The council: "Did you hear anyone mumble beforehand that they intended to flee with this treasure?"

Pritchett: "No."

The council: "Do you not realise that such serious offences were punishable with the death sentence?"

Pritchett: "Yes, but I was only an apprentice of the captain and had no say in the matter."

After questioning, Abraham Pritchett returned to his chains in the barracks room.

The council met on December 9 to review the cases of the prisoners and untangle the obviously conflicting testimony. They summoned Lloyd, who had recently returned from Norman's Island:

The council: "Did you show the right place where you hid the money?"

Lloyd: "Yes, I showed the right place where I gave the markings."

The council: "Did you find the money as promised?"

Lloyd: "No, to my amazement we dug up all the places where we found nothing but twenty one and a half pesos that were strewn around the sand."

The council: "Did you hear who dug up the money and carried it away?"

Lloyd: "Yes. The people of Tortola and the three who were brought back to the island."

The questions switched to the subject of Blackstock. Lloyd told them that Blackstock kept his share but his son-in-law, James Moorehouse, went with Lloyd to bury his share.

Council: "Did you go with them to shore in order to help hide the silver and the money?"

Lloyd: "Yes, I definitely went to shore in order to witness where the money and the silver was being hidden and I was thinking about how to report this to one or other government, so that everything would be returned to the rightful owner."

Council: "When you were a passenger on board [at Ocracoke], were you blackmailed and talked into it by Blackstock, Moorehouse and Charles McClair?"

Lloyd: "When I returned from shore and got back on board, I noticed that these people went to the captain, where they talked behind closed doors and when they reappeared, I witnessed that the captain gave orders to set sail immediately. I objected, but Blackstock threatened me that if I spoke up again that he would bash my brains in."

Council: "Did you help in the whole plot to escape with the ship?"

Lloyd: "No, Dames, Moorehouse, Jonathan Deacon, and Isaac Raye raised the sails and Blackstock went and stood behind the helm after he had raised the anchor."

Council: "Did the Spanish people know that something was out of the ordinary when they saw that the sloop set sail without them?"

Lloyd: "Yes, they lowered a dingy named *Dog the Wind* and begged Blackstock with tears in their eyes to come back, but Blackstock didn't care and he even took his hat off and waved good bye."

The council had heard enough. The Dutch guards escorted Lloyd back to the barracks room.

Governor Heyliger was in possession of not only the "pirates" but now over 17,000 pesos in treasure and Lloyd's sloop as well. His next order of business was to dispose of Lloyd and his "associates." He could, in good conscience, keep his one-third salvage fee for saving the English and the Spanish the trouble of hanging Owen Lloyd.

Heyliger convened the council after Owen Lloyd's final testimony. The members reviewed the statements of each and to each the sentence was read. Governor Heyliger addressed Owen Lloyd:

> The accused, according to his own confessions, sailed on the Zeeflower in N. Carolina, supposedly as a passenger, loaded with monies, cochineal, indigo, silk and tobacco which he had unloaded from a Spanish ship without protest, had sailed on the barque to

Noorman's Island, and that he had in this way been an accomplice in the theft of said goods, as well in helping to hide and bury the goods and monies on Noorman's Island.... The accused failed to report any of it to any government and since such grave offences and proofs cannot be tolerated or endured in any well-regulated place where trade takes place and where good laws are established and enforced the accused should be condemned in this place where criminal justice is customarily applied, to be hung from a rope at the gallows until death follows, and for his dead body to remain suspended until it is consumed by the air, and that the proceeds from the aforementioned barque and other effects after deduction of expenses should be confiscated and forfeited, two thirds of which to be allocated to the state and one third to the R.O. officer.

The same sentence was handed down to Zebulon Wade, Abraham Pritchett, and James McMahon. They were all going to hang.

The Wreck of the Nuestra Senora de los Remedios (alias La Ninfa) a prize to the Royal family Privateers, taken 5 February 1746. And Lost in November following, near Beachey head on the Coast of Sussex.

Chapter Seven

The Unfortunate Spaniard

Ocracoke Inlet, on Board the Sloop Mary, October 20, 1750

ohn Lloyd and Captain Fitz-Randolph were in a panic. They had driven into shallow water and were hard aground. The outgoing tide that had carried Owen and the *Seaflower* to a successful escape had left them stranded with no hope of getting off. Because of the current and the distance to shore, they didn't dare attempt the swim.

The Spaniards had pursued the *Seaflower* all the way to the bar at the inlet's mouth in their ship's boat, but seeing that the situation was hopeless, they turned back into the ebbing tide, rowing laboriously towards the *Mary*. The Spaniards approached, brandishing their muskets and pistols and shouting to discourage escape. John Lloyd and the others realized the treasure was no longer theirs. With nothing left to get shot over, they raised their hands in submission.

The Spaniards boarded the *Mary* in a blind rage. They pushed and shoved the would-be pirates, then tied them up. The *Mary* was brought alongside the *Guadalupe* and the prisoners were locked in the former treasure hold of the galleon. The hatch was closed and six guards were placed on board the *Mary* to protect the treasure. In the confusion, they had missed the one-legged John Lloyd. He had hidden in loose sails piled on deck. Lloyd could scarcely breathe as he listened to the jabbering of the Spaniards shuffling about the deck.

That night, the Spaniards started to unload treasure from the *Mary*. They discovered four chests of silver with their seals broken, missing a bag of coins in each. The bulkhead that separated the cargo hold from the crew's quarters had a hole leading to the crew's quarters. This situation caused a great deal of confusion and commotion. John Lloyd knew it was only a matter of time before he would be discovered, but with the added guards on board he was afraid to move. John lay there all night contemplating an escape while thinking about Owen. He was the lucky one as usual and now was a very free, and a very rich, man.

The next morning, the Spaniards, not wanting a replay of the sloops sailing away, began stowing the sails that were heaped on deck. John Lloyd listened as their footsteps closed in on him. He rehearsed in his mind what to do. His only path to freedom was overboard. He checked his wooden leg; it was secure. When the sail in which he was hiding was unfolded, he sprang like a cornered cat for the rail and dropped into the skiff. Before he could untie the line, the Spaniards had seized him. He was shoved into the hold of the *Guadalupe*, joining Fitz-Randolph and the others.

Tomás Carriedo set to questioning Lloyd and Captain Fitz-Randolph in hopes of getting some information—most importantly, where Owen Lloyd was headed. When they refused to talk, he boarded the *Mary* and searched for the missing money. After going through every box and trunk on board, he recovered 1,379 pieces of eight, most of which was in Captain Fitz-Randolph's chest. Fitz-Randolph, however, still refused to cooperate.

Carriedo returned to his cabin, and with deep regrets, began a letter to Juan Manuel Bonilla.

New Bern, North Carolina

Governor Johnston and Colonel Innes had been entertaining Bonilla after concluding a contract for HMS *Scorpion* to carry his treasure to Virginia. Bonilla stared out of the window of Governor Johnston's study, watching the wind-driven rain. He had been worried about the frequent storms at the inlet and wondered how his ship and the two chartered sloops were doing. He was concerned that the anchors might drag and drive the treasure-laden vessels onto a sandbar. If that happened, the Bankers would probably declare a shipwreck.

Bonilla's chilling thoughts were interrupted by a knock at the study door. A messenger begged permission to enter as he had an urgent letter from Ocracoke.

Bonilla was handed a letter and returned to the light of the window. Governor Johnston and Innes watched. They were as anxious as Bonilla to learn more about what was happening. Bonilla's hands began to shake and all of the color drained from his normally ruddy face. It was the letter from Tomás Carriedo:

The Unfortunate Spaniard

My Brother and Dear Sir. The time has come in which our fortitude in such distress must endure the bad fortune which in so many ways is attempting to humiliate you in its adversities. I am saddened to use my pen to give you a bad piece of news...

Bonilla read on as his brother-in-law detailed the events that had taken place from the time he left the *Guadalupe* and the actions of the one-legged man and his brother, the "pilot of the accursed packetboat." Carriedo expressed his concern that their former prisoner, Thomas Wright, who had left the day before for Charleston, might be involved. "Perhaps there was a chosen location for such insolence," Carriedo surmised. But, he thought, since the one sloop was captured, the other sloop might have changed its plans.

His suspicions were probably well founded, for Thomas Wright was well known in the Carolinas. When Governor Johnston had heard of his presence, he noted in a letter to his agent in London that, "your old friend Thomas Wright of Charleston is among the Spaniards at Ocacock incognito." He described him as their "great Oracle" and noted he was advising the Spaniards to pay no heed to the North Carolina officials. Wright could have gone back home to Charleston anytime he wanted, but instead he remained on the scene. This is what made Carriedo suspicious now.

In his letter, Carriedo attempted to console Bonilla, saying that he and the crew felt sorry for him and that he was certainly not responsible for the recent events. "It can only be attributed to the compassion of the Almighty who permits these sad reversals of fortune," Carriedo lamented. "May God protect you for many years."

Bonilla's hands still trembled as he thought of his bad luck, of the losses he'd incurred at the hands of the English three years before when his *Nuestra Señora de los Remedios* had been captured and later wrecked, and of the pressing needs of his family back in Cádiz—his wife Maria and their five children. And then there was his mother-in-law and partner, Dona Angela de Prado y Sarmiento. His voice cracked when he told Innes and the governor what had happened.

After Bonilla regained his composure, he sent specific instructions to Carriedo that the prisoners be separated from each other, particularly Captain Fitz-Randolph and *Pata de Palo*, "Peg Leg" as they had begun to call John Lloyd. "And care must be taken that in all that I am taking in writing, that there be nothing missing....

It is assumed that this infamy is an arrangement with men of the devil."

Bonilla's state of mind can be clearly deduced from his comments to the Marqués de Ensenada, the secretary of the marine back in Spain, as he would later write on November 11. The recent events had "very nearly left me in the hands of death and in a very fragile and delicate state of health indeed." Being fifty-one and in a weakened state, Bonilla may have come close to cardiac arrest.

Governor Johnston sent express messages to the West Indies and impressed two local sloops, one to go north and the other south, to scour all of the ports, inlets, and creeks in search of the *Seaflower*. Johnston then departed for his home in Edenton while Bonilla headed for Ocracoke. The sloops would later return empty handed.

Ocracoke Inlet

After Carriedo had finished loading the treasure back onto the *Guadalupe*, the prisoners were moved to the *Mary* and locked below decks. A sloop from Edenton arrived to take the prisoners to New Bern under the guard of eight Spaniards. It was Governor Johnston's intent to "take the testimonies of their notorious crimes," but John Oliver, who was given charge by Carriedo, tricked the Spaniards into putting down their weapons. There was gunfire and a Spaniard was seriously wounded after John Lloyd and Captain Fitz-Randolph made their move. The would-be pirates made their escape in a canoe and quickly blended in with the Bankers on shore.

William Waller had not been on the *Mary* when she was captured. He had left the sloop after a falling out earlier with Captain Fitz-Randolph. Waller did not participate in the theft, but he was approached by Joseph Jackson, who gave him an oznabrig bag with 450 pieces of eight and a letter addressed to his father, James Jackson, in Woodbridge, New Jersey. Waller was told to deliver 213 of pieces of eight to Jackson's father and the rest were his to keep. Waller later got more money as it was distributed. He then set sail for Middletown, New Jersey, with Captain Anderson, who had no idea he was carrying stolen money with him.

When Anderson found out about it, he admonished Waller, telling him that he would not have let him sail if he had known about the theft. After they arrived at Sandy Hook, New Jersey, Captain Anderson put Waller on a sloop bound for Woodbridge where he landed on October 27. Waller made his way to Robert Fitz-Randolph's house, where he also lived. Here, he sent for Mary Jackson, the daughter of James Jackson, to deliver to him the pieces of eight. As for his own share, he ended up spending and loaning out nearly all of it. The word spread, and soon enough Waller was arrested. He was taken to Perth Amboy, interrogated, and put in jail. On November 16, he testified about their robbery at Ocracoke, the Fitz-Randolph brothers making several visits to the open treasure chests, and sharing the booty with their father and the other crew. Waller was unaware of what took place after he had left for New Jersey.

Meanwhile, HMS *Scorpion* had cleared Cape Fear River, headed north, and crossed the Ocracoke bar in fair weather at 2 p.m. on October 28, eight days too late. Half of the *Guadalupe* treasure was well on its way to the Caribbean. By 6 p.m., she was anchored close to Bonilla's galleon. Manuel de Echanis was already there with soldiers from *La Galga*, but they also had arrived too late. The *Scorpion* took control of the *Mary* and, in the middle of a gale, had to send over a stream anchor to keep her in place.

The *Scorpion's* presence at Ocracoke was a deterrent to not only the Bankers who still were lusting for the *Guadalupe*, but also the customs officers who wanted to take control. They did make one attempt to seize the vessel on November 6 when the customs collector at Bath demanded that the *Scorpion's* captain assist them in doing so. Captain Randall declined, since he was under the orders of Governor Johnston. Johnston, however, had his own ideas for the treasure.

On November 4, Bonilla had entered into a new contract with Governor Johnston to have the *Scorpion* transport the valuables that had been aboard the *Mary*, now stored on the *Guadalupe*, directly back to Spain. This was done with the help of *La Galga's* Lt. Manuel Echanis acting as interpreter. They agreed that the fees would be at the same rate that the English paid to ship their silver back to Europe and the islands aboard their men-of-war. The freight was to be paid by the House of Trade in Cádiz. Accordingly, on November 8, the crew of the *Scorpion* began moving the iron ballast to the after hold in preparation of loading the treasure. The *Guadalupe's* boatswain, Pedro Rodriguez, seeing that the treasure was now being taken away for good, opposed Bonilla's orders and tried to stop the removal of treasure until his wages and those of his fellow Spaniards were paid.

Bonilla, with Captain Randall's assistance, confined him on board the *Scorpion*.

For the next two days, the treasure from the *Guadalupe* was transferred onto the *Scorpion,* while other crew went ashore to retrieve the cochineal and likewise loaded it on board. Bonilla was given a receipt for the following:

In silver coin.	150,000 pesos.
1 chest of silverware	560 pesos.
1 chest of silverware with gold and other jewels	24,000 pesos.
1 small chest for Joseph Guitian	5,000 pesos.
1 dozen plates, spoons, and forks	120 pesos.
134 sacks of grana (cochineal)	61,908 pesos.
Total valued at	241,588 pesos.

Bonilla breathed with great relief once the treasure had been safely stored. The next day, while the English celebrated King George's birthday with a fifteen-gun salute, Bonilla took up his quill and filed a detailed report to the Marqués de Ensenada, not admitting to any of his negligence in the theft of the treasure:

> Finding myself without any recourse to a Superior to suppress the continual Extraordinary excesses and proceedings will induce your Excellency to think and Consider the danger that the whole was in and that it was exposed to worse Consequences if I had not intervened with my greatest Diligence, Prudence and Patience, which I did make use of to avoid the worst.

Most of his crew by now had deserted and those that remained had been following the lead of Pedro Rodriguez. Rodriguez's influence was terminated when, on the following day of November 12, he was transferred to an English sloop bound for Virginia, where Captain Huony would take responsibility. Carriedo and Felipe García, the *Guadalupe* pilot, went aboard the *Scorpion* to return to Spain with the cargo. Two other Spaniards named Julián Rodríguez and Joseph del Duque joined them. Bonilla paid 135 pesos to Randall for their fare. The following night, just hours before the *Scorpion* was to sail for Spain, Captain Randall received an order from Governor Johnston directing him to sail to Brunswick Town on the Cape Fear River, 140 miles to the south. It was "recommended" that Bonilla go

The Unfortunate Spaniard

with him as there were "some matters of great consequence." Bonilla agreed. On November 14, the beleaguered Spaniard boarded the *Scorpion* and set sail for Brunswick.

While the *Scorpion* was en route to Cape Fear with Captain Bonilla and his treasure, the Governor of North Carolina wrote a report to the Duke of Bedford in London about his activities as they related to the Spaniards. Governor Johnston said it had been tempting to execute the laws of trade in the strictest sense because the Spaniards had "transgressed them all," and that it would be "Cruel to take Advantage of the Ignorance and obstinacy of the Spanish officers," no doubt Bonilla topping that list. With the theft of Bonilla's treasure still at the forefront, an event that Colonel Innes predicted, Johnston advised the Duke that "it was not in the power of man to prevent their plaguing and Injuring one another, and fooling away the largest part of a Valuable Cargo."

Johnston, after informing the Duke of the "delicate care" he afforded the Spaniards in recognition of the fragile peace that existed between the two crowns, reminded the Duke that his salary was now twelve years in arrears and that taking care of the Spaniards had been a personal expense to him. He confessed to feeling justified in seizing the *Guadalupe* and all of her remaining cargo to reimburse himself and His Majesty's Officers in North Carolina. Because of his move to have the *Scorpion* take possession of the remaining treasure and cargo, he, Johnston, was personally responsible for foiling plans of the "inferior Officers of the Customs."

On November 22, the *Scorpion* anchored off Brunswick in the Cape Fear River and commenced the loading of water and supplies and conducting routine maintenance in preparation for their transatlantic voyage. Bonilla was surprised to find Thomas Child, The king's Attorney General for North Carolina, and Colonel Innes waiting for him. They had gotten word of the *Scorpion's* arrival two days before when she had anchored downriver opposite Johnston's Fort. After Innes had come down the river from his plantation, he boarded the *Scorpion* and presented orders from Governor Johnston that they were there to collect a ten percent duty for all of the treasure on board as well as the other items that had been sent to Virginia. That total of that cargo was a little over a quarter million pieces of eight. Apparently, getting paid by the House of Trade in Cádiz was a gamble that Johnston didn't want to take. Bonilla was taken aback. He was under the impression that his previous agreement with Johnston was for fees that were customary for the trip from America to Europe. But his hands were tied and he acquiesced, with the stipulation that these duties be paid to the King of England. That, Child responded, would not be the case. The money was for the governor and his officers. With that, Bonilla dug in his heels, reminding Child that he had been forced into port on account of storms and did not conduct commerce with the inhabitants. Governor Johnston had heard otherwise, having received reports that Bonilla had expended several thousand pieces of eight trading with local vessels for supplies and services and that contrary to the laws of trade, he had unloaded and reloaded the galleon twice without permission. Child came down to eight percent, which was refused, and then six percent, which Bonilla also rejected. When Child got Bonilla to agree to four percent, he sent an express to Governor Johnston for his authorization.

Governor Johnston was not alone in his demand for a share of Bonilla's treasure. Governor James Glen of South Carolina had gotten word of the *Scorpion*'s arrival at Brunswick. He sent his own order demanding 180,000 dollars as recompense for the Governor of Havana's seizure of English vessels taken as prizes since the end of the war. Word was sent to Johnston in New Bern about the South Carolina governor's demand. Johnston refused to execute the order, saying that the *Scorpion* was loaded and on her way to Spain. But that didn't settle the issue. Five English captains had come into Brunswick and lodged complaints of the grave injustices inflicted on the Englishmen in Havana. They claimed there were sixteen English vessels being held there. The captains were headed for Virginia with dispatches from Governor Glen to seize the effects of the *Nuestra Señora de Los Godos* stored at John Hunter's warehouse in Hampton. Bonilla hired a courier to warn Captain Pumarejo to get his treasure out of Hampton as soon as possible. At that moment, the *Dorothy* was loading there with Pumarejo's valuables. Standing by were twenty-two soldiers from the warship *La Galga* who would be traveling with the treasure back to Spain. She departed for Cádiz on December 31. Later, the Duke of Bedford wrote Governor Glenn that should King George get wind of his grab for the treasure, "You will no longer suffer to remain in your Government."

On December 16, 1750, Captain Randal hoisted a flag to signal that they were ready to sail. The next morning, in the midst of gale winds and rain, Colonel Innes rowed out to the warship with some armed guards carrying Johnston's latest demand. He wanted four and one half percent for not only what was on board the *Scorpion* but also what had been sent to Virginia. There was no charge for the treasure that Lloyd had stolen. But Johnston also demanded another two and a half percent for freight. After reviewing the orders, Captain Randal gave permission for Innes to send the four slaves he had brought along to go into the hold. Each one hauled out a heavy chest of silver putting it into Innes's boat. Bonilla protested to no avail and could do nothing more than watch as the 12,000 pieces of eight headed for shore. At Brunswick, the chests of silver were turned over to Thomas Child, who departed for New Bern to meet with the eagerly awaiting governor.

Bonilla was so angered and distressed he was unable to write so he ordered Tomás Carriedo to file a report about the recent events. Once it was witnessed by his pilot, Felipe García, and his surgeon, Diego Chavera, Bonilla took the report and bade Carriedo goodbye as he was making ready to leave for Spain.

Bonilla, with García and Chavera, ferried up the river thirteen miles to the town of Wilmington and landed at the new wharf at the foot of Dock Street. The recent rains had turned the unpaved streets into slippery mud. Bonilla was not impressed with Wilmington, which was not much more than a village. There was a courthouse, a tavern, and houses that took in guests. The buildings were haphazardly laid out. The new prison caught his eye. He envisioned Owen Lloyd on the inside.

Downriver, the gale winds that hammered Cape Fear prevented the *Scorpion* from leaving immediately. This was not a good time to be crossing the Atlantic with the frequency of the northern gales. Two crewmen were charged with mutiny and a third for desertion after trying to avoid the hazardous journey. At 10 a.m. on December 26, HMS *Scorpion* set sail for Cádiz, leaving Bonilla with a few crew, little money, and his battered, and nearly useless, galleon.

After seeing the *Scorpion* off, Bonilla sat down to pen an update to the Marqués de Ensenada relating the most recent events. He was angry, frustrated, and becoming a bit insecure. He didn't even know what day it was. In his letter, he reiterated the events as Carriedo had recorded in his letter that was drafted after the treasure chests had been removed from the *Scorpion*. He added little more for Ensenada's enlightenment other than complaining that the agreement he had struck with Governor Johnston in New Bern, which he had reported earlier to Ensenada, had been broken.

Bonilla set out for New Bern to find the governor to try to reclaim the silver. When he arrived, he found himself not just arguing over the 12,000 pieces of eight taken from him, but money Governor Johnston said Bonilla owed him for the two sloops that were impressed to go after Owen Lloyd but had returned unsuccessful. Bonilla demanded that Johnston be liable for the charges and that Fitz-Randolph's sloop, the *Mary*, be sold to help cover the value of the silver that had been stolen by his crew.

Bonilla's standing in Spain meant nothing to Governor Johnston, but apparently Bonilla thought it did. Nevertheless, Bonilla was in North Carolina now, a place where the inhabitants had little use for the Spanish and where most of them, in Bonilla's eyes, were backward and lazy. One contemporary visitor said, "There is no place in the World where the inhabitants live with less labor than in North Carolina." Their main occupation was the raising of hogs, which took so little work, as they fended for themselves grazing in the woods. Governor William Byrd of Virginia commented in 1728, "The Inhabitants of North Carolina devour so much swine's flesh, that it fills them full of gross Humours." As for their religious practices, "They do not know Sunday from any other day." His ship's surgeon and interpreter, Diego Chavera, was not able to explain these things, leaving Bonilla to feel superior to these North Carolinians. Johnston needed no interpreter to understand Bonilla's insolent attitude. After hearing his repeated complaints about his ill treatment and refusal to reimburse his expenses, the governor summoned some guards and delivered him to the New Bern jail. Bonilla was already in debt to some of the other English, so Johnston may have done this for his own protection as well. The jail was the same one that had held Respaldiza's men in September and the same jail that John Lloyd and the Fitz-Randolphs had been headed for but saved by their daring escape. The irony could not have been lost on Bonilla. He was in jail while he thought Owen Lloyd was a free man.

Chapter Eight
The Empty Gallows

Christian Lloyd stood on the shores of the family home, gazing hopelessly across the azure sea to the island of St. Eustatius. On the opposite side of the blue-green slopes of Mt. Mazinga stood Fortress Oranje where her husband was scheduled to be hanged. It was late December and Thomas Hobson, who had arrived earlier after being let go by Governor Heyliger, delivered the bad news. When Hobson had finished his story, Christian saw a glimmer of hope. Heyliger needed permission from The Netherlands to carry out the death sentence. The sentence was on hold. Christian and her brother, Charles, quizzed Hobson on every detail of the fort and the room where Lloyd and the rest were chained. They listened intently as he described the routine of the guards. Charles thought for a moment and looked optimistically into the terrified eyes of his sister. "I have a plan."

The last two years had been difficult for her and Owen. The war had left them devastated and their future uncertain. It was only five months ago that she was waiting for him to return to St. Kitts, where they were to start their lives over. But now the unthinkable was going to happen. Ordinarily, the Christmas season was one of great celebration for Christian's family, but now the peace and tranquility of the Caines plantation was shattered. At this moment, she was scared to death but she was not alone. The fear and loneliness she felt was shared by a woman named Mercy Wade far away in a little town in Massachusetts.

The news of Lloyd's deeds, his return to St. Kitts, his capture at St. Eustatius, and his pending death sentence, spread like wildfire around the island. Life at St. Kitts had become routine since the war ended, but now St. Kitts was the epicenter of an international brouhaha. The whole island was abuzz about Lloyd and what might be going on at the Caines plantation. The prevailing feeling was surely sympathy for Lloyd. Many reflected on whether they would have done the same thing had they been at Ocracoke.

St. Eustatius

Commandant Ravene maintained maximum security over his prisoners: Lloyd, Wade, and the others lay chained to the floor in the barracks building. At the beginning of every watch, their chains and shackles were checked. There was a guard posted with them in the same room as well as outside the barracks door. But no amount of security could protect against Lloyd's charisma. He began the seduction of his guards. Lloyd befriended Jan Jansen, a thirty-year-old corporal from Switzerland, and Jan Fredricks, a soldier of twenty-six.

When Thomas Hobson had returned to St. Kitts, he told Charles Caines that before he left St. Eustatius he had befriended Jan Schraeders, the assistant constable who, like Hobson, was only fourteen. Caines realized that he would have to get word to Owen that they would try and get him out but that they needed cooperation from the inside. Caines went over to St. Eustatius and presented himself and his sister to Governor Heyliger and requested permission to visit Lloyd. The request seemed harmless enough, so Heyliger consented, and Lloyd was able to visit with his family. When the opportunity presented itself, Christian gave Lloyd the escape plan.

Because the fort was situated above the town and a little way from the harbor, it was clear that only a night escape would be possible. Thomas Hobson had explained the schedule of the changing of the guards and their positions within and without the barracks room. Cooperation from more than the young assistant constable was going to be necessary. Lloyd would have to persuade some of the other guards to help. Promises of more buried treasure on Norman's Island would not work on the guards, as they knew that Lloyd had failed to uncover any more treasure with Commandant Ravene, treasure that might now save his life. It was going to take cash in hand to do the convincing, as well as a promised share of any other treasure yet to be had. Any guard who would commit such a treasonous act would be on the run for a long time.

When Lloyd received the message from the Caines plantation about an escape plan, he went to work on his new friends, the guards. Jansen and Fredricks certainly felt compassion for Lloyd and the others; after all, their only crime was to steal from the hated Spaniards. The Dutch had no use for these former enemies, who still harassed their shipping and harbored their runaway slaves. Lloyd convinced them that it made no sense to hang him for something he would have been praised for doing only two years before. It was the same logic he had used on himself at Ocracoke only a few months ago. It apparently worked again.

The silver-tongued Lloyd easily convinced Jansen and Fredricks to help. Now a complicated and dangerous escape plan could be coordinated with his family at St. Kitts. The date was set; it would be after the changing of the guard at midnight, January 26.

At 8 p.m. on the 26th, Corporal Adolf Trippel took charge of the prisoners and everything seemed normal. Corporal Christian Praat came inside and prepared to go to sleep in the same room with the prisoners. Lloyd, Wade, and the others were unusually quiet and pretended to be sleepy, hoping to get Praat as relaxed and off guard as possible. At 10 p.m., Trippel entered the room and inspected the prisoners' shackles and chains and found them in good order. He then turned the watch over to yet another guard, Corporal Johan Casper Leverworst. Every quarter hour the guards would call out to each other to guarantee that each was in place and that the fort was secure. A little after 11 p.m., Sergeant Jacob Raapzaet stopped by to check the prisoners and noted nothing unusual. At midnight, Corporal Leverworst again inspected the chains and found them fastened properly. The prisoners appeared to be asleep.

Under the clock in the courtyard, the guard was changed, leaving Private Pieter Dewitte in charge. The sentries gave an "all's well." Above, on the rampart, Jan Fredricks took his assigned position and the guarding of the barracks door was turned over to Corporal Jansen. After waiting for all of the guards to get settled at their posts, Jansen quietly opened the door and unlocked Lloyd from his chains without disturbing the sleeping guard. Jansen then resumed his station outside the door. Lloyd, now in possession of the keys, proceeded to free Wade, Pritchett, and McMahon. They remained in their positions, pretending to still be locked, and waited for Jansen's signal. At 1 a.m. the sentries again gave an "all's well."

Corporal Jansen opened the door and Lloyd, Wade, Pritchett, and McMahon tiptoed out and started up the stone rampart. Jansen stayed behind, guarding the rear. Lloyd was looking for Fredricks on the rampart who would show the way over the wall. Seeing someone, he said in a muffled voice, "Who is there?" Underneath the clock, Dewitte, thinking it was Fredricks, said, "Are you crazy, the clock has already struck one!" Dewitte then looked up at the rampart and in the darkness saw movement, but he thought it was Sergeant Raapzaet. Jansen, fearful that they were about to be discovered, walked over to the clock and told Dewitte that he better keep a sharp lookout as Commandant Ravene had just come into the fort. Jansen then caught up with Lloyd, Fredricks, and the rest, and they all slipped over the wall at the south end of the fort. They ran stumbling over each other in the dark down the coast road and made their way to a beach about a mile and a half south of town where Schraeders and Caines were waiting. Lloyd, Wade, Pritchett, McMahon, and the three guards fell breathless into the waiting boat. The sail was raised and they made for the dimly lit silhouette of St. Kitts. As they approached, the sun was peeking over the horizon. It was a glorious morning. Alive and safe, they trod up the hill to the great house. Christian was waiting; she had not slept a wink that night.

Corporal Praat woke up only minutes after his prisoners had made their escape and noticed he was now alone in the room. Bolting out of bed, he alerted Sergeant Raapzaet and he in turn alerted Commandant Ravene. Ravene ordered all troops to head for the harbor beach and scour the coastline before it was too late. They would have no luck. When the soldiers regrouped at the fort, roll call was taken and the three guards, Schraeders, Jansen, and Fredricks, were found to be missing.

The next morning, Governor Heyliger convened an inquiry. He questioned all of the guards involved in the incident, including his trusted commandant. Statements were submitted in writing and witnessed.

Heyliger was furious. He knew it was unlikely he would ever see the prisoners or his deserting soldiers again. A month after the escape, he convened a trial and convicted Jansen, Schraeders, and Fredricks in absentia:

> Those summoned should be condemned to being taken to the place where criminal justice is customarily carried out, to be shot by arquebus until death follows, and for their body to be buried underneath the gallows next to the moat by order of the Court.

On January 31, Heyliger issued a summons for Lloyd and the others. Though pointless in regaining the captives, it did show the authorities in The Netherlands that he was making every effort to recapture the "pirates."

Meanwhile, Zebulon Wade, Abraham Pritchett, James McMahon, and Thomas Hobson would have to risk returning home to the American colonies, as they had no money and nowhere else to go. At St. Kitts, Owen and Christian made plans for a speedy departure for St. Thomas. He needed money to not only repay those who helped him escape but money to start a new life. On February 5, before leaving, he signed a power of attorney over to Thomas Caines, Charles' cousin, which gave him the ability to collect any money owed to him around the island of St. Kitts. In early February, he and Christian set sail for St. Thomas.

The island of St. Thomas was legendary for harboring thieves and pirates. It was first colonized by Denmark in 1671 and populated with Danish convicts. They proved to be poor laborers, so slaves were brought in. There was little communication between the island and Denmark and the governors found that they could get what they needed by operating as a free port. This attracted thieves and pirates who brought their plunder to trade. This situation was of great concern to the English government. In 1682, William Stapleton, the governor of the Leeward Islands, referred to St. Thomas, then governed by Adolph Esmit, as a "bad neighbor." The following year the French pirate, John Hamlin, reputed to be an "arch-murderer and torturer," was given protection. The protection of criminals was not isolated to one governor. In 1699, Captain Kidd, who had plundered a great many vessels at Madagascar and in the Caribbean, sought the protection of Governor Johan Lorenson. Lorenson turned him away but allowed a man named Burk to bring in treasure and goods from Kidd's ship, declaring once again that St. Thomas was a free port.

Owen Lloyd had struck a deal with Governor Christian Suhm three months earlier. He told Lloyd that if he brought his wife he would make him a citizen. Owen Lloyd had now joined the ranks of the many thieves and pirates who had previously claimed St. Thomas as their home.

Basseterre, St. Kitts

Chapter Nine

The Governors' Greed

Tortola, December 1750

"You very well know Sir that Pirates are of no Nation as they are enemies to all, and therefore no nation is further chargeable on Account of their actions than to execute Justice upon them when they fall into their hands...." So wrote Lt. General Gilbert Fleming to the governor of Puerto Rico, Agustin de Pareja. It was just the year before that Fleming had described Puerto Rico to the Duke of Bedford as a "Pirates Island." For the moment, he was talking about Owen Lloyd.

It was December 20, 1750, and Lt. General Gilbert Fleming, who was presently at Tortola, had dispatched Major James Young to Puerto Rico with a letter addressed to Governor Pareja. In it, Fleming reminded the governor that Spaniards had been given refuge and protection by the English government after the recent storm. Fleming hoped that the robbery and piracy at North Carolina wouldn't diminish the new friendship between the English and Spanish nations. He went on to assure the Spanish governor:

> The moment I had intelligence of the late Piracy at North Carolina and the Transactions at Norman's Island I came from the remotest part of my Government to an island (usually subject at this season to dangerous fevers) to inquire myself into this affair and not only to search for the Perpetrators of this Villany, but also to snatch out of the hands of those, who think themselves entitled to all they can find, all Plate and Effects the Pirates left behind them and I can possible discover in order to have it restored whom it belongs...

Fleming added that, despite the continued "injuries and depredations committed all at once by the subjects of Your Excellency's Government upon the poor people of the Virgin Islands," he would still do whatever he could to recover the Spaniard's treasure. He assured the governor that upon his return to Antigua he would provide him with "an account of my success which I already conjecture (tho' it will fall short of my wishes) will be ample proof of the good intentions of my Royal Master...."

Governor Pareja sent a message back to Fleming carried by Manuel Franco, his captain of the infantry. Pareja skipped the normal flowery and polite greeting and demanded in the name of the King of Spain that the treasure must be restored, meaning turned over to him. He also wanted Owen Lloyd:

> Your excellency will also be pleased to order the Captain and all belonging to the said ship into custody and punish with the utmost rigor...that it might be an Example to others and terrify them from committing such base actions against the King and Master....

By now Fleming knew that Lloyd had stopped at St. Thomas. Upon his arrival at Tortola, he made inquiries to Governor Suhm as to Lloyd's whereabouts. He then spent the next two weeks trying to recover money found at Norman's Island by the inhabitants of Tortola.

In Barbados, the hue and cry finally reached Commodore Francis Holburne aboard HMS *Tavistock* about Lloyd and the *Seaflower* running away with the treasure from Ocracoke. He ordered the warships, *Shark* and *Otter*, to go "in search of her" and hopefully the treasure-laden sloop "won't escape them both." The *Shark* sailed for Tobago and Trinidad while the *Otter*, under Captain MacDonald, departed English Harbor, Antigua, sailing for St. Kitts in squally weather.

By December 24, Fleming had made an accounting of his treasure recoveries, which he submitted to the Duke of Bedford. It included treasure found not only at Tortola, but also at Anquilla, Antigua, St. Thomas, and St. Eustatius.

When Fleming had compiled this list, nothing of significance had been turned in the previous week and there were apparently no new finds on Norman's Island. He had Ralph Payne's letter of November 30, which fingered John Haynes as having 40,000 pieces of eight, Robert Hack with 30,000, Rebecca Purcell with

20,000, and Adrianna Jeff with "two canoe loads." Nothing was recovered from Hynde or Hack. However, these reported findings did not reconcile with his meager recoveries.

Fleming left Tortola on December 25 anxious to get home. He enjoyed the satisfaction of knowing Owen Lloyd had been captured at St. Eustatius. Besides the "inconveniences" of Tortola, he complained that several inhabitants and some of his staff were taken with a fever that was spreading around the islands. He wrote to the Duke of Bedford with an update on the search for stolen treasure:

> Besides the difficulty of bringing ignorant and wantious people to reason and gain their interest, a greater mischief was, that they search in bodies, were equal sharers, and most of them needy or transient people and negroes, and the mass of treasure was dissipated in such hands beyond recovery.

En route to St. Kitts, Fleming stopped at Anguilla and turned over Chalwell and the other prisoners to Governor Gumbs. Fleming knew that the people of Tortola could not be trusted to guard one of their own. There he discovered that Daniel Smith's brother, John, had also been involved with Blackstock. It was John who gave up the money to Gumbs. Smith still refused to confess where the additional money was hidden. Fleming ordered Daniel Smith and his brother to remain in confinement to await prosecution as "accessories after the fact and punishable as principle offenders," since they acted with full knowledge of Blackstock's role in the piracy and attempted to assist in his escape.

Fleming could have saved his breath. No sooner had he departed for home than the Smith brothers escaped "by the favours of some liberties" given by Governor Gumbs, who happened to be their uncle. The brothers fled there in the schooner with the silver William Blackstock had carried to Anguilla. Not long afterward, they returned in a Danish vessel to one of the little harbors of Anguilla to get their silver back from their uncle. They turned on Gumbs and threatened to burn his house down and "carry off his negroes to Puerto Rico." They then fled back to St. Croix.

Meanwhile, the *Otter* had arrived at Basseterre Harbor, St. Kitts on the evening of December 25. After stopping there for intelligence, she proceeded to Sandy Point, just up the coast from Basseterre, where Captain MacDonald met with Lt.

General Fleming on December 29. Fleming had just returned from Anguilla and was still aboard and anchored off shore. Here, they learned that Lloyd and the others had been apprehended and of the episode with the Smith brothers who had fled to St. Croix. The *Otter* then proceeded to St. Thomas where she anchored in the harbor at 8 a.m. on January 4 and made plans to fix a leak in her starboard bow. Captain Macdonald took the boat ashore in heavy rain. He had orders to meet with Governor Suhm and demand the return of the *Seaflower* and all of the cargo Lloyd had abandoned. In his written request, which would be translated for the governor into Danish, he invoked the treaty of 1669 made between Great Britain and Denmark. Macdonald recited the relevant articles about illegal seizure or detention of vessels and the harboring of "Pirates or such like Robbers." He made it clear that Great Britain considered the *Seaflower* to be English property. Suhm, with the help of a translator, returned his written response. The cagey governor had his own interpretation of the treaty. He rebuked MacDonald for his misinterpretation of the treaty and made it clear that he wasn't going to surrender the *Seaflower* claiming he had no knowledge that the sloop belonged to any subject of King George and that since the cargo was Spanish goods, his position was that the sloop belonged to Spanish subjects and that he would undertake the return of both the sloop and cargo to them. Suhm had no intentions of returning the property to the Spaniards as he was already trying to obfuscate the issue with the governor of Puerto Rico who had made demands of his own. The *Otter* weighed anchor the following day, touched at St. Croix to gain intelligence on the Smith brothers, then returned to St. Kitts on January 10 after a three day stop at St. Eustatius.

Governor Gumbs, humiliated and embarrassed, made three trips to St. Croix to get back his nephews and the money brought to Anguilla by Blackstock. He claimed to have interrogated thirty people in his unsuccessful quest. Fleming sent Major Young with a letter to Governor Suhm at St. Thomas about this and begged his assistance in apprehending the Smith brothers and to send them to one of the English islands for punishment.

St. Thomas, December 31, 1750

In late December, Don Manuel Franco, captain of the infantry at Puerto Rico, was dispatched with letters to Governors Suhm and Fleming. He encountered bad weather on the way and his vessel entered St. Thomas leaking and dismasted on the 31st. Franco came ashore and met with Suhm, delivering Pareja's letter.

Suhm responded in writing on January 16, totally ignoring the issue of the stolen treasure, and asked Pareja to treat his two deputies, Mathias Hyldloft and Stephen Desbroses, well while they were there negotiating the runaway slave issue. Suhm then presented him with a gift:

> You'll pardon me that I took the liberty of sending you a pipe of Madeira wine, 22 loaves of white sugar and 2 hams from my reserves, as I was informed that there is a lack of it in Puerto Rico. I beg you to accept it. I'm highly sorry that the sterility of the island does not allow me to find something else to please your Highness with and to show my obedience.

London, England

Word had arrived about Lloyd and his daring theft. On December 31, Spain's ambassador, Ricardo Wall, wrote to José Carvajal y Lancaster, Spain's prime minister, informing him of the news:

> With regard to this act of bad faith and unfair treatment, I have talked effectively with the Ministers who have said that immediately they will send orders to their Governors to find and hang the culprits of this act. I replied that the important issue is to discover where the effects have been taken and afterwards the guilty men can be punished according to their laws.

Wall was confident that "His Majesty will take measures in those ports to search for these criminals and the stolen cargo although it is feared that this may be an act of piracy."

Since news had to travel by ship across the Atlantic, Ambassador Wall and the English ministers did not yet know the good news that Lloyd had been captured and sentenced to hang at St. Eustatius.

At Madrid, the Marqués de Ensenada received Bonilla's letters from Ocracoke which had been forwarded by the Consules in Cádiz. In the Consules' cover letter, they told Ensenda that they hoped that King Ferdinand would dispatch war ships to the West Indian ports in the hopes of intercepting Lloyd and the stolen treasure.

The Consules characterized the acts of both Owen Lloyd and Gabriel Johnston as "violent proceedings" and asked Ensenada to solicit the Court in England to force the English official involved to turn over the treasure and to "find Lloyd and punish the Delinquents in such a manner as to terrify others in the future."

Antigua

Gilbert Fleming arrived at Antigua on January 5 and released a "private letter" to the *Antigua Gazette* which the paper printed on January 8. The letter had stated that 150,000 dollars had been recovered at Norman's Island by the inhabitants of Tortola, "one half of which had fallen to the share of the negroes, the first discoverers of the treasure." The numerous statements that the "negroes" made off with a large sum of money was questionable. But Fleming was done with it. Lloyd was in prison and, thankfully, he wasn't the one to administer the death penalty to a former hero of St. Kitts and the son-in-law of an old friend.

Captain Franco departed Puerto Rico, stopped at Tortola, and then proceeded on to Antigua. On January 25, he presented himself to Fleming with orders from Governor Pareja demanding that Fleming release the money recovered at Norman's Island and capture Owen Lloyd and his crew. He was still unaware that Lloyd, Wade, and the others were in prison at St. Eustatius. Fleming read the demand:

> Your Excellency will also be pleased to Order the Captain and all belonging to said ship into Custody and punish'd with the utmost Rigour of the Law that it might be an Example to others and Terrify them from Committing such base actions against the King, my Master.

Franco also asked Fleming's assistance in getting Governor Suhm in St. Thomas to turn over the cochineal, indigo, and vanilla impounded there after being abandoned with the *Seaflower*.

When Franco returned to Puerto Rico, Governor Pareja asked why Suhm failed to address the issue of the stolen treasure. Franco told him that he pretended to not understand. Pareja then wrote Suhm another letter and thanked him for the gift of the wine, sugar, and hams. In light of the gifts, Pareja said diplomatically that he understood that "an answer would be forthcoming when Your Lordship found himself capable of doing so."

Ocracoke, North Carolina

Bonilla had left the *Guadalupe* at Ocracoke under guard of Pedro de Ortega, and thirty-four other men. On January 1, 1751, a severe storm from the west threatened the galleon as she was aground in shallow water without anchor cables. On January 5, the pilot, John Oliver, came over and helped them move the ship into deeper water and away from Bonilla's packetboat.

A week later, Ortega wrote to Bonilla at his new residence at the New Bern prison with a plea for help. He was still in custody over his disagreement with Governor Johnston. Ortega was nearly out of money and could not afford to pay the men who were still employed. He told Bonilla he would hold them off until he could get there. But the weather was his greatest concern: "The cold is unbearable, it is necessary for Your Honour to get us away from this intolerable situation in all brevity as our patience is waning and our strength has left us. Your Honour is advised. I say no more." As if this was not enough, he added a side note: "We are penniless, completely devastated and our surroundings more unbearable than Your Honour can imagine."

Ortega wasn't exaggerating. Other reports had the Chesapeake Bay in Virginia frozen over. The Spaniards weren't prepared for this kind of weather. They had left Havana in the sweltering heat of mid-August expecting to be in Cádiz by the end of September.

In jail, shivering from the cold, Bonilla was tormented by visions of Owen Lloyd with his money and relaxing on some Caribbean island. He didn't know that, at the time, Lloyd was in prison at St. Eustatius waiting to be executed. Governor Johnston, anxious to get the arrogant Spaniard out of North Carolina to avoid his complaints about the 12,000 pesos, contacted John Watson and Alexander Cairnes, two prominent merchants in Suffolk, Virginia, who were also correspondents with Robert and John Lidderdale, Bonilla's insurers in London. They agreed to represent Bonilla and made arrangements to guarantee Bonilla's bail and to dispose of the *Guadalupe*.

Bonilla sent James Campbell, a merchant from New Bern, to assist Ortega at Ocracoke, check on the *Guadalupe*, and return with some cash to get him out of jail. Colonel Innes had paid part of his bail, which Bonilla guaranteed with a personal note. The remaining 385 pesos owed was paid to Joseph Balch, justice of the peace. Bonilla was fortunate to be bailed out with the intervention of Watson & Cairnes, for Campbell was late returning.

After twenty-five days of languishing in jail, Bonilla was released, but not before paying yet another fee to the constable and sentry who had been guarding him. Bonilla checked into the local inn in town and made plans to depart for Edenton for a meeting with a man whom he was now beginning to see as his nemesis: Governor Gabriel Johnston.

St. Thomas

In early February, while Owen Lloyd was en route to St. Thomas, Governor Suhm advertised the upcoming auction of the *Seaflower* (renamed the *Elizabeth*) and her cargo of one hundred bags of cochineal, six bags of indigo, three chests of vanilla, and eighty-two tanned hides. The auction was to take place on February 16 at the warehouse of Mr. Peter de Wint, a wealthy merchant of St. Thomas. Notices were sent to St. John's and St. Croix and word also reached St. Eustatius.

On auction day, the sloop with all its rigging, apparel, and cargo was presented for sale. People from all over the Caribbean and as far away as New York flocked to St. Thomas. The sloop was ultimately sold to Gert Sprewart de Wint for 505 pieces of eight. Items such as the compass, speaking trumpet, and roasting pan were sold to various individuals for an additional eighteen and a half pesos. The cargo of dyes and vanilla fetched 37,302 pieces of eight, bringing the total proceeds to 37,825 pesos and five reales. To facilitate a successful auction, some of the local residents were given up to six months to pay; those from other islands had to pay in cash. The proceeds were paid into the island treasury. When news of the auction reached Bonilla where he became outraged and later wrote that Governor Suhm had acted in very bad faith. Under the law, Bonilla stated that he was obliged to have waited a year before selling these goods. Bonilla felt that this was especially true in this case because it was public knowledge that the cargo "had been stolen by a pirate."

As for de Wint, the proud new owner of the *Seaflower*, he insisted that he be paid a third of the total auction proceeds since it was he who had discovered the abandoned sloop in the West India Company harbor. Suhm, being a good friend, contacted the officials in Denmark of the West India Company and recommended that he get the reward.

North Carolina

While Bonilla was in jail in New Bern, Gabriel Johnston had returned to his home at Edenton. When Bonilla was released, he made the seventy-mile journey to apply for further assistance because he could no longer maintain the expense of guarding his ship at Ocracoke. Remembering his recent stay in New Bern, he politely asked for his 12,000 pesos back. Johnston ignored him and suggested that he turn the *Guadalupe* over to Watson & Cairnes. They recommended that he auction the galleon and the remaining equipment left on board, including her cannon, sails, and rigging. His attorneys took a complete inventory of the ship and then placed an advertisement in the *Virginia Gazette* of February 18 announcing the auction. The sale was to be held at Edenton in early March. The notice stated that the ship could be inspected at the harbor of Core Banks on the south side of Ocracoke Inlet and an inventory of the ship could be inspected at Suffolk, Virginia, at the house of Watson & Cairnes or at Andrew Sproul's in Norfolk.

Governor Johnston explained that there was nothing more he could do. He recommended that Bonilla move on to Suffolk, where he could be properly taken care of by his agents and supervise the shipment of the remaining cargo back to Spain.

Bonilla and Chavera set off on horseback traveling north from Edenton and around the Dismal Swamp. On February 24, they arrived at Suffolk, a new but thriving town founded eight years before on the Nansemond River eighteen miles southwest of Norfolk. There, they met with David Meade, a prosperous merchant and planter whose plantation adjoined the town at the river's edge. Meade was also a partner of John Watson and Alexander Cairnes and was well known in Williamsburg.

When Bonilla arrived, he turned over to Meade 460 pesos that he had brought from Ocracoke. Bonilla was told that to be properly represented, Meade and his partners would have to handle his financial affairs. They also wanted to make sure that they would be compensated for their services. Bonilla would be relying on them for everything from transportation and supplies to his clothes washing. All of his expenses would be managed through Meade and his partners. Bonilla and John Watson traveled to Williamsburg to meet with Virginia's new acting governor, Lewis Burwell. Thomas Lee, former president of the council and acting governor, had passed away the previous November. Also traveling with them was Samuel Ormes, a noted apothecary formerly of London and now a neighbor and personal friend of Governor Johnston. Bonilla had been in a poor state of health and Ormes was as close to a doctor as he could readily find.

Williamsburg, Virginia

Bonilla was in the capitol of Virginia; he found it to be the most civilized place he had yet been in since he left Havana. He was now at the courthouse, anxiously pacing the wooden floor while Benjamin Waller, the clerk of the general court, drew up a power of attorney that Bonilla was granting John Watson. He was going to be his agent in the West Indies on a mission to recover the stolen treasure. He also drafted a testimonial about the robbery and advice on how to handle Thomas Child and the recovery of his 12,000 pieces of eight. With the *Guadalupe* set to be auctioned and his treasure carried safely to Cádiz by the *Scorpion*, Bonilla's only goal now was the recovery of his treasure found at Norman's Island and the capture of Owen Lloyd. Bonilla chose Watson because he was not only a man of moral character and well respected, but he possessed a powerful build. Both traits would serve him well in his pursuit of Lloyd and wresting treasure from the unruly inhabitants of the Virgin Islands.

Lt. General Fleming, now back at Antigua, wrote Governor Suhm on February 25 about the Smith brothers having fled to St. Croix from Anguilla. Not only did he want them to stand "Tryal for the Crimes they are charged with," but he also wanted the schooner they had fled with to St. Croix. Suhm politely and tactfully declined:

"Sir nothing should give me more Content than to know in

Reality with what pleasure I am willing to be at your service... but am Obliged to see those goods preserved, that I may have them delivered into the right Owners out of which reason I will still wait two Months to see if any of them should come in this Space of Time to reclaim those goods in Natura which then shall be delivered unto them after having pay'd the expenses, but in case of the Contrary, and that none of them come in, this Time shall I be obliged to put everything to a Public sale and secure the money to be restored unto the owners when they come."

Governor Suhm did give Captain Fraser an inventory of the dye and other valuables left on board the *Seaflower* to turn over to Fleming on his return to Antigua. Suhm gave all appearances to be willing to cooperate with the English. He had to simply because Denmark's King Frederick V was married to Louisa of Hanover, daughter of King George II of England.

Fleming's assistant, Major James Young, arrived at St. Thomas on March 1 and presented a letter to Governor Suhm. Owen Lloyd was there, but Young did not yet know it. Suhm thought about the request. He informed Fleming that he was aware of the events in North Carolina and what Owen Lloyd had done; however, he did not acknowledge Lloyd's presence on St. Thomas. But Suhm did say that the Smith brothers were indeed citizens—plantation owners of St. Croix who had "retired" there—and that he had John Smith in custody. Daniel had fled several days before to the Dutch Island of Curaçoa. Furthermore, the schooner that they had brought to St. Croix had disappeared. Since they were Danish citizens, they would stand trial there, and "they were sure to get punishment by his King's law and mercy." He would not be turning them over to the English. As for the schooner, he said he would seize it if it ever returned. Suhm, tongue-in-cheek, added that he was a great friend of the English and would gladly capture and turn over any "English bandit" for punishment who happened to arrive at St. Thomas.

When Young arrived at Antigua, he found that Fleming had left and returned to his plantation at St. Kitts. Major Young caught up with him there and presented the letter. It was now mid-April. Fleming studied Governor Suhm's promise to prosecute the Smith brothers and drafted another request to have Daniel Smith's schooner returned. Young was dispatched to St. Thomas to make the delivery.

Fleming pretended to be impressed with Suhm's "honesty" and interest in "justice:"

> It is with the greatest Satisfaction to me that you have raised my esteem and that of all the World by your attention to my application, and your proceeding against the two Smiths, and assurances You are pleased to give me that they shall be prosecuted to a perfect restitution and deserved punishment. I shall give John Baker, Esq. His Majesty's Solicitor General, directions to prepare and Transmit to your Honour the proofs that your forms may require in order to the prosecution of these Two very bad men, and entreat the Favour of you to permit Mr. Solicitor to correspond with your honour on this occasion, if my Distance so far from you as Antigua should make it necessary.
>
> The motives Your honour mentions to a perfect Friendship and good Harmony between the subjects of both Nations are very Strongly impressed upon me, and I have besides so high esteem for your personal merit as makes me with great regard and respect Sir
>
> Your Honour's most Obedient and humble servant,
>
> Gilbert Fleming.

Suffolk, Virginia

After getting settled in Suffolk, Bonilla was anxious to update his family about his situation. He addressed a letter to Messrs. Mauman and Macé, his agents in Lisbon, Portugal. These merchants had connections in both London and Cádiz. David Meade covered this letter with his own of February 27:

> As his wife, friends, and those others interested in his fate may think that he still is in the hands of designing men it may tend to their quiet to enquire our Characters of Mr. Robert Carey & Co in Wattling Street London and Messrs. Robert and John Lidderdale merchants in Leadenhall Street London who are our

separate correspondents there... As Captain Bonilla is likely to be here until a return to this may be had from Spain, his wife and friends will no doubt be anxious to write him. Therefore please acquaint them that any letters they send to these gentlemen in London or to Messrs. Dunlop & Peter in Glasgow, will be duly forwarded here.

By the middle of March, news of Lloyd's apprehension had reached Suffolk but not that of his subsequent escape. Bonilla was elated and he wrote a letter to the Consules in Cádiz about Lloyd's arrest and his own efforts in Suffolk to return the cargo. David Meade wrote a cover letter for Bonilla, which included the news that Governor Payne at St. Christopher's was believed to have recovered over 20,000 pesos and expected to get more. Between the time that Bonilla wrote his good news and Meade wrote his cover letter, they received word of Lloyd's escape from St. Eustatius. The guards, Meade lamented, "seem to have been highly bribed, else they would not have ventured their lives in such a desperate case."

In an attempt to lift his spirits, Meade told Bonilla that he had maintained a good relationship with St. Eustatius's governor in recent years and believed "he will exert himself in endeavors to apprehend these villains." Watson & Cairnes also had a correspondent relationship with Robert and John Lidderdale, merchants of London. They were Bonilla's insurers and were designated the receivers of the money that would hopefully be recovered in the Caribbean.

Bonilla was reminded of his unfair treatment and neglect at the hands of American officials when a hue and cry arose over some convicts who had commandeered a ship at Cape Hatteras, locking the captain and his mate in a cabin and vandalizing the ship. Governor Johnston issued an order for their apprehension. Bonilla felt that he hadn't received this kind of cooperation. Governor Johnston's assistance had been minimal and he had taken 12,000 pesos for his trouble. But the last time Bonilla complained, he wound up in jail. This time he kept his frustrations to himself.

On March 13, the sloop, *True Patriot*, arrived at Yorktown, Virginia, with news from Bristol about the ship *Jubilee*. After the *Jubilee* left Virginia for Spain carrying Spaniards, there had been an uprising, no doubt instigated by Pedro Rodriguez, Bonilla's former boatswain. The mutineers' plot to murder the crew and run away with the ship failed. The English were able to subdue the attack, shooting several Spaniards, including Rodriguez, and locking the others below decks.

On March 17, Meade sent John Stallings to Norfolk to arrange for a charter vessel for Bonilla's anticipated return to Cádiz. A week later, Bonilla returned to Edenton with Don Diego Chavera to witness the auction of the *Guadalupe*. With the auction producing no takers, the galleon was registered to David Meade so that he could assume legal custody of her. Plans were then made to move the ship from Ocracoke to Suffolk so that repairs could be completed. Bonilla gave 2,200 pieces of eight to Meade on his return to Suffolk for safekeeping and Meade took title to the ship. Bonilla's plans to return to Spain were postponed.

Bonilla's cash was dwindling fast. He had a little over 3,500 pesos remaining. Bonilla's self-indulgent surgeon and interpreter, Don Diego Chavera, was now getting a grasp on how valuable he was. He took a liking to some fine Holland and Cambrick cloth that John Watson was happy to purchase for him. This expense was accordingly charged against Bonilla. Both John Watson and Alexander Cairnes took full advantage of this open-ended arrangement. They were reimbursed for new clothes and shoes, clothes washing, new glasses, and frequent sessions at the taverns. Chavera was now in their employ as interpreter. They lavished him with sundries paid for by Bonilla. These Englishmen, who were the only friends Bonilla had, continued to make advances of money on his behalf.

Bonilla's *Guadalupe* was safe for the moment at Ocracoke and almost half of his treasure had now been returned to Spain in the *Scorpion*. He longed to be with his family and it was looking as if that just might happen soon. Little did Bonilla know that, trapped in a strange land and surrounded by a language and culture he did not understand, his problems had only just begun. What had happened at Teach's Hole on October 20, 1750, would torment him for years to come.

Hampton, Virginia

Bonilla's attorney and agent, John Watson, hired the ship, *Caesar*, lying at the Hampton wharf, to carry him to St. Kitts. Bonilla had contracted with him to go to the West Indies to recover as much of his treasure as possible and, with luck, return with Owen Lloyd. The *Caesar* was a 232-ton vessel, crewed with eighteen men, armed with two cannon, and owned by John King & Co. of Bristol, England. John Watson was armed with his broad power of attorney just granted by Bonilla. With him was Diego Chavera of the *Guadalupe* acting as interpreter and a teenaged youth named Thomas Gibson, the son of his partner, James Gibson, who would take his place in case of serious illness or death. The ship was loaded with "sea stock," which included a hogshead of beer and some wine, all paid for by Bonilla, who remained behind in Virginia to manage his cargo and his ship. Captain Sword of the *Caesar* was fortunate to be transporting a cargo of oats, hoops, tar, turpentine, shingles, corn, pork, and other Virginia produce to St. Kitts. This would be a profitable voyage.

On March 29, 1751, the *Caesar* cleared Hampton for St. Kitts. That same day, David Meade sent a letter addressed to the Consules in Cádiz. He protested on Bonilla's behalf the actions of North Carolina's Governor and put some blame on Captain Randall of the *Scorpion*, who had arrived safely at Cádiz on January 28, 1751:

> From Don Juan's account of the treatment he met in North Carolina he hath been very severely handled, especially in taking from him four chests of silver which we think illegal.... He had bills of lading for the whole money shipped in the Scorpion Sloop of War and that Captain Randall delivered these four chests without Captain Bonilla's license, barely upon an order either real or pretended from the Governor of North Carolina.... We imagine that you would persist that the Captain of the Scorpion should refund the whole money he gave bills of lading for, the end of which we suppose will be Captain Randall's complaining to the Lords of the Admiralty in London, and appealing to the order he had for quitting that money, which will revert the affair to North Carolina, and will (in that way) come with much more weight than our proceeding in the matter, as we are only in private stations.

The *Caesar* arrived at Basseterre, St. Kitts, on April 21, 1751. After getting established on shore, Watson hired John Baker, Esq. as his attorney. Baker was solicitor-general of the Leeward Islands and a prominent citizen of St. Kitts. On Baker's advice, Watson appeared before the Honorable Richard Wilson, Chief Justice of the Court of the King's Bench, and produced the power of attorney granted by Bonilla, which Judge Wilson then ordered entered into the court records of the island.

Watson had much catching up to do. He had heard of Lloyd's escape from the fort at St. Eustatius but had no idea that half of the Caribbean was now involved in some fashion either with Bonilla's treasure or the pursuit of Owen Lloyd.

The following week, after getting acquainted with John Baker, Watson dispatched a letter to Charles Caines at Dieppe Bay and demanded that he relinquish the treasure still in his possession. On the 30th, Watson hired horses and traveled the coast road from Basseterre to the Caines plantation. His intent was to "take evidence," and hopefully to gain a further confession as to the location of more of Lloyd's loot.

As expected, Charles Caines was cooperative since his family had held prominent posts in the island government over the years. He readily produced 5,347 ½ pesos, a silver basin, a silver cup, a serving dish, eight plates, six spoons, and a salt shaker. He admitted to having 495 pieces of eight, which he refused to return because he said his brother-in-law, Owen Lloyd, owed it to him, presumably for money Caines advanced as bribes for the fort guards at St. Eustatius.

Watson remained in St. Kitts until the first week of May making inquiries about the stolen treasure and enjoying himself at Robert Nichols' tavern in Basseterre. Watson, Gibson, and Chavera then set sail for St. John's, Antigua, to meet Lt. General Gilbert Fleming whom they had missed before his departure from St. Kitts.

On May 7, Watson arrived at Antigua. Landing some distance from the fort, it was necessary for them to hire transport from there to John Lindsay's Tavern. Watson found that the local taverns were the best place to obtain the latest gossip and to discern the character of the officials he was preparing to meet. He hired Charles Wager Mann as his legal representative. Boarding for the three of them was secured at the inn of Mrs. Crispen. Once situated, Don Diego Chavera began complaining about his shoes (apparently he saw some new shoes he liked) so Watson purchased a new pair and as usual, recorded the expense for Bonilla's later reimbursement.

Watson met with Lt. General Fleming and related Bonilla's misfortunes and

The Governors' Greed

presented his contract and power of attorney enabling him to recover the treasure and hopefully Owen Lloyd as well. He tried to impress upon Fleming that it was in both their interests as servants of King George to do all they could to help the unfortunate Spaniard. This was now a matter of national concern. Watson produced his power of attorney from Bonilla, which was then ordered recorded by John Watkins, justice with the Court of Common Pleas. In spite of the power of attorney, Fleming said he still needed to hear from the Duke of Bedford in England on the matter of returning the treasure.

Watson now made preparations for Tortola. He was convinced that there was more treasure to be recovered and he consulted with Ashton Warner, the attorney general of Antigua, on how best to deal with the notorious inhabitants of the Virgin Islands.

Before leaving, Watson presented petitions on May 13 and 21 officially requesting the return of the stolen cargo for the English Crown. Watson's best chance for recovering any money for Bonilla would be for the English authorities rather than individual finders, not to mention his bonus was tied to his success.

Back in England, the Duke of Bedford consulted with the solicitors general and the ambassador to Spain, Ricardo Wall, about Governor Johnston's actions. He also evaluated the actions of Gilbert Fleming taken at Tortola.

Before the Duke of Bedford's ruling reached Fleming, Watson made Fleming an offer he couldn't refuse. Watson, after being stonewalled, realized that Fleming would have to be bought. He offered Fleming £1,000, "for his extraordinary trouble rescuing the treasure from many doubtful and desperate hands." This is how the bribe would be accounted for in Fleming's official statement. To himself, Fleming felt only somewhat compensated. In September 1743, Spanish privateers had raided his plantation at the south end of St. Kitts and absconded with fifty-two of his slaves.

Fleming went with Watson to St. Kitts and then made an accounting of his expenses incurred while going about the job of retrieving Bonilla's treasure from the people of Tortola. Fleming listed the expense of the sloop, *Christian*, and another for the shallop owned by Captain Dean. There were items for large quantities of rum and supplies and food for his servants and guards at Tortola. He also sought reimbursement for his lodging with Captain John Purcell. And he did not forget his friend, Governor Benjamin Gumbs of Anguilla. He authorized him to submit his own accounting and keep a portion for his own "extraordinary trouble." Out of the 1,120½ pesos Gumbs recovered from Blackstock, 600 pesos were turned over to Watson in June. Bonilla's fortune continued to dwindle.

After it was all added up, Fleming gave Watson the net of nearly 20,000 pesos, plus cochineal and some silver plate. This was a hefty sum, but still far from 150,000 pesos that Owen Lloyd had carried to the Caribbean.

St. Thomas

On May 1, while John Watson was still at St. Kitts, a vessel from Cumaná, Venezuela, stopped there, having first been to St. Thomas. Juan Bernardo Santiago and Juan Andrés García gave statements to Watson that, while at St. Thomas, they learned that Owen Lloyd was careening a small sloop which he had used to pick up treasure, allegedly buried at St. John's, St. Croix, St. Martins, and Montserrat. Rumor had it that Lloyd had given Governor Suhm 30,000 pesos as protection money and had bought "one or two haciendas." It was at this time that Watson learned of the recent auction and that Governor Heyliger of St. Eustatius and Governor Suhm had bought a great deal of the cochineal.

On May 23, Watson wrote a report to Bonilla in Virginia about what he had learned and described the actions of Governor Suhm. When referring to Lloyd, he said, "It is such a wicked thing for having made him a resident of that island and announcing publicly that he was under his protection." Watson promised Bonilla he would continue in his effort to reclaim the stolen treasure and if things worked out as hoped, he would be back in Virginia within two or three months.

Hampton, Virginia

The dogwoods were blooming as winter gave way to spring. In Virginia, the beleaguered Bonilla was busy handling details on his cargo now stored at John Hunter's warehouse on Hampton River. On April 7, Alexander Cairnes paid Hunter £387 on Bonilla's behalf for warehouse storage and the cargo was then transferred on board the 180-ton ship, *Polly*, with Hugh Crawford as master. The *Polly* had arrived from Ocracoke on April 12 having been sent from London by the Lidderdale Company, Meade's correspondents and Bonilla's insurers.

The pressure to get out of Virginia was mounting. On April 15, 1751, the *Virginia Gazette* published a reprint from Boston excoriating the Spanish for seizing ships and imprisoning English crews after the peace had been declared. "Might it not be here queried, whether the Spaniards ought to have been all seized till every capture they have made on the English since the Peace were restored or are the English resolved to treat them as Gallinas (chickens) as they call us...."

On May 4, Captain Crawford, representing the owners of the *Polly*, signed a contract with Watson & Cairnes, on behalf of Bonilla, to freight as much as possible of the *Guadalupe* cargo stored at Hunter's warehouse to Cádiz. The contract also included passage for ten Spaniards and adequate provisions for them. Five of those ten were to serve as crew at no compensation. (In the end, sixteen Spaniards would make the trip.)

At Hampton, the loading of the *Polly* was supervised by Don Pedro Ortega, but under the watchful eye of Alexander Cairnes. Bonilla spent some time at the docks as well. From Hampton, Bonilla ferried to and from Suffolk, where he sometimes stayed with David Meade. Although Meade was hospitable, Bonilla was forced to buy his own bed in Edenton and transport it to Suffolk.

The *Polly* sailed May 10 with plans to return to Virginia via London. In order to maximize profits for the voyage, David Meade sent a letter with the *Polly* to the Consules in Cádiz to set up a cargo for Captain Crawford to carry from Cádiz to London. The shipping contract had already guaranteed a cargo whether one was available or not.

On May 15, David Meade wrote to the Consules in Cádiz to inform them that the *Polly* had been loaded and to transmit the shipping contract ahead of her departure. Bonilla was considering selling the dye wood cargo in Suffolk since the cost of freight to Spain would eat up its value.

Two days later, Bonilla, Ortega, and Cairnes met at Mother Hawkins' tavern to discuss the status of the *Polly*. They no doubt were eyed with great curiosity by the seaman and sea captains of Hampton who were friends of Owen Lloyd. The three of them then ferried to Suffolk where plans were formulated for bringing the *Guadalupe* into Hampton Roads and then up the Nansemond River to Suffolk.

Meade also advised the Consules that the receipt given Bonilla by Captain Randall of the *Scorpion* had been previously transmitted to them via London. After accounting with the Consules for the *Scorpion's* cargo, they would then prosecute those in North Carolina who had taken advantage of Bonilla. He also informed the Consules that Watson was in the West Indies but some late news from those islands said his voyage might be unsuccessful due to some national reprisals, apparently over the issue of the slaves running away to Puerto Rico.

On May 18, Robert and John Lidderdale also wrote the Consules from London and vouched for the "Universal Good Character" of David Meade and gladly reported to them that Bonilla "could not have fallen into better Hands for capacity or integrity" with their partners in Suffolk, Virginia, namely John Watson and Alexander Cairnes.

Bonilla, sadly, still remained in Virginia. He bid farewell to yet more of his fellow Spaniards when the *Polly* cleared Hampton. He could not leave as he still had to attend to his ship and he was anxiously awaiting the return of Watson from the West Indies.

En route to Spain, the *Polly* was boarded by two Algerian men-of-war. Captain Crawford knew that if the Spaniards on board were detected, his ship would have been seized by the pirates. But at the risk of his own ship and crew, he concealed the Spaniards below, whereby the *Polly* was released and allowed to proceed on to Spain.

Perth Amboy, New Jersey

William Waller, who had rifled the treasure chests stored on the *Mary* at Ocracoke had been recaptured after his escape from the Perth Amboy jail. Governor Jonathan Belcher wrote the Duke of Bedford on June 18, 1751, that he had recovered 317 pieces of eight and that they were now "lying in the publick Treasury of This Province." No attempt was made to return the money to Bonilla.

Antigua

Watson departed Antigua destined for the island of Montserrat, thirty-five miles to the southwest. He had hired Captain Christopher Mardenbrough, a mariner from St. Kitts, for the voyage. He stayed at Montserrat for two days and called at the tavern of Matthew Dyer, inquiring among the patrons if they had any knowledge about Owen Lloyd or any money that was rumoured to have been left there by Lloyd. With no success, he then sailed on to St. Kitts.

When Watson arrived, Fleming delivered to him the six bags of cochineal that Governor Gumbs had taken from Blackstock in Anguilla. On June 6, he hired Negroes to load the cochineal aboard a sloop for shipment to England, but it was then unloaded on the orders of the customs collector, Henry Brouncker. It was obvious that he did not want to cooperate with Watson as he "imagined himself restrained by the parliamentary ruling entitled *An Act for Encouraging and Increasing the Shipping and Navigation.*" The customs collector cited the fourth clause, which said that no goods could be brought into England or its territories other than English goods or they would be forfeited.

Watson prepared to travel to the other islands in pursuit of more treasure. What had already been recovered was shipped to Antigua in three wooden casks specially made for that purpose. Before departing for St. Eustatius, he purchased a broadsword to present to Governor Heyliger. On June 19, after clearing his tavern bill, he boarded a sloop owned by Captain Hedges destined for St. Eustatius.

Following a day's sail, Watson arrived at the Dutch island and on the next day called on Governor Heyliger and presented the sword with his written demand that the treasure or its cash equivalent be turned over to him:

> Furthermore, I request that you would register the lists of the load, both the money and goods, with the secretary of the islands and that you would make the effort to send a statement of the account, addressed to Messrs Meade, Watson and Cairnes, Merchants in Nansemond, Virginia. Sir, your consent to the above will make my indebtedness to you even greater. Your much obliged, very obedient, and very humble servant.
>
> J. Watson
> for Don Juan Manuel de Bonilla

Days later, Governor Heyliger convened his council in a special meeting and examined Watson's request. They gave him their stock answer: such a release could only come from the authorities in Europe. The next day, Watson paid the secretary, Johan de Graf, fees for filing his petition and made ready to call upon Governor Suhm at St. Thomas. He purchased another presentation sword, called at the barbershop, and took Chavera and Gibson to the local tavern. Chavera complained about his breeches needing mending. Watson indulged him and hired a seamstress. Captain Hedges' sloop was underway again.

In late June, John Watson arrived at St. Thomas and was taken to the home of Stephen Desbroses, councilman of the island. Desbroses was a Frenchmen, indicative of the multinational populace of the Danish Islands whose citizens were not only Danish, but English, Dutch, and French. Stephen Desbroses had been the first to alert the governor of Puerto Rico that Owen Lloyd had arrived at St. Thomas from Norman's Island in a sloop loaded with Spanish treasure.

In preparation for his meeting with Suhm, Watson found a translator and paid to have a formal protest drawn up against the governor. He believed that armed with Bonilla's power of attorney, a professional demeanor, and an order from Gilbert Fleming, he would prevail in his request. In preparation for his meeting, he also dropped by the local tavern, where he questioned its patrons about what they knew about Lloyd, the stolen treasure, and what involvement the governor had in the affair.

On June 29, Watson signed the newly drafted protest, which was delivered to Suhm, but he refused to meet with him. In the protest, Watson had detailed all of the events starting with the hurricane and Bonilla's misfortunes in Ocracoke. This meant nothing to Suhm. Watson flat-out accused Governor Suhm for having some of the "Bullion Plate." He also made a demand for Owen Lloyd and any of his accomplices

> But in case that the Laws of Denmark are such as your Honour cannot Deliver him or them up your Petitioner then prays that your honour would be pleased to order him or Them to be immediately seized and kept in safe Custody that he or they may take their Tryals here and your petitioner will soon as possible send Down from Antigua the Necessary Evidences to appear against him or them and your petitioner shall pray.

In due course, the protest was delivered to Governor Suhm, who dictated a response the next day that was translated into English for Watson's convenience. Suhm acknowledged the events in North Carolina, but seemed to place the blame of "running away with the sloop" upon Zebulon Wade, not Owen Lloyd. Suhm then addressed the auctioned cargo and the demand for Lloyd:

> You were informed that I have recovered and in my Possession a great part of the wrought plate, merchandise and other Effects Embarq'd in the said Sloop. In Consequence of that Power given

unto you, you demand that I will account for the Expenses and restore and deliver up unto You all What has been found here. I Should be very Glad to settle this Affair with you at this time; But as the Owners have retarded so long either to come themselves or to send any other Person lawfully empowered in his Place I have been obliged to have these Effects that are found here consisting of Cochineal, Indigo, Vanilla, and hides (but no silver Either plate or money) put upon publick sale. The cochineal being on the point of being spoiled by the humidity of the Sloop, and that the said Effects could be sold to a greater advantage to the owner. I have been obliged to give Credit, that thereby the terms of Payment are not payable before the month of August. And as it was entirely unknown to me When the Owners were to come I have been oblig'd to report this affair unto the Royal Compagnie. In Consequence of which, and before I receive orders and Answer from Europe, I cannot settle this Affair. But be pleased to persuade yourself that as soon as I receive orders from Europe which I expect very Soon and the repayment for the Effects are perform'd, I will directly give you notice of it and I expect that when you come You will have all possible Justice done. Concerning to deliver Owen Lloyd unto Your Hand, I cannot satisfy Your demand as I am thoroughly convinc'd that he hast not committed any Murder, and I have not heard that any of his crew to this day have been seized and punish'd, and as I have granted him Protection I shall not Break it by no Means. I find it unnecessary to have any Evidence heard against him in this Affair so I shall not let him be Sentenc'd and punish'd here when he has not committed any Crimes under my Jurisdiction. I am Sir,

    Your most willing Serv.
    C. Suhm

Suhm refused to recognize John Watson's power of attorney from Bonilla, the true owner of the cargo. He had said at the beginning, he was holding the property for the Spaniards and was waiting for them to come make their claim.

Where he had acknowledged before that Lloyd had committed a crime and should be apprehended, he now overlooked that and said he deserved protection because he hadn't committed any "murder." Watson realized there was no way to force Suhm to comply, but in one final act, he filed another protest with Johan George Hollenberg, Esq., secretary of the island, that was accepted and recorded. He asked if Suhm had any other answer besides the one he had just read and he warned:

> As for not delivering up Owen Lloyd to be try'd in an English Government or having him Try'd in this Island agreeable to the Tenor of the said petition and that you would protest for all Costs, Losses, & Damages that have already or may hereafter be sustained by the aforesaid Don Juan Manuel Bonilla, I am Sir
> Your most hum^L Serv.
> J^o Watson

Unknown to Suhm or Watson, Fleming had requested Commodore Holburne to send HMS *Shark* to St. Thomas with his order that Lloyd be surrendered to him as he had just found out that Governor Suhm had made Lloyd a burgher (citizen) of St. Thomas. The *Shark* also called at the other islands of St. Eustatius, St. Croix, Puerto Rico, Virgin Gorda, Tortola, and Norman's Island before returning to St. Kitts without Lloyd or any additional treasure.

Suffolk, Virginia

It was the end of July and Bonilla was at the town wharf at the end of Main Street when he observed the *Guadalupe* coming up the river in tow behind the eighty-ton brig, the *Nansemond*. Bonilla had been waiting since June 10, when David Meade dispatched Captain John Hews in the *Nansemond* for Ocracoke to bring back the *Guadalupe*.

There had been no takers at the auction in Edenton, North Carolina, earlier in the year.

After arriving at Ocracoke, the *Nansemond's* crew had prepared the dilapidated galleon for her return to Hampton Roads. On July 30, under sunny skies, the *Guadalupe*, commanded by Cornelius Campbell and a crew of twelve, arrived in

Hampton Roads and was towed up the river to Suffolk where she was moored at the town dock. Bonilla's remaining crew, who were being lodged in town at the inn of Mathias Jones, were now able to move on board the *Guadalupe* and begin more elaborate repairs.

The Caribbean

After leaving St. Thomas and the intractable Suhm, Watson, Gibson, and Chavera went on to St. Croix where they called at the tavern and made inquiries into the missing money and Lloyd's previous visit there. Watson had no luck.

From St. Croix, Watson then proceeded on to Tortola, where he was received by Governor James Purcell.

On July 8, Governor Purcell commenced hearings and examinations of the residents to find those who were still in possession of money recovered from Norman's Island. That included the one-third salvage allowed by Gilbert Fleming in December. It may be recalled that Purcell was in London when the treasure had been discovered at Norman's Island. Watson stayed with Purcell for twelve days and monitored the examinations and recorded the additional recoveries of treasure.

At St Kitts, Gilbert Fleming reinforced and made public the treaty with Spain as ordered by the Duke of Bedford. He also instituted a prosecution in chancery against those who had found and concealed treasure.

After Watson returned to St. Kitts, he petitioned the Lord's Commissioners of His Majesties Treasury on July 28 to release the cochineal that the customs collector had embargoed, arguing that "Cochineal is a Commodity that is of no use in St. Kitts and of a perishable nature." Warning that this would result in a loss of "many thousands of pounds," Fleming directed the customs collector to release the cochineal so it could be shipped to Robert and John Lidderdale in London. Gilbert Fleming certified as to its origin and that it was exempt from the laws of trade. But the customs collector held firm and still refused to release the cochineal.

Watson's interpreter, Diego Chavera, had been complaining that he was out of money. Chavera knew his value as translator for Watson and took every opportunity to take advantage of Bonilla. Watson complied, dipping once again into Bonilla's expense account. Watson then bought some canvas to be fashioned into bags to carry the treasure he confiscated at Tortola for shipment to London. The customs collector finally relinquished the cochineal, which was loaded with the silver on board Hedges' sloop and the three of them escorted the cargo over to Antigua, where it would be shipped to England.

Upon their arrival at Antigua, Watson met James Doig and Charles Wager Mann at Lindsey's Tavern. While enjoying a bowl of arrack punch, Watson and his assistants related their adventures in the other islands as he pursued Owen Lloyd and Bonilla's treasure.

On July 27, James Doig and John Halliday, Antigua merchants now in Watson's employ, wrote to Bonilla and reported on Watson's success. They told him that the treasure deposited with them was on its way to London and was being delivered to the Lidderdales. They were also apparently acquainted with Owen Lloyd or someone close to him, as they wrote:

> In regard to the said Lloyd who, on behalf of his agents and friends is being protected, we do not know if Your Honour would care to agree with the said scoundrel so as to recover what is possible of the referred to treasure and other effects and thereby remove all other accusations and in that way not to concern Yourself in seeking peace with the English government with an end that he can remain with his home and family and not be accused and tried as a criminal.

In the same letter they referred to the treasure as being "stealthily robbed by the villain Zebulon Wade." It appeared that Doig and Halliday had already heard Lloyd's version of the events. Contrary to this belief, Wade was now back home in Scituate, Massachusetts, trying to start his life over again, wishing he had never met Owen Lloyd. Wade appeared to be under no threat of arrest.

At last, Watson returned to St. Kitts, where he paid Captain Hedges for his services, and then he, Gibson, and Chavera bought some rum, wine, and limes. On July 27, they boarded the *Caesar*, which had been waiting for them, and sailed for Hampton, Virginia. Watson's job in the Caribbean was finished. It had been quite an adventure and what some might even call a holiday as he travelled from island to island at Bonilla's expense. His meetings with the governors were frustrating, however, as he discovered the avarice of these supposedly trustworthy officials.

On August 24, 1751, the *Caesar* arrived triumphantly in Hampton. Bonilla, Pedro Ortega, and some other crew left Suffolk and ferried to Hampton to meet with Watson and to get a firsthand account of their successes in the Caribbean. The good news elevated Bonilla's spirits as he had been recently in the care of Dr. Alexander Jameson of Williamsburg while Watson was in the Caribbean. The incredible stress of the past twelve months had made him quite ill.

Watson surely had stories to tell of his pursuit of treasure in the Caribbean. He would recount them many times to anyone who cared to listen. The week after his arrival, John Blair, a member of the Virginia Council and resident of Williamsburg, invited him to dinner where Watson regaled his guests with his electrifying narration of his pursuit of Lloyd and the Spanish money.

Watson made a final accounting; then he and Alexander Cairnes presented their statement to Bonilla. Short on cash, he signed a note for £748 for his balance due.

Bonilla had not seen his family for two years; but there was going to be another delay. Bonilla received word from his London insurers that he was expected to go to England to account for his lost treasure. He rehired Watson to go with him and began preparations for departure. He traveled to Norfolk where he purchased some new clothes and found a ship that would take them to Cádiz.

There was nothing more for him to do in Virginia. The *Guadalupe* was safe at Suffolk undergoing repairs, his crew were all gone, his fortune decimated. He regretted leaving America without retribution from Governor Johnston but he knew that he would be pleading his case against him in London. He also was going to hire agents to negotiate return of his property from Denmark and the Netherlands.

Bonilla and Watson departed Hampton, Virginia, for Cádiz, Spain, in early September, where he would finally see his family and check on his cargo. From there, he and Watson would travel to London in the hopes of regaining money recovered in the Caribbean as well as North Carolina. Bonilla was glad to be gone from English America, but he would find that the other European nations were just as difficult when it came to stolen Spanish treasure.

LONDINUM
URBS PRAECIPUA REGNI ANGLIAE.

Chapter Ten

Silver and the Embassies

London, December 1, 1751

Juan Manuel Bonilla and John Watson descended the wooden gangway that bridged the wharf to their ship. Just to their left, London Bridge spanned the River Thames and to their right was the Custom House and the infamous Tower of London which had housed many a pirate and political prisoner. Just before berthing, they had passed Execution Dock, the notorious hanging place for pirates. One notable was Captain Kidd in 1701. Bonilla certainly took notice: he was here because of piracy and he had been the victim. He hoped that Owen Lloyd would join Captain Kidd in his pirate afterlife.

From Virginia, Bonilla had first landed at Cádiz to visit with his family and tend to his affairs. It had been two years since he had last seen them. Unfortunately, he could not remain long, as his appearance in London was overdue. The last time Bonilla was in London was in 1747 when he had come to plead his case about the capture and subsequent loss of his *Nuestra Señora de los Remedios* that had been taken by the English privateer, George Walker. He had hoped then that he would never have to return.

London's cobblestone streets reeked from dead animals and the contents of chamber pots dumped out of open windows of dilapidated and soot-stained tenement buildings; the air was thick with smoke; there were gin houses and coffee houses everywhere to nourish those of its nearly 700,000 inhabitants who could afford the water substitutes. The Thames was the primary source for drinking water as well as a repository for all manner of human and animal refuse. So here he was again, but this time he was in the middle of an international brouhaha concerning his personal fortune, a situation made more tenuous because of a fragile peace agreement between two former warring nations.

He and Watson climbed into a waiting carriage and made for Leadenhall Street a half mile away where his insurers, Robert and John Lidderdale, maintained their offices.

Lloyd's theft of the *Guadalupe* treasure had sent shockwaves throughout the Caribbean that would ripple across the Atlantic for years. He created a truly international state of affairs. Lloyd had been the instigator, but the governors of North Carolina, St. Thomas, and St Eustatius, out of greed and hatred of the Spanish nation, dipped their own fingers into the pot of gold, skimming off what they could. There were four countries and their colonial territories embroiled in the mess: Spain, England, Denmark, and The Netherlands. England was quick to cooperate with Spain since the disaster had happened on their colonial turf, and in the wake of war, the fragile relationships between the ambassadors and ministers in London and Madrid had to be maintained. Denmark and the Netherlands were another story. As Captain Bonilla sought help recovering the *Guadalupe's* treasure, he discovered much to his chagrin that he would have to hire agents in each European capital to represent his interests and guide him through the bureaucratic maze.

Bonilla's problems with the European governments had started long before he had stepped into the din of the London streets. On February 22, 1751, while Bonilla was still in Suffolk, Virginia, Spain's ambassador to London, Ricardo Wall, had paid a personal visit to the Duke of Bedford in London and informed him of the actions of Governor Gabriel Johnston and his attorney general, Thomas Child. Wall complained of the Spaniards' unjust treatment in North Carolina and Virginia at the hands of the English government. Bedford, who seemed distracted by other affairs of state, said he would look into the alleged excesses and illegalities but that, at first glance, the fees charged by Governor Johnston did not appear out of line. He told Wall, rather glibly, that between their two courts, it was not necessary for these issues to become so strained and be approached so rigorously, when it is known that there is sufficient confidence and trust between them. The Spanish "have the best disposition towards us in the world."

Frustrated by his failure to get the Duke of Bedford to take action, Wall sent several coded messages to José Carvajal y Lancaster, Spain's secretary of state, about the meeting and England's lack of immediate cooperation.

Carvajal passed the reports on to King Ferdinand at his summer retreat at Aranjuez, south of Madrid. The king instructed Carvajal to respond back to Ambassador Wall and convey to the English Duke the message that this was still not satisfactory to the Spanish Crown. Vague promises were not enough: "Your Excellency is to communicate in the most strict words that the amount charged for the mentioned rights of salvage be returned." He reminded Wall that the contract between Bonilla and Governor Johnston for the *Scorpion* to carry the treasure to Spain was to be in line with other shipping charges to Europe. The two percent freight charge was deemed excessive and an insult. Ambassador Wall was also instructed to communicate the downright unfairness of taking advantage of distressed vessels brought in by bad weather. Examples of English ships being assisted on the coast of Spain were offered. King Ferdinand failed to acknowledge that English ships were still being captured by the Spanish and taken into Havana—an overlooked fact that did not help Wall in his negotiations.

Despite the setback, Wall felt things were progressing. He had reports from Virginia that President Thomas Lee had taken "all measures to repair the two Spanish and the Portuguese ships." Even more pleasing to him was the knowledge that Owen Lloyd was in prison at St. Eustatius and was being taken under guard to Norman's Island to recover the remaining treasure. Because of the delays in communication, he was not yet aware of his escape. And, it looked like the Duke of Bedford was starting to come around.

Bedford quietly agreed with the Spanish position concerning the exorbitant salvage and freight costs. The legal opinion of the solicitors general, Messrs. Paul, Ryder, and Murray, was submitted to the Duke on June 15. In it, they stated "by Fleming's own account" the salvage claimed at Tortola was much more than that claimed by Governor Johnston in North Carolina, since Fleming allowed each finder to keep a third. Furthermore, they were of the opinion that:

> these Effects ought to have been seized by the president and Council of Tortola, and restored without any other Salvage than for necessary Charges and expenses. We are also of the opinion that whoever has any part of these Effects in their possession, which they have got by Seizure or delivery by the pirates, are liable to restore them to the rightful owners.

The solicitors' opinion was that the treasure had been taken from the *Scorpion* by "Violence" and was confiscated without merit. At Tortola, the governor and officials were instructed to give "the required punishment to the thieves." The solicitors directed Governor Johnston to deposit "in safe hands" all the treasure confiscated except two percent for freight, but this would only apply to that which was transported to Spain. Johnston would be entitled to no "Duty or Gratification" and he was instructed to wait for further orders from the king on procedures to return the stolen treasure. As for the other governors, they were to return what treasure they had. The solicitors made no statement about Governor Johnston's salary being £12,000 in arrears.

The orders were given but Johnston did not yield the treasure. The Duke sent copies of his orders to England's ambassador, Benjamin Keene, in Madrid, so that he could personally present them to his Spanish counterparts as proof of the English Crown's efforts to effect restitution.

While Spain's ambassador and the English ministers in London fretted over the inactions of Governor Gabriel Johnston and the recovery of money in the English Caribbean Islands of Tortola, St. Kitts, and Antigua, Spain's ambassadors to Denmark and The Netherlands were making their cases against their own errant Caribbean governors who still held a sizable portion of Bonilla's treasure.

The Hague

Weeks before Bonilla came to the sooty streets of London, Spain's ambassador to The Netherlands, the Marqués del Puerto, had read a memorandum of facts from the States General, or Parliament, which served as the Dutch governing body. Wigged and robed ministers listened intently as the memorandum described the theft of the treasure at North Carolina by Owen Lloyd and his brother. The Marqués also related the efforts of John Watson to recover the treasure confiscated from Lloyd, Wade, Pritchett, and McMahon by Governor Heyliger at St. Eustatius. He said that Heyliger had deferred decision on the matter to their "High Mightynesses." They had recently received Heyliger's letter on the issue dated August 23rd, a month after he had turned John Watson away. On October 13, 1751, the Marqués pleaded:

You will also be aware of how important it is for the reputation of justice and equity that the money and the above mentioned effects be returned fast and in their entirety. They escaped successively from the fury of the waves which nearly swallowed them and from the hands of the thieves which took them away. It is therefore just that they should be given back to their proprietors, and it would be inhuman to postpone their restitution.

The King is convinced that your High Authorities will consider it a point of honour and will therefore send precise orders to the Governor of St. Eustatius according to which he has to deliver everything to the agent of the Captain of the La Guadeloupe frigate. I've been ordered to request from your High Authorities a fast and favourable response.

The Marqués took the opportunity to say that, in London, the court was persuaded to intervene vigorously, not only to recover the money and effects, but to "punish the authors of such a horrible crime."

When the Marqués learned of the contents of Heyliger's letter and his version of the late events at St. Eustatius, he prepared another memorandum. Heyliger's version of events, he wrote, "didn't entirely correspond to the truth." Without any hesitation he said that Governor Christian Suhm had participated in a scheme with Heyliger, saying that Heyliger had rigged the auction of the cochineal, indigo, and other goods so that he would emerge the purchaser at an unreasonably low price. There seemed to be some truth to this accusation, as bags of cochineal were sold for between 150 and 180 pesos when the actual value was around 560. The Marqués demanded not only restitution of the 17,369 pesos and 470 ounces of silverware that Heyliger openly admitted he had, but also compensation for the fraudulent auction that he now characterized as "a real villainy." "Your High Authorities certainly are aware of it and their well-known feelings of equity will dictate to them whatever has to be done to administer justice to the Commander of St Eustatius. He will receive the punishment he deserves and there will be a reimbursement to the legal owners of the money and the other goods which he and his associates took away so inhumanely."

Copies of the memos were ordered sent to representatives of the king and the General Chartered West-Indian Company at the Presidial Chamber of Amsterdam. Copies were also sent to Mr. van Wassenaar, the Dutch Ambassador at the court of Spain.

In ill health, Ambassador Ricardo Wall left London for Spain, appointing his secretary, Don Felix José Abreu y Bertodano, to carry on his duties until he could return. Abreu was instructed to visit Lord Holderness, senior secretary of state who had oversight over the American colonies, to ask that orders be sent again to the colonial governors to return the missing cargo stolen from Bonilla's ship. Abreu had received communications from John Watson indicating that Gilbert Fleming guaranteed that the money recovered from the finders at Tortola would be shipped from Antigua and that James Doig and John Halliday, Watson's agents, were posting security in the amount of £20,000 for the shipment of treasure to London.

After Bonilla's arrival in London, he learned that Owen Lloyd, who by this time had escaped from St. Eustatius and was under the protection of Governor Suhm at St. Thomas, had made overtures through friends in Antigua to the effect that, if he would be permitted to go free and return to his family in St. Kitts, he would be willing to negotiate the return of more of the stolen cargo. As for Governor Suhm, Bonilla felt that he had acted in very bad faith when he proceeded to auction the captured sloop and goods without waiting a year as prescribed by law. Fortunately, Bonilla was able to report to the Consules in Cádiz that Watson had managed to recover and safeguard at Antigua the sum of 107,265.5 pesos. This was not only silver but the value of some recovered cochineal as well and also what Gilbert Fleming had recovered. Watson had successful meetings at St. Eustatius and St. Thomas but nothing more could be done on those islands until the officials at The Hague and Copenhagen gave permission to relinquish the treasure.

The following week, on December 9, Bonilla conveyed to the House of Trade in Cádiz a list of the auctioned cargo obtained by Watson while he was at St. Thomas. On a second front, Bonilla was doing his own battle against the English officials. These included Thomas Child, the former attorney general of North

Carolina, who left there in May and was now in London acting as a prosecutor.

James Abercromby, North Carolina's agent in London, wrote to Johnston shortly after Bonilla's arrival to inform him that Bonilla had already applied to Ambassador Wall to have restitution from North Carolina's governor of the 12,000 pieces of eight seized from the *Scorpion*. He assured him that Watson "was his friend in this matter" and had portrayed Johnston's actions in a favorable light. He enumerated the great efforts of Johnston to preserve Bonilla's ship and treasure. The idea was to lead Wall to believe that the 5,000 pieces of eight "gratuity" claimed by Johnston was reasonable. The balance was for actual expenses or had been retained by Colonel Innes and Thomas Child. James Abercromby became the eyes and ears for Johnston in London. Besides his £100 annual salary from North Carolina he had an arrangement with Johnston, who paid him £50 more a year for his "special interests." While Watson was tending to Bonilla he was also reporting to Abercromby.

Ambassador Wall decided to wait for the testimonies of Tomás Carriedo and Felipe García on the matter. Before pressing the English Crown further, he wanted all of the facts on the conduct of Child and Colonel Innes at Wilmington.

As the weeks passed, Bonilla received more news that some of the cochineal sold at St. Thomas was tied up at customs in Holland. This was apparently the same that Governor Heyliger had purchased on auction day through his bookkeeper. On the 16th of December, 14,000 pesos from Antigua arrived, money he badly needed. The frustrated Spanish captain continued to write letters to the officials in Spain about his stolen cargo but by March 2, he had only received one letter from home.

Thomas Child was again called upon to give his account of treasure taken by himself and Innes. Bonilla had submitted his version of events and now John Watson was called to render his opinion. Watson delayed his report knowing that Bonilla was set to leave.

Captain Bonilla had been making preparations to return home since he had arrived in London. In January, he had bought a 435-ton English ship, the *York*, and was outfitting her for his planned departure from England. John Watson was growing weary wanting to return home and was now complaining about "his tribulations and travels." Bonilla agreed to let him out of his contract. Nicolas Magens, a merchant from Savage Garden in London, was designated to take the place of Watson. Magens was affiliated with James Doig and John Halliday in

Antigua, who were acting as Bonilla's representatives there. He was also known in many European circles and was an expert on marine insurance. The issue of the money owed by The Netherlands and Denmark would have to be settled by diplomats and agents in those countries. The matter of the 12,000 pieces of eight taken from the *Scorpion* was now in the hands of Felix Abreu and the English court.

Bonilla received more news of his treasure. On March 2nd, in his letter to the House of Trade, he mentioned having received word that:

> One of the main pirates who participated in the robbery is in Ireland and Nicolás Magens has written about this to someone in Dublin… This man does not know him but will track him down. This pirate must be wealthy for he was one of the principals and not only did he get a large part [of the booty] but he also later robbed his associates. He does not appear to be a big spender and I estimate his fortune to be more than 50,000 pesos… I am writing this apart from the rest of my news because it is not information for public knowledge until the pirate is caught and you know how quickly the ink of the pen travels.

By July 1752, Magens had identified the pirate in Ireland that he had previously told Bonilla about. It was William Dames, the Irishman from Maryland who had joined in with Blackstock at Ocracoke and was later marooned by Lloyd at Norman's Island. He assured Bonilla that "I will not rest in my pursuit of that thief in some part of the world."

Magens seemed to be an able and ambitious representative for Bonilla in London. After his return from Antigua, he appointed William Gideon Deutz, a Burgermiester in Amsterdam, to represent Bonilla in that city, and Justus Fabritius, merchant and a director of the West India Company, to liaison in Copenhagen.

On March 3, Watson wrote to Governor Suhm at St. Thomas telling him that he was no longer attorney for Bonilla but reminded him that he had left an "order" for him to pay Doig and Halliday at Antigua any recoveries made of money or effects. If this responsibility was not executed before the receipt of his letter, then "Mr. Bonilla expects from your Honour to be paid for it without any further detention at Copenhagen where the Spanish minister is charged with it."

Bonilla continued to wait it out in London hoping for news of a break in the diplomatic log jam and treasure shipments from Antigua. He needed money not only for himself but also to start reimbursing the other merchants and passengers who had lost cargo at Ocracoke. By the end of March, he received word that he could leave and began his final preparations.

In June, Watson received a package of letters from home, which included a provocative letter from Governor Johnston to Bonilla. Abercromby reported to Johnston that he had "soothed matters" with Bonilla, telling him cooperation was necessary for a proper defense.

Bonilla hoped that the matter would have been settled, but by early July he could wait no more and departed London for Cádiz on board the *York* with a much diminished view of Englishmen: "although these are rich men, it is a fact that as a nation it is very greedy and without the least scruples."

On July 17, 1752, Gabriel Johnston died at Eden House, his plantation across the river from Edenton. When he died, his salary was £13,000 in arrears with the king. The treasure taken from Bonilla had proved a godsend. Johnston left many "turbulent" creditors, who openly complained. Abercromby continued to prosecute his salary arrears in London and as he told Samuel Ormes, not only Johnston's friend and neighbor but Bonilla's former physician, he would "continue my endeavors to put an end & extinguish the Spanish minister's claim." He wanted to protect the governor's wife and family from any forced restitution by Bonilla or his agents.

His widow, Frances, later married John Rutherford of New Hanover County, North Carolina, who took charge of settling the estate, which would take many years. There is no record that Johnston or his estate ever reimbursed Bonilla.

After his arrival in Spain, Bonilla renamed his ship *La Reina de los Angeles*, alias the *Peregrina*, and made further preparations for another trading voyage to Vera Cruz. He began disbursing from what little cash he had to some of the merchants who had shipped on the *Guadalupe*. His insurers denied coverage for his loses suffered in North Carolina.

St. Eustatius

On July 8, 1752, Governor Heyliger, having been advised by letters from the West India Company of the investigation into his actions and conduct, wrote the West India Company and the council. They acknowledged the visit of John Watson the year before and had told him that the treasure should be returned to Bonilla only on orders of the authorities in The Netherlands. Watson, it will be recalled, had left instructions that the treasure would have to be forwarded to London in the care of Robert and John Lidderdale after the release was granted.

Heyliger acted offended by the investigation. He addressed each allegation that had been levied against him by the Spanish ambassador, the Marqués del Puerto, arguing that "the proof and the evidence are bright like the sunshine in the firmament. I never undertook anything in this affair without the presence of the entire council and everything that was done to the last iota has been reported to your High Authorities."

The Marqués had alleged that the auction at St. Thomas was rigged by Governor Suhm and Heyliger. "It is clear," Heyliger responded, "that the Ambassador will not have known that St. Thomas belongs to the King of Denmark and not to your High Mighty. If he had been aware of that, he would not have stated that I had asked the Governor of St. Thomas to hold a bogus auction." He said that he became aware of the auction by a letter from St. Croix. Heyliger admitted that he had sent his bookkeeper, Paul Anjot, to the auction for the purpose of buying some cochineal but told him to offer the highest price.

Heyliger pointed to the fact that when John Watson had called on him in the previous July, he obviously trusted him because he left without taking any treasure and trusted Heyliger to forward it when the permission was granted in the Netherlands. If this logic wasn't convincing enough, he tried to discredit Watson and Gilbert Fleming by pointing to the fact that Fleming had received "a gift of 2,000 pesos" from Watson and was reimbursed 4,000 in expenses. Heyliger claimed to have been offered the same deal, but: "the King of Spain did not have enough money to bribe me to do something that I did not deem fair and legal, because that I had informed my Lord Superiors of the affair and was awaiting further orders and that I would not do anything until I had been advised."

The Council of St. Eustatius backed Heyliger in every regard. In a letter accompanying his letter to the West India Company, they stated that the Marqués de Puerto was "badly informed" and that all of the treasure had been inventoried including the items bought at St. Thomas and deposited with the treasury. Lloyd's schooner, the one he brought from St. Croix, had been put to auction, and the expenses of sending Commandant Ravene to Norman's Island were deducted. The Council again took the opportunity to make a statement about the runaway slaves at Puerto Rico and demanded their recovery, a remark that was certainly intended for the Spanish ambassador.

At the meeting of the Board of Ten of the West India Company on September 25, the case was reviewed and on October 14, 1752, the decision was reached. They determined that there was no wrongdoing on the part of Governor Heyliger and that orders were being sent to him to deliver as quickly as possible all of the money and silverware to Bonilla.

In their final report, they stated that their actions corresponded to "the famous honesty of the King of Spain." No further interventions were necessary and that extracts of the proceedings were being sent to Ambassadors del Puerto at Amsterdam and van Wassenear at Madrid.

Governor Heyliger was at Spanish Town in the Virgin Islands with Governor Purcell and John Baker of St. Kitts on November 19, 1752, and died two days later without having surrendered any treasure to Bonilla or to the Spanish government. His widow would now be faced with that responsibility.

London

John Halliday, the man handling Bonilla's affairs at Antigua, was advised to go ahead and forward any of Bonilla's effects still situated in Antigua. The six bags of cochineal quarantined at St. Kitts were being forwarded to London on the ship *Houston*. She arrived that August and the cochineal was sold. Magens received £1,000 from Messrs. Claude Johnson and Son in Antigua and was promised £1,000 more within the next month.

Halliday and James Doig had been to St. Thomas in an attempt to recover the cochineal left over from the auction and still under the control of Governor Suhm. Suhm told them to take their demands directly to Copenhagen. As for Owen Lloyd, he was still under the protection of Suhm. It was Halliday's hope that Denmark would intervene and order his arrest. Halliday was sure that Lloyd had hidden a considerable amount of the treasure that could be recovered if not for Suhm giving him protection.

Magens, in turn, reported to Bonilla his latest successes and said that he was meeting with Abreu to discuss the action against Thomas Child but he "feared the procedure will be slow but I do not doubt that one day or another some compensation will be received either from him or the Governor."

In December 1752, Magens filed a new report with Bonilla, who was in Cádiz, stating that the Danish court said that nothing further could be done until proof had been given as to who the legitimate owners of the cargo left at St. Thomas were. By this time, Suhm had forwarded to Denmark the proceeds of the auction. He had little choice now that John Watson had informed the embassies. Denmark was engaged in another delaying tactic that would hopefully wear Bonilla's resolve. The Consules in Cádiz had tried to put the responsibility on Denmark and England in September to pursue prosecutions against the "aggressors" concerning the piracy. That included Thomas Child and Governor Johnston. The request also included a demand for the treasure at St. Thomas and for Owen Lloyd's surrender as well, "because a pirate is everywhere deemed a common enemy."

The Danish court's tactics were taken in stride by Magens. He put aside his frustration and played the diplomatic game. He met with the Danish ambassador and served him with clear documentation that the effects saved were from the *Guadalupe*. This included descriptions, quantities, and merchant marks. The Dutch ambassador was notified as well.

Besides the pursuit of the *Guadalupe* treasure and Owen Lloyd, Bonilla was preparing for his next voyage with the *Peregrina*. Cargoes needed to be hired and purchased. Bonilla's mother-in-law was again his partner.

While this effort was getting underway, across the Atlantic his last command, the *Nuestra Señora de Guadalupe*, was also preparing for her return to Spain. Bonilla needed to get his ship home to help fund his next Vera Cruz venture.

Norfolk, Virginia

HMS *Triton*, under Captain Matthew Whitwell, was ordered to escort the *Guadalupe* back to Spain with Captain Charles Elliot acting as her commander. The *Virginia Gazette* of October 23, 1752, advertised for sailors who were willing to sign on as crew. The aging galleon was entirely manned by Englishmen, since all of the former Spanish crewmen had returned to Spain. The *Guadalupe* set sail for Cádiz on December 20. Five days out, she sprung a leak, forcing the crew to man a pump constantly. On January 29, about one hundred leagues from Cádiz, she hoisted a distress signal for the *Triton* and threw overboard her remaining cannon to gain some freeboard. The *Triton* was not able to maneuver in close enough to render assistance due to the rough seas.

They were having great difficulty in keeping the ship afloat and the ship was unable to carry any sail. Captain Elliot was able to transfer over to the *Triton* carrying a letter signed by him and two mates attesting to the serious condition of the *Guadalupe*. Captain Whitwell sent some of his crew over to inspect her only after the seas had calmed. If not for this reprieve in the weather, the *Guadalupe* would have been lost.

Whitwell's crew was able to cut away the bowsprit to ease the stem where most of the water was coming from. They then made for Madeira arriving on February 19. However, the *Guadalupe's* ordeal was not over. Two days later, a gale arose and drove her out to sea, anchors dragging. The crew cut the cables, raised her foresail, and ran with the wind. Captain Whitwell was unable to send his boats to assist as the seas were running too high. Whitwell, ashore, perceived the "public good" in saving the Spaniards' ship. He offered a "large sum" to some Portuguese sailors to swim out to a boat that could carry them with orders for Lt. Thomas Pembles aboard the *Triton*. Prembles was ordered to immediately proceed after the *Guadalupe*, and if necessary, follow her to Cádiz and leave him at Madiera. The *Triton* slipped her cables and proceeded after her, firing several cannon as a signal to speak with them. But the distance between them was seven miles and soon the *Triton* lost sight of her.

The *Guadalupe* was not seen again until she arrived just outside Cádiz Bay, damaged and leaking. At last, two and a half years after her departure from this same city, the *Guadalupe* was home. The ship, for which Bonilla had shelled out 28,000 pieces of eight in 1749, was now a skeleton of her former self and nearly worthless. But, with little consolation, she was the only ship of the 1750 fleet that would return to Spain. The *Triton* returned to her station in Virginia after retrieving Captain Whitwell at Madeira. The fortunes of Juan Manuel Bonilla had been dealt another blow.

Despite this setback, Bonilla's future began to look a little brighter. Governor Johnston had died, but his former attorney general was accessible and now in London, ready to face, rather than evade, the issue. In February of 1753, at

Westminster, England, Child was facing investigation by the Board of Trade and the persistent demands of Nicolas Magens for the return of the 12,000 pieces of eight. Magens had also sent authorization to William Gideon and John Deutz in Amsterdam to name suitable agents to forward the treasure still in the hands of widow Heyliger at St. Eustatius. Three thousand pesos and the silverware had already been sent to Amsterdam aboard the ship *Zorg & Rust*. The remainder was going by ship to London and to save money, without insurance, in care of the Lidderdales. By May 17, 1753, Magens reported that 12,839 pesos had been returned out of the 17,369 pesos and 470 ounces of silverware originally seized by Heyliger. The balance was charged as commissions and freight. This was the last of Owen Lloyd's booty to leave the Caribbean.

Bonilla welcomed the money, which he so desperately needed to fund his voyage to Vera Cruz. But officials in Copenhagen and St. Thomas still refused to cooperate.

Two years had now passed since Magens had taken over from Watson, and so far, Magens's letters to Copenhagen had not recovered a single piece of eight. In his latest letter dated October 12 to the Consules of Cádiz, Magens's frustration started to show: "...so much time is wasted in writing letters and awaiting responses from such faraway places, it is not as easy as they say to prove the truth."

Magens frequented Lloyd's Coffee House on Lombard Street in London as did many other ship captains, owners, insurers, and common seaman. Here one could learn about the latest news in the shipping industry as well as local gossip. The plight of Juan Manuel Bonilla was becoming well known. Just recently, John Boydell published some engravings of the famous maritime artist John Brookings. Brookings had drawn two scenes from the 1747 capture and later sinking of Bonilla's former ship, the *Nuestra Señora de los Remedios*. Bonilla's bad luck and his alleged abuse of the insurance underwriters were the subject of many exchanges. Some would smile when the name Owen Lloyd was mentioned. This did not dampen Magens' loyalty to his cause, however.

The Spanish bureaucracy was now heaping more demands on Bonilla. He had to assemble all of his expense reports, starting with Owen Lloyd being hired to tow his ship into Ocracoke. He had spent 31,802 pesos during his stay in Virginia and North Carolina. Bonilla also had to account for his treasure recoveries to date while continuing his plans to leave in the *Peregrina*. He now had five backers, including Don Joseph Respaldiza, who was with him in the 1750 voyage and also lost his own ship, the *Nuestra Señora de Soledad*, at Drum Inlet in North Carolina. Respaldiza had been very supportive of him at Ocracoke while he endured his own problems with a mutinous crew and the obstinate governor of North Carolina.

Copenhagen

The West India Company sent its ruling to Governor Suhm at St. Thomas about Gert Sprewart de Wint's request to be awarded one third of the value of the *Seaflower* and her cargo for claiming to be the first one to sound the alarm on Lloyd. Suhm, who never admitted that he knew of Lloyd's presence, was told that only a court had the power to make such an award. The officials in Denmark were not prepared to disburse to anyone until the claims of Bonilla could be disposed of and they were in no hurry to do that.

Cádiz

On November 26, 1753, Bonilla boarded the *Peregrina* in much the same way he had the *Guadalupe* in 1749, with great fanfare and personal good-byes. Bonilla had the backing once again of his mother-in-law. This was probably going to be his last chance at financial recovery. At fifty-three, he was getting a little old for the transatlantic crossings and he still had young children and a wife to support and little choice on how to make a living.

The *Peregrina* was armed with twenty-eight cannon, rifles, pistols, swords, pikes, and hatchets, and loaded to capacity with cargo. Tomás Carriedo, his long-suffering brother-in-law, was designated master for the voyage. As usual for Bonilla, there was some controversy related to his cargo. The port officials determined that he was overloaded and removed 200 barrels, of which eleven were empty and belonged to Bonilla. The customs officials were perplexed.

With a ship's compliment of ninety-eight men and boys, they departed Cádiz with the two war ships, *Asia* and *Fuerte,* under Don Juan de Langara. The convoy sailed to the Canary Islands where they became separated. The fleet was seen in the distance by the lookout on the topmast, but Bonilla made no attempt to catch up.

On January 24, 1754, the *Peregrina*, still sailing alone, was close to St. Martin. Crown decrees specified ships must carry at least ninety days worth of water and now with only fifty-nine days behind them they were nearly out, with only three and a half barrels remaining. This shortage may have had something to do with the empty barrels removed just prior to sailing. Had he loaded sufficient water in Spain, he could have made Havana as planned to reprovision for his final leg to Vera Cruz. But Bonilla, suspiciously, set his course for San Antonio Bay, Puerto Rico.

Some of his crew took exception to the decision, San Antonio being farther west than the port of San Juan on the north coast of Puerto Rico. San Antonio was a very remote area and the chance of taking on water and supplies was slim. Bonilla said that in San Juan he would be required to spend more than 500 pesos on gifts for the governor and bishop, but this made no sense as his officers pointed out to him that he could enter the bay of San Francisco at no charge and get water. The *Peregrina* sailed west past the bay of San Francisco, as suggested to Bonilla.

The *Peregrina* continued along the coast in light breezes, arriving at the Bay of San Antonio on January 25. The pilot warned him that he was unfamiliar with the bay, so a launch was sent ahead to take soundings and light a signal fire on the beach as the sun was going down. Bonilla did not order any sails furled. Instead, he and his ship boldly headed into the bay. Presently, the *Peregrina* shuddered to a stop, having driven onto a sandbar. Bonilla acted as if he was not too concerned. He gave no orders to preserve the cargo or attempt to free the ship. Fortunately, the weather remained calm.

Four hours later, however, the *Peregrina* began to take on water and it was decided to carry some of the cargo ashore. Bonilla retreated to his cabin and went to bed. Awakened the next morning by a junior officer, he discovered that his brother-in-law, Carriedo, had gone ashore at midnight and had been hiding in the hills where he was discovered that morning. When Carriedo was returned at 11 a.m., the crew started to unload one of the cannons, but Bonilla came on deck and ordered all activity stopped. Carriedo went ashore again, saying he was going to seek assistance from some nearby schooners. The passengers were distraught. None of Bonilla's actions made any sense to them, especially since he was so slow to react and remained nearly oblivious to the situation. It seemed as if their voyage was being doomed deliberately by the arrogant Spaniard.

That afternoon, Don Juan de Langara, either by coincidence or by design, arrived with his warships *Asia* and *Fuerte* and rendered assistance. Finding that half of Bonilla's crew had deserted to the hills and that the others were too tired to work, he took charge and ordered crews from both ships to unload the *Peregrina* and store the cargo on the beach. The *Peregrina* was pulled off the bar, whence it was found that her keel was missing and the hull in need of an overhaul. While repairs were being made, Langara suggested to officials in Puerto Rico that an inquiry into Bonilla's conduct was necessary, as there were passengers and crew who had questioned his actions. After the inquiry, Bonilla was exonerated. But in spite of the fact that the pilot had warned Bonilla about entering the bay, Langara found "only the pilot to be guilty of over self-confidence which made him dare to come into a port unknown to himself with only the aid of a map which was not worthy of an opinion amongst those of the profession." The repairs to the *Peregrina* were completed by March 11 and Langara left with the warships for Vera Cruz the next day.

As the *Peregrina* sailed on to Vera Cruz, Tomás Carriedo died at sea. He was replaced by Manuel Prieto. When the *Peregrina* arrived at Vera Cruz on May 30, the passengers and some crew complained to the port officials that Bonilla and his pilot "had planned this mischievously and with ill intention." The Viceroy ordered a hearing to re-examine the conduct of Bonilla and his pilot. Bonilla was charged with incompetence and irresponsibility. Unfortunately, his star witness, Tomás Carriedo, was not alive to testify for him.

During the inquiry, Bonilla testified in his defense that he had lost more cargo than anyone else as he was the one with the most cargo registered—more than a million pesos worth. Evidence was presented to the contrary about the value of his cargo. Most of it was iron and steel. The court concluded that Bonilla's cargo was worth less than ten percent of his claimed damages.

When the judge rendered his decision, he considered evidence presented against Bonilla in regards to his previous loss of the *Guadalupe*:

> After abandoning the ship, he tried to reclaim the insurance in London where the ship was insured. However his underwriters dispatched a ship, it was no surprise to find the Guadalupe anchored and safe, but abandoned. It was outfitted and sailed to Cádiz where Bonilla was obliged to take responsibility for it, pay for the expenses of its return, and not be eligible for collecting any insurance. This incident is enough to presume Bonilla's ill intentions regarding the grounding of the Peregrina.

The authorities in Puerto Rico asked the viceroy to "charge Captain Bonilla to pay those who had interests in the cargo…the complete amount of the same according to its value at Cádiz as well as the costs ensued in this kingdom and delays and consequences as a result of the running aground at San Antonio Añasco."

On October 23, while still in Vera Cruz, Bonilla wrote the merchant guild in Cádiz about his perceived mistreatment. He made it clear that the governor of Puerto Rico had cleared him of misconduct and the incident was only a mishap and that the viceroy of Mexico had convened a hearing based on malicious rumors:

> They proceeded to make accusations against me—based on evil intentions—such have never been seen or heard from anyone in our merchant circle which your Excellency will see, as if I had acted with malice and was openly pronounced as such. This unwanted incident is worthy of the utmost attention because I have been dispossessed of what is mine based on unfound suspicion and not only this, they also used a belligerent lawyer, well known in the courts, to strip me not only of my honour and assets, but also affect my life in ways not known to our group of merchants in such manner that has greatly perturbed my spirit and sense of dignity. I have been obliged to abandon all my dependencies and as I have been embargoed, I am unable to meet my debts, notwithstanding the fact that I have the wherewithal. I advise Your Excellency of this so that, in time, my rights may be demanded.

Just as the *Guadalupe* had been laid up in Virginia, the *Peregrina* remained in Vera Cruz for nearly two years. Before her departure in early 1756, she was loaded with sugar, cocoa, and dye wood. Bonilla had a relatively small consignment of silver—only 7, 819 pieces of eight. Bonilla was not on board, as he had returned to Spain ahead of her departure to give his sister Juana the painful news that her husband Tomás had died at sea. The *Peregrina* sailed into the Bay of Cádiz on March 19, 1756, under the command of Pedro Manuel de Ortega, the *Guadalupe's* former pilot.

All of this while the quest continued for the money stolen from the *Guadalupe*.

Cádiz

In early June 1754, the Consules held a meeting to discuss the distribution of 24,920 pesos previously received by the Spanish treasury from recovered cargo and treasure. Only a few of the cargo owners presented themselves, and hence it was suggested that the total be divvied up only between them.

Later, on August 8, Nicolas Magens reported to the Consules that he had the final accounting from his friend John Duetz, Burgermeister in Amsterdam, of the treasure turned over by Heyliger's widow. He also forwarded the news that John Watson was back in Virginia. His job had been finished in London but he was still engaged to proceed against the heirs of Governor Gabriel Johnston in North Carolina, who still owed Bonilla the 12,000 pieces of eight as ordered by King George II in 1751. He was also still negotiating with the Danish Court to recover the value of the effects sold at the auction at St. Thomas.

London

Nicolas Magens was still working to recover balances owed Bonilla. In April of 1755, he wrote to Don Geronimo Ariscum with the Consules in Cádiz and reported that the Spanish warships *Castilla* and *Europa* would be returning from Havana with treasure from Vera Cruz that was being sent on Bonilla's account. It was expected that the treasure would be applied to the outstanding balances of those who still remained unpaid by Bonilla. The following year, conflicts arose between France and England over the latter's westward expansion in the North American colonies. This would lead to all-out war, bringing in other European countries, and would last seven years. Magens' progress with the Danish ambassador ground to a halt.

On August 27, 1758, Queen Barbara of Spain died, throwing Ferdinand into extreme melancholy, and he began isolating himself. Bonilla's fortunes were still tied to negotiations with Denmark, which had completely stalled for the past three years. The Spanish ambassador to Denmark, Juan Domingo Pignatelli, was now Bonilla's representative, and he hired the Baron von Bernstorff, privy councilor in charge of foreign affairs in Copenhagen, to replace Just Fabritius, who accomplished nothing during the war. Another petition was filed demanding the value of 37,825 pesos and again outlining the historical circumstances surrounding the theft of the treasure from the *Guadalupe*. Bonilla had gotten nowhere in the last eight years.

St. Thomas

The international drama that had been playing out since Owen Lloyd had stolen Bonilla's treasure was about to be recast with a new set of players. In 1759, Governor Christian Suhm of St. Thomas died. He had been replaced the year before by Harrien Felchenhauer. The Danish Court continued to drag its feet over the 37,825 pesos from the auction of Bonilla's goods in 1751. With Suhm dead, it would be impossible to recover any money from him. King Ferdinand VI died on August 10. His half brother, Carlos, gave up his title as King of Naples, and arrived at Barcelona, Spain, October 17, 1759, to assume rule of the Spanish Empire as Carlos III. Bonilla's problems were of little concern now to any of those whom Bonilla continued to petition.

Cádiz, January 1759

Bonilla was nearly broke, and his largest asset was the money still owed to him from Denmark. In January, he received word that for some reason the governor of Jamaica was now claiming the money that was owed Spain by Denmark. This claim went nowhere. The officials in Copenhagen were demanding that a new claim be filed by Bonilla to clarify the issue. Bonilla's spirits plummeted, as did his health. At sixty years old, the strain of Bonilla's personal finances was taking its toll.

Knowing that his end was near, Bonilla prepared his will. On October 25, 1759, he wrote "I am gravely ill and bed ridden." He reflected back on the misfortunes of his life, particularly what had happened at Ocracoke. To be spared his life and his ship from the hurricane, and then meet the humiliating and financially devastating fate delivered to him by Owen Lloyd, was bringing Bonilla to a premature end. He died later that day.

Bonilla was a religious man. He thought of the Church and regretted that there was nothing to leave her. In his will he said, "I have so few possessions because of the many misfortunes which I have experienced in my business and also because of all my dependents, so much so, that I have been left without any fortune."

Also in his will, Bonilla described his remaining estate. He said that he only had 8,000 pesos in hand. But he owed approximately 11,000 pesos to "people whose names I cannot remember." He also had some valuable receivables. Bonilla was owed money by Don Lope de Morales of Havana, "a sum left when I last set sail from that city and which I gave to Antonio Parladorio to be used for the purchase of 600 arrobas of sugar." He also described a certain cargo that he was unable to sell when he was last in Vera Cruz to a value of 1,000 pesos. This was left with a Francisco Vaso Ibáñez, a merchant in Mexico, to sell for him. He listed another portion of money owed from some canvas and muskets that were not sold in Vera Cruz. And regarding the last remaining sums due to him from his stolen cargo of 1750:

> I declare that I should have that which belongs to me in the amount of 20,000 pesos, the value of 100 sacks of cochineal and other effects which have been sold in the court of Denmark. These are deposited under judicial order and it is my hope that the outcome is favourable. As well, I have an interest in the value of 18 of these same 100 sacks which became my responsibility via the merchant house of this city, Gilli y Montao.

Before he died, he also filled out a list of nine shippers' marks for consignments of ten sacks of cochineal and four of indigo that had been auctioned at St. Thomas, but were not in the cargo manifest of the *Guadalupe* issued at Vera Cruz. Bonilla could have possibly disavowed their existence but the Consulado now had a record of these thanks to John Watson's efforts. Apparently the owners were still insisting on being reimbursed, even though their cargo had been smuggled.

Bonilla's real estate interests included: in Cádiz, "the sixth part of a ground floor on the Calle de Comedias...which is presently occupied by the merchant house, Prasca y Arbore." In Puerto de Santa Maria just north of Cádiz there were also two adjoining properties, a house with two floors and a lot located on the Calle de la Palma. There was also a hacienda with olive trees and a property in that same town. In Cádiz, he resided on the Calle del Veedor. Bonilla was succeeded by his wife, Doña María Agustina de Utrera, and six children.

He regretted to his wife that she would have to use her remaining dowry to pay for his funeral. His desire was to be "dressed in the habit of St. Francis," but he did not care where he was buried. Shortly after he died, Bonilla was laid to rest in the vegetable garden of the Franciscan Convento de los Descalzos, known as "San Diego" in Cádiz. Funeral masses were said the following day at the church of San Diego.

London, England, September 1760

Nicolas Magens, now working for Bonilla's widow, became so desperate for results that he offered a "large compensation" to a secretary of the King of Denmark for assistance in recovering the money. His petition and offer of a reward went unheeded. The Royal West India Company was now defunct. On January 7, 1760, the Chamber of Customs replaced the Chamber of Revenue that was established in 1754 and which in turn had replaced the West India and Guinea Company. This bureaucratic change would force Bonilla's agents to start over from scratch.

Copenhagen

In the first week of September, 1761, Don Joseph Cadalso arrived in Copenhagen with a power of attorney from the Consulado in Cádiz. He was owner of part of the stolen cargo and was representing Bonilla's interests as well. Cadalso called on Juan Domingo Pignatelli, the Spanish ambassador in Copenhagen, to help present his case. Cadalso had been told that he would have to prove not only Bonilla's interest in the *Guadalupe* cargo but actual ownership of the ship itself.

On September 12, Pignatelli threw down the gauntlet, notifying Baron von Bernstorff, Denmark's minister of foreign affairs, that Cadalso was there to collect the money and had brought with him all of the documents necessary to prove his case once again. He informed Bernstorff that once Cadalso had complied, he would have "to prove, in this case like in all others, his sentiments towards the Spanish state." In other words, no more talk, just give us the money:

As these facts have all been proven by justifying and convincing documents, the delegate from Spain has every reason for hoping the equity and justice of the Danish crown which will give the required orders for the restitution of the 37,825 pesos and 5 reales…, as recorded by the accounts received from the Commander of St. Thomas.

Ambassador Pignatelli advised Ricardo Wall in Madrid that Cadalso had made his proper presentation. He said that Baron von Bernstorff had assured him that he would present this evidence to the king and take great care that this matter be resolved efficiently. "I will follow this with the utmost energy so that His Majesty's vassals need not endure further lack of consideration."

Perhaps the stress had gotten to him or perhaps he had some congenital time bomb, but on September 22, Joseph Cadalso came down with a fever and his condition deteriorated rapidly from there. The best doctor in the city was called but to no avail. Joseph Cadalso died at 5 a.m. on October 4 "of a swollen chest." Once again Bonilla, or rather his widow, was without legal representation. To make matters worse, in January, 1762, Spain officially entered the conflict now known as the Seven Years War, siding with France.

Copenhagen

On February 15, 1763, King Frederick V of Denmark reached his decision. If he got the legal documentation from Spain, he would make the payment from the royal treasury. On the 21st, Baron von Bernstorff acknowledged this to Pignatelli. The next day Pignatelli wrote to Ricardo Wall and advised him that Joseph Constant would be presenting the power of attorney left to him by Cadalso before he died. This was done and the Danish treasury was at last forthcoming. On March 29, Joseph Constant received 27,623 pesos, 3.75 reales, which represented the total of 37,825 pesos less charges and expenses.

Joseph Constant then carried letters of exchange for the money to Cádiz, where it was turned over to the treasurer of the Camara de Indias, Don Juan de Garay. Here they analyzed the auction document secured by John Watson and compared the shipper's marks for each bag of cochineal, indigo, chests of vanilla, and the eighty two hides sold at St. Thomas twelve years before. They made an accounting to each shipper including Juan Manuel Bonilla. Expenses were then prorated against each and the final division was computed.

Cádiz

On June 19, 1764, the treasurer of the Consulado, Joseph Perez de Vargas, disbursed the money to the cargo owners who shipped aboard the *Guadalupe* in 1750. Bonilla's share, 9,819 pesos 4 reales, was paid to his widow on June 23, 1764, finally putting an end to Juan Manuel Bonilla's quest for his lost treasure.

Bonilla's family resumed their lives. His oldest son, Antonio, became a brigadier and his youngest son, Juan Manuel, an army commander in Vera Cruz, Mexico. His son, Francisco, was already a Franciscan priest. All six children shared in the properties in Puerto de Santa Maria when their mother, María Agustina, later died.

Zebulon Wade had safely returned to Scituate, Massachusetts, after his escape from the fort at St. Eustatius. His life was never the same. Records indicate that he did not return to the coastwise trade. He died in 1759 at the age of forty-nine. His first mate, Abraham Pritchett, would become a captain and carried on trade between Ocracoke and Boston just as he had done with Wade on the *Seaflower*. He no doubt shared his tales of adventure with William Howard, Blackbeard's former quartermaster, who acquired Ocracoke Island in 1759. The other crew, Isaac Raye, James Moorehouse, Thomas Hobson, James McMahon, Enoch Collins, and Jonathan Deacon, resumed their previous lives, but now they had an adventure to share with anyone who would listen. William Dames became a church warden and prominent citizen in Queen Annes's County, Maryland, on the Eastern Shore of the Chesapeake Bay. In 1769, he donated 100,000 bricks to the new St. Paul's Church in Centerville, Maryland. The one-eyed William Blackstock assumed the role of "planter" in Pasquotank County, North Carolina. He also ran a tavern.

For the fate of Owen Lloyd and his treasure, we must wait.

Part Two

RETURN TO TREASURE ISLAND

It is not the bullet that kills you, it is fate.
Arabian Proverb

"It was like any other seaman's chest on the outside, the initial "B" burned on the top of it with a hot iron..."—Jim Hawkins, Chapter Four, "The Seaman's Chest," *Treasure Island*.

Chapter Eleven

Return to Treasure Island

The forty-one-foot ketch called *Antiquity* cleared the east end of St. John, Virgin Islands, sailing southeast on a port tack as the green peaks of Norman Island came into view. The blue Caribbean waters were lightly flecked with white as the ever-present trade winds lathered the wave crests. Her present course would place the determined vessel just west of the rocky sentinels called the Indians, which protruded out of the sea guarding the entrance to Man-of-War Bay, the planned anchorage for the night. Captain David DeCuir hailed his young mate from below deck in preparation for anchoring. On board were two passengers who were secretly reveling at the sight of this wild and beautiful island while contemplating the buried treasure left by Owen Lloyd. It was January 20, 2000. The millennium had just changed. The passengers were my wife, Delphine, and me.

Our trip to Norman Island was more accidental than planned. In the fall of 1999, Delphine informed me that her employer, First Horizon Home Loans, Inc., was sending us to St. Thomas for their annual production meeting. Delphine suggested that instead of returning home after her meetings were over, we should charter a sailboat and cruise the British Virgin Islands. When she suggested a bareboat charter, I told her that I was totally unfamiliar with the waters there, and since it was just the two of us, I was not so sure. She suggested a crewed vessel, but again, I was negative about it because I pictured it as a potential bad blind date. She ignored me and went on the Internet in the evenings checking out sailboats and charter services. I didn't pay much attention to her until she asked me to look at one particular boat called *Antiquity*. The web page advertised scuba diving, treasure hunting, and underwater photography, and most importantly, good food. *Antiquity* certainly got my attention. The captain was David DeCuir, who said he was originally from Louisiana and described himself as, besides being a treasure hunter, a gourmet Cajun chef. With his beard, he looked like a pirate and that awakened my boyish curiosity. So, I agreed with Delphine to go ahead and book it. I looked forward to the opportunity to see Norman Island, as it was now called, for the first time.

As the days counted down to our trip, old memories returned. My introduction to the story of Owen Lloyd and Norman Island had happened twenty years before when I began earnestly researching the 1750 fleet. My primary goal then was locating the remains of *La Galga*, which had been escorting the *Guadalupe* back to Spain. In 1978, I had found a letter from Captain Daniel Huony to the governor of Maryland that gave specific directions to finding his lost ship. He said that it had run ashore two ship lengths north of the Maryland-Virginia line on Assateague Island. This was my first introduction to the 1750 Spanish fleet. My life would not be the same after that, as it led me on an odyssey that lasted more than three years. More than two centuries after she drove ashore on Assateague Island, *La Galga's* location would finally be discovered: she was buried beneath the sands of Assateague.

We arrived at St. Thomas and stayed at the Frenchman's Reef Hotel where Delphine's convention had been booked. Here, we got plenty of sun and relaxed in our free time, all the while anticipating our upcoming adventure aboard *Antiquity*.

On sailing day, our instructions were to go to the bar and restaurant, Molly Molone's, located at American Yacht Harbor, Red Hook, at the east end of St. Thomas. Captain DeCuir would find us. I had already decided that I would not discuss my personal interest in Norman Island or my future book plans on *La Galga* and the *Guadalupe* treasure since at the time I had no idea when I would start or what new facts my research would find. I was looking forward, however, to some diving and the chance to see Norman Island in person.

When we arrived just before noon we immediately recognized *Antiquity* lying at anchor in the harbor. She was a beautiful forty-one-foot Morgan Out Island trimmed in burgundy. Captain Dave was coming in on the dingy and we recognized him even though he had shaved his beard.

Captain Dave is a short, muscular, tanned man, with graying blonde hair, evidence of his many years at sea. After he came up to the restaurant, we went over and introduced ourselves. Dave joined us at our table where Delphine and I had ordered some beers and were already mentally aboard. Captain Dave asked us what we had in mind for the trip. We said we really didn't know except that we wanted to go to Norman and Anegada Islands. Dave quickly outlined our route. We would spend the first night at Leinster Bay, St. John, which is directly opposite Soper's Hole, West End, Tortola. In the morning, we would sail there and clear customs. From Soper's Hole we would go to Norman and dive, then stay the night. The following day we would sail to Virgin Gorda, then Anegada, and work our way back at the end of the week. As we would later find out, Dave DeCuir had come to the islands twenty years before, vowing to only stay a year. As he explained it, his year had not yet ended. The beauty of the islands had taken him prisoner.

Nodding towards the boat, Dave said, "Well guys, if you're ready, come on aboard and meet Erica, your crew for the week. Times' a'wastin!"

Sailing around St. John, Delphine and I were quickly taken in by the beauty of the green and brown mountainous islands that protrude from the blue Caribbean. Columbus was equally impressed, for it was he that gave the Virgin Islands their name. When he sighted these islands in 1493, he was reminded of St. Ursula and her 11,000 virgins.

The sailing was peaceful and enjoyable, and the service aboard spoiled us. We were not used to being waited on hand and foot.

After clearing customs the next morning at Tortola, we anchored for lunch at New Found Bay, St. John, where we were served Captain Dave's Crawfish etoufeè. Mealtime became something to look forward to. Afterwards, we set our course for Norman Island.

As *Antiquity* approached Norman, we rounded the rocks called The Indians near the entrance to Man-of-War Bay, furled the sails, and prepared to anchor.

Man-of-War Bay, also known as the Bight, was quite crowded with assorted motor and sailing craft. At the head of the bay was a sandy beach with a restaurant, Billy Bones. Billy Bones was a fictional character in Robert Louis Stevenson's *Treasure Island*. He was the mate of the *Walrus*, the pirate ship of Captain James Flint. He was also the ailing sea captain who, at the beginning of the story, died at the Admiral Benbow Inn leaving a mysterious sea chest. Jim Hawkins and his mother discovered a treasure map in the chest that marked a treasure buried in 1750 on a deserted Caribbean island. This map launched an expedition to return

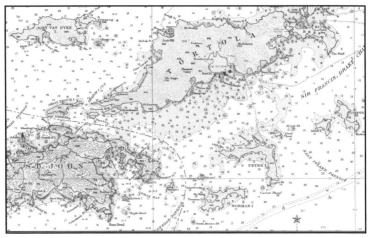

The Virgin Islands from NOAA Chart #25641, 1976.

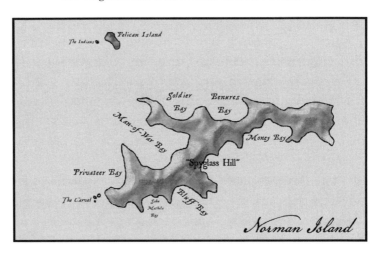

to that island to recover the pirate loot.

The restaurant was a tribute to what the locals believe is Stevenson's *Treasure Island*. Some tourist literature briefly describes Owen Lloyd's visit to the island in 1750.

The restaurant, which was built in 1997, is open on all sides, surrounded by the sand beach, and is only yards from the water's edge. It has a bright red metal roof displaying the name "Billy Bones" in large white letters. At the pier is the dinghy dock where patrons of the restaurant land, coming from all sizes of sail and motor yachts. On the south side of the bay, there was a small black ship riding at anchor, called the *William Thornton* but popularly called the *Willie T.*— it too was a restaurant. Pleasure boats were tied up along its floating dock. Man-of-War Bay is the most popular anchorage in the Virgin Islands as it is large, deep, and quite protected, features that no doubt interested Owen Lloyd.

I took in every detail. It was here in this bay that I was sure that some of the treasure that belonged to William Blackstock, William Dames, and the old man, Charles McClair, had been buried. Blackstock's deposition hinted at this bay.

In 1750, Norman Island was described as an uninhabited island. Today, the only residents are the staff of Billy Bones, now known as Pirate's Bight, who rotate on and off the island from nearby Tortola. There are staff quarters whose foundation is an old stone building left from the late eighteenth century.

Antiquity anchored at the north side of the bay and close to the restaurant. Captain Dave and I climbed into his dinghy, a fourteen-foot McKee craft and motored out to the Indians and got in an afternoon dive exploring the coral reef that surrounds them. Afterwards, we all went ashore to decompress at Billy Bones, grazing on conch fritters and beer. Every afternoon, one of the bartenders dressed in a pirate bandana brings out a miniature cannon, which is fired promptly at five signaling happy hour. The pirate theme is played to the hilt. Although Owen Lloyd committed an act of piracy, he falls way short of the modern-day image of a murderous buccaneer, but he was equally adventurous.

That evening on the boat, while enjoying another cold one, Dave cooked fresh lobster and steak on the grill. We began to talk more openly about wreck diving and treasure hunting. Inevitably, the subject turned to Norman Island and the treasure said to be hidden there. He was familiar with a story of treasure found over a hundred years ago in the caves at Treasure Point, located at the entrance to Man-of-War Bay. He explained his long fascination with the island and told me of some artifacts that he had discovered in the area. He told me of numerous depressions in the ground where treasure hunters have dug for their fortunes over the centuries. Dave had gotten to know Valerie Sims, owner of the restaurant and one of the owners of Norman at the time, and had received permission to use his metal detector in his quest for artifacts. I admitted to Dave that I knew quite a bit about the treasure, the people who buried it, and the saga of the 1750 fleet. This revelation surprised Captain Dave at first, but then he looked me straight in the eye and said, "It's no accident you are here, John." In hindsight, I really knew very little about Owen Lloyd's adventure at that time.

That night, from the deck of *Antiquity*, we listened to the Caribbean rhythms and laughter emanating from Billy Bones, which was carried across the water by the balmy trade winds. This was, without a doubt, a "treasure island"— it felt like home.

———◆———

Ever since Owen Lloyd departed Norman for St. Thomas, there have been treasure stories, treasure hunts, rumors, and mysteries told about Norman Island. One story that supposedly took place in the 1850s was related in the June 22, 1889, issue of *The Daily Light* of San Antonio, Texas. It described the caves at the entrance to Man-of-War Bay:

> One morning about thirty years ago a fisherman of one of the Virgin Islands arrived at Road Town, Tortola, the capital, with a story that a large schooner was anchored off the coast of Norman's Island and that her boats were moving along the shore. The island being uninhabited, there could be no question of smuggling; nevertheless, the circumstance was so extraordinary that an expedition was at once organized to investigate.
>
> On arrival off the point indicated by the fisherman, the schooner was, sure enough, in sight, but was already far off, making all sail to the westward. A dim suspicion of the real facts of the case induced the party now to extend their investigations into the "Bat Hole," a deep sea-tunneled cavern extending far into the bowels of the island, and that bore the reputation of having been the treasure vault of pirates in olden days. Tradition peopled the place with ghosts and other undesirable inhabitants, and so nothing could induce the fisherman to colonize despite its excellent fisheries.
>
> The old fisherman took the exploring party to his own settlement nearby, and there they were furnished with boats, torches, etc., and thus equipped they made sail once more for Norman's Island. They entered the cavern despite the protests of thousands of bats that rushed around the torches. On either side was a narrow sandy beach sloped from the perpendicular

walls, leaving a channel of more or less uniform width, in which the boat could with difficulty be turned. After a search of half an hour or so, the explorers came to a spot where the solid wall of the cavern had only recently been attacked with a pick. The pick itself lay prone on the pile of debris that littered the beach below.

On closer investigation, the debris was found to consist of mason work, and to have formed the walling up of a vaulted chamber sunk into the rock, about four feet square. Scattered about among the fragments were found a few pieces of Spanish gold and silver coin and a jeweled sword hilt, together with a sheet of paper, on which were written explicit instructions for the finding of the vault, in which it was stated that a vast quantity of treasure had been stored away by Captain Kidd and some of his companions.

There was nothing mysterious about the paper. It was simply a memorandum, far more exact than grammatical in the instrument it contained, written on an ordinary sheet of foolscap paper. Attached was said to be a chart of the island, but this was not found. As there were no means of obtaining the identity of the schooner no action could be taken in the matter by the local government. But that a long hidden piratical treasure had been carried off there was no room to doubt, in the face of the discoveries made. As to its having been Capt. Kidd's may of course be questioned, but there does not appear to be any reason to doubt the assertion of the memorandum that had so truthfully guided the treasure hunters to the goal of their desires.

It seems that the legend of Kidd's treasure may have supplanted the actual historical facts surrounding the events of 1750. The allusion to the Washington Irving tale, *The Money Diggers*, in 1843, a highly imaginative story about uncovering Captain Kidd's treasure, seems to prove that the foregoing account written in 1889 is full of embellishments if not totally untrue. But what is true is that there was a legendary treasure buried at Norman Island thanks to Owen Lloyd. Kidd did visit the area in 1699 when he called on the governor of St.

Thomas for protection, just as Owen Lloyd had in 1750.

As the sun rose above the hills behind Billy Bones, we were awakened by the smell of frying bacon and brewed coffee from the galley. Dave was preparing another great meal—eggs Benedict. At breakfast, we outlined our plans for the day. We were going to pay the legendary caves at Treasure Point a visit.

"I beheld great heaps of coin and quadrilaterals built of bars o gold."— Jim Hawkins, Chapter Thirty-Three, "The Fall of the Chieftain," *Treasure Island*. From Wikimedia Commons.

When we arrived at the caves, we found them flushed with shallow crystal clear water and inundated with tropical fish, which have become accustomed to hand-feeding by the tourists. While we explored the caves we did not see any of the bats that were reported to haunt them the century before. Dave said that the caves had changed a lot. Evidently, years ago some aggressive treasure hunters

Antiquity

"It's child's play to find the stuff now. I've half a mind to dine first."—Long John Silver, Chapter Thirty-Two, *Treasure Island*. BOTTOM LEFT: Dave DeCuir, Captain of *Antiquity*. BOTTOM RIGHT: The author. Photos by Dave DeCuir and the author.

Norman Island

TOP: Entrance to Man-of-War Bay, Norman Island. LEFT: Billy Bones bar and restaurant, now known as Pirate's Bight. ABOVE: Mooring buoy inside the Man-of-War Bay, "Pay at Billy Bones." LEFT OPPOSITE: Signal cannon starts Happy Hour. BOTTOM LEFT: The *Willie T.*, floating bar and restaurant, short for the *William Thornton*. BOTTOM RIGHT: Left to right. The author, Delphine, Shane, and Madeline. Photo by Dave DeCuir. All others by the author.

The Treasure Point Caves

"As we passed the two-pointed hill, we could see the black mouth of Ben Gunn's cave."
—Jim Hawkins, Chapter Thirty-Three, *Treasure Island*.

The Treasure Point caves. MIDDLE LEFT: Captain Dave DeCuir. BOTTOM LEFT: The author is hand feeding the fish. Photo by Dave DeCuir. All others by the author.

Man of War Bay
also known as The Bight

TOP: Man-of-War Bay, Norman Island. St. John in background. LEFT: Employee housing and gift shop built on eighteenth century foundation. RIGHT: Artifacts on display in the gift shop, some of which were found by Dave DeCuir. The sand beach here is the best in Man-of-War Bay. Treasure may have been buried here. Photos by the author.

"'Ah,' said he, 'this here is a sweet spot, this island—a sweet spot for a lad to get ashore on. You'll bathe, and you'll climb trees, and you'll hunt goats, you will, and you'll get aloft on them hills like a goat yourself.'"—Long John Silver, Chapter Twelve, *Treasure Island*.

TOP: Stones piled centuries ago to make a landing. What was once above the water is now submerged. Photo by the author. BOTTOM: Stone dock as seen from underwater. Photo by Madeline Amrhein.

Pirates Bight
formerly Billy Bones

TOP LEFT. Shane Cook, in background, Delphine, the author and Madeline. Photo by Dave DeCuir. TOP RIGHT: Front to back, Madeline, Shane, Delphine, Dave De DeCuir, and Doris. LEFT: Behind the bar. BELOW: The Amrhein family wrestling lobsters. BOTTOM LEFT: The author and his wife Delphine taking a swim in Man-of-War Bay. Photo by Dave DeCuir. Madeline and Jordan make the famous jump from the *Willie T.* Other photos by the author.

Inside Man-of-War Bay

"Old man if you have any money, bring it out, I will take care of it for you or these people will take your life for it." So said Abraham Chalwell, the president of the council of Tortola, to Charles McClair after he discovered him on Norman Island. Two areas in Man-of-War Bay where treasure may have been buried. Photos by the author

Soldier Bay

"*We all pulled round again to Rum Cove, the nearest point for Ben Gunn's treasure-house.*"— Jim Hawkins, Chapter Thirty-Three, *Treasure Island*.

TOP: *Antiquity* at anchor in Soldier Bay. Tortola in background. Photo by Dave DeCuir. LEFT: Captain Dave takes Shane and Madeline ashore to explore the ruins. Photo by the author. BELOW LEFT: The author descends to bottom of Soldier Bay. Photo by Dave DeCuir.

The Soldier Bay Ruins

"They had clapped a stout loghouse fit to hold two score of people on a pinch and loopholed for musketry"—Dr. Livesey, Chapter Sixteen, *Treasure Island*. Dave DeCuir showed us these ruins that overlook Soldier Bay. We found evidence that this spot had been attacked centuries ago. TOP: The stairs are still largely intact. LEFT: Loophole for muskets. BOTTOM LEFT: Madeline and Shane exploring the area around the ruins. Photo by Dave DeCuir. ABOVE: Stone perimeter wall of compound. Photos by the author.

Benures Bay

TOP: Photo taken by Dave DeCuir as *Antiquity* sails to Benures Bay. BOTTOM: These rock outcroppings located outside Benures Bay look like the remnants of caves that may have been blasted. Photo by the author.

Benures Bay

TOP: Benures Bay as seen from near the ruins. Peter Island in background. Photo by the author. LEFT: *Antiquity* at anchor in Benures Bay. BOTTOM LEFT: On the shore of Benures bay is a pit that either once held treasure or was dug while in search of it centuries ago. Photos by Dave DeCuir.

"The doctor opened the seals with great care, and there fell out the map of an island, with latitude and longitude, soundings, names of hills and bays and inlets, and every particular that would be needed to bring a ship to a safe anchorage upon its shores." —Jim Hawkins, Chapter Six, The Captain's Papers, *Treasure Island*.

TOP: Privateer Bay lies just south of the Treasure Point caves. The small rock on right is called the Carvel. MIDDLE RIGHT: The Treasure Point caves with "Spyglass Hill" in background. BOTTOM RIGHT: The author and his daughter, Madeline, pose below the Carvel. Photo by Dave DeCuir.

"Lloyd advised them to go to Norman's Island, one of the keys or little islands near Tortola and uninhabited, as a proper place to share their Booty."—William Blackstock. Privateer Bay was the likely anchorage for the *Seaflower*.

"Spyglass Hill"

"I climbed a thousand times to that tall hill they call the Spy-glass, and from the top enjoyed the most wonderful and changing prospects."—Jim Hawkins, Chapter Seven, *Treasure Island.*

TOP: "Spyglass Hill" as seen from the north side of Man-of-War Bay. Pirates bar on left. BOTTOM: Man-of-War Bay and Tortola in background as seen from "Spyglass Hill." Photos by the author.

Money Bay

"We not only looked down upon the anchorage and Skeleton Island, but saw—clear across the spit and the eastern lowlands—a great field of open sea upon the east."—Jim Hawkins, Chapter Thirty-Two, *Treasure Island*. Money Bay, on south side of Norman Island, as seen from the top of "Spyglass Hill." Photo by Shane Cook.

Money Bay

TOP LEFT: "Spyglass Hill" (distant) as seen from present day Money Bay. TOP RIGHT: Bluff Bay on south side of Norman Island as seen from "Spyglass Hill." MIDDLE: This Bay is most likely the real Money Bay. BOTTOM LEFT: Boulders at top of "Spyglass Hill" marked with graffiti by an unknown fraternity brother. BOTTOM RIGHT: View of Norman taken on south side. Photos by the author.

The Dead Man's Chest or Dead Chest Island

"Fifteen men on the Dead Man's Chest Yo-Ho-ho, and a bottle of rum!"
—The pirates' shanty, *Treasure Island*.

"At first I had supposed 'the dead man's chest' to be that identical big box of his upstairs in the front room, and the thought had been mingled in my nightmares with that of the one-legged seafaring man."—Jim Hawkins, Chapter One, *Treasure Island*.

TOP: Dead Chest Island, made famous in Robert Louis Stevenson's *Treasure Island*. Stevenson said it was the "seed" for his story. It lies on the opposite side of Peter island, four miles from Norman Island. LEFT: Shane Cook explores the remains of the RMS *Rhone* which sank in 1867. The site is where the 1977 movie, *The Deep*, was filmed. Photo by the author. BOTTOM LEFT: Inside the wreckage of the *Rhone*. Photo by Dave DeCuir.

dynamited the grottos and altered their appearance. None of the caves seemed to fit the description found in the 1889 account, as they are not very deep. The Treasure Point caves, however, are something right out of *Treasure Island*.

There is yet another story of treasure having being found in the caves. Valerie Sims, the owner of the island in 2000, is the great-great-granddaughter of Henry Creque of Anegada Island. She will swear that as handed down in her family traditions, Henry found treasure in the caves, which is what prompted him to buy the island in 1894. His initial investment of forty pounds brought the Creque heirs several million dollars when the island was sold to its current owner, Dr. Henry Jarecki. Billy Bones then became known as "Pirates" in 2001.

Norman Island is supposedly named after a Dutch pirate named Norman who relocated there from Anegada and brought his booty to this deserted island. In 1666, the English took control of the Virgin Islands, which have remained British ever since. The brief references found in tourist literature associating Norman Island with the treasure buried in 1750 were based on Harold T. Wilkins' book, *Pirate Treasure*, published in 1937. This book also recounted other pirate treasures through history. Wilkins devoted a chapter to the stolen *Guadalupe* cargo. The primary source for his story was the same microfilmed documents I had found at the Library of Congress in 1980. The most significant of them was the deposition of William Blackstock.

In 1750, Norman Island was owned by the Phipps Family of St. Kitts. It probably came into their possession shortly after their arrival at St. Kitts and Antigua about 1675. Fourteen years later, their cousin, William Phipps, salvaged the Spanish galleon, *Nuestra Señora de Concepcion*, which sank in 1641 off of Santo Domingo. William Phipps was knighted for his successful exploits of salvaging over £200,000 in treasure from nine fathoms of water with a diving bell and Indian divers. He returned to England and surrendered the agreed portion to his investors and the Crown. Soon afterwards, he was named the first royal governor of Massachusetts in 1692. In 1746, six Phipps brothers and their nephew comprised half of the St. Kitts Assembly. They would variously occupy the assembly into the 1750s. Owen Lloyd may well have known the Phipps brothers, as his brother-in-law, Charles Caines, and Charles's cousin, Thomas Caines, were both prominent men of the island at the time.

After our brief visit to Norman Island, *Antiquity* set sail for Virgin Gorda and Anegada. Before we knew it the week was over and we were back at Molly Molone's calling a cab to get us to the airport. We said goodbye to Dave, but it was obvious to the three of us that we would get together again, now bonded by the history and allure of Norman Island. In just one week we had become old friends.

Twelve months passed soon enough and I found myself once again in the Virgin Islands aboard *Antiquity*. This time we had our kids, Shane and Madeline, with us for a two-week cruise. Shane was twenty-three at the time and certified to dive. Madeline, who was only twelve, had to be content to float on the surface, enviously watching us explore the seabed below.

Since we had the luxury of two weeks, we not only revisited Norman, Anegada and Virgin Gorda, but laid over at Jost Van Dyke as well. When we arrived at Norman Island, Dave took us exploring to the top of the hills surrounding Man-of-War Bay. From the hilltops, we could see all of Man-of-War Bay and, to the north across Drakes Channel, Tortola. The trade winds cooled us after the heated climb to the top. Dave showed us the ruins of several structures, which appeared to be eighteenth century. I told Dave that I was sure they had to post date 1750, as Norman Island was described as uninhabited and destitute at that time. The most impressive was a foundation of a building on top of the hill overlooking Soldier Bay. The foundation, which must have supported a second floor made of wood and thatch, was made from ballast stones, native rock, cut coral, and brick. The entrance stairway was still largely intact. On the north side, overlooking Soldier Bay, were openings made in the wall for muskets. These conjured up images of the loopholes in the blockhouse walls of the stockade in Stevenson's *Treasure Island*.

There was a lot of other evidence of former habitation. Besides aloe, which Dave explained was often found around old ruins on the islands, there were old tamarind trees and pottery shards scattered about the areas of ruins. There were large pieces of old black glass rum bottles, lead fragments, and other metal. Shane found two small cannonballs, which looked to be swivel gun or grape shot caliber, embedded in the hill below the ruins overlooking Soldier Bay. It appeared obvious that this site had been attacked long ago. I found a small turquoise slave bead lying on the ground.

Below the ruins and at the head of Man-of-War Bay, Dave pointed out a stone formation just below the surface of the water and joining the shore. Dave said that this had to be an old dock, now submerged. Madeline and I dove in to inspect it and from what we saw, I had to agree with him. The fact that there was nearly a foot of water over the stone platform demonstrated a marked increase in sea level since it was built or subsidence that had occurred as a result of the earthquakes that have traumatized the islands over the centuries.

Columbine Map. Courtesy of Library of Congress Map Division.

It appears that this bay did not receive its name until 1789 when it was surveyed by Lt. E.H. Columbine of HMS *Sybil*. On New Year's day, the *Sybil* "came too in 13 fm^s in a bay at the west end of Normand's Island." The log described a bay with no name. The map prepared from Columbine's survey contained the new names. What influenced these names may have been some previous naval engagement within the bay. The log of the *Sybil* says that they remained for four days while Lt. Columbine surveyed the shoreline and sounded the ocean bottom. While this was going on, some of the crew were "working up junk," no doubt a reference to salvaging items from a wreck. We explored a ballast pile in the bay that may have been the subject of the *Sybil*'s salvage. Columbine labeled this bay Man-of-War

Bay on his chart but it was not named in the ship's log.

I was quick to realize how fortunate we were to have met up with Dave. He readily shared his knowledge gained from years of explorations. He was truly the "Man of the Island," but he wasn't clad in tattered goatskins as was Stevenson's Ben Gunn.

Having promised Shane and Madeline that they would see the other islands, we left for Virgin Gorda with our end destination to be Anegada and to dive the inside of the treacherous reef in the hopes of a discovering a wreck.

Once outside Man-of-War Bay, *Antiquity* rounded Peter Island and entered Sir Francis Drake Channel, so named because of the voyage Drake made through the Virgins in 1595. We took note of the little domed island called Dead Chest Island lying about a thousand yards to the east of Peter Island. On the other side of Peter Island is Norman Island. Dead Chest Island was said to be where Blackbeard marooned some of his men. There are two small islands between St. John and Tortola called Big Thatch and Little Thatch Islands said to be named after Blackbeard, "Thatch" being one of his aliases. Fact or not, Dead Chest Island became immortalized in *Treasure Island*. On the first page of Stevenson's tale is a little sea shanty that the pirates often sang: "Fifteen men on the Dead Man's Chest Yo-Ho-Ho, and a bottle of rum!"

On the return leg from Anegada, we stopped at Salt Island and put Delphine, Madeline, and Doris, our crew for that trip, ashore to meet the island's only resident, an aged black man who evaporates seawater and sells the salt. This island has been known for this practice for centuries.

While they were ashore, we motored the tender out to the buoy marking the site of the wreck of the RMS *Rhone*, a steel-hulled British mail steamer that succumbed to the great hurricane of October 29, 1867, and made famous as the dive location in the 1977 movie, *The Deep*. After she had wrecked, her wooden mast protruded from the water for years and was even noted by Charles Kingsley in his book *At Last: A Christmas in the West Indies*, published in 1871. Shane, Dave, and I descended to the wreck with cameras and explored her tangled remains.

Luckily, the following year, we returned once again to Norman Island. On this trip, my goal was to examine the likely spots that Lloyd and his crew could have buried treasure. My starting point was establishing the anchorage of the *Seaflower*.

As a side adventure, Shane convinced me to climb "Spyglass Hill." In *Treasure*

Island, Long John Silver described the hills on the fictional island: "There are three hills in a row running south'ard—fore, main, and mizzen, sir. But the main—that's the big un, with the cloud on it—they usually calls the Spy-glass." Today, on Norman Island, the tallest hill, or "main," has been dubbed unofficially, "Spyglass Hill."

The climb left me totally red-faced and out of breath, but it was worth it, as we got some spectacular views of the south side of the island.

Now armed with recent research, I found that Soldier Bay, on the north shore of Norman, could have been named after the visits of the soldiers sent by Governor Heyliger of St. Eustatius with Owen Lloyd as their prisoner and more soldiers who arrived shortly after that under the command of Lt. General Gilbert Fleming.

Owen Lloyd chose to bury his treasure at Norman's, now called Norman Island, for some undisclosed reason. He needed protection and he needed someplace close by to act as his bank, someplace where he could make periodic withdrawals. With plans to live at St. Thomas, Norman Island was a perfect match. St. Thomas had the reputation for harboring thieves and pirates.

Lloyd was headed to the West Indies to join his wife in St. Kitts but he needed to get rid of William Blackstock first. The *Seaflower* first sighted land at Anegada and Spanish Town or more commonly called today, Virgin Gorda. He needed supplies but opted not to land in a British port. Instead he proceeded on to the then-Danish island of St. John and entered Crawl, now correctly called Coral Bay, on the east end of the island. St. John lies between St. Thomas and Norman Island.

St. Thomas was owned by Denmark and had a protected harbor guarded by Fort Christian at Charlotte Amalie. St. Thomas also had the reputation as being a safe haven for troublemakers since the days before Captain Kidd at the end of the seventeenth century. By the early eighteenth century it was widely known that "any pirate for a small matter of money may be naterlized Deane." It seems a certainty that Owen Lloyd knew well ahead of time what his opportunities would be at St. Thomas.

Thanks to archival records of the event, the modern-day treasure hunter or adventurer can estimate just what treasure was buried on Norman and what the later recoveries were.

At Ocracoke, North Carolina, inventories were taken of the treasure that was loaded onto each sloop. Bonilla claimed that he had loaded fifty-five chests of pieces of eight on board the *Seaflower*. Lloyd's crew later testified at St. Eustatius that there were only fifty chests to be divided up. According to Abraham Pritchett there had been an argument on Norman during the division because some had heard an English official at Ocracoke say there were more than fifty chests that were divided. When HMS *Scorpion* arrived at Cadiz on January 28, 1751, with the treasure taken from John Lloyd's sloop, the House of Trade made this observation about what had been taken by Owen Lloyd on the *Seaflower*:

> According to a rumor there were 55 chests of silver at 3,000 pesos each on the English sloop which made off from Virginia, this made a total of 165,000 pesos. There are 37,707 pesos missing to complete the register which would come to a total of 202,707 pesos. Don Juan Manuel Bonilla should clarify this with his representative and against the total amount of the register and that sent to Cádiz. That in Virginia and what was on the sloop which took off should make up the difference according to the sources.

The *Seaflower* had only stopped at St. John before arriving at Norman and it would have been impossible for Lloyd to have offloaded the other five chests in front of the crew. He may have found a space in the bilge and relocated the money while underway to the Virgin Islands. This would have been similar to the situation on the *Mary* at Ocracoke when Fitz-Randolph's crew cut a hole in the bulkhead and removed some bags of silver.

Lloyd told Governor Heyliger at St. Eustatius that he only had eight to ten thousand pieces of eight on board when he left Norman Island. He also testified that he bought a sloop at St. Croix for 3,000. Heyliger siezed 5,702 pieces of eight from Lloyd and Wade and later another 11,167 pieces of eight from Abraham Pritchett. These recoveries alone proved to Heyliger that Lloyd was lying. There is more evidence that Lloyd retained more than can be deduced from the archival documents. When Bonilla arrived at London in December 1751 he was told that

Lloyd, although still under the protection of the governor of St. Thomas, made contacts through friends at Antigua that if he was given freedom to return to his family at St. Kitts he would be willing to negotiate the return of more of the cargo. He was not taken up on that offer.

Knowing Bonilla's conduct in 1753, when he took the *Peregrina* to Veracruz and attempted to scam his insurers, he might have inflated his losses. But then the total load on the *Seaflower* was computed by his brother-in-law, Tomas Carreido, just after the theft and while Bonilla was in New Bern. There is a possibility Bonilla was setting up Zebulon Wade. Upon arrival at Norfolk, he could have made a demand for fifty-five chests when there were only fifty.

On December 13, 1750, Fleming filled out his report on the treasure he recovered and these were the individuals who were found to have recovered pieces of eight at Norman Island:

Thomas Stephens	3689
Christopher Hodge & James Pasea	3007 ½
Abraham Chalwell Sr.	2100
Abraham Chalwell, Jr.	4902
George Wickham	5100
Lewis Higgs	2460
Absolom Zegers	900
William Ronan	78
Mrs. Rebecca Purcell	1212 ½
Adrianna Jeff	508
Peter Hodge	400
William Pickering	246
John Downing	210

Early accounts said that President Chalwell's son had twenty bags of coins, that John Haynes had thirty bags, and that Mrs. Adrianna Jeff had made off from the island with two canoe loads of money, jewels and plate. Then there were other reports from Ireland in 1751 that William Dames had at least 50,000 pieces of eight. It was documented that Dames persuaded some of the finders to turn over some of the money to him. Later, in the summer of 1751, John Watson returned and made additional recoveries from the people of Tortola.

There is reason to believe that Rebecca Purcell may have withheld the truth about her findings. When her husband, John, died in 1771, he was then the lieutenant governor of Tortola and the Virgin Islands, having succeeded his brother James at that post in 1751. He was also the owner of Norman Island at the time. In his will, he left £7,000 each to his two daughters, Francis and Margaret. His son, John, got Norman Island as well as plantations on Tortola and "Spanish Bay" (probably Virgin Gorda). John Purcell, the brother of James Purcell, the lieutenant governor in 1750, was a very rich man.

Interestingly enough, you can find many place names on Tortola that are derived from the names associated with the 1750 treasure episode. On that island you will find Fleming Street, the districts of Chalwell and Pasea Estate, Burt Pt., Nibbs, Pickering, Fort Purcel, Hodge Estate, and James Young.

The question for the modern adventure seeker is, "Is there any money left on Norman Island?" Owen Lloyd, under threat of death, returned to show the locations to the Dutch officials and was only able to recover twenty-one and a half pieces of eight. Was he so bold as to withhold the location of his own loot? Did he already know that he would make his escape from St. Eustatius? And if he was out of money, how did he manage to win the affections of Governor Suhm of St. Thomas who gave him protection?

Owen Lloyd was a very clever character. Would he have left Blackstock, Dames, and McClair at Norman if all of his treasure was buried at Norman? The records show that what was recovered at St. Kitts and St. Eustatius exceeded 20,000 pieces of eight. He left St. Thomas in a hurry, taking all the money with him to St. Croix. He left none if his money with the *Seaflower*. Lloyd left St. Thomas for St. Croix, where he spent 3,000 pieces of eight on a new vessel. Because Lloyd obviously had money to bribe Governor Suhm at St. Thomas and he could not produce any more treasure at Norman when he was taken back in chains, St. Croix becomes the prime location of his "bank."

The anchorage of the *Seaflower* is not specifically identified in the historical record but can be easily deduced. The *Seaflower* was observed by Thomas Wallis when he came out from Tortola in his coble, a small sailing craft, which suggests that he saw the *Seaflower* either on the north or west side of Norman Island. The south side is open to the sea, which is often rough and totally out of sight from boats going in and out of Tortola. On the north side is Benures Bay, which is much larger than Soldier Bay. Captain Dave pointed out an unnatural hole in the ground in this bay area. It is large enough to have accommodated several treasure chests or it could be the result of blasting from early treasure hunts. This bay is in plain view of Peter Island only two miles away. My guess is that Lloyd would have been hesitant to anchor here in front of unseen eyes.

St. Croix was the most likely location for Owen Lloyd to hide his treasure.

Man-of-War Bay provides several good hiding places for treasure and was out of view from Peter Island and Tortola. The records say without a doubt that the treasure was buried and there are only a few locations with a sandy beach for hiding chests or bags of coins. Most of the shoreline is hard or rocky. The best place is at the head of the bay where Pirates Bar is located but there are other spots rimming the bay as well.

From the anchorage in Privateer Bay, each individual could row into Man-of-War Bay, go ashore, and hide his share unobserved from the *Seaflower*. Some statements by Lloyd suggest that he was present when everyone buried their shares. This may have prompted Blackstock, Dames, and McClair to stay behind in order to protect what was theirs. It also is unlikely that the *Seaflower* would have entered the bay because they would have been trapped by any vessel that might come in and surprise them. It seems certain that on November 14, 1750, it was in this bay that Blackstock, Dames, and McClair were marooned, either by their choice, or Lloyd's. But would Owen Lloyd bury his own share in the vicinity of the others? Would he leave Blackstock in a place where he and the others could accidentally stumble on his burial spot? He seems to have been too clever for that. He and Zebulon Wade had apparently only buried part of their loot, keeping the majority of it on board the *Seaflower*. Abraham Pritchett had testified that everyone brought the largest part of their share on land except for James Moorehouse.

At Norman, the treasure hunts would resume over the years. One can easily picture the young and old alike sailing over to Norman from the neighboring islands of Tortola, St. John, or Virgin Gorda for an afternoon treasure hunt. There may have been some success by the owner of neighboring Peter Island. A writer from Tortola in the first half on the nineteenth century reported that there was still a legend surrounding the island, "not unlike that of the 'Money Diggers.'" *Money Diggers* was written in 1824 by Washington Irving. This same writer from Tortola reported to their correspondent in London that there had been blasting on the island recently performed by "the Norman Island treasure company" and that the company's prospectus declared that it "cannot fail to bring ample returns." This adventure was no doubt a hunt for Owen Lloyd's treasure. There is no documented proof of any success. However, there is a story that predates this adventure that may shed light on what Lloyd may have left.

In May 1806, Captain Thomas Southey visited Peter Island, which lies between Dead Chest and Norman and about two miles north of Norman. He went to the home of the island's owner which was situated on a cliff with a commanding view of the bay. The old man told Southey that he was worth £60,000. Southey had to be more than surprised when he saw the man's humble surroundings. The house had only a ground floor with a roof of shingles that projected six to eight feet out and had glassless windows with shutters. In the center room there were hanging ears of corn; a fishing net on a chair; in another corner, another fishing net; a fowling piece, a spy glass, and a looking glass. He had a library that consisted of a prayer book, almanac, and one volume of the *Navy Chronicle*. In an adjoining room, he had various machines for extracting the seeds from cotton, a crop that had been cultivated for many years in the Virgin Islands. Ranging outside were an abundance of goats, turkeys, fowls, a bull, a cow, pigs, dogs, and cats. There were several young Negro girls running around naked. In Southey's words it was "a kind of Robinson Crusoe spot." The description of the proprietor matched that of the house: "The old man was dressed in a large broad-brimmed white hat, which appeared to have been in use for half a century; a white night cap covered his bald head; his blue jacket had lapels buttoned back; his duck waistcoat had flaps down to his knees; the trousers were of the same material. His elderly wife was dressed like an "Egyptian mummy." The £60,000 in 1806 would be worth several million dollars today. The question remains unanswered as to how he accumulated such wealth or if in fact Southey saw it firsthand. Southy reported that he had lived on Peter Island for twenty years and at Tortola for twenty years before that. It's not known if he was alive in 1750 but what is certain is that he lived among those who had vivid memories of where treasure had been discovered on Norman Island. Southey's book was published in London in 1827. This account may have been the inspiration for the treasure hunt by the Norman Island Treasure Company twenty years later.

Money Bay

On the south side of the island facing St. Croix is a large cove called "Money Bay." The origin is uncertain, but it dates back to maps of the island of the early 1800s. In 1980, when I had first read about Owen Lloyd's theft of the treasure and his trip to Norman, I examined old and new maps of the island and became intrigued with Money Bay.
There is no doubt in my mind that it was named after discoveries of Lloyd's treasure. But it seems unlikely that it could be the harbor where the treasure was buried. It not only would have been a tricky anchorage for the *Seaflower*, but it was not visible from Tortola. The record seems to indicate that Thomas Wallis, who had sailed out to the *Seaflower*, had come out from there because they could be seen from across the water at Tortola. That would have been impossible from Money Bay. There are a number of bays or coves around Norman Island. Most are very small and hardly deserve the characterization as a bay. Man-of-War Bay is by far the largest. Blackstock seemed to be describing this bay, as it was unnamed at the time, when he and President Chalwell of Tortola went back to inspect the tobacco and went from that spot to "another part of the bay" to recover the

Early Nineteenth Century Virgin Island Maps. Courtesy of Library of Congress Map Division. These early maps place Money Bay west of its present location.

cochineal.

When I told Dave I wanted to go to Money Bay, he cautioned that it can be tricky as there are almost always ocean swells and winds on that side of the island. Nonetheless, he agreed to go, so Shane, Dave, and I set off in *Antiquity's* tender and motored around the island. After being nearly swamped while rounding the windward end, we were rewarded with a spectacular view of the rock cliffs draping the east end of the island. We reached Money Bay and found a beautiful sand beach. It seemed to be a nice place to bury treasure but it would have been a long row from Privateer Bay at the west end, the place I had theorized the *Seaflower* had anchored. The *Seaflower* would have been too exposed to the wind anchoring outside of Money Bay. I hunted with Dave's detector but found nothing.

When we left, we continued westward around the island for more spectacular views, looking carefully at every small bay and cove to get an idea of accessibility and to determine whether the ground was soft enough to bury something.

The dilemma of placing Lloyd's treasure at Money Bay was solved after careful study of several nineteenth century charts. They proved that the present location for Money Bay was in error. Older maps indicated it was a small bay much closer to the Man-of-War Bay and Privateer Bay. It was now conceivable that some of the *Seaflower* crew could have rowed around the west end of Norman to find a burial place. On a later trip and with these questions in mind, we set out in *Antiquity's* tender to search the beach just east of the rock promontory that bordered what I believe might be the original Money Bay. When we arrived, we found the entire beach littered with debris; milk jugs, beer and soda cans, fishnets, and other detritus deposited by the currents and trade winds. If coins were left here they would be impossible to locate with a metal detector since the flotsam contained various forms of metal. The south coast of Norman can only be characterized as wild and unfriendly. The hills descend to what little sand and stone beach rims the shore. The views from Spyglass Hill of this side of the island are spectacular, however.

Captain Dave DeCuir with his wife Claudia. He found his treasure in the Virgin Islands.

Delphine and I would return to Norman for the next five years aboard *Antiquity*, hoping to make some discovery that would illuminate the story of Owen Lloyd's treasure. But research would soon take us over the horizon to another island in search of Owen Lloyd. One hundred and thirty miles to the southeast of Norman is the island of St. Kitts where Owen Lloyd's brother-in-law ran a successful plantation. And it was here on this island that the great-grandfather of Robert Louis Stevenson met his untimely end.

Robert Louis Stevenson

Chapter Twelve

Stevenson's First Book

"And now admire the finger of predestination."
— Robert Louis Stevenson, *My First Book*

Robert Louis Stevenson was seven years old before he could read. He was the only son of Margaret Balfour and Thomas Stevenson, a Scottish lighthouse engineer in Edinburgh. Louis, as he was called, was plagued from infancy with several respiratory illnesses and digestive disorders which certainly interfered with his schooling. That was not the whole problem as he would later admit. He was lazy and delighted more in oral storytelling. Because his father traveled with his job and his mother suffered from her own respiratory problems, they hired a nanny, Alison Cunningham, to help with his care and upbringing. "Cummy" as she was affectionately known, entertained Louis with not only stories of the Bible, but legends of pirates, smugglers, witches, and fairies.

From his earliest days, he attempted writing stories. At six he was dictating them to his invalid mother. His health kept him out of school and he had trouble making friends. At thirteen he was in boarding school and wrote stories for the school magazine. One was a tale of eighteenth century wreckers. As a teenager, he retreated from reality into fantasy, while his physical weaknesses became more obvious to others as well as himself. He longed to be a writer and he loved history. At sixteen he wrote a sixteen-page pamphlet, *A Pentland Rising*, which his father paid for the printing of 100 copies. Young Stevenson would soon have a chance meeting with R. M. Ballantyne, the author of *Coral Island*, one of the many stories that would influence him when he later wrote *Treasure Island*. At age seventeen, he entered Edinburgh University. Those that knew him remembered that he took no notes and seldom listened to the lectures. He did make notes of his own literary fancies inside and outside the classroom. Stevenson did not engage in sports as other boys his age. He found them irrational and boring, but then his physical limitations were an obstacle even if he had been tempted to engage. Instead, he exercised his mind and traveled vicariously through his extensive reading.

At the university, his father expected him to prepare himself for the family profession of lighthouse engineering, but Stevenson had no desire to be an engineer. After much debate with his father, he agreed to prepare instead for the Scottish bar.

In 1873, Stevenson contracted a severe respiratory illness and went to the French Riviera to recuperate. He regained his strength and returned home the following spring. In July 1875, after finishing at the university, he was called to the Scottish bar but he never practiced. In fact, he never worked. His father had given him an advance against his inheritance so Stevenson, assuming the airs of a true Bohemian, only considered writing as a way of life.

Grez-Sur-Loing, France, July 6, 1876

The twenty-six-year-old Robert Louis Stevenson arrived at the Hotel Chevillon, fifty-five miles southeast of Paris where his cousin, Robert Alan Mowbry Stevenson, was entertaining a group of art students. His cousin was recognized as a man of great intelligence and was a gifted painter, musician, philosopher, and art critic. Seated at the table with him was a woman named Fanny Osbourne who had come to Paris from San Francisco. With her were her eighteen-year-old daughter, Belle, and her eight-year-old son, Sam. Fanny had come to Europe to find herself. She had been beckoned to Paris to study art. Mostly though, she wanted to get away from her philandering husband, a court stenographer and a former miner who loved wild women and whiskey. When she had arrived at Paris, there was a third child, Hervey, who was five. He had taken ill shortly after their arrival, and, after a slow descent, he died on April 5, leaving Fanny paralyzed with grief. When his end was near, she had summoned her husband, Sam, to rush to Paris, but he arrived only days before his son's death. They each blamed the other for their common loss. Her husband pleaded for reconciliation, but that was interrupted when the doctor informed them that their son Sam needed to get out of Paris or he would contract tuberculosis. Her husband declared he was returning to San Francisco, and after seeing him off at the train, Fanny and her children boarded a coach that took them to the Hotel Chevillon.

When Robert Louis Stevenson saw Fanny he immediately fell in love with her, but he held those feelings in check when he learned that she was married. The grieving mother, however, had already found his cousin Bob to be quite attractive. Bob enjoyed her intellectual charms but was taken with Fanny's daughter, Belle, who was ten years younger than he. Fanny had been introduced to Bob quite by chance. Fanny and young Sam were fishing in the river when Bob Stevenson rowed past and found Fanny's fishhook snagged in his collar forcing him to land the boat to disengage it. Fanny, Belle, and Sam were then introduced around to the other artists. It was only a few days later that Robert Louis Stevenson would arrive from Edinburgh.

Robert Louis Stevenson endeared himself to Fanny's children and made a place for himself at the nightly dinner table. Fanny soon realized that there would be no relationship with cousin Bob and began to submit to the boyish charms of Louis. The twenty-six-year-old Stevenson was ten years her junior. When Fanny returned to art school in Paris in January of 1877, Robert Louis Stevenson followed her. They became close friends, but Stevenson did not know how to cross the threshold of physical intimacy with her. And now looming was the return of her husband who had announced he was coming to fetch his family home. Stevenson decided to return home to Scotland and fretted over the reality of never seeing Fanny again.

Sam arrived by train in May, and what Fanny anticipated as a very uncomfortable reunion became a return to their former lost marriage. After a week of familial happiness, Sam insisted that they go to Grez so he could meet Fanny's new friends and experience her new world. Fanny fought the notion, as she wanted to protect the precious independence she had discovered there.

Fanny's intellectual friends found Sam's wild-west swagger and his roving eye offensive. To them, he was just a roughneck, a cowboy. Sam soon found his way into the bedrooms of some of the local ladies. Then a letter arrived for him from San Francisco from his mistress. Fanny, at last, had had enough and demanded that he leave. But Sam still had the control. Fanny was dependent on his allowance. Sam said there would be no more money for her and that he was taking Belle and Sam back to California. The children protested so much that Sam relinquished after their promise to return to Oakland by June the next year.

On June 9, 1877, Sam Osbourne arrived in London, where he boarded a ship for Montreal and then a train to San Francisco. Twelve days later, Robert Louis Stevenson left London for Grez to reunite with Fanny. Where they had practiced discretion before, they held nothing back now. Fanny and Louis were now lovers and the talk of the village.

In July 1878, Fanny and Louis went to London. She was preparing for her scheduled return to California. Louis pleaded with her to ask for a divorce, a concept that Fanny found difficult to consider in these Victorian times. He even begged her to stay on until he could get the money he would need to travel with her. Fanny rejected that notion because of the problems his presence would make in California. Stevenson extracted a promise from her that she would call him if she needed him. After she left, Stevenson returned to France where he travelled alone for several weeks; his only company was his donkey and thoughts of Fanny. He ate sparingly and slept under the stars.

After Fanny returned to Oakland, she became ill and she sank into a serious depression, compounded by hearing and vision problems. The stress of her compromised relationships was becoming too much to bear. Fanny ultimately asked for a divorce and was refused. Sam wanted another chance at reconciliation so he proposed that the family would take a holiday in Monterey, a charming southern California town about 150 miles south of San Francisco. Here, Sam rented an entire wing of a large house known as the Casa Bonifacio. It was his intention to put their past indiscretions behind them because he loved his children and did not want the disgrace of divorce to haunt them.

He would travel to Monterey on weekends and return to his stenographer's job at the courthouse in San Francisco during the week. It also gave him the opportunity to hunt loose women without his family around. The weekly separations had an unintended effect: Fanny resumed her fantasies of divorce and the charming Scotsman she left behind in Europe. On July 30, 1879, while still in Monterey, Fanny telegraphed Louis in Scotland. It is not known what her short message said, but he answered saying, "Hold tight, I will be with you in one month."

Stevenson left for London, and when he arrived he begged his friends, his mentors in literature, and his parents for money to make the trip to California. His parents were aghast that he was taking up with a married woman. They all were convinced that if he went it would be the end of a career in writing that had only just begun.

Stevenson obtained a small advance on some future essays, told his parents that he would see them the following day, but instead, boarded the *Devonia* for New York on August 7 with a second-class ticket. After descending the gangway in New York, Stevenson rode train after train until he covered the 2,600 grueling miles to Monterey. When he arrived on August 30, 1879, his already gangly frame had shed fifteen pounds and he had aggravated respiratory problems. When Fanny's ten-year-old son, Sam, saw him, he was shocked. When he had first met Stevenson at Grez he was eight. He never realized that Stevenson, even then, was in ill health.

Unfortunately, Fanny's husband was to arrive at Monterey the next day. Stevenson knew he needed to get out of the way and spent his last seven dollars on a room at the French Hotel two blocks away. After Sam's visit, Stevenson was rejected by Fanny, who again entertained second thoughts about her contemplated divorce. She told Stevenson that he had to leave as she was taking care of her sister Nellie who had diphtheria. Little Sam and Belle were sent to live in a hotel. She promised Stevenson she would send for him when Nellie had recovered.

In September, Stevenson had gotten a wire from London for £30 and was now able to fend for himself. While Fanny was taking care of her sister, he decided to take an adventure into the backcountry. Being ill didn't discourage him, as just about everything he did in life was accompanied by physical discomfort from his lifelong infirmities. Once into the countryside, he became dizzy and fell out of his saddle and could only crawl to a nearby tree where he stayed for three days. An old bear hunter came upon him and took him to his ranch eighteen miles outside of Monterey and nursed him back to health.

Fanny's daughter, Belle, had her own love affair going with Joe Strong, a young and handsome artist who was becoming well known in California. She and Joe left for Oakland, where her parents maintained a cottage across the bay from San Francisco. Joe asked for Sam's permission to marry Belle, knowing that her mother was against it. While Louis was travelling the countryside, Fanny returned to Oakland and found out about her daughter's marriage. She was furious with her husband for allowing it. Perhaps his selfish act was retaliation for her own admission of her affair with Stevenson. Whatever it was, it marked the end of her marriage. When Stevenson returned to Monterey, Fanny had finally committed herself to the idea of divorce. She and Louis were now able to make plans for their own wedding.

Young Sam did not understand what was going on. He heard the fights between his mother and father. He sensed that things were not right between them and he loved them both. His life was about to change. He would recount forty years later that Robert Louis Stevenson had taken him for a walk one day and, instead of telling an imaginative pirate or Indian tale for his amusement, he was quiet. Then, all a sudden he spoke, "I want to tell you something. You may not like it, but I hope you will. I am going to marry your mother." Sam was not sure how to react. He loved his father, but there was a magic about this man called Stevenson. Hand in hand, they both returned to the house.

Fanny was encouraged to leave Stevenson in Monterey, who was still living at the French Hotel, and return to Oakland and finish the divorce. She anguished over this as she felt that there was no one else in the world to care for her sickly lover. After she, young Sam, and her sister Nellie left, Stevenson collapsed in a heap, vomiting blood. He was found two days later by Jules Simoneau, the owner of a restaurant where Stevenson took his daily meals. Simoneau took Stevenson home and saved his life.

Stevenson recovered enough to find work writing articles for the local paper, *The Monterey Californian*. Back in San Francisco, Sam Osbourne was trying to see what kind of money the Stevenson clan had before he reached any agreement with Fanny on a cash settlement in their divorce.

It was November 4, 1879, when Robert Louis Stevenson and his future brother-in-law, Adolpho Sanchez, who was now engaged to Nellie, shared an unusual outing. The two took a buggy ride from Monterey to the mission church of San Carlos Borroméo in Carmel. This was the second mission out of the nine missions founded by Father Junípero Serra. San Diego had been the first. This was also Father Serra's favorite mission which he had made his headquarters the last fourteen years of his life. Father Serra died there in 1784 and was buried beneath the sanctuary floor.

Once a year, on November 4th, Father Angelo Delfino Casanova traveled to Carmel from his parish in Monterey to say mass within in the ruined walls of the mission, celebrating the feast day of San Carlos. The mass was followed by a gathering which not only included Catholics, but Protestants, friends, and strangers alike. Everyone was welcome. Some of the aged Indians, remnants of Father Serra's flock, would raise their voices in reverent song, reciting perfect

Latin, which brought Stevenson to comment later, "There you may hear God served with perhaps more touching circumstances than any other temple under heaven…." Stevenson was brought to tears as he had never witnessed such reverence and devotion. It was later said that nothing interested him more deeply in Monterey than the old mission at Carmel. It was in 1749, it will be recalled, that Father Serra had made the voyage from Spain to the New World aboard the *Nuestra Señora de Guadalupe* captained by Juan Manuel Bonilla. His ship was saved by a miracle without which the missions may never have been founded nor a treasure buried on a deserted Caribbean Island.

Stevenson learned that Father Casanova was trying to raise funds for the

Father Juniperro Serra. From the book by his biographer Francisco Palou. *Relacion historica de la vida y apostolicas tareas del venerable padre fray Junípero Serra, y de las misiones que fundo en la California Septentrional, y nuevos establecimientos de Monterey.* 1787. Copyright The Huntington Library. By his prayers on the feast day of St. Barbara, the Spanish galleon, *Nuestra Señora de Guadalupe*, was saved from a hurricane. Without this miracle there would have been no *Treasure Island*.

The mission church of St. Charles Borremeo at Carmel, California. Photo taken around the time of Stevenson's visit. Father Junípero Serra is buried beneath the sanctuary floor. Courtesy of the Monterey Historical Society.

preservation of the mission, charging ten cents a person to those who came to visit

When Stevenson was there, a new roof had been built over the sacristy but leaving the rest of the church to the open air. When Stevenson returned to Monterey, he wrote an editorial the following week in the *Monterey Californian* making an appeal for the restoration of Father Serra's mission: "When I think how that bell first sounded from the Mission Church among the Indians of Carmello, and the echoes of the hills of Monterey first learned the accustomed note, I am moved, by sentiment, to pray for restitution or at least repair." In 1882, after the confirmation was made of Father Serra's remains in his burial vault, the restoration was well underway.

Today, Father Serra is known as the Apostle of California. His legacy is everywhere in southern California. Besides the numerous statues of him throughout that part of the state, there is also one in the Statuary Hall at the U.S. Capitol. No one knows of his historic bond with a Spanish galleon and buried treasure.

Stevenson's health declined again. He came down with malaria and his tuberculosis was eating at his lungs. Fanny was warned by her friends not to bring him to San Francisco or to return to Monterey until the divorce was final because of the obvious scandal. Fearing that news of his death was imminent, Fanny fell into a deep depression.

Fanny and Sam's divorce was soon finalized and Stevenson's plans for marriage proceeded, but Fanny was cautioned by her friends not to get remarried right away. She and Louis continued to live apart. Stevenson arrived in San Francisco a few days before Christmas, looking much like a walking cadaver, and found a room at 608 Bush Street. On Christmas Eve, Stevenson received a telegram from his home in Scotland that his father, Thomas, was dying. He sent word back to his mother that unfortunately he could not return, as he would not desert Fanny.

Stevenson spent Christmas alone over the holidays. Stevenson poured himself into his writing; it was a welcome diversion from hunger and his longing for Fanny. He had barely enough money to survive. He weighed only a hundred pounds, but still had the strength and charity to set aside his writing to care for the four-year-old son of the woman who ran the boarding house. She credited Stevenson with saving her son's life, but Stevenson then collapsed from exhaustion. Fanny travelled daily by ferry from East Oakland to the boarding house in San Francisco in all manner of weather to care for him. In April, she brought him to East Oakland and put him up in the Tubb's Hotel. Here he suffered a hemorrhage. Fanny then moved Stevenson to Sam's house and set up his bed in the parlor, moved her bed downstairs, and devoted herself to bringing him back. There was vomiting, diarrhea, cramping and cold sweats. He spit up blood. Stevenson fought for his life, determined that he would marry Fanny and someday become a success at his writing. Fanny knew that if he lived that he would achieve both fame and money. In May, she moved him to her cottage at East Oakland.

The Statue of Father Junípero Serra in the Statuary Hall at the U. S. Capitol. In his hand is a miniature of the mission church which was his favorite and where he is buried.

The turning point came when Stevenson's father recovered and he realized that he did not want to lose his only son. He accepted the idea of his marriage to Fanny and sent him a letter saying so and promised him £250 annually. This good news lifted Stevenson's spirits enough that he began to recover.

On May 20, 1880, Fanny and Louis were married. Three days later they set out on their honeymoon to the north of San Francisco with young Sam and their dog, a setter-spaniel named ChuChu. Short of funds, Fanny suggested they find an old miner's shack and live as squatters. A local storekeeper directed them to an abandoned silver mine that Stevenson dubbed "Silverado." Fanny took to making a home out of a wooden platform and old crates. Stevenson mostly watched as this veteran pioneer woman went about her chores. His health improved so much that Fanny was able to write to Louis's mother on July 16 that they were headed for Scotland. On August 7, they cleared New York harbor, one year to the day that he had left home.

Stevenson carried with him a great archive of firsthand experiences from which he drew his travel writings. Before he arrived in California he had written *An Inland Voyage*, a story of his travels in France in a canoe with a friend. A year later, still in France, he wrote *Travels With a Donkey in the Cévennes*. From his American adventures he wrote *The Amateur Emigrant*, *Journey Across the Plains*, *Silverado Squatters*, and *Old and New Pacific Capitals*. All of these were short stories published later and none of them impressed his parents or his wife and stepson. Even his mentors in literature had mixed reviews. Stevenson wanted to write a novel, a full-length fictional story. Only then, he felt, could he stand proudly with his peers.

On October 8, 1880, Stevenson and his new family arrived in England. His health was once again on the slide and he, Fanny, and young Sam traveled to Davos, Switzerland, to stay at a sanatorium for the winter. At the time, it was a popular resort for people with lung ailments.

In the spring, the Stevensons found themselves in France. Louis had another hemorrhage and was again out of funds. His father sent them money to pay their hotel bill and they were then off for Scotland. They arrived to cold, rainy weather at the summerhouse his father had rented near Pitlochry. The wet weather there proved to be detrimental to his health. The entire Stevenson clan then picked up and moved, hopefully to find milder weather at the village of Braemar. It was here, one rainy afternoon in late August 1881, in a cottage owned by the late

Mrs. McGregor, that Stevenson began to write *Treasure Island*. His enthusiastic thirteen-year-old stepson later recalled the events of that day which were recorded in the preface to Stevenson's *My First Book* written in 1894 shortly before he died:

> That idolized stepfather of mine was the most inspiring playfellow in the world—which made it seem all the sadder that he was unable to write a book worth reading.... One rainy morning busy with a box of paints...I happened to be tinting the map of an island I had drawn. Stevenson came in as I was finishing it and with his affectionate interest in everything I was doing, he leaned over my shoulder, and was soon elaborating the map and naming it. I will never forget the thrill of Skeleton Island, Spy Glass Hill, nor the heart stirring climax of the three red crosses! And the great climax still when we wrote down the words "Treasure Island" at the top right hand corner! And he seemed to know so much about it too—the pirates, the buried treasure, the man who had been marooned on the island. "Oh, for a story about it," I exclaimed, in a heaven of enchantment, and somehow conscious of his own enthusiasm for the idea.
>
> Then, after writing in more names, he put the map in his pocket, and I can recall the little feeling of disappointment I had at losing it. After all, it was my map, and had already become very precious owing to its association with pirates, and the fact that it had been found in an old sea chest which had been lost and forgotten for years and years. But my step-father took it away, and the next day at noon I was called up mysteriously to his bedroom (he always spent the mornings writing in bed), and the first thing I saw was my beloved map lying on the coverlet. Still wondering why I had been summoned so specially, and not a little proud, and expectant, I was told to sit down while my step-father took up some sheets of manuscript, and began to read aloud the first chapter of *Treasure Island*.
>
> Thus one of the greatest, the most universal of all romances came to be written, and that I should have had a share in its

inception has always been to me a source of inexpressible pleasure. Had it not been for me, and my childish box of paints, there would have been no such book as *Treasure Island*.

When Stevenson arrived at the idea for *Treasure Island*, the story's main character was going to be the one-legged pirate, Long John Silver. He was owner of a tavern in Bristol, England, who had been hired as a cook to serve aboard the *Hispaniola* in her voyage to return to a Caribbean island to recover a cache of buried treasure. Stevenson had first dubbed his opus, *The Sea Cook or Treasure Island; A Story for Boys*. Long John was in the forefront of Stevenson's mind as he was introduced in the first chapter as "the seafaring man with one leg" before we even knew his name. The reader finally meets Long John Silver in Chapter Seven when he is hired as the ship's cook and we learn that his missing leg is attributed to an injury while serving under Admiral Edward Hawke. Edward Hawke was a real eighteenth century naval hero. His first experience in naval combat was in 1744 at the Battle of Toulon when he was a captain. He was promoted to Admiral in 1747 and led a British fleet to a decisive victory against France. This reference to Hawke is the first hint of the time period that he envisions for *Treasure Island*. Stevenson did not readily disclose the actual dates he had in mind as on the very first page he begins "in the year of grace 17—." This was when the narrator, Jim Hawkins, begins to retell his story. But his continuing narrative reveals more. In Chapter Six, when Billy Bones's sea chest is opened and the map of Treasure Island is discovered, there was also a note book with the date, June 12, 1745, which referred to some money due. This was the only date given in the book. Later in Chapter Sixteen, Dr. Livesey mentions having been wounded at Fontenoy, a battle between the English and the French in 1745. But these dates don't tell us exactly when the treasure was buried but rather help ascertain the year the *Hispaniola* sailed for Treasure Island.

As the story was written, Stevenson would read each chapter aloud to his family in the afternoons. He would discuss his story with his father, who not only encouraged him, but gave him ideas. Stevenson knew he needed help to keep the story going and wanted to add realism to his fictional narrative. At the end of his third chapter he wrote to his mentor and friend, W.E. Henley in London: "I want the best book about Buccaneers that can be had—the latter B's above all, Blackbeard and sich." Henley arrived with a copy of Captain Charles Johnson's *A General History of the Robberies and Murders of the Most Notorious Pirates* while Stevenson was writing

Chapter Ten, "The Voyage." Johnson's *History* had been published in 1724, and today is still considered the best authority on pirates of that era. However, it only covered the "Golden Age" of piracy, which ended about that time. Johnson's *History* was from another time period than what Stevenson was already writing about.

In Chapter Ten, "The Voyage," the reader is introduced to the coxswain, Israel Hands, who in real life had sailed with Blackbeard in 1718. Israel Hands was the only pirate whose life was spared when Blackbeard's crew was taken at Ocracoke. But Stevenson took the opportunity to have him killed.

It is also in this chapter that we meet Long John's parrot, Cap'n Flint, which Stevenson later freely admitted he borrowed from *Robinson Crusoe*. With the parrot, Stevenson created a character in its own right, as he was often heard squawking, "Pieces of Eight! Pieces of Eight!" Long John Silver tells young Hawkins that if anybody has seen more wickedness than this bird "it must be the Devil himself." He describes the parrot as having been to Madagascar, and Malabar, Porto Bello, and with the great Cap'n England. Long John goes on to tell young Hawkins that "she was at the fishing up of the wrecked plate ships (the Spanish fleet lost on coast of Florida in 1715). It's there she learned to say, 'Pieces of eight.'" These details were all gleaned from Johnson's *History*.

The next chapter, "What I heard in the Apple Barrel," includes more from Johnson's *History*. The previous chapter had ended with Jim Hawkins climbing into the apple barrel on deck and being lulled to sleep. Hawkins awakens to hear Long John Silver conversing with some of the other crew. It is here that Hawkins learns of Silver's mutinous plot to take over the ship. With Hawkins listening in for the reader, Stevenson now tells us that Long John had in fact lost his leg with Edward England at Corso Castle on the coast of Guinea in the same broadside "that old Pew lost his deadlights." But that event described by Johnson happened in 1722. In this same chapter, Long John Silver tells us he is fifty years old. If he had been with Edward England in 1722, as Stevenson suggests in this chapter, he would have been only twelve at the time he lost his leg. Stevenson obviously was trying to associate his favorite character, Long John Silver, with some real pirates, but he did not change the actual time frame of *Treasure Island* to further that end. That mid-course correction was merely brought on by his reaction to the fascinating history found Johnson's *Pirates*. Stevenson knew from the beginning that his story was going to be set in the mid-eighteenth century, a time period when piracy on the high seas had greatly diminished. He had been consistent with this premise for the first ten chapters until he read *Pirates*.

Stevenson was either unsure about giving an exact date for the treasure to be buried in his narrative or he wanted to keep it a secret. In his story, the only reference of how the treasure got to Treasure Island is that an infamous pirate named James Flint, "the bloodthirstiest buccaneer that sailed," had buried his ill-gotten gain on a deserted Caribbean Island. Billy Bones was his mate and Long John Silver was his quartermaster when the treasure was buried. But they did not witness the location—Flint had killed the six crewmen that did. Never mentioned were the details of how Flint came by the treasure.

"One more step, Mr. Hands, and I'll blow your brains out! Dead men don't bite, you know,"—Jim Hawkins, Chapter Twenty Six, "Israel Hands," *Treasure Island*.

Stevenson's First Book

The map of Treasure Island says the treasure was buried in August of 1750, but the date on the map did not come from Stevenson. It came from his father, Thomas. What made Thomas pick 1750, the year that the greatest non-war piracy had taken place, rivaling anything from the Golden Age? Even Blackbeard never made such a haul as did Owen Lloyd in that year.

The idea for the story of *Treasure Island* all started with a map that Stevenson and his stepson had playfully constructed to amuse themselves that fateful rainy day. As he labeled the map, he created the story, so the map had to accompany the book. The story was started in August 1881, sold to *Young Folks* magazine that September before it was finished, serialized in *Young Folks* in 1882 without the map, and in 1883, when the manuscript was sent to Cassell and Co., his publisher, Stevenson sent in his original map. When the proofs were returned, the map was missing. When Stevenson inquired about it, his publisher claimed to have never received it. Three years had passed, and without a copy, Stevenson was forced to go back to every detail of his story so he could reconstruct the map. He did this in his father's office, and when he was done, his father made his own notations. Below the words "Treasure Island," which now appeared on the lower right of the map, he wrote in "August 1750, J.F." The "J.F." was for James Flint. We know that this took place because Stevenson said in *My First Book* that his father "forged the signature of Captain Flint and [wrote in] the sailing directions of Billy Bones." The original map of *Treasure Island* was labeled in the upper right corner, as later attested to by his stepson, Samuel Osbourne.

If one reads his tale carefully, a time period for the return trip to Treasure Island in the *Hispaniola* can be easily deduced. First there is the treasure map. The notation at the bottom says that Captain James Flint gave the treasure map to Billy Bones in 1754 at Savannah, Georgia, as he lay dying of alcoholism, specifically an addiction to rum. Stevenson recounted this event in his narrative, so the voyage definitely follows 1754.

Stevenson used the term "the immortal Hawke" when referring to the first instance of Long John's account of his missing leg. He did not achieve such notoriety until 1759, after the Battle of Quiberon Bay in November of that year in which he prevented the French invasion of Great Britain. That reference would

219

put the year of the *Treasure Island* adventure starting no sooner than 1760. As for when Long John Silver lost his leg, it would have been 1744 or later, not in 1722 at Corso Castle. Stevenson was no stranger to British naval history, as he wrote an essay called "The English Admirals," published in the July 1878 issue of *Cornhill Magazine*. There is no doubt Stevenson had a date in mind and he didn't want to give it to us. If he had been true to form he would have picked a time in the first quarter of the eighteenth century when many of the pirate legends like Blackbeard roamed the seas. And contrary to his knowledge of a real pirate treasure buried in 1820 on an island in the Pacific called Cocos Island, he neither chose that time frame nor that location for his Treasure Island. Stevenson gave an account of the treasure hunts going on at Cocos Island in an article attributed to him published in the *Monterey Californian* on December 16, 1879. He had moved to San Francisco shortly after that and began his wedding plans with Fanny Osbourne.

Stevenson documented more of his father's influence in *My First Book*:

> My father caught fire at once with all the romance and childishness of his original nature. His own stories, that every night of his life he put himself to sleep with, dealt perpetually with ships, roadside inns, robbers, old sailors, and commercial travelers before the age of steam…he not only heard with delight the daily chapter, but set himself actively to collaborate. When the time came for Billy Bones's chest to be ransacked, he must have passed the better part of a day preparing, on the back of a legal envelope, an inventory of its contents, which I exactly followed; and the name of "Flints old ship," the *Walrus*, was given at his particular request.

Stevenson may have accidentally tipped his hand on the where he got the idea for the map in the seaman's chest. In the front matter of *Treasure Island* is a poem dedicated "TO THE HESITATING PURCHASER." In it, he acknowledges three authors, W. G. H. Kingston, R. M. Ballantyne, and James Fenimore Cooper. All three were an influence in the creation of *Treasure Island*. In 1849, Cooper wrote

The Sea Lions: The Lost Sealers. In Chapter Three, Cooper tells a story of an oath of secrecy, a sea chest, and a map with a key that will lead to a fortune.

Stevenson's father was the source for another scene. The idea of the apple barrel found in Chapter Eleven, "What I Heard in the Apple Barrel," was borrowed from real life. Stevenson's grandfather, Robert Stevenson, had great admiration for a Captain Soutar who worked for Scotland's Lighthouse Board. Stevenson's grandfather was aboard his vessel one night and crept into the apple barrel on deck. Captain Soutar was indulging himself with an after-dinner glass of whiskey when Stevenson's grandfather overheard him talking. Soutar had put aside his smooth and distinguished air of a respectable seaman as the young Stevenson "listened with wonder to a vulgar and truculent ruffian." Thus, this story was passed from father to son.

Robert Louis Stevenson was born into a family of lighthouse engineers in Edinburgh, Scotland. This proximity to the sea would influence his forbears and later himself. His father was born in 1818 to Robert Stevenson, who had acquired the knowledge of lighthouse engineering from his stepfather, Thomas Smith. Robert's real father was Alan Stevenson, said to be a West Indian merchant who, with his brother Hugh, managed a trading business at St. Kitts. Robert Louis Stevenson wrote that the beginning of his own story began with the deaths of his great uncle, Hugh Stevenson, who died at Tobago on April 16, 1774, and a month later when his great grandfather, Alan Stevenson, died at St. Kitts on May 26. Robert Louis Stevenson recalled:

> With these two brothers my story begins. Their deaths were simultaneous. Their lives unusually brief and full. Tradition whispered me in childhood they were owners of an islet near St. Kitts; and it is certain they had risen to be at the head of considerable interests in the West Indies, which Hugh managed abroad and Alan at home, at an age when others are still curveting a clerk's stool. My kinsman, Mr. Stevenson of Stirling, has heard his father mention that there had been something "romantic" about Alan's marriage; and alas he has forgotten what.

There hung in the house of this young family, and successfully in those of my grandfather and father, an oil painting of a ship of many tons burthen. Doubtless the brothers had an interest in the vessel; I was told she belonged to them outright; and the picture was preserved through years of hardship, and remains to this day in possession of the family, the only memorial of my great-grandshire Alan. It was on this ship that he sailed in his last adventure, summoned to the West Indies by Hugh. An agent had proved unfaithful on a serious scale; and it used to be told me in my childhood how the brothers pursued him from one island to another in an open boat, were exposed to the pernicious dews of the tropics, and simultaneously struck down.

Alan and Hugh Stevenson were born in Glasgow, on the River Clyde, which in the eighteenth century was Scotland's gateway to the Caribbean. It was here that sugar—white gold—was imported from the West Indies. Their father, Robert Stevenson, was born in 1720 in Glasgow. Records show he was a maltman, manufacturing malt for the production of beer and whiskey. Also needed in that process was sugar. His sister, Elizabeth, had married Alexander Brown, a sugar refiner from Glasgow with interests in St. Kitts. In November 1750, when the first news of the events at Ocracoke reached Glasgow, he was thirty years old and his son Hugh had been born the year before. Alan was born in 1752.

The newspapers in Glasgow and Edinburgh carried updates from America on Bonilla's plight. And certainly the newspapers from Antigua, Barbados, and Jamaica would have been read in Glasgow because of the large sugar interests there. Owen Lloyd's adventures would most likely have been told in them. Unfortunately, those papers did not survive. From Virginia, passengers and crews of vessels that routinely traveled to Glasgow in the trade would ferry the latest gossip told at Mother Hawkins' tavern to the Merchant's Hall in Glasgow where it would be distributed. Bonilla's insurers were two Scotsmen in London, Robert and John Lidderdale. They maintained correspondents in Glasgow, the merchant firm of Dunlop & Peter. William and James Dunlop regularly sent ships to Hampton,

Virginia. The *London Magazine* of February 1751, distributed throughout England and the American colonies, featured an article entitled "Spanish Treasure Embezzled." It was actually a letter that had been written from St. Kitts to the magazine dated December 16, 1750. The letter stated that Captain Lloyd was "now in chains at St. Eustatius" for stealing money that belonged to "the Viceroy of Mexico." It also stated that "it is imagined that Lloyd has murdered some Spaniards, and run away with the treasure." Fifty-two chests of treasure were said to be buried at Norman Island but were later recovered by the people of Tortola. It said that at St. Kitts, coins minted in 1749 and 1750, part of Lloyd's loot, were being passed in the course of daily commerce. Lloyd had to have already been well known throughout the island by most of the plantation owners because of his capture of the French slave ship. Over 300 slaves had been sold and dispersed around the island. And now, newly minted pieces of eight were circulating around St. Kitts thanks to him. For some, these freshly minted pieces of eight may have even had a collector's value as they were believed to have belonged to the "Viceroy of Mexico."

St. Kitts had become the epicenter of the 1750 event. Owen Lloyd's brother-in-law, Charles Caines, it will be recalled, maintained a prosperous plantation at St. Kitts and was a member of the assembly when the treasure was stolen. He and his son were both members of the council in 1774 when Alan and Hugh Stevenson were at St. Kitts.

In the 1770s, the Scottish merchants, James Milliken and William McDowell, who both owned land in St. Kitts and in Glasgow, were partners in the firm of Alexander Houstoun & Co. who traded with St. Kitts. There was also the South Street Sugar House in Glasgow and the St. Christopher's Sugar House in Edinburgh. So when Alan and Hugh Stevenson set off for the West Indies to make their own fortunes, like Milliken and McDowell, they might have been quite familiar with the story of Owen Lloyd and the prospects of buried treasure.

We may not know the real reason the Stevenson brothers went to St. Kitts but we know of two major events in 1772 that would have affected their lives and fortunes. In June of that year, there was a near collapse of the banking system in Scotland brought on in part by speculation in the West Indian sugar business and the exchange of nearly worthless bank notes. Hard currency was scarce in Glasgow and Edinburgh. Two months later, on August 31, the Leeward Islands were ravaged by a hurricane like no one had yet seen. At Antigua, ships were drove ashore, nearly every structure damaged or destroyed, people sought unprotected shelter in the cane fields; at St. Croix, the seas were said to be seventy feet high, nearly one half of the houses in Christiansted were damaged or destroyed; at St. Eustatius they had similar damage and reported that "there is not a barrel of flour on the island for sale, the country provisions are all out and they expected a famine to occur. At St. Kitts, the *St. Christopher's Gazette* of September 2 was able to report:

> We inserted in our last the account of the hard wind from the S. W. with some accidents which attended the same, which, to this island's inexpressible grief, were no more than a prelude of our destruction: for on Monday last, at the dawn of day, our angry hemisphere predicted violence from the N. E. which by degrees broke forth upon us with such a rage, not be paralleled in memory by the oldest man living. Nothing escaped its fury. The wind shifted to S. W. which brought on us such a horrible scene of destruction till eight o'clock in the evening that is beyond the power of man to relate. Scarce a house, sugar mill, tree, or plant in this town but was blown down or very much damaged. The loss of lives was considerable. The loss was computed to be in excess of £500,000.

It would take years for the islands to recover and the sugar merchants in Scotland surely suffered.

At the onset of the banking collapse, Robert Louis Stevenson's grandfather was born to Alan and Jean Stevenson in Glasgow on June 8, 1772. Soon after that, Alan traveled to St. Kitts and assumed the job of store clerk. He may have joined his brother Hugh who was probably already there. Robert Louis Stevenson had surmised in his book, *A family of Engineers*, that Hugh's death in 1774 was probably announced by letter in Glasgow because the circumstances of his death are known today. That letter most likely would have come from Alan upon his return to St. Kitts or from someone close to him. Alan died shortly afterwards.

Stevenson's family tradition says the brothers "were owners of an islet near St. Kitts." There are no islets, or small islands, near St. Kitts except for the Virgin Islands, 130 miles northwest. The records of St. Kitts show that the brothers did not own property at St. Kitts. As for the details of the brothers' pursuit of a "defrauding partner" in an open boat, we have little to go on. Stevenson said that Alan was "summoned to the West Indies" by Hugh. Since Alan was already working there as a store clerk, the notion that Hugh had "summoned" Alan to the West Indies may have been merely to join him in the reconstruction necessary at St. Kitts. Once there, the most likely scenario is that Alan and Hugh left St. Kitts together in pursuit of an unnamed agent. Stevenson said that in the words of his grandfather the location of the adventure took place "in these lawless parts and lawless times." "These lawless times" may be a reference to the anarchy that might be expected after the devastation on the 1772 hurricane. Generally, St. Kitts was an ordered society. However, the Virgin Islands were a problem. George Suckling wrote in 1780 about the difficulties in this island chain. There had been no legislature until 1773 and there were many ownership disputes over land in the islands. Hugh, being single, might have ventured here in search of a wife before being victimized, as Suckling said "in no place can a man have a better chance of meeting with an agreeable companion for life, than in the Virgin Islands." Hugh's plans may have been not unlike the Scottish merchants Milliken and McDowell who had married their fortunes at St. Kitts. A number of plantation owners at St. Kitts had satellites at Tortola. Hugh may have purchased (or thought he did) "an islet" or land thereon in the Virgin Islands. The land was cheap as witnessed by the sale of Norman Island to Henry Creque in 1894 for forty pounds. The land records that might answer that question are in very bad condition today and cannot be examined.

On November 13, 1773, Ralph Payne, son of the deputy governor of St. Kitts in 1750 and governor in chief of the Leeward Islands, convened a house

225

of representatives that consisted of eleven members. One of them was Abraham Chalwell, whose father had been president of the council at Tortola in 1750. Both father and son partook in the stolen treasure at Norman Island. Chalwell, Sr. had been arrested by Gilbert Fleming for withholding some. Another member was George Nibbs who, as collector of customs at Tortola in 1750, was charged with selling blank customs forms at that time. Payne instructed them to make no decision on real estate disputes until a proper court could be convened.

There is scant record of Alan Stevenson. Contrary to the family tradition, the records for the time period tell us that Alan and Hugh were not owners of a ship out of Glasgow. Alan left no property to his young widow. Glasgow records show that Hugh owned a tenement with his mother. They were not prosperous merchants as had been romanticized in the family. A similar tradition that has since been debunked was attributed to the Scottish merchants Milliken and McDowell who, as the story goes, served as soldiers before ascending to wealth and prominence. The historian, Stuart M. Nisbet, has documented that they were only slave overseers when they arrived at Nevis and St. Kitts. For Hugh and Alan Stevenson, it appears that they both may have worked in the business owned by their uncle, Alexander Brown, the sugar merchant, before he died in 1769. All we can say for sure now is that Alan left St. Kitts to rendezvous with Hugh, where they would begin their pursuit of a defrauding business partner in an open boat which would lead to their premature deaths.

Robert Louis Stevenson regretted that "Thus from a few scraps of paper bearing little beyond dates, we construct the outlines of the tragedy that shadow the cradle of Robert Stevenson." Robert Stevenson was only two years old when his father Alan died mysteriously at St. Kitts. His mother, Jean, lived on until 1820, long enough to see her grandson, Robert Louis Stevenson's father, born in 1818. Her son Robert did not die until 1850, the year of Robert Louis Stevenson's birth. For years, his father heard stories of St. Kitts and of his grandparents. Was Thomas's insistence on the date of August 1750 to bury the treasure just an unrelated coincidence with the adventure of Owen Lloyd?

After Stevenson published *Treasure Island* in book form in 1883, it became a huge success. His peers and critics were quick to analyze the story and his obvious sources traced to the available literature that appeared to have influenced his "creativity." The world was so captivated by Stevenson's romantic tale that his source material had become well documented before he died. We will never know for sure if Stevenson was knowledgeable of the events of 1750, but it is easily demonstrated what did influence his writing of *Treasure Island*. After *Treasure Island* was published, his critics began pointing out other works that Stevenson had obviously borrowed from. For example, Charles Kingsley's *At Last: A Christmas in the West Indies*, written in 1871, was admittedly used by Stevenson. Kingsley, when describing the British Virgins, refers to Dead Chest Island as "the Dead Man's Chest." Adding the word "Man's" was his idea because no map has ever showed this island as "Dead *Man's* Chest." This may have been influenced by the small bay called "Deadman's Bay" on Peter Island just opposite Dead Chest. In a letter to Sidney Colvin in 1884, a year after *Treasure Island* was serialized, Stevenson admitted, "T.I. came out of Kingsley's *At Last*; where I got the 'Dead Man's Chest'—and that was the seed." Dead Chest Island lies only five miles from Norman Island. In 1887, in a letter to a journalist, he said that his *Treasure Island* sea shanty which chorus sang "Yo-ho-ho and a bottle of rum!," "was his own invention entirely; founded on the name of one of the Buccaneer Islets." Stevenson did not acknowledge the Negro hymn that Kingsley had heard:

'Ya-he-ho-o-hu'—followed the chorus.

'Captain he go to him cabin, he drink him wine and whiskey—'

'Ya-he,' etc.

'You go to America? You as well go to heaven.'

'Ya-he,' etc.

Stevenson certainly would have read Kingsley's impressions of St. Kitts included here. "It is not till the traveler arrives at St. Kitts that he sees what a West Indian island is. The 'Mother of the Antilles,' as she is called, is worthy of her name."

In 1894, in *My First Book*, Stevenson adds to his confession: "I am now upon a painful chapter. No doubt the parrot once belonged to Robinson Crusoe. No doubt the skeleton is conveyed from Poe. I think little of these, they are trifles and details…The stockade I am told is from *Masterman Ready*. It may be, I care not a jot."

As for other aspects of the story, Stevenson was quick to give credit where it was due:

> It is my debt to Washington Irving that exercises my conscience, and justly so, for I believe plagiarism was rarely carried farther. I chanced to pick up *Tales of a Traveler* some years ago, with a view to an anthology of prose narrative, and the book flew up and struck me: Billy Bones, his chest, the company in the parlor, the whole inner spirit and a good deal of material detail of my first chapters—all were there, all were the property of Washington Irving. But had no guess of it then as I sat writing by the fireside, in what seemed the springtides of a somewhat pedestrian inspiration; nor yet day by day, after lunch, as I read aloud my morning's work to the family it seemed to me original as sin; it seemed to belong to me like my right eye.

Three years after *Treasure Island* was written, Stevenson confided in Edward Purcell, a literary critic: "I had no idea what a cruelly bold adapter I was, till I found the whole first part of *Treasure Island* in what I had read (I believe, but I am not sure) for nearly twenty years: Washington Irving's *Treasure Seekers*."

For years, Stevenson carried the imagery of buried treasure with him until 1881 when *Treasure Island* was written. Stevenson not only adapted a story of buried treasure but used real life people in his creation of characters.

Treasure Island's strongest and most memorable character is Long John Silver. Stevenson looked to his admired friend, W. E. Henley, a Scottish writer and poet living in London, as his model for this character because it was the combination of his amputated foot and strength of character that prompted Stevenson to admit to him later, "It was the sight of your maimed strength and masterfulness that begot John Silver…." And for the missing leg, he had several true amputees, including Admiral Benbow to choose from. Stevenson used his visual experiences in California to describe the scenery of *Treasure Island*.

Stevenson picked James Flint to be captain of the pirate ship, *Walrus*. This name was probably taken from James Flint, Scottish author and traveler who wrote *Letters from America* in 1822. Stevenson probably read this book before setting out on his adventure to America to reunite with his future wife. Squire Trelawney was supposedly taken from Edward Trelawny, the adventurer, who was friends with the poets Lord Byron and Percy Shelly. Coincidentally, in 1750, the governor of Jamaica was also named Edward Trelawny. Captain Alexander Smollet was given command of the *Hispaniola* for the trip to Treasure Island. Tobias Smollet, 1721-1771, considered to be Scotland's first novelist, must have been the inspiration for Stevenson's make-believe captain as he was in real life a surgeon in the British Navy, wrote about the Caribbean, and translated the adventures of Don Quixote from Spanish. He also was at Cartagena in 1741 when Don Daniel Huony was wounded. He was the future captain of *La Galga*, the armed escort of the 1750 fleet.

Frank Gwyn, one of Stevenson's biographers, observed: "the whole of his book is constructed out of materials found in other books. Stevenson utilizes all his resources all that he read and all that he had observed." The *New York Times* of February 11, 1884, reviewed *Treasure Island* and said that it would have been fairer to dedicate the book to Edgar Alan Poe, rather than his stepson since "it is the story called 'The Gold Bug' with many pleasant and clever amplifications." Poe's story was written in 1843 before Stevenson was born.

In 1750, it was not the fictional pirate, James Flint, who buried his pirate loot on Treasure Island, but a merchant captain from Flintshire, Wales, named Owen Lloyd. It was Robert Louis Stevenson who then took the whole world back to dig it up. Nearly a century ago, a writer summed it best:

> Stevenson too could have organized an expedition. But Stevenson was of Scotch lineage, and he knew of a way of getting far more treasure out of the map than he ever could have dug from the island in its centre. Stevenson's was buried treasure too, and not easy to come by. But by hard work, he dug it out, and when success had crowned his efforts, the treasure was not only his but all the world's.

Before Stevenson died in 1894, he had more to say about the genesis of *Treasure Island* and how it began with the help of his stepson, Sam Osbourne, and his map of an island. This map became the chief part of Stevenson's plot. And as Stevenson said in 1894, "I might say it was the whole."

Stevenson recognized his stepson's influence from the very beginning. On August 25, 1881, after just getting started on *Treasure Island*, Stevenson wrote a letter to William E. Henley telling him that he had begun a new story:

> I am now on another lay for the moment, purely owing to Lloyd, this one; but I believe there's more coin in it than in any amount of Crawlers: now see here, "The Sea Cook, or Treasure Island: A story for Boys."

By this time Stevenson's stepson did not choose to be called Sam as was his natural father. He used his middle name "Lloyd." He had been named after a friend of his father's and a dear companion of his mother, a treasure hunter in California named JOHN LLOYD.

Samuel Lloyd Osbourne, the step-son of Robert Louis Stevenson. He was the inspiration for *Treasure Island*. © The Writers' Museum, Edinburgh Museums & Galleries.

Chapter Thirteen

The Hunt for Lloyd

It was in 1978 when I first read an account of the *Nuestra Señora de Guadalupe*, Juan Manuel Bonilla, and Owen Lloyd. I had read a series of eighteenth century newspaper accounts about the loss of the 1750 fleet while doing research on *La Galga*, with the goal of finding that shipwreck. The story of Owen Lloyd was intriguing, although very little was said about him in the contemporary accounts. Two years later at the Library of Congress, I discovered documents from the Public Record Office in London related to the theft of the treasure. Here, I found out about Owen's one-legged brother, John, and William Blackstock. All I was able to learn then about Owen and John Lloyd was that they were brothers, that Owen married the daughter of a Colonel Caines at Dieppe (pronounced "dep") Bay, St. Kitts, and that John Lloyd had a wooden leg. These microfilmed documents contained the deposition of William Blackstock after he was captured and correspondence from Lt. General Gilbert Fleming of the Leeward Islands, Governor Ralph Payne of St. Kitts, and council minutes from Tortola. Blackstock was the one who described John Lloyd's wooden leg. The parallel between John Lloyd and Long John Silver in *Treasure Island* did not go unnoticed. I reread *Treasure Island* and was reminded that Stevenson's *Treasure Island* contained a map dated August 1750. It was in August of 1750 that the hurricane brought the galleon of Juan Manuel Bonilla to Ocracoke putting the treasure within the grasp of one enterprising Owen Lloyd.

At the Library of Congress, I easily found a wealth of information on Robert Louis Stevenson, how *Treasure Island* was written, and the fascinating story of Stevenson's chance meeting with Fanny Osbourne whom he would later marry. When I read about his stepson being named after a Welshman named John Lloyd, who was Sam Osbourne's best friend in a mining camp in Nevada, I realized it was a coincidence that could not be ignored.

This intriguing story took a back seat to my quest for *La Galga*, the warship that was escorting the treasure fleet in which Bonilla had sailed. I found the wreck in 1983, but I would have to wait until 2001 to pick up the trail of Owen Lloyd. When that day arrived, I was also researching and writing *The Hidden Galleon*, the complete history of *La Galga*, her captain, and my discovery of that shipwreck at Assateague Island eighteen years before. Now, with a small army of researchers and possessing the time and money for the project, I set out on an adventure, or rather an obsession, to hunt for Owen Lloyd in the archives of Europe and America as well as numerous exploration trips to Norman Island. That manhunt now expanded to include a miner named John Lloyd who lived in the next century.

Austin, Nevada, June, 1864

John Lloyd stood on the doorway of his cabin nested on the hillside of the Sierra Nevada mining camp that bordered the Reese River. Off in the distance he could see a stage coach churning up the dusty road as it thundered into Austin. Close by in another cabin was Sam Osbourne, another miner, who had been anxiously awaiting the arrival of his wife, Fanny.

Lloyd watched as Sam walked into town to greet the stage. He had heard so much about Sam's beautiful wife. He already felt like he knew her.

Sam beamed as he watched his twenty-four year old wife step from the coach followed by his six year old daughter, Isobel. After the hugs and tears that came with a joyous reunion, Sam Osbourne escorted his wife and daughter up the mountain trail to his cabin.

John Lloyd found Fanny to be even more enchanting than Sam had described. He immediately bonded with Fanny and Isobel who reciprocated his affection. John became one of the family.

John Lloyd had no family in America. He had come over from England in 1860 at the age of twenty-two to seek his fortune and find a new life. The news of gold and silver discoveries in the American West had spread through Europe luring many young men and women to cross the Atlantic.

John and Sam had met while working the mines. They soon became best friends and bought a mine together. Sam Osbourne had come to Nevada quite by chance.

Sam and Fanny Vandegrift were married on Christmas Eve of 1857. She was only seventeen and Sam was twenty. It was said that it had been love at first sight. The following year their daughter Isobel was born. It was a happy union but then the Civil War broke out and Sam and his best friend, George Mason, volunteered for duty in the Union Army. In January 1863, Fanny's sister, Jo, married George. But George's health was failing from the tuberculosis that he had contracted during the war. The following week, Sam borrowed some money to take his brother-in-law to San Francisco for the recuperative mild and dry climate.

Once George was established and comfortable, Sam was going to return to Indiana. Unfortunately, George died on board the steamer and was buried on the Isthmus of Panama. Sam proceeded on to San Francisco. His intentions had been to return home but he became enraptured with the California climate and the fever of the budding Gold Rush. With his remaining money, he purchased what he hoped would be a profitable silver mine in Nevada. He sent for Fanny and Isobel, or "Belle" as she was called, to join him in San Francisco. Fanny, without hesitation, accepted the invitation and liquidated everything. She booked passage on a steamer from New York to take her and Belle to the Isthmus of Panama where they transferred on board a rickety train for an overland trip to the Pacific and then shipped aboard another steamer for San Francisco. Her journey was grueling and hampered by delays. When she arrived at San Francisco, she found that Sam had lost patience and left the day before but he had left instructions for her on how to find him at the Austin mining camp. The next day, June 21, she boarded the stage coach and headed for Austin.

Life was difficult in the mining camp—there was little comfort, scarce supplies, and Indians—but Fanny had that creative, hard-working pioneer spirit which helped her survive.

The mine that Osbourne and Lloyd had bought became a sinkhole for cash and never returned a profit. By March of 1865, Sam and John realized they had had enough. The optimistic treasure hunters left for Virginia City, home of the Comstock Lode, the greatest vein of silver found in the 1800s.

After a few weeks in Virginia City, Belle became ill and Fanny suffered from exhaustion. Sam decided that Fanny and Belle needed to return to San Francisco to get some sea air. On April 8, they booked passage on the stage coach to California leaving Sam and John behind. Sam was relieved.

Fanny Osbourne, not only the future Mrs. Robert Louis Stevenson, but close friend and suspected lover of John Lloyd.

Two days later, news arrived that the Civil War was over and that the North had won. The overly exuberant inhabitants of Virginia City quickly descended on the saloons and stayed drunk for days. Then came the sobering news of Lincoln's assassination. There were riots in San Francisco forcing Fanny to return home to Virginia City.

To Fanny's dismay, she found that Sam had taken up with a widow named Betty Kelly who was running a boarding house in town. Because Mrs. Kelly was lacking in furnishings, Sam even took all of their marital possessions out of the cabin to use at the boarding house. When Fanny realized that she had a philandering husband, one that had probably never been faithful, she fell into an angry tirade. Sam wanted freedom and reverted to whoring and card playing with the other miners. He returned to prospecting. On March 28, 1866, Sam left Virginia City with a caravan of miners.

While winter approached, Fanny remained in Virginia City and watched the town wither as the mines played out. John Lloyd maintained his daily visits with Fanny and took care of her and Belle as much as she would allow. That December, Lloyd realized that the economic situation in Virginia City was becoming worse by the day. He announced to Fanny that he had to go back to San Francisco. Fanny pleaded with him that she needed another week to wait for Sam to return but by the end of that week, Lloyd said they could wait no more. The last stage until spring was leaving for San Francisco. Fanny's last act was to leave a message for Sam scrawled on the cabin walls saying that she had returned to San Francisco to the same hotel that he had put them up at two years before.

Fanny and Belle checked into the Occidental Hotel, the most expensive in San Francisco which was owned by friends of her husband. John Lloyd went off to find his own lodging. Shortly after checking in, Fanny heard that Sam

The Hunt for Lloyd

and his crew had been ambushed and massacred by Indians; there had been no survivors.

John Lloyd was devastated by the news. Not only had he lost his best friend, he fully expected Fanny to leave San Francisco and return to Indiana. To his surprise, Fanny announced with her usual grit and determination that she would stay in San Francisco and return to her former work as a seamstress, much to the relief of Lloyd. She and Belle then relocated to the more affordable hotel where Lloyd was staying.

At the hotel, John Lloyd continued his visits with Fanny but she was so stricken with grief that she refused to go out. Lloyd was very devoted to Fanny and Belle. He gave up his one day off a week to be with them. Lloyd would take Belle down to the wharfs to see the ships where he entertained her with stories. He would often rent a boat and row amongst the anchored ships hoping to be invited aboard after a friendly wave. Once aboard, Belle later recalled, he would tell the ship's crew that he was searching for his two brothers who had run away to sea.

By day, John Lloyd worked as a messenger at one of the many San Francisco banks. At night, he studied law books borrowed from the library.

In early October, Fanny's life took another reversal. Her husband Sam showed up, very much alive. He recounted how he had escaped death not just from the Indians, but from thirst, snakebite, and a ricocheted bullet to the head as well. Regarding the Indian ambush, he related that he and his partner, Sam Orr, had fallen behind the mining caravan and were not discovered by the Indians but they had suffered great hardship in the desert thereafter.

Fanny and Sam resumed their marriage. She never spoke of the widow Kelly affair again. Sam obtained a job as court stenographer and moved Fanny and Belle into a house on 5th Street. Belle was happy to have her beloved father back and John Lloyd resumed his daily visits at supper time.

On April 28, 1868, a son was born. It had been a difficult pregnancy and Sam had started whoring again. He had moved out and found an apartment which he shared with a divorcée. But in a feeble effort to console Fanny, he told her that the woman meant nothing to him. Once again, John Lloyd was there to fill the void in her life.

When Fanny wrote home to her family in Clayton, she never talked of her husband or of her pregnancy but she did go to great length to describe her friend, John Lloyd. "The more one knows him and how reliable and straightforward he is the more you like him."

A month after the baby had arrived, Fanny packed her bags and left for home in Indiana retracing her steps across the Isthmus of Panama, boarding a steamer for New York, and from there back to Clayton. During the voyage, she baptized the boy Samuel Lloyd Osbourne in recognition of her loyal and devoted companion, John Lloyd.

Fanny enjoyed being back home with her parents—at first. Before long, however, her father was telling her that her place was with her husband in San Francisco and that moving back would be best for her two children. After receiving a plea from Sam, Fanny took her father's advice and returned. This time by rail as the transcontinental railroad had been completed just weeks before. Her married life once again returned to normal but Fanny had changed. She sought to change herself and engage life like she hadn't before. It was at this time that Fanny, with her daughter Belle, took up art lessons with Virgil Williams, a noted artist in San Francisco. At this same time, her husband Sam, Virgil Williams, John Lloyd and a group of journalists established the Bohemian Club, an exclusive society of intellectuals and business men which still exists today.

For the next three years, the Osbourne family prospered. John Lloyd would visit every Sunday taking Belle and his young namesake for a stroll and a story. Sam's family was his family. Fanny soon had another son named Hervey whom she adored, maybe more than the other two. Hervey was a frail child. With the love and protection she heaped on Hervey, there was little room for her husband's romantic advances. Sam moved out to another apartment and took in another woman, supporting her and Fanny with his stenographer's meager paycheck. John Lloyd's visits stopped upon his marriage to a Swedish woman named Christina in 1873.

Fanny continued to live in the cottage in East Oakland but dreamed of far off horizons. In March of 1875, she announced to Sam that she was taking the three children and going to art school in Antwerp, Belgium. Sam was told that he had to fund her trip or else there might be a divorce. This created quite a stir at the Bohemian Club. John Lloyd and another lawyer named Timothy Rearden, both confidants of Fanny, condemned the plan but she was determined and couldn't be swayed. On April 28, 1875, she headed east for New York to board the ship that would take her and her three children across the Atlantic for her historic meeting with Robert Louis Stevenson.

The Hunt for Lloyd

Stevenson arrived in Monterey, California, in August of 1879, after a grueling journey which included a transatlantic voyage, and a 2,800 mile train ride through deserts, mountains, and unpredictable Indian territory. He had come to marry the soon-to-be divorced Fanny Osbourne. John Lloyd and Timothy Rearden were quite curious to meet the struggling writer. Rearden traveled to Monterey and got acquainted with Stevenson after a long stroll on the beach. Afterwards at the Bohemian Club, Rearden told Sam Osbourne and John Lloyd that he had a favorable impression of him. At the end of December, Stevenson left Monterey for San Francisco for his much anticipated union.

Although Fanny was now divorced, the wedding would not take place until May. In the meantime, Stevenson moved into a boarding house on Bush Street and visited with Fanny when she crossed the bay from Oakland. Fanny introduced him to Virgil Williams, her artist friend and mentor, who maintained his art studio adjacent to the Bohemian Club over top of the California Market at 430 Pine Street. Virgil Williams was impressed with the Scotsman and they became quick friends. While Fanny was away in Oakland, Stevenson would visit Williams and then loiter about the Bohemian Club where he got to know John Lloyd and some of the other members. John Lloyd was certainly a frequent visitor. He shared a law office with Henry Hyde on California Street just two blocks from the Bohemian Club. What took place between the two is unrecorded.

Lloyd apparently had yet to extinguish his romantic interest in Fanny, even after seven years of marriage to Christina. After Fanny and Stevenson were married, John Lloyd revealed his jealous feelings when he expressed his criticism of Fanny's new mate. Not even Sam Osbourne, the ex-husband, recorded such sentiments.

Fanny never forgot her earlier relationship with Lloyd. She wrote to her friend Dora Williams after the earthquake and fire of 1906 inquiring after the welfare of the John Lloyds: send my "kindest regards to the Lloyds if you see them. I can feel nothing but kindness, when it comes to the bedrock, for any living soul."

When Robert Louis Stevenson visited the Bohemian Club there were a number of journalists and artists as members. They would certainly have been interested in the struggling and starving Bohemian from Scotland. When questioned of his past achievements he would have undoubtedly referred to his short stint at

The Monterey Californian which ended just weeks before. One of the last articles written by Stevenson was on December 23, 1879. It was a follow up article about buried treasure that he had written the week before. Stevenson reported that "The 'Buried Treasure' article that appeared in the *Californian* last week has been the topic since of no little conversation among many of our citizens." There was probably equal interest at the Bohemian Club. Did John Lloyd ever express any personal interest in the subject? If so, perhaps he had his own story to tell.

St. Kitts, July 2002

I was holding the Register of court documents at the archives at St. Kitts at Basseterre carefully turning the centuries-old, stained and discolored pages looking for reference to Owen Lloyd. I was there because I had just one clue for Owen Lloyd: he had married the daughter of a Colonel Caines from St. Kitts. I realized my hunt for Lloyd could begin and end right here.

When our family had decided to go back to the Virgin Islands and spend some time at Norman Island in July of 2002 we also decided that we would go to Antigua and St. Kitts after our week with Captain Dave on board *Antiquity*. I really wanted to see these islands and there was a possibility of doing some local research. I contacted Mrs. Victoria O'Flaherty at the archives in St. Kitts and told her of my planned visit. She said to ask for her on my arrival.

When Delphine and I landed at the St. Kitts airport we immediately noticed and appreciated the unique beauty of the island. I also noticed something else. In the airport, I saw a sign that said "Caines Car Rentals." I took this as a good omen that perhaps I might find something here after all. The cab driver delivered us to the Ocean Terrace Inn where we registered and went to our room. Delphine said she wanted to rest, so I grabbed my notebook and headed to downtown Basseterre to the St. Kitts Government Building which housed the archives.

As I went into the office, I thought to myself that since it was so small, there must not be much here and I probably wouldn't find anything. I had hoped for years that I might find out what happened to Owen Lloyd at this archive. I also hoped that I would have found him alive and well long after 1750. I knew that he had escaped from prison at St. Eustatius.

Mrs. O'Flaherty came out, I introduced myself, and she recollected my earlier

The Hunt for Lloyd

phone call. She asked what I was looking for and I told her I wanted anything on the Lloyd or Caines families from 1750. I felt certain that she would say something like "Oh, you must be looking for Owen Lloyd, the pirate who stole that treasure." But I got no such reaction. She said that there would certainly be something on Caines as they were a prominent and well-known family centuries ago. As for Lloyd, she said I would not find anything. She went into the vault and brought out the General Register book which mostly indexed land transactions and wills. The only seating was a small desk and chair located in the vestibule that is really an exterior courtyard and my only protection from the weather was the second floor walkway overhead. She wished me luck and she returned to her office. I was able to locate the year 1750 in short order and started looking for "Lloyd" and "Caines." Within minutes, I was up to 1752 where I saw two entries, both titled "Lloyd to Caines." I rushed back to Victoria's office, trying to remain calm. I told her what I had found. She returned with me to the book on my desk and I pointed to the reference. She frowned at this and said that that particular book was in very bad condition and was doubtful that it could be opened. I groaned with disappointment. I think she felt sorry for me coming all the way from North Carolina, so she went to the vault and retrieved the volume.

The covers appeared to be in good shape. They were held closed by a brass

ABOVE: This book contains Owen Lloyd's power of attorney to Thomas Caines found at St. Kitts. It was granted days after his escape from the fort at St. Eustatius. Note the brass reinforcing and clasp. Photo by the author.
RIGHT: Owen Lloyd's power of attorney to Thomas Caines. Courtesy National Archives of St. Kitts. Photo by the author.

clasp which she carefully released. She slowly opened the book and we found that all of the pages were dark brown with age and extremely fragile. All of the pages had also broken from the spine. The page numbers in the upper corner could be read so we carefully opened it to the exact page. Reading the text was somewhat difficult because of discoloration. The excitement was unbearable. I was sweating more than the outside temperature demanded. I read and made notes. There was a power of attorney from Captain Owen Lloyd dated February 5, 1751, to Thomas Caines, Charles' cousin. It was witnessed by an Abraham Pritchett—whom I did not know at the time—and an Isaac John Finch. The instrument was not recorded until May 9, 1752, and only Isaac Finch was present on that date to swear to its authenticity.

At first, I didn't understand what the power of attorney was for. Lloyd had authorized Thomas Caines to go about St. Kitts to collect any money that was due him. I knew he had escaped from St. Eustatius and this document proved that he stayed awhile at St. Kitts before fleeing to St. Thomas. The words of the document said more than their intent. It was clear that his wife's family had come to his aid. He needed cash to pay back the bribery money and to fund his escape to St. Thomas.

The other document was a release of his dower interests to his brother-in-law, Charles Caines. It looked like he was being disowned. In this document,

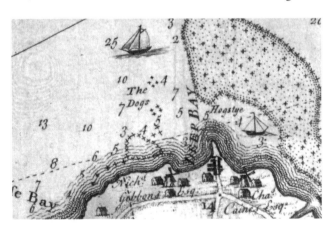

I found Owen's wife's name, Christian, who had gotten £1,100 current money of St. Kitts as well as two slaves, Mariana and Celia when her father died in 1737. She had inherited a small fortune. Her sister, Sarah, who had died

Dieppe Bay at the north end of St. Kitts. Note the plantation of Charles Caines to the right of town. To the left of town is the plantation of Nicholas Gibbons who was Owen Lloyd's former employer and owned the sloop when Owen Lloyd captured the French slave ship in 1745. From the map of Lt. Samuel Baker, RN, 1753. Courtesy of the National Archives of England.

before she was eighteen, had been promised £900 pounds and the slave "Arabelia," as well as "three new negroes out of the ship." Sarah's inheritance was to be divided between her mother, Christian, and Charles. Owen was releasing any right he might have as the survivor of Christian. This document was dated September 15, 1752, and was executed by power of attorney given Thomas Caines. Owen Lloyd was apparently still on the run.

I also located a reference to the will of Charles Caines, Sr., Christian's father, but it unfortunately turned up missing. I told Mrs. O'Flaherty that I was going to the Caines' estate the next day and she showed me a map of the island drawn in 1753 by Samuel Baker. It showed the Caines' plantation and even the windmill located on his property. She explained that the plantation was now in ruins and unoccupied. Before I left, she introduced me to Lindon Williams of the St. Christopher's Heritage Society who later proved to be very helpful in further research into the Caines plantation.

I returned to my hotel where I found Delphine waking up. She asked routinely if I had found anything interesting at the archive. When I explained to her what I had just seen she was incredulous. "Did you photograph the pages?" she asked. I told her that I had left the camera behind and no, I had not. She insisted I go back, so I called Mrs. O'Flaherty and asked permission to do it the next day, which she reluctantly agreed to do. "This is the last time I want to open that book!," she vowed.

The next morning, we hired a cab to tour the island. One of our stops was the fort at Brimstone Hill. This had to be the most impressive of all fortifications I had ever seen. It took a hundred years to complete starting in the 1690s. Although I was impressed with everything I saw, I could not get my mind off visiting the Caines plantation and getting back in the afternoon to photograph the book.

We arrived at the Caines Estate, as it is called today, to find many of the stone structures crumbled and falling down. The stone base of the windmill was intact, a vacant two story home of twentieth century origin stood at the end of the drive which was flanked by two stone gate columns. It was very simple, but at the same time, quite spectacular. There were other buildings there for the production of sugar and rum such as a boiling house, curing house, and caretaker's house—all in disrepair. But in spite of the disintegrating walls, the overgrowth of vegetation, and trash scattered about, it was easy to imagine this classic eighteenth century sugar plantation as it was two and a half centuries ago. I tried to picture Owen and

Christian walking about. Delphine and I stood on the black sand beach looking northwest over the Caribbean where we could plainly see Mt. Mazinga towering over St. Eustatius. It was easy to empathize with the anxiety Christian felt as she probably stood in this same spot centuries ago and looked at the island prison that held her husband. Their lives would never be the same again.

We later had lunch at the Turtle Beach Bar and Grille at the south end of the island. Just before getting to the bar we drove by the remains of the windmill marking one of the former plantations of Gilbert Fleming, Lt. Governor of the Leeward Islands in 1750. Besides getting a spectacular view of Nevis at Turtle Beach, you sometimes can see the wild monkeys coming by for a handout or jumping up on the bar to ask for a cup of water or a rum punch. The monkeys are friendly but you're not to touch them as they can inflict a vicious bite. Gilbert Fleming suffered such a bite in 1752. We saw Wilbur, the pet pig, rooting around. The food and the island atmosphere were memorable. Several years later, I learned that it was sold and torn down for a resort.

After lunch, Delphine and I arrived at the archives. When Mrs. O'Flaherty, betraying her own insistence that she would not do it again, brought out the book, Delphine reacted much the same way I did the day before. The clasp was again separated and the book opened. The appearance alone of the book told many stories. It had survived numerous hurricanes, fires, and wars over the last two hundred and fifty years and inside was Owen Lloyd's escape plan. We took the relevant photographs and resumed our experience of St. Kitts.

In late January 2002, Victoria Stapells, who in 1980 had worked so diligently for me in the archives of Spain while I was pursuing *La Galga*, made a great discovery of another bundle of documents at the Archivo General de Indias in Seville. This bundle labeled *"Consulados 861"* contained over four hundred pages of information on the events at Ocracoke, the theft of the treasure, and the aftermath. It was here that I learned that John Lloyd had been captured, but it was also documented that he and Fitz-Randolph escaped by wounding a Spanish guard before they were to be locked in the New Bern jail. After their struggle with the Spaniards, they then made their escape in a canoe. These documents also mentioned Owen bribing the guards at St. Eustatius and making his escape which I did know from my research in 1980. These documents, however, did not answer the questions that plagued me.

I resumed the hunt for Lloyd in California, not for Owen, but John Lloyd the Welshman miner. I enlisted the help of John Flora, of ancestryexperts.com who took the few clues that I had and was able to locate Fanny Stevenson's friend through census records and obituary notices. He produced the next clue that would take the hunt back across the Atlantic. According to his record at the crematorium, John Lloyd was born at the Isle of Man, a relatively small island off the west coast of Wales. The 1900 census for California disclosed that he had been born in June of 1838 and had immigrated in 1860 and was naturalized in 1868. John Lloyd had married a Swedish woman named Christina in 1873. The census record said his nativity was England, not the Isle of Man. At the Isle of Man, Carol Carine resumed the search but she could find no match among the few Lloyd families at the Isle of Man. The trail went dead here. The passenger lists from England did not record his entry into New York, Philadelphia or New Orleans. He most likely went straight to Panama, crossed the isthmus, and took a steamer to San Francisco, but there was no record that would confirm it. The census of 1841 and 1851 did not show Lloyd or his parents at the Isle of Man and in Wales and England there was a maze of John Lloyds. The name Lloyd is as frequent there as Smith is in the United States. It seemed I had jumped into the proverbial haystack.

Spain and England looked to be the chief repositories of documents that would relate to the 1750 event. I needed a researcher in London and contacted Simon Niziol to research the records at the National Archives in Kew and the National Maritime Museum in Greenwich. Taking the hint from *Treasure Island* that Long John Silver lost his leg under Admiral Hawke in the British navy, I had Simon begin by looking for a John Lloyd in the British admiralty records. I had found a Captain John Lloyd of HMS *Glasgow* who in 1748 brought the news of the end of the war to Virginia. Simon was able to dismiss him soon enough, but that clue led him into the admiralty records related to the Greenwich Naval Hospital in search of a missing leg that once belonged to a John Lloyd.

Simon Niziol's search in the records of the Greenwich Naval Hospital opened a large door in the investigation. He located an application for admission to the hospital, now the museum, filed March 29, 1753, by a midshipman named John Lloyd. This John Lloyd had only one leg. This of course created a lot of excitement, but as Simon cautioned, we had no proof that it was our John Lloyd. We would have to keep digging.

Before long, Simon discovered another clue. In August, Simon emailed and said that there was more on the one-legged Lloyd. John Lloyd had checked into Greenwich Hospital on April 11, 1753 and never left. He was "discharged dead" in 1761. But he left behind some valuable clues. The records stated he was born in Wales, was forty-five years old, and last served on the *Happy*, a vessel classified as a snow. He was married and said he last lived with "Cap'n Lloyd." Another notation said he had lost his left leg. In the margin was written "privateer." It was obvious that it referred to a previous injury as the war had ended in 1748 and privateering had ceased at that time.

Using my microfilm copies of the *New York Gazette, Maryland Gazette, Boston News Letter*, and the *South Carolina Gazette*, I searched for a snow named *Happy* but I had no luck. However, I did start to find references to a merchant captain with the name of Lloyd sailing between Boston, North Carolina, and St. Kitts. The *Boston News Letter* did not reveal his first name or his vessel's name for the entries in 1743 and 1744. I searched for the port records of Boston but it was in vain: records for this time period did not survive. However, the port records did survive for Hampton, Virginia, New York, New Jersey, and other ports. I had read from a note in the *Maryland Gazette* that a Captain Lloyd had come into Virginia from Jamaica in early 1748. Copies of the *Virginia Gazette* were not available from 1747 to the end of 1750 as they did not survive or the paper was interrupted so I could not check there.

I had picked up the trail but I needed more. There were more countries which could contain documents. Demark owned St. Thomas in the eighteenth century and St. Eustatius is still part of the Netherlands today.

I emailed the National Archives of the Netherlands at The Hague and asked them if they had any 1750 documents related to St. Eustatius. They got back to me right away and said that the government records for St. Eustatius started in 1781. Earlier records had been destroyed by the devastating hurricane of 1772 and later by the British in 1781. I learned that some of these valuable documents were actually used as toilet paper by the British occupiers. This was a disappointment but not a surprise. Next stop: Denmark.

I contacted Peter Phister in Copenhagen to translate some Danish documents that I located in our National Archives. These documents were acquired when the United States bought St. Thomas, St. John, and St. Croix from Denmark in 1917.

The Hunt for Lloyd

From my research in Spain and England I knew that the last known location for Owen Lloyd was St. Thomas in 1751, so the archives of Denmark would hopefully give some more clues. The website for the Danish Archives was helpful, so I sent Peter the documents I had and a list of targets and instructions.

In early October, I started thinking again about St. Eustatius and how unfortunate that the records had been destroyed there. *There?* The records were destroyed *there,* not in the Netherlands. I realized that correspondence from *there* to the homeland could have survived. On October 10, I emailed Nicole Brandt at the Nationaal Archief and asked her to look specifically for correspondence *from* the colony and any maps and plans of the island. On October 29, I received an email from Victor van den Bergh of the archive. He said that they did, in fact, have correspondence from St. Eustatius as I had asked and it contained information on Owen Lloyd and Zebulon Wade and the stolen treasure. He also had some maps and plans of St. Eustatius and Fortress Oranje that I would be interested in. Two days later, he emailed again to say he had located ninety pages in all. He would translate the Lloyd and Wade depositions. The other documents would have to be done by a translator because he could not get to them. The remaining documents included the depositions of Abraham Pritchett, James McMahan, and Thomas Hobson, the cabin boy, and records of The States General which reviewed the conduct of Governor Heyliger.

With these documents, I was able to determine the names of every crewman aboard the *Seaflower* when she fled Ocracoke with the treasure. This would be the only place in four countries that these names were recorded. Being a resident of North Carolina, I was pleased to discover names of North Carolinians involved in the event: Abraham Pritchett, Thomas Hobson, and the one-eyed Scotsman, William Blackstock. These depositions also described where the other men were from which would later prove to be valuable in locating more clues. Other documents described in detail the escape from the fort. I had never imagined that such a find would be made! This discovery was a major turning point in the "hunt for Lloyd." These documents contained the keys that would unlock doors that would lead me to finally meet Owen Lloyd. It seems that Victor van den Bergh was as excited as I was for when he was finished, his email message exclaimed "It has been a pleasure to look for documents to illustrate this nice story that fits so well in the Caribbean atmosphere." The remaining translations were done by Anne Lee of europeantranslation.net in London England.

First page of the interrogation of Owen Lloyd while prisoner at St. Eustatius. Courtesy of the Naational Archief, The Netherlands.

Owen Lloyd's deposition gave more clues that would help tie the John Lloyd at Greenwich to being his brother. Owen Lloyd testified as having been born in the month of May in Wales and his age was "thirty" in November 1750. He said he last lived in Virginia. I had already found that John and Owen were brothers from William Blackstock's deposition. The Spaniards called John Lloyd the father of Owen Lloyd. This I attribute to the language differences. But it seemed to clear up the question as to who was older and now I was a step closer in tying the two Welshmen with John Lloyd the reputed lover of Fanny Stevenson.

The port records for Hampton, Virginia, are preserved in the National Archives in London. The Collector of Customs was located at Hampton, not Norfolk, and was responsible for all commercial shipping in the lower James River. I had Simon check them for a Captain Lloyd returning from Jamaica in 1748. In December, he emailed back that the records for early 1748 did not survive but he had made a great discovery anyway. He went back several years and found Owen Lloyd coming into Hampton on the sloop *Elizabeth* which was built in New England in 1743 and owned by Owen Lloyd and Company of St. Kitts. The fact that Lloyd's sloop was New England built pointed to the likelihood that the *Boston News Letter* had in fact described Owen Lloyd's activities during 1743 and 1744.

Now that I had established the connection between Owen Lloyd and Virginia, I resumed my searches in the *Virginia Gazette* and the port records of Hampton on microfilm at the John D. Rockefeller Library in Williamsburg. I not only located more information on Owen Lloyd but found numerous references to a snow called the *Happy*. She traded routinely between the Upper James River and Whitehaven, England. Learning this was another step, I thought, toward connecting Owen and the John Lloyd at the Greenwich Hospital. I even found a reference to the *Happy* being involved with a Spanish register ship which I believed was the incident where John lost his leg. Seven years later I would find that this *Happy* was merely a red herring.

In early February 2004, I made a routine research trip to Norfolk and went to the local history room at the Kirn Memorial Library. While there, I noticed that they had microfilm copies of Norfolk County court records which included wills and deeds for the mid-eighteenth century. I thought it might be worthwhile to look for Lloyd in these records even though I assumed that Owen Lloyd probably was not a property owner in Virginia, especially since his wife Christian was from

St. Kitts.

After threading the microfilm onto the machine, I went to the index at the beginning. Scanning the index, I found several references of "Lloyd to Hutchings." By this point I knew that John Hutchings was Lloyd's employer, so I was certain that I had located more on the right Owen Lloyd. My assumptions proved correct, but it was not a deed for real estate. There were two mortgages recorded in favor of Hutchings. One mortgage dated July 3, 1747, was secured by eighteen slaves who were enumerated in the document by Owen Lloyd. They were probably part of the twenty-four slaves listed in the customs records for his trip from St. Kitts in 1746. The second mortgage document, dated November 2, 1747, was from Christian Lloyd, acting as attorney for Owen, which mortgaged their home furnishings and personal possessions to Hutchings. The security appeared to have been given for money already received by Owen Lloyd. This was done while Owen had skippered Hutchings' ship, the *Rawleigh*, to Jamaica. Owen and Christian were identified as residents of the "Burrough of Norfolk." It appeared that Lloyd desperately needed money, most likely to bail out his brother. This was before he stole the treasure and got himself in trouble. There was still more. On April 2, 1748, the mortgage was extended and increased probably to cover accrued interest. Lloyd now owed £572, sixteen shillings, and three pence. The mortgage was recorded November 17, 1748, and Lloyd was not present to acknowledge it.

On May 9, 1750, Lloyd signed a final release of his security over to John Hutchings. I also found a release of a secured slave named Maria and her four children on this same day to Captain Maisterson of HMS *Hector* and statements about Lloyd having been apprehended by Maisterson and confined on board the *Hector*. (The *Hector's* log, which I later examined, does not mention this.) This document also identified Lloyd as a resident at that time of Elizabeth City County where Hampton, Virginia, is located just across the water from Norfolk. His residence at that moment was the county jail. Sheriff Armistead was holding him for multiple reasons. He not only was being held until John Hutchings could arrive to get Lloyd to sign a release on his mortgaged slaves, but a Mary Brodie had also filed suit against him. Hutchings then signed a bond for Lloyd in the amount of £250 on May 10 at Norfolk.

The following document was actually a letter written by Owen Lloyd on May 11, 1750, from the jail in Hampton and for some unknown reason recorded with the deeds:

The Hunt for Lloyd

> To John Hutchings, Esq., Norfolk:
>
> Sir I have sent over your bond and hope you will send the Negroes by the Bearer, my wife tells me that you seem to promise her some Favours if she would come over to Norfolk, she doesn't care to work on Account of Arabella and her children Crying about her which would give her a great deal of uneasiness. You have several small trifles that will be of little service to you and would at present be of great service to us. I leave it lay and owe Honour what you please to send us, soon after you walked out of Goal I was arrested on account of Pettit and am told there is two writs taken out by Johnston for his Servant which is to be served tomorrow. I am totally ruined, what to do I know not. Captain Armistead is very strict and hard with me. If you can help doing anything I shall acknowledge your Favours and am Sir you're your Distressed and Unfortunate Humble Servant, Owen Lloyd
>
> Hampton Goal
> May 11, 1750

John Hutchings was not only a prosperous merchant but he was three times a mayor of Norfolk and served in the House of Burgesses from 1738 to 1756. Lloyd worked for a very powerful man. Thanks to his intercession, Lloyd was released and it probably explains why the letter was recorded.

These documents were recorded in Norfolk on August 27, just before the hurricane would reach Norfolk and the Lloyd brothers were preparing to leave for St. Kitts. And there I saw a familiar name: the slave woman, Arabella. I had seen her name in the St. Kitts documents.

I had never seen an entry like this filed with wills and deeds. Having examined thousands of deeds located in different counties and states over the years, I was totally surprised. These documents identified Owen Lloyd as now a resident of Hampton. With this new discovery, I knew that I was closing in on Lloyd. The message to John Hutchings said one thing, but to me it was a message that meant something else:

251

> *To John:*
> *I know you are looking for me. Follow these clues that I have left for you, you are going to find what you need to know.*
>
> *Owen*

I then discovered a roll of film in the drawer entitled "Marriage Bonds 1708-1752." I threaded it on the machine and started scanning. I was still guessing that Owen Lloyd had married in St. Kitts and there would be nothing there. For him there was not. But there was a marriage license for John Lloyd to marry an Elizabeth Hall. It was signed by John Lloyd but the space for Elizabeth was blank. It was dated February 17, 1750. Days later, I traveled to the courthouse at Hampton to see the Elizabeth City County records. The deeds were not indexed so I had to wade through many pages of old script, but I found a deed to Owen Lloyd dated June 7, 1749, from a Charles White for a lot and buildings inside the town of Hampton. There was no lot number given, but by the description of the lot, I was able to ascertain that he was near the west end of Queen Street on the north side and quite close to St. John's Episcopal Church which was the Anglican parish church in Lloyd's day.

In the records of wills at Norfolk, I found that John Lloyd had witnessed the deathbed testament of a John Drury on March 2, 1751. This was confusing to me. It seemed so unlikely that he would show himself in public after his narrow escape from his Spanish guards at Ocracoke. It appeared that there might be more than one John Lloyd in Norfolk. The proof I needed was just pages away. While searching the Court Orders for 1751, I found an entry dated for the court session of January 28, 1751:

> John Lloyd against Don Pedro Rodriguiz in trespass, the Sheriff having returned not to be found is dismissed.

Pedro Rodriguiz had been sent back to Spain aboard the *Jubilee*. To clear his name, John Lloyd had gone on the offense and filed a suit against Bonilla's boatswain, an act that seemed to take incredible nerve and arrogance on the part of John Lloyd. This not only proved that this was *the* John Lloyd, but also it said a lot about the attitude of the English towards the Spanish at that time. John Lloyd appeared to be a free man while his brother was waiting to be hung at St. Eustatius. But then Owen had actually succeeded in stealing the Spanish treasure.

On March 5, 1751, John Lloyd and his wife Elizabeth sold their tenement located on the west side of Church Street in Norfolk situated between William Nimmo, a prominent lawyer, and Francis Dyson, to a William Freeman. This was probably between St. Paul's Church and City Hall Avenue today. Elizabeth Lloyd's signature was substituted with her mark, "X" indicting that John Lloyd had married an illiterate lower class woman. It is most likely that Owen Lloyd lived here as well up until he married in 1746.

There was one last discovery in the court records: John Lloyd served on a jury as late as August 17, 1751, in a case of trespass. This was my last reference to John Lloyd in Norfolk. It appeared that the trail had gone cold. The next time he appeared was two years later at Greenwich Hospital. Those records said he had last lived with "Cap'n Lloyd." Unfortunately, it did not say where. I turned again to my European researchers for help.

Part of my research was to scour all of the colonial newspapers looking for clues. It was a tedious process. One item I found was a list of captures made by the Spanish during the year 1747. An entry said that a Captain Lloyd, with a cargo of Madeira wine, had been captured and taken to Havana. On October 8, 2003, Victoria Stapells emailed me with the news that she had found record of John Lloyd's capture on the *Elizabeth*. She said that the tip from me about a cargo of Madeira wine had made it certain. She had located a list of prizes captured by the *Nuestra Señora del Carmen*, Captain Don Pedro Garaicochea, from April 10 to July 20, 1747, between Bermuda and the coast of Virginia. So now we knew that John Lloyd had the distinction of being captured by probably the greatest Spanish privateer of the war and taken to Havana! Even if the *Elizabeth* had been armed, she was no match for Garaicochea's thirty-six guns. Another chance discovery I would make would not only put the icing on the cake but gave me a clue to the identity of the sloop that Owen and John would sail on in September of 1750. After John Lloyd took command of the *Elizabeth*, he signed an agreement with Alexander MacKenzie of Hampton to ship grain to Madeira—"as much as the vessel can receive"—and return from Madeira with seventy pipes of wine or a greater number if possible. For some reason John Lloyd decided to have the agreement recorded at the courthouse. A hundred years ago, someone had come across a few stray pages of eighteenth century documents at the courthouse. There were six pages in all. Included in the discovery was the shipping contract between John Lloyd and MacKenzie. These six pages were published in the *William and Mary Quarterly* in 1912 and then listed in a master index of various historical publications. If not for this index, the discovery and publication of the contract, and John Lloyd's insistence that it be recorded, I would not have been able to establish why the cannon had been removed from the *Elizabeth*, but most important, it provided a direct clue to the identity of the sloop that carried the Lloyds to their fateful encounter with Bonilla at Ocracoke. In the shipping records for Hampton, Virginia, recorded by Wilson Cary, was an entry for a small sloop called the *Hannah* which was owned by MacKenzie and had left immediately after the hurricane for Montserrat, an island near St. Kitts. The shipping contract not only proved a relationship between MacKenzie and Lloyd but that they also had both suffered a loss by the Spanish privateer Don Pedro Garaicochea. The shipping contract also told me that his sloop was named after his wife because Hannah MacKenzie witnessed the contract between John Lloyd and her husband. The *Hannah* was thirteen years old and reaching the end of her useful life when she sprung a leak and then sank at Ocracoke. The port records for Hampton showed that she never returned. Had they travelled on a more seaworthy vessel they wouldn't have arrived at Ocracoke, encountered the *Guadalupe*, and absconded with Bonilla's treasure. The *Hannah* had now secured her place in history.

Finding Owen's brother John in the Havana prison put some other facts into a clearer perspective. Owen Lloyd had cleared Jamaica in the *Rawleigh* for Virginia on November 4, 1747. The Virginia port records and the *Virginia Gazette* did not survive for this time period but the *Maryland Gazette* of February 24, 1748, featured news from Williamsburg dated February 4 that Captain Lloyd had "lately arrived from Jamaica" and brought news of Garaicochea fitting out his privateers and that he was destined for the Virginia Capes by the end of March. His account seemed first hand as if Owen Lloyd had been to Havana. It also appeared that his return voyage from Jamaica took unusually long which is further evidence that he detoured to Havana under a flag of truce before returning home. This evidence also explained the mortgages of Lloyd's furniture and slaves. He needed the money to bail out his brother. The Jamaica records said he left in ballast and had no cargo at risk. It was upon his return to Hampton that his legal problems seemed to begin.

In November, 2002, Peter Phister in Denmark had found a cryptic note on Lloyd at St. Thomas. The record described an "Owen Layd" and his wife renting a house in St. Thomas from a Jean Malleville in 1751. He was able to determine

Part of the accounting of the auction of the *Seaflower* and her contents in February of 1751 by Governor Christian Suhm at St. Thomas. Note that the sloop of Zebulon Wade is now called the *Elizabeth*. No doubt that Owen Lloyd renamed the *Seaflower* to not only avoid detection but to perfect his revenge against the Spaniards for the seizure of his own sloop in 1747, also named the *Elizabeth*. This English translation was given to John Watson in July of 1751 by Governor Suhm. It was later filed by representatives of Juan Manuel Bonilla in his case against the Danish Crown. Courtesy of the Statens Arkiver Rigsarkavit, Denmark.

A page from the expense account of Juan Manuel Bonilla while he was in Hampton Roads, Virginia, repairing his galleon and coordinating the recovery of his treasure in the Caribbean. Note the expenses in Hampton at Mrs. Hawkins' tavern and the inn of Janet Wheeler. In Suffolk he incurred expenses at the inn of Mathias Jones and his clothes were washed by Sarah Johns, a woman whose name was lost to history until this document was discovered in Denmark. Courtesy of the Statens Arkiver Rigsarkavit, Denmark.

that the Malleville family owned two plantations on the island and a house in town. Governor Christian Suhm was married to Maria Malleville. The records of 1754, however, no longer mentioned Lloyd. I told Peter to expand his search in time and types of records. He did, but for months he continued to report no results.

On November 24, 2003, Peter sent me "Great News" as the subject of his email predicted. His message, colored with his Danish accent, began:

> Hi John, after all these failure, have I very good news to you. I think, that I have found all, what you want and

more. Names like Owen Lloyd, Zebulon Wade, Gilbert Fleming, Suhm, Juan Manuel Bonilla, John Watson and others turned up.

His discovery was found in the section, *Chamber of Customs 1760-1848*. It was truly a great find and indeed great news. It included mostly documents from 1750-1753. At least some of the documents had been saved from the shipwreck of the *Princesse Wilhelmine Caroline* whose captain, Nicolai Hoyer, saved and delivered them to Denmark in December of 1752. These documents had been filed here because the dispute between Bonilla and his heirs and Denmark over the money retained by Christian Suhm, the errant governor of St. Thomas, was not settled until 1764. There was correspondence from Suhm, Lt. General Gilbert Fleming of the Leewards; a transcript of proceedings at Tortola about additional recoveries of treasure; detailed expense accounts of Alexander Cairnes and John Watson in Virginia as they acted as agents for Bonilla; and detailed expenses of John Watson's trip to the West Indies as he traveled to St. Kitts, Antigua, Montserrat, St. Thomas, St. Croix, and Tortola in search of Bonilla's treasure. There were also copies of records of the auction of the *Seaflower* at St. Thomas and powers of attorney recorded at St. Kitts and Antigua. Some of the documents still had the wax seals, although broken. It was truly a gold mine, but it did nothing to further the outcome of Owen Lloyd, except to say that Governor Suhm had been protecting him.

In Spain, Victoria was finding more documents on the aftermath of the treasure and about relations and correspondence with Denmark, England, and the Netherlands. They portrayed what an international controversy Lloyd had created. This discovery, in turn, prompted more searches in The Netherlands and Denmark where the diplomatic and heads of state sections yielded even more details of Bonilla's relentless pursuit of his stolen cargo. But there was still no mention of Lloyd after 1751.

I then pursued the names of the rest of the *Seaflower* crew in the hopes of a new lead. It seemed that no one died as a result of their misadventure. But still, no mention of Owen Lloyd.

Owen Lloyd's deposition at St. Eustatius described William Blackstock as being from North Carolina. When I searched the familysearch.org website for Blackstock in North Carolina, I found a John Blackstock born in 1751 in

Pasquotank County. This interested me since the county seat was Elizabeth City, only forty-five minutes from home. I thought it might be worthwhile to go to the courthouse and take a look.

I searched the land records and found several transactions of land conveyed to William Blackstock. The first referred to him as a "trader." This was in 1757. Other transactions called him a "planter." The evidence was still inconclusive that this Blackstock was "the one-eyed Scotsman;" however, the fact that his son was born in 1751 in North Carolina suggested that he not only was in North Carolina in 1750 but this was indeed the one-eyed nemesis of Owen Lloyd. More records showed that he kept a tavern at his house in 1761 and died the next year leaving John an orphan.

I started to leave the courthouse but my instinct said *look for Lloyd* which I did. I found that on May 2, 1750, a John Lloyd had purchased 150 acres on the west side of Arenuse Creek on the Pasquotank River opposite Elizabeth City. *But was this the same John Lloyd?* The answer came quickly. This same Lloyd then sold the land on August 18, 1752, two years to the day the Spanish fleet left Havana, which was recorded November 29, 1753. In the deed were two startling revelations. The first was that John Lloyd was described as a captain formerly of Norfolk, Virginia. The second and most important, was this statement:

> The true intent that James Montier do pay and cause to be paid twenty pounds lawful money of Great Britain in the hands of Mr. George Keith merchant in London at or upon the arrival of the aforesaid John Lloyd in London and within eighteen months from date hereof then this indenture to be void but if fault be made in payment of twenty pounds to the said Lloyd when he arrives in London…

This priceless tidbit now placed John Lloyd in London in proximity to the time of the one-legged John Lloyd checking into the Naval Hospital in Greenwich in April 1753. Once again, I discovered language in a deed that would ordinarily not be found in such an instrument. That might be incredible enough, but when I left the courthouse, the historical marker outside told the rest of the story. The records that I had just seen had been saved in a barn during the Civil War when the Federal troops invaded Elizabeth City and burned the courthouse in 1862. Had these records not survived, this invaluable link that bridged the gap between records found in London and those in Virginia would never have been found. *You are going to find what you need to know.*

On June 13, 1946, Merritt and Goldie Hooper purchased a tract of land on the west side and at the mouth of Arenuse Creek, the same land that John Lloyd owned two centuries before. They subdivided the land and called it "Treasure Point" as it is known today. This is truly a remarkable coincidence as there are no American records which associate John Lloyd with the theft of treasure at Ocracoke. There was no way for the Hoopers to have known.

The clue left by John Lloyd in the Greenwich Hospital records seemed to give the next location for the whereabouts of Owen Lloyd. He said he last lived with "Cap'n Lloyd." But this could be most anywhere—St. Kitts, St. Thomas, St. Croix, England, or Wales. There was no record of Owen Lloyd at St. Thomas after 1751. I was not much closer to solving that mystery of Lloyd's ultimate fate.

In the summer of 2003, my hunt for Lloyd in the archives was put on hold. I was going to resume the hunt at St. Kitts. From St. Kitts we were going to St. Eustatius, and from there to Norman Island, where we would again sail aboard *Antiquity* with Captain Dave.

After landing in St. Kitts, we returned to the Ocean Terrace Inn at Basseterre. We revisited the Caines' plantation for a closer look and more pictures. We now had a complete description of the ruins and the building

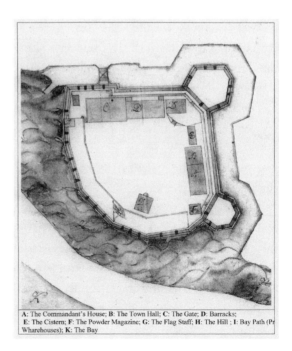

Diagram of Fortress Orange at St. Eustatius around the time of Owen Lloyd's capture and imprisonment. Courtesy of the Nationaal Archief, The Netherlands.

A: The Commandant's House; B: The Town Hall; C: The Gate; D: Barracks; E: The Cistern; F: The Powder Magazine; G: The Flag Staff; H: The Hill ; I: Bay Path (Pr Wharehouses); K: The Bay

functions that had been provided to me by Lindon Williams of the St. Christopher's Heritage Society. We inspected the ruins containing the "coppers," the large iron boiling pots that were used to process the sugar. We got inside the caretaker's house that showed evidence of some modern renovation. The most intact structure was the windmill which I entered and photographed. I had read that when these mills were being operated by slaves, an ax was kept nearby in case an arm got into the millworks—there was no stopping the mill. A grim thought indeed.

For the trip to St. Eustatius, which was only nine miles from the Caines Estate by water, I chose to fly; it seemed the only way we were guaranteed to get there. We had to fly to St. Martin's first, and then over to Statia, as it is popularly called, since we were entering a Dutch possession. The kids did not like this inconvenience but they soon forgot all about that when we donned our snorkeling gear and explored the submerged ruins in the harbor that lay directly in front of Fort Oranje. The fort sits atop a steep cliff providing a commanding view of the Caribbean.

Besides the stone foundations of the eighteenth century warehouses we saw the remains of the old stone sea wall built in 1828 and several old anchors and a small cannon lying on the bottom.

Now that the kids were sufficiently engaged, we set off for the fort, climbing the steep walkway up the hill known as the "Slave Path" as it was said to be an escape route from town. By its location it was probably used by everyone as it was the closest route from the town and fort on the hill to the docks, warehouses, and shops that lined the waterfront. It was quite a climb but we soon arrived at the fort entrance. We could see the moat with a small bridge over it that we followed on into the inside of the perimeter. Luckily, it being summer, there were no other tourists inside.

Fortress Oranje was first built by the French in 1629 as first occupiers of the island. It was a small fort which was left abandoned several years later. In 1639, the Dutch took possession and rebuilt and enlarged it. Between this time and 1750, the flag had changed fourteen times, with the French and English managing some short occupations. St. Eustatius became a center of trade between Europe and North America and was a thriving commercial hub. Tobacco, cotton, and coffee had been the chief produce of the island until about 1740. After this, Statia became a great trading center and sugar and rum from the neighboring islands would pass through here. The harbor would be filled with ships from all over the Caribbean, Europe, and the North American colonies. It was here that Owen Lloyd and crew thought that they could "blend in" and hide their true identities. But some of them started spending like drunken sailors which alerted Governor Heyliger that Owen Lloyd was anchored in the harbor.

Having the complete story of Lloyd's escape loaded into my memory and a contemporary plan of the fort provided me by Victor van den Bergh, I strolled the inside perimeter and was able to match most of the existing structures with the old plan. There were the Constable's Quarters at the gate above the jail, barracks buildings, the cistern, and the flag pole. I was trying to figure out which wall Lloyd and the others must have gone over. The English records had described Lloyd as having been locked in the cistern. I always wondered about this. It did not seem to make sense since they still needed to store water. Besides, I wondered, how did they get him in and out of a watertight structure. The Dutch document referred to Lloyd being in a room with a locked door. This could not be the cistern. However, the Dutch word for "barracks" was "ciseren" which was clearly labeled on the fort plan. There were several barracks buildings (labeled "D" in the diagram). One barracks building in the upper right had changed. The old original structure was probably wood as a new and different configured building was there today. Its construction date was indicated as 1899 and it had been used as a prison. In the description of the escape,

Copy of the power of attorney granted by Juan Manuel Bonilla to John Watson to enable him to recover any treasure found there. It was supposedly recorded at the courthouse in Antigua. No record of it can be found there today. Its counterpart at St. Kitts is missing as well. Courtesy of the Statens Arkiver Rigsarkavit, Denmark.

the records mention a rampart that must have been very close to the prison room. It seems most likely that Owen Lloyd, Zebulon Wade, and the others were held in a building at this spot. The south and east walls were most likely the ones they went over since the north and west exposures dropped off at the cliff. Had they gone over these walls, they would have had to skirt the narrow perimeter of the fort and would have risked being seen by the other guards. The entrance to the fort was on the east side which could have been used if it was unguarded by the sentry. The most likely place was the southerly wall, an easy drop to the ground. Then, as I speculated, they would have quickly gained the road out of town before heading south along the coast. The only other way out would have been a direct route down the "slave path" to the harbor. I ruled this out, however, since it would have been risky for Lloyd and his gang; also, if something had gone wrong, his accomplices who were waiting with the boat would have been discovered as well. It seemed likely that his rescuers would not have risked coming into the harbor in the presence of all of the other vessels. The issue of getting underway in an uncertain wind would also have been considered. The records did not say what they did after they left the fort since they made a clean getaway.

At the end of the day we flew back to St. Martin and from there to St. Kitts. The next stop was Norman Island.

After the summer ended in 2004, we began looking forward to the Christmas season but the kids had made plans of their own. Delphine and I decided that we should go some place warm. We both arrived at the idea of returning to St. Kitts. That island was becoming more and more like home, so we booked ten days at the Ocean Terrace Inn starting December 17. We also decided that an overnight trip to Antigua to stay at the Admiral's Inn at the southern end of the island would add to the adventure. Situated in Nelson's Dockyard surrounded by eighteenth century buildings which formerly housed the British Navy, the inn itself is a converted storage building and engineer's quarters from the days of Admiral Nelson. Besides picture taking in the islands, my goal was to verify that the archives of both islands had a copy of the power of attorney and inventory of the stolen treasure that Peter found in Denmark. These documents were certified as recorded in the courthouses of St. Kitts and Antigua when John Watson arrived there in April of 1751.

On Monday after landing, we took a taxi to downtown St. John's. Our first stop was to visit the Antigua and Barbuda Museum. The building was the

Veracruz, Mexico

The *Nuestra Señora de Guadalupe,* the galleon of Juan Manuel Bonilla, was loaded with treasure at Veracruz, Mexico, in the spring of 1750. Some of her treasure would be buried on a deserted island in the Caribbean.

TOP LEFT: The fort of San Juan de Ulúa as seen from the town of Veracruz. Photo courtesy of Wikimedia Commons. TOP RIGHT: The landing where the galleons could tie up and enter the gate of the fort. Note the mooring rings. Photo by the author.
MIDDLE RIGHT: The author poses with a mooring ring with date 1734. Bonilla's galleon could have tied up here. Photo by park service employee. BOTTOM LEFT: The only remaining section of the wall around Veracruz. BOTTOM RIGHT: Inside the fort you can see the treasure rooms or warehouse where billions of treasures were once stored. Photo by the author.

263

Veracruz

TOP LEFT: The watchtower of the governor's house as seen from the central plaza of Veracruz. The tower enabled the governor to keep a watchful eye on the galleons in the harbor. TOP RIGHT: The Iglesia Mayor, or cathedral, that borders the plaza. MIDDLE RIGHT: The Convento de San Francisco, now a Holiday Inn, is where Father Junípero Serra would have stayed after the *Nuestra Señora de Guadalupe* was saved from certain doom by the prayers of Father Serra and the other priests on the feast day of St. Barbara. Part of this book was written here while the author and his wife visited Veracruz. BOTTOM RIGHT: The inside courtyard of the governor's house and town council building.

Havana, Cuba

TOP: The Governor's castle in Havana. This is where John Lloyd and other prisoners were held in 1747 during King George's War and often in peacetime when the Spaniards could get away with it. Photo courtesy of Wikimedia Commons. BOTTOM: Morro Castle and the entrance to Havana harbor. On August 18, 1750, *Nuestra Señora de Guadalupe* and the other ships of the fleet sailed through this gateway. Photo by Richard Johnston.

Hampton Roads, Virginia

Norfolk. When Owen and John Lloyd were married here, the church was known as the Borough Church. The church was built in 1739 and her interior was burned out when the British leveled Norfolk in 1776 during the American Revolution. It was later christened St. Paul's in 1832. Photos by the author.

Hampton. LEFT: On Queen Street opposite the location of Owen Lloyd's former house. Behind the trees is St. John's Episcopal Church, which was built in 1728. Christian Lloyd would have been a regular worshiper here while Owen was at sea. MIDDLE LEFT: The town wharf at the foot of King Street. Photo taken from in front of what used to be Mrs. Hawkin's Tavern. On a hot summer evening you might still see Owen Lloyd and his peg-legged brother making their way to the tavern for a "noggin of rum." Photos by the author.

Suffolk. BOTTOM LEFT: On July 30, 1751 the *Nuestra Señora de Guadalupe* arrived at customs in Hampton from Ocracoke, NC. She was then towed to Suffolk on the Nansemond River and berthed at the wharf at the foot of Main Street. She remained here under the supervision of David Meade, whose plantation adjoined left, until December 20, 1752, when she was escorted back to Cádiz, Spain, by HMS *Triton*. Before the *Guadalupe* had arrived, some of the Spaniards stayed at the inn of Mathias Jones up the hill. Photo by the author.

Ocracoke, North Carolina

Ocracoke Inlet lies nineteen miles east of the mainland. Bonilla described the inlet in 1750: "The Road is made by several Sand Hills and Banks and several stony Banks that come out of the Sea." It took Owen Lloyd three days to tow the *Guadalupe* into the inlet. Bonilla later regretted his help. Photo by author.

Bonilla took his treasure to the house of John Oliver, "there being no other House on these desert places." *"Some Englishmen rushed in one night and took from the guardroom some Firearms but could do nothing on Account of the resistance made."* ABOVE: The author holds a very old brick found among some of more recent origin that probably came from John Oliver's house. Photo by Jim Breashears. RIGHT: Nearby well which dates to early eighteenth century located on Springer's Point. Photo by author.

Springer's Point, Ocracoke Island.

TOP LEFT: Springer's Point and Teach's Hole. This is where John Oliver, the harbor pilot, lived and also where Juan Manuel Bonilla, Owen Lloyd, and Blackbeard roamed about. Today, it is a nature preserve owned by the North Carolina Land Trust. NEXT DOWN: The entrance to Old Slough. The *Nuestra Señora de Guadalupe* would have anchored nearby. This picture was taken at 2 p.m. on October 20, the exact time that the *Seaflower* unmoored and Owen Lloyd escaped with fifty chests of pieces of eight. The preserve has a number of live oaks and cedar trees that most likely date to 1750. There are beautiful walking trails that take you beneath gnarled old oaks to the sandy beach that overlooks Teach's Hole. Photos by the author.

St. Kitts

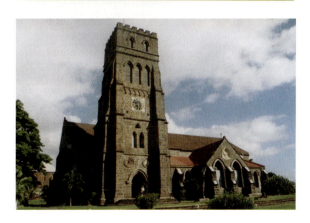

Besides being the central location for the treasure drama in the Caribbean, St. Kitts is an unspoiled tourist destination today. TOP: Sunset Beach. The Island of Nevis can be seen in distant background. MIDDLE LEFT: View of St. Eustatius from the fort at top of Brimstone Hill. BOTTOM: St. Georges's church. It was here that Alan Stevenson, the great grandfather of Robert Louis Stevenson was buried. Also buried here is Elizabeth Lloyd. Photos by the author.

Shadwell House, St. Kitts

This was the home of Lieutenant General Gilbert Fleming, second in command of the Leeward Islands. Many of the operatives in the treasure drama would have come for the formal dinners frequently held here: Charles Caines, Owen Lloyd's brother-in-law, was a member of the assembly in 1750; the Phipps brothers were members of the assembly and owners of Norman Island; James Purcell was Deputy Governor of the British Virgin Islands and a plantation owner of St. Kitts; his brother John Purcell succeeded him in 1751 and was later owner of Norman Island; John Baker was Solicitor General of the Leeward Islands and a resident of St. Kitts. Most likely Governor Johannes Heyliger of St. Eustatius who, for a time, held Owen Lloyd in his prison, would have come as well. Photos by Carla Astaphan. Shadwell was for sale at the time of this writing.

The Caines Plantation, St. Kitts

Owen Lloyd's ultimate destination. Here, he wanted to reunite with his wife and live a life of ease paid for with the treasure of Juan Manuel Bonilla. TOP LEFT: Great house (ca.1940) built over the foundation of original house. TOP RIGHT: The stable. LEFT: The base of the windmill used to grind the sugar cane. BELOW LEFT AND RIGHT: Remains of the storage house. BOTTOM LEFT AND RIGHT: The caretaker's house. Photos by the author.

The Caines Plantation

TOP: The remains of the windmill as seen from the beach. Mount Misery looms in the background. MIDDLE: St. John's Church, located two miles southeast of the Caines plantation where the family worshiped. Many prayers were said here while Owen Lloyd awaited his execution at St. Eustatius. BELOW: St. Eustatius as seen from the black sand beach in front of the Caines plantation. Photos by the author.

St. Eustatius

TOP: The entrance to Fortress Oranje. You can see the moat on the right of the bridge. Photo by the author.

MIDDLE: A view from inside of the fort looking west. Photo by the author.

BOTTOM: The building over the entrance of the fort was the constable's house. Photo by the author.

St. Eustatius

TOP: Leading from the top of the hill next to the fort is a paved walkway descending to the lower town. Today it is called the "slave path." Actually, this walkway would have been used by anyone wanting to get from the lower town, (below) to the upper town where the people lived. Photo by the author.

UPPER MIDDLE: The ruins of the lower town where there were hundreds of shops, taverns, and warehouses. It was here that Isaac Raye, Jonathan Deacon, and James Moorehouse went ashore to spend some of their loot, which attracted the attention of the governor. Owen Lloyd and Zebulon Wade were captured and put in the fortress prison (below). Photo by the author.

LOWER MIDDLE: The walls of Fortress Oranje as seen from the ruins of the town below. Owen Lloyd would not have gone over this wall. Photo by the author.

BOTTOM: Just off the shoreline of the lower town are the ruins of a collapsed sea wall. Also a small cannon and an anchor can be seen. Shane and Madeline are inspecting the anchor. Photo by the author.

St. Eustatius

TOP: A view of the fort from the upper town. Note the moat which fronts the fort to the left of the gate. Dutch records say that the gallows that would hang Owen Lloyd and his associates was next to the moat. Photo by the author.

UPPER MIDDLE: The western and north western exposures of the fort are next to a very steep cliff. This was not the escape route that Lloyd would have taken. Photo by the author.

LOWER MIDDLE: A close look at the northwestern face of the fort (opposite) shows that if one went over the wall they would be forced to run into town and close to the entrance gate. Photo by the author.

BOTTOM: It's a short drop to the ground on the southern face of the fort. But to accomplish this Lloyd had to have cooperation from at least one of the guards. It is this wall that the author theorizes was Owen Lloyd's escape route. From there he, Wade, Pritchett, and McMahon could easily run south along the coast to a waiting boat. Photo by the author.

Antigua

TOP: The courthouse at St. John's, Antigua was only recently finished when Gilbert Fleming addressed the joint sessions of the council and assembly just before departing for Norman Island. MIDDLE LEFT: Inside the courthouse, which houses the Antigua and Barbuda Museum today. BELOW: The Admiral's Inn at English Harbor at the south end of Antigua. It was from this harbor that HMS *Otter* would venture out in pursuit of the stolen treasure and Owen Lloyd. The author stayed here during his visit. Photos by author.

St. Thomas

TOP: Fort Christian, Charlotte Amalie, St. Thomas, USVI. The oldest building in the Virgin Islands. This was the home of Governor Christian Suhm, who gave Owen Lloyd protection. Owen Lloyd probably made numerous visits here until he ended up dead at St. Croix. Photo courtesy of Wikimedia Commons. LEFT: Salt River, St. Croix may be the burial place for Owen Lloyd. BOTTOM: The waterfront today at Charlotte Amalie has undergone drastic changes since 1750, when piers and wharfs extended out into the harbor. That area has now been filled in. Owen Lloyd spent many an idle hour walking the waterfront and ducking into taverns during the last year and a half of his life until his past deeds finally caught up with him. Middle and bottom photos by Captain Dave DeCuir.

Cádiz, Spain

TOP: The fort, Santa Catalina, at the mouth of Cádiz Bay. The *Nuestra Señora de Guadalupe* sailed past here on August 31, 1749, on her way to the New World with Father Junípero Serra, one of the seminal figures in the 18th-century history of California. In late February 1753, she returned to Cádiz, the only ship of the 1750 fleet to survive the hurricane and make it back to Spain. Photo by author. LEFT: Statue of Father Junípero Serra at the mission church of St. Charles Borremeo in Carmel, California. Without his miracle on the feast day of St. Barbara in 1749, there would have been no *Treasure Island*.

Juan Manuel Bonilla was buried in the vegetable garden in front of the Franciscan convent known as the Convento de los Descalzos. The convent was originally on the site of the present post office building seen BELOW RIGHT. The Plaza de las Flores stands before it now. The statue is of Lucius Junius Moderatus Columella, Roman writer. Photo courtesy of Wikimedia Commons. BELOW LEFT: Bonilla's funeral mass was said at the church of San Diego the following day. Photo by the author.

The Hunt for Lloyd

former courthouse built in 1749 where Gilbert Fleming addressed the Council and Assembly of Antigua just before he left for Tortola to pursue the treasure recovered at Norman Island. From there we went to the archives.

At the front desk, I showed the receptionist my reference, "Book Z, pages 142-143." By the time I finished explaining what this was, the archive director, Dr. Marian Blair, who I had e-mailed months before in regards to the reference, came out to help. She said that coincidentally she was working on it just that morning. She brought out Book "Z." We consulted the index and found nothing. We then scanned the pages for dates, discovering the book ended in 1737, not 1751 as my reference suggested. Dr. Blair then retrieved the book and index for 1751. There was nothing listed for Bonilla, Watson, Chavera, Gibson, or Governor Gabriel Johnston from North Carolina. It appeared that the record groups had survived, but there was no explanation why the Denmark reference did not check out. I told Dr. Blair I was visiting the archives of St. Kitts on Wednesday, and that I would email her my findings.

At the time, I didn't realize that I was pursuing Owen Lloyd in much the same way that John Watson had two and a half centuries before.

Our two days in Antigua were great, but I was anxious to get back to St. Kitts. On Wednesday, I called on Victoria O'Flaherty, the archive director. She brought out the same Register I had used to locate Owen Lloyd's power of attorney on my last visit. There were no entries related to my reference. She then brought out "Book P" so we could look for pages 507-508 as the Denmark document had certified. That book ended about page 270 and the end of 1750, not 1751. There was more head scratching. Book Q which covered 1751-52 did not contain the documents either. I had noted that in the index there were numbers in the left margin which Victoria explained were sequential document numbers. I also had noted that the entire index from 1720 to 1780 had the same handwriting. This told me that the Books P and Q were most likely recopied at a later date without the documents I was looking for—meaning that they had been removed centuries ago. I realized it was possible that Charles Caines may have had enough influence to have the document removed. Then later, the books were transcribed and re-indexed leaving no trace of Bonilla's power of attorney.

The possibility that the documents were never recorded or that the documents could have been removed immediately after they were filed was a very interesting thought. Both scenarios suggest that Lloyd's connection with the powerful Caines family and the English hatred for the Spanish may have been the motivation to protect Owen Lloyd or possibly the reputation of his wife. But this premise would suggest that he could return to St. Kitts. I found no evidence that he did. Another possibility was that they were merely lost in the great hurricane of 1772. The hurricane had slammed Antigua as well but would this hurricane destroy the powers of attorney of both islands while leaving the remaining documents largely intact?

After hours of fruitless internet searches for Lloyd in Wales and England, I contacted the National Library of Wales for help. Owen stated in his deposition that he was born in the month of May in Wales. John Lloyd stated at Greenwich Hospital that he was born in Wales and was forty-five years old in 1753. That put his birth year at 1708-09. Owen had affection for the name Elizabeth—he had named his own sloop *Elizabet*h and renamed the *Seaflower* the *Elizabeth*—so I guessed it must have been his mother's name. With these facts, I hoped to triangulate on the correct Owen Lloyd.

At the library, a research assistant named Llona Jones found a Lloyd family in Rhuddlan, a small town near the north coast of Wales that matched. She identified John, born January 19, 1709; Owen born May 28, 1715; another brother named Vincent born in 1716; and a sister, Elizabeth, born January 7, 1714. All of the pieces fit with the exception of Owen's deposition which stated he was thirty, not thirty-five. The age difference easily was attributed to a transcription error made because of language differences when his statement was taken in 1750. But had it not been for Owen stating his birth month it may not have been possible to make this connection. None of the others with Lloyd volunteered their birth month. No wills or death records could be found for any of them at Ruddlan. *Was Owen speaking to me again?*

In the town of Ruddlan was an estate known as Bodrhyddan that owned several plantations at St. Kitts. That cinched the identity because I knew that Lloyd had a trading relationship with St. Kitts. But there was no record found of Owen Lloyd returning home to Wales. I was running out of clues. Everyone of the *Seaflower* crew was accounted for and alive after 1750 except for Owen Lloyd. His last known location was St. Thomas in 1751. I was now certain that the John Lloyd at Greenwich was his brother, evidenced by John's statement that he had last lived with "Cap'n Lloyd." That statement was made April 11, 1753, when he signed into the hospital. In the intervening time was he living with

Owen? Was this in London? Or was it in St. Thomas? Was it at his house in Hampton, Virginia? Did Owen take John to London? It was obvious from the deed conveyance in North Carolina by John Lloyd, who was unaccounted for since August of 1751 when he served on the jury in Norfolk, that by August 18, 1752, he intended to go to London.

The trail was once again going cold. At St. Kitts, I could find nothing more on Owen or Christian Lloyd. The court register did not list a will for either one, or for that matter, any possible children. Church records for the various parishes were consulted. Death, marriage, and baptismal records revealed no new clues. Many hours were spent combing old newspapers and port records for anyone named Lloyd commanding or owning a vessel. Church records for St. Thomas were also consulted. They were unreadable and in Danish. It was a dead end. The Danish, Dutch, Spanish, and English archives never mentioned him again after 1751.

It was around January 2006 that I had an idea. What if I consulted a psychic to help in the search? It seemed a bit far-fetched, but I had an amazing experience in 1983 with a man named Bill Holloway who had proven psychic ability. When my partners and I were searching for *La Galga*, I had concluded that *La Galga* was not to be found in the ocean but was buried under Assateague Island. I recalled that Holloway had advised one of my partners the year before that the wreck was not in the ocean. Because it seemed to contradict all logic, we had ignored him. After I realized that he had predicted the location a year before our own research brought us to that conclusion, it was decided to bring him to Assateague Island to help with the search. Within the hour he had me walking over a piece of it which was detected with a magnetometer. Additional research led to the discovery of new documents that independently proved that the shipwreck was buried beneath the island. Using the internet and court records, I attempted to locate him in Virginia Beach at his last known address. I had no luck. The idea of using a psychic intrigued me but finding someone with real psychic ability was daunting. It is not something to be found in the Yellow Pages. I scrapped the idea—temporarily.

One day in February, I went to bed a little earlier than usual. Sleep did not come as hoped. Frustrated, I turned on the television to a show about a psychic who had solved a murder. A woman named Pam Coronado had had a vivid dream about her own murder. It turned out that she merely "witnessed" parts of a real murder of someone else, including the face of the perpetrator. She went to the police and with other evidence, the missing woman was found and the crime was solved. It was an impressive display. As soon as the show was over, I went to the Internet and found her web site. Here, I found that she was doing a new series with The Discovery Channel where she and another psychic were used to help police in various cases around the country. She had even assisted law enforcement in the Washington, DC, sniper shootings. She made some amazing predictions in that case.

I contacted Pam and we set up an appointment. She seemed at little hesitant when I told her that I needed her in a missing person case that was two-and-a-half centuries old but she agreed and we proceeded with a phone conference. Pam lives in California so travel was out of the question.

I will have to admit that this whole thing made me feel bit nervous and foolish, but I decided to go with it. Pam said that I should just start by telling her about the 1750 event and what I knew about Lloyd. I ended the story by telling her he was last seen at St. Thomas. And then she had the vision.

Pam began to relate that Owen Lloyd had become restless while confined at St. Thomas. He had been afforded protection by Governor Suhm there but he needed a change of scenery so he went over to St. Croix forty miles south of St. Thomas. When he arrived at Christiansted, St. Croix, he went ashore to go into the tavern. Pam said he was recognized by someone whom he had double crossed in the past. A pistol was drawn and Owen Lloyd was shot. She said it happened in 1752. Pam vividly described someone in a bluecoat, military style. She saw someone with a wooden leg and that Owen Lloyd was put in a small boat and carried out of Christiansted to a cove west of town. That would have been Salt River. As for the shooter, she could shed no light other than she thought it was revenge for a double cross.

It was an interesting story but I had no way of knowing if it was true. The records I had seen said he was still there in 1751 when John Watson was sent to the Caribbean to recover the treasure.

The only readily-available source that I found that would cover 1752 was the church register for St. Thomas which was on microfilm and could be borrowed from the Mormon Church's genealogical collection in Utah. I had used it before but I couldn't read it because it was on negative film and the original documents were in Danish and bad shape, making it even more difficult to read.

The Hunt for Lloyd

When the microfilm arrived, I went to the local Mormon Church to view it on their film reader. Since I could make out some dates, I went to the beginning of 1752 and started studying the film with great difficulty. I looked for recognizable words and in particular "Owen Lloyd." I was nearly done with 1752 when I detected a capital "O" and a capital "L." It looked like it could be Owen Lloyd. I then printed out the document and carried it home and scanned the copy into the computer. I was then able to change the image from negative to positive and alter the contrast and brightness. There it was, Owen Lloyd for sure and on the same line I could also make out "Christiana Caines." The rest was in Danish but I could see the date—December 7, 1752— and another date of January 25, 1753. I emailed the enhanced image to Denmark where Peter Phister could decipher only about half of the words. What was certain is that Owen Lloyd died in December of 1752. This was later clarified when, at the very end of this project, I enlisted the help of Dr. Birgit Christensen who located the original and provided a full translation. Apparently, Lloyd had not died immediately. He had declared a will on December 7 and was dead by January 25 when his will was proved. The document did not say anything of how or where he had died, but Pam Coronado had called it right. For Owen Lloyd to declare a will, he must have known he was

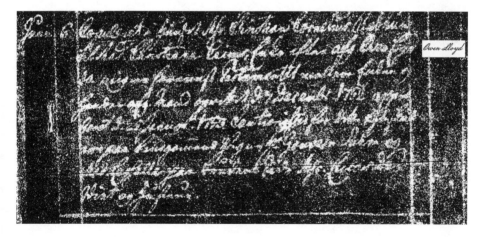

This document was discovered by the author only after the insistence of Pam Coronado, a psychic, who had a clear vision of Owen Lloyd's demise at St. Croix in 1752. Although it mentions the probate of the will of Owen Lloyd, it is actually a marriage document of Lloyd's wife to Christian Cornelius Rebhun of St. Thomas in June of 1753. Courtesy of the Provincial Archives of Zealand in Copenhagen, Denmark, and the Church of Jesus Christ of Latter Day Saints who microfilmed the document.

dying or that people were out to kill him. Given this, it seemed Pam's vision at St. Croix could not be dismissed..

The remainder of Dr. Christensen's translation was a shocker. The document I had found was not a church burial record but a marriage document. The reference to Lloyd's will was for the purpose of declaring Christiana a widow and was free to remarry. Christiana Lloyd had remarried a German named Christian Cornelius Rebhun on June 23, 1753. He was in the regiment on St. Thomas and later became surgeon. The witness for the groom was Governor Suhm. The witness for her was Lucas de Wint who was one of the purchasers of items at the auction of the *Seaflower*. Dr. Christensen also confirmed that there was no separate death or burial record for Owen Lloyd at St. Thomas. She said that the records seemed to be complete for that time period. St. Croix now became likely place for Lloyd's grave. The St. Croix records are incomplete and no record of Lloyd's burial can be found.

Christiansted, St. Croix as it would have appeared when Owen Lloyd visited here and where he most likely met his end. Courtesy of the Danish National Maritime Museum, Copenhagen, Denmark.

Pam Coronado's version of events must be strongly considered. First, we have to analyze who would have had the motive to carry out the shooting. It was unlikely that Zebulon Wade, William Blackstock, or any others of the *Seaflower* crew would have returned to the Virgin Islands. One candidate could be one of the Dutch guards who helped him escape prison at St. Eustatius and ultimately were on the run themselves. Owen Lloyd probably made them promises of buried treasure which he failed to deliver on. St. Croix would have been a safe haven for any of them.

Another suspect—although a surprising one to be sure—might have been his brother, John. He had a motive since he always seemed to pay the price for his brother's schemes. He had great plans to retire to his one hundred and fifty acres on Pasquotank River, North Carolina. There was enough time between selling his land in North Carolina in August of 1752 and when he showed up at Greenwich in late March 1753.

Another theory involved a suspected conspiracy between Governor Suhm, Governor Heyliger of St. Eustatius, and Lt. General Fleming at St. Kitts. Heyliger and Fleming wanted Lloyd to hang but they were prevented by Suhm while he gave him protection at St. Thomas. That protection would probably only last as long as the remaining cash that Lloyd had hidden. After that, Lloyd would have been a liability to him.

Pam Coronado had more to say on this theory. Owen had not only come to St. Croix to get away from St. Thomas, but he had hidden some money around St. Croix and was there to retrieve it. She said he hid it in three places—on the east end, on the south side, and on the west end. She said he avoided the northwest coast. Pam had no idea what we were going to talk about at that time so she would have had no way to prepare for this line of questioning. It was only after getting off the phone and consulting a nautical chart did I discover that—although the other areas would have been accessible—there was no way to anchor or safely go ashore on the northwest coast because of rocky shorelines and a steep drop off. Her suggestion coincided with my own theory that Lloyd needed a bank to keep his money. Norman Island was doubtful; Owen was too smart to leave all of his money there for Blackstock and Dames to discover. They weren't with him when he, Wade, Hobson, Moorehouse, Deacon, and Raye, stopped there in his flight from St. Thomas to St. Kitts in November of 1750. With the idea that Lloyd had prepared a will, it seemed likely that he would have given his wife a map or written instructions on retrieving any remaining treasure.

On October 27, 1752, John Baker, the Solicitor General for the Leeward Islands rendezvoused with Heyliger at St. Croix. His diary made no mention of the intended business. A later entry for November 25th says that while he was dining at Lt. General Fleming's at St. Kitts, word had arrived that Heyliger had died at Spanish Town in the Virgin Islands. A parenthetical notation said that "When we left him last Sunday at Spanish Town, Governor [John] Purcell was with him." This statement implies that both Baker and Fleming were with Heyliger at Spanish Town. Governor Purcell, if not then, soon would be the owner of Norman Island. In any event, the island was in his jurisdiction. All of these men could be said to have a motive. If not justice, greed was the motivator.

Most likely it was both. Until Owen Lloyd was captured, tried, and hung, he would have been an unresolved issue. With dwindling tribute being paid to Suhm, he could have been a willing co-conspirator. For John Baker, the Solicitor General of the Leeward Islands, the news of Lloyd's demise the following month would have been of great interest. He made no mention of it in his diary. If there was such a conspiracy, it could have played out two ways. The first would be simply paying someone to find Lloyd and shoot him. The second would be to find Lloyd and then force him at gunpoint to reveal the location of his buried loot. This could explain Pam Coronado's vision of Lloyd being placed in a small boat and taking off. At that point it made no difference whether he was able to produce any money or not. He would have been shot and buried in a shallow sandy grave.

Once Owen was dead, Christian Lloyd had a great deal to fear. Lloyd undoubtedly had bragged that he still had a lot of money hidden which was probably what kept him in the good graces of Governor Suhm. But the truth was that he was probably tapped out. A reexamination of the power of attorney granted Thomas Caines at St. Kitts gives hint of his desperation. It was made out in February of 1751 but wasn't recorded until May 19, 1752. It can be inferred that at this point he was in need of money. While he was holed up at St. Thomas, Thomas Caines, still retaining power of attorney from Lloyd, signed away Owen Lloyd's marital rights of property and money Christian had inherited from her father.

If Lloyd knew he was near his end, as suggested by the reference to a will, Lloyd's secret of the treasure's location would have been entrusted to his wife. It is reasonable to conclude that Lloyd would have named her in his will and made her executrix. The will that was probated January 23, 1753, cannot be found but it wouldn't have addressed any buried treasure anyway. It would have addressed his other assets the most valuable of which would have been his house on Queen

Psychic investigator, Pam Coronado, with the author at Chincoteague Island, Virginia. Here she described in detail her impressions of not only Owen Lloyd, but of Mrs. Hawkins' tavern in Hampton, Virginia.

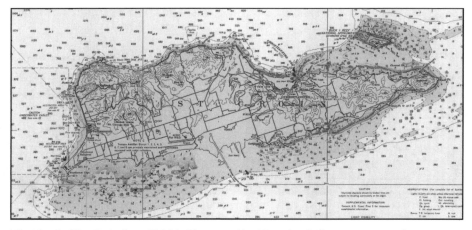

The island of St. Croix from NOAA Chart #25641. Note the shallow water at southwest corner, south side, and east end. Pam Coronado believes that Owen Lloyd distributed some of his treasure here.

Street in Hampton, Virginia.

Christian Lloyd was now the target of designing men who believed that she knew the location of buried treasure. There was nothing at St. Kitts to sustain herself as her brother, Charles Caines, had inherited the family plantation. And according to Pam Coronado, she had children to look out for. Whether it was real love or another marriage of convenience, Christiana Lloyd married Christian Cornelius Rebhun in 1753. She and her new husband do not show up in the tax lists as land owners on St. Thomas or St. Croix for 1754 and 1755. According to the church records of St. Thomas for 1755, she was present during several baptisms as a godmother, one of which was for the child of Lucas de Wint's overseer. In January 1758, when Governor Suhm's daughter, Maria, was born, Christian Rebhun and his wife were not present. St. Thomas baptismal records indicate that there were no children between Christiana Lloyd and Rebhun.

It wasn't long before I turned to Pam with help on another subject—John Lloyd of San Francisco and Lloyd Osbourne, the stepson of Robert Louis Stevenson. I emailed her pictures of Sam, Fanny, and Lloyd Osbourne while we talked and told her of the coincidence of Lloyd Osbourne being named after John Lloyd who might be connected with the Lloyd brothers who stole the treasure in 1750. Her first reaction was to "get a chill down her spine" and said she saw a connection. In later discussions, she said she wasn't so sure. I was too far in to walk away from that unlikely coincidence so I asked for her help in tracking John Lloyd and his parents. She felt that Vincent Lloyd, the younger brother of John and Owen, was where I needed to look.

We also examined Stevenson's relatives, Alan and Hugh Stevenson, who had died in 1774. I described what Robert Louis Stevenson said about them: that they were merchants with business interests at St. Kitts. I told her that Stevenson said that they died of a fever while pursuing a former employee or agent in the Caribbean who had defrauded them. Without hesitation Pam said that she felt that they were not merchants, but treasure hunters. Of course one could take that to mean that they were at St. Kitts to seek their fortunes just as many young men did in the Caribbean at the time. Pam described their travels in the open boat that Stevenson himself had documented. She said "I'm tasting something salty.

Something salty made them sick." She did not know that she was describing salt pork, a staple for seamen. If they were travelling in an open boat, the pork could have spoiled in the heat. The Stevenson brothers may have died of trichinosis, an illness characterized by prolonged joint pains, muscle aches, and fevers. It is interesting to note that Trichinosis is a slow death—and the two brothers died forty days apart.

With Owen Lloyd finally accounted for, the only thing left was to find out if he had any children and what may have become of his wife Christian. The parish records for St. John's Cabosterre, the Anglican church attended by the Caines family, did not have a marriage record for Owen and Christian. There was no death record and no record of children. The records for the time period seemed nearly complete. I had reached the conclusion that Owen and Christian had gotten married in Norfolk, Virginia, after he had arrived there in 1746. Although the marriage bonds for 1750 were intact and documented his brother's marriage, the earlier years seemed to be incomplete. I did not find Owen's marriage bond. It seemed highly probable that the marriage did take place there because I had found a deed dated May 12, 1746, for six slaves sold to Owen Lloyd which was witnessed by John Lloyd and Charles Caines. Charles' presence in Norfolk was a strong indicator that he was there for the wedding. It was the seller of the slaves to Owen which finalized that conclusion. Owen bought the six slaves from a "spinstress from St. Kitts" named Christian Malone. A later document related to Lloyd was witnessed by "Christiana" Malone. At Hampton, I discovered a power of attorney from Christian Malone to John Riddell dated August 7, 1753. This was most likely filed so she could recover the value of the house on Queen Street. Another document located showed that Charles Caines' daughter, Susanna, was married to George Riddle and living in Williamsburg, Virginia, in 1781.

The name Christian or Christiana was not a very common name in those days. It seemed more than a coincidence that not only was there someone named Christiana from St. Kitts who was known to Charles Caines, but that Charles Caines happened to be in Norfolk at the same time. The logical conclusion was that he was there for the wedding of his sister who must have been married before. Christian Lloyd first appears in the Norfolk deed book on November 13, 1747, when she mortgaged her furniture to John Hutchings. In the St. Thomas marriage record she had reverted back to her maiden name of Caines.

During a consultation with Pam Coronado, she described at least two children belonging to Christian. The older child was from a previous marriage. I told her of the Malone theory which she not only confirmed but gave me the name of Christian's former husband, "John" Malone. She described John Malone as a lot older than Christian and the marriage was loveless, probably one of convenience. Pam depicted a scene of children crying, wondering where their father was. This may give a special meaning to what Owen Lloyd said in his letter to John Hutchings in May of 1750 while he was in jail: "she [Christian] doesn't care to work on Account of Arabella and her children Crying about her which would give her a great deal of uneasiness." It is unclear whose children are referenced here, the slave Arabella's or Christian's.

At St. Kitts, I found the will of Christiana Malone in the index for 1765. But the will itself could not be viewed as the book that contains it is crumbling to pieces. It is uncertain when Christiana returned from St. Thomas or when she separated from her husband, Christian Rebhun.

On November 3, 1753, four months after her marriage, a Pieter Klog, an official with the West India Company, appeared at the house occupied by Rebhun and his new wife in St. Thomas. He came to take their last will, apparently summoned by Rebhun. In his preamble, Klog noted that they were both "in a perfect state of health." The will made each sole heir of the other as long as each did not remarry. Another provision allowed the heirs of each of them to inherit after the last one dies. There was a small contribution to the Lutheran Church and the poor. A reaffirmation of this will was made on April 27, 1770. It noted that Christiana had previously "left this world by death." What is puzzling is that Dr. Rebhun, as he was now called, prepared another will in May of 1769 as he was going to Europe and was concerned about the risks of the voyage. He mentions having recently sold his sugar plantation. He listed two sisters and brother as heirs. By 1772, he was noticed at Denmark as having died. These documents found in the Danish archives depict something less than a happy marriage for Owen Lloyd's former wife. She chose to use the name Malone in her power of attorney filed on August 7, 1753, at Hampton, Virginia. Christiana most likely was hiding her assets from her new husband. And when she returned to that name again at St. Kitts in 1765, it is reasonable to conclude that she fled St. Thomas and her third husband and resumed the name Malone, making her hard to find.

Christian Lloyd would have certainly divulged the names of her surviving children in her will at St. Kitts. One might be Peter Malone, a sailor whose death at St. Kitts in 1779 was recorded at St. John's church at Dieppe Bay. If this is Owen Lloyd's stepson, he would have been eight years old in 1750. At St. Anne's in Sandy Point on the west side of the island, there was a marriage of a Thomas Lloyd on July 23, 1771, who was a carpenter and died the following year on December 2, 1772. From the transcripts of the death records of St. George's Church at Basseterre, St. Kitts, located at the British Library in London, I learned that an Elizabeth Lloyd was buried there in 1759. This could have been the daughter of Owen Lloyd or even the wife of his brother, John. Fifteen years later on, May 26, 1774, Alan Stevenson, the great grandfather of Robert Louis Stevenson, would also be buried there. He was twenty-two years old when he died. In that year, Charles Caines still ran his plantation and often served on the Assembly. He lived on until 1799.

Within the cracked pages of the will of Christiana Malone, the legacy of Owen Lloyd might be discovered. I found that it would take at least $10,000 to reconstruct and preserve the book, money that neither I nor the St. Kitts archives had to spend. Any lineage from Owen and Christian Lloyd has a dead end at St. Kitts.

—⋙·◆·⋘—

Tracing John Lloyd, the former lover of Fanny Stevenson and an acquaintance to the author himself was proving very difficult. There were just too many Lloyds. I needed help—and lots of it—because it seemed sorting them out might be impossible.

There were conflicting clues. John Lloyd's cremation record said that he was born in the Isle of Man, yet there was no record of him there. That information was most likely given by his wife, and there was evidence in her death record that she was an alcoholic, but it could have come from a business associate. The only solid clues to start with were in the census data of 1900 San Francisco which gave his birth as June 1838, however, voter registration records gave conflicting years of birth. He stated that he was born in England and so were his mother and father. This seemed to contradict that he was a Welshman as suggested by Stevenson's stepdaughter, Belle. In 1937, when she wrote about the mining camp at Austin, Nevada, she had called John Lloyd a Welshman. This was in contrast to describing his cabin mate, Tom Reid, as an Englishman. But we know that Belle knew him

Long John Silver and Jim Hawkins at the Bristol Docks.
From *Treasure Island*, Cassell and Co. Ltd, 1907, illustration by Wal Paget.

"I was standing on the dock, when, by the merest accident, I fell in talk with him. I found he was an old sailor, kept a public-house, knew all the seafaring men in Bristol, had lost his health ashore, and wanted a good berth as cook to get to sea again. He had hobbled down there that morning, he said, to get a smell of the salt. I was monstrously touched--so would you have been--and, out of pure pity, I engaged him on the spot to be ship's cook. Long John Silver, he is called, and has lost a leg; but that I regarded as a recommendation, since he lost it in his country's service, under the immortal Hawke. He has no pension, Livesey. Imagine the abominable age we live in!" Squire John Trelawney, Chapter Seven, *Treasure Island*.

It was this line in *Treasure Island* that led the author to the British Admiralty records in search of John Lloyd and his missing leg. Because of that search, it was found that Owen Lloyd had been in the Royal Navy as well.

The Hunt for Lloyd

TOP: Greenwich Hospital (ca. 1750). Greenwich, England, longitude 0° 0' 0" located down river from London. The hospital was built in 1699. Today it is the Naval Observatory and National Maritime Museum. John Lloyd checked in on April 11, 1753 and was discharged dead on June 26, 1761. This former midshipman certainly had a story to tell his fellow pensioners about what he and his brother Owen had done at Ocracoke Inlet, North Carolina, on October 20, 1750. No doubt Blackbeard was mentioned as he was outdone by the Lloyd brothers. ©National Maritime Museum, Greenwich, London.

LEFT: A Greenwich pensioner wearing his "timber toe" pointing to the hospital across the Thames. ©National Maritime Museum, Greenwich, London. MIDDLE: One of the colonnades where John Lloyd would have "hobbled" about while idling his time. RIGHT: Monument inscription at Greenwich. Photos by Dianne Strang. BOTTOM LEFT: The signature of John Lloyd on his marriage bond found at the Kirn Memorial Library, Norfolk, Virginia.

well and John Lloyd may have last lived in Wales or had family ties there.

I dove into the online census records for the United Kingdom. There were hundreds of John Lloyd's and I also had to recognize that the right John Lloyd could have been missed during census taking.

Since I had reached a dead end with Owen's family, I decided that I could not ignore the possibility that his brother, John, may have had children to support while he was at the Royal Navy Hospital at Greenwich because he was married, which he acknowledged when he was admitted. I found that the National Archives in England had some relevant records. I was most fortunate to connect with Dianne Strang of Back to My Roots Genealogy services in London to do the search. She soon became infected with the hunt and began tracing John Lloyd's navy record. It was in this exercise that she located him aboard the sloop-of war, *Happy*, specifically, a snow of fourteen guns. And serving with him as captain was his uncle, James Lloyd, who would also be with him at the hospital. During the war, Captain James Lloyd had various commands has he fought the Spanish and the French. At the Battle of Toulon in the Mediterranean off of France in 1744, he commanded the seventy-gun warship, HMS *Nassau*. Another notable there was Captain Edward Hawke who in *Treasure Island* commanded the ship where Long John Silver said he lost his leg. Hawke would later become Admiral of the Fleet. Captain Lloyd and Captain Hawke were both court martialed for their actions at the Battle of Toulon and both were exonerated. Hawke would later become Admiral of the Fleet. James Lloyd became Lieutenant Governor of the Royal Navy Hospital in 1747 and remained there until 1761 when he died only months before his one-legged nephew.

Documenting James Lloyd as Lt. Governor of the Greenwich Hospital cleared up the meaning of John Lloyd's statement that he had last lived with "Cap'n Lloyd." He apparently took advantage of his uncle's position and roomed with him in the governor's apartment until a slot opened for his admission. During his eight years at the hospital, he certainly would have entertained his fellow pensioners who had previously fought the Spanish and French in the wars of the last half century with stories of stolen Spanish treasure. Lloyd was one of the few who could claim a perfect revenge on their former enemy.

Dianne continued to dog the admiralty records and found that shortly after John had left the *Happy*, his brother Owen signed on as midshipman at Charleston, South Carolina. The *Happy* had been hauled ashore "abreast of ye New Market

House" when he arrived there and then was taken into Townsend's Creek for more repairs. With the ship in dry dock, Owen and Uncle James probably had a lot of free time to patronize the many taverns in this historic seaport town. Here, they would have heard stories retold about Blackbeard's blockade of Charleston harbor fourteen years before. It seemed that Owen was always one step behind the notorious pirate until he caught up with his legend at Ocracoke.

Dianne suggested that Owen must have had previous Royal Navy experience and probably left another navy vessel to join with his uncle. He could have come out of Jamaica. If he followed in his brothers footsteps, he might have started as a servant before being elevated to able bodied seaman. His service came to an abrupt end in 1735. The *Happy* returned to Deptford, England, where he transferred to HMS *Alborough* and travelled about the coast of England until his discharge in October of 1735 at Grimsby on the east coast of England, one hundred and forty miles from Rhuddlan.

On November 13, 1760, ten years to the day that Owen buried his treasure, Captain James Lloyd made out his will. This will became a roadmap into the Lloyd family tree. There was a brother, Cornelius, three sisters, and three nieces but no children. There was John, his nephew, who got "such part of my apparel as my executors shall think most proper for his use" and an annual allowance of ten pounds. This allowance was to be spread out weekly; no doubt it was beer money and he couldn't be trusted with a lump sum. James Lloyd referred to a "kinsman" named John Lloyd of Ormskirk, England, who was quite an enigma until Dianne was able to determine that this John was probably a half brother of Uncle James. He had left an interest in a mortgage that he held on a farm outside of Rhuddlan called Cwybr occupied by his brother, Cornelius. Dianne had opened a gaping hole in the wall that I had hit years before. I couldn't help but wonder: *Was this a doorway to Fanny Stevenson's supposed lover?*

———◆———

It was 1981 when I started my research into the connection between Owen Lloyd and John Lloyd, acquaintance of Robert Louis Stevenson. There was one book that gave me great insight into the relationship between Fanny Osbourne and John Lloyd. Fanny's daughter, Belle, wrote her autobiography in 1937 which gave an account of how Fanny and John Lloyd met in Nevada and their lives together in San Francisco. She referred to him as a Welshman and reminisced that while they lived in the same boarding house in San Francisco in 1867: "There were many bright spots even there and the brightest of all was John Lloyd."

Just after beginning this project, I happened to pick up a book at a Dollar General store called *Fanny Stevenson, A Romance of Destiny* published in 1995 and written by Alexandra LaPierre. For the cost of one dollar, I read a marvelous account on the life of Fanny Vandegrift, the future wife of Robert Louis Stevenson. LaPierre was obviously obsessed with the character of Fanny and her fateful meeting with Stevenson. She followed in Fanny's footsteps as her research led her around the world. Following close behind her in her quest for that story was Claire Harman who published *Myself & the Other Fellow, A life of Robert Louis Stevenson* in 2005. Harman was captivated with the relationship between John Lloyd and Fanny, going so far as to infer from her research that they were lovers. Neither biographer knew anything about the Lloyd connection with *Treasure Island*. It is from these two biographies that my own research into their relationships begins.

Now that Dianne Strang had established the ancestral tree of Owen Lloyd's family she began the painstaking task of preparing an inventory of all the John Lloyds that were born in 1838 in England to parents who were also born there. The first United Kingdom census was in 1841. From that list she would then search for these same John Lloyds in the 1851 census using place of birth and parents names to create a match. Then she proceeded to the 1861 census to see if each John Lloyd was still present or not, since according to records in California, our target had immigrated in 1860. By 1860, John Lloyd would have been twenty-two, and unfortunately like most young men, would have left home by that time.

Because of her detailed research we were able to establish that a number of Flintshire Lloyds moved into England in the neighboring counties of Lancashire, Cheshire, and Shropshire that bordered Owen Lloyd's former home. She found an interesting candidate that led us both to believe that we had found our man. Dianne found one man named John Lloyd who fit the research parameters. The birth indexes for England and Wales said he was born in the second quarter of 1838 which ends in June, the same month that was John Lloyd's stated birth month in the 1900 San Francisco census. He had a brother and a sister that were born on Mold, in Flintshire, Wales, one hundred and thirty miles south of Rhuddlan. John's father, who was born in 1804, was named Phillip, a rare given name in the Lloyd family. Owen and John had a younger brother Phillip who died shortly after birth. And Uncle James had a niece named Philippa Lyon. It seemed certain we had a relative of John and Owen as we had a statistical match.

The 1900 California census was the only one that disclosed birth months. We had no other way to confirm the June birth month and we had no way of knowing who the census taker was talking to. We could not close the case until his birth certificate was located. When it was, we found that this John Lloyd was born in May of 1838, not June as was recorded by the census taker in 1900. I then realized that even a birth or baptismal record that proved a June birth would not solve the mystery. Only a will or some other document tying John Lloyd in San Francisco with a family member in Wales or England would absolutely prove or disprove the suspected connection to the family of Owen Lloyd. A will for this John's father could not be located. The haystack multiplied.

In tracing one line of the Lloyd family in Wales I found a possible remnant of Owen's legacy. I discovered a clue, or rather a coincidence, in the census for Wales in 1851. There were three brothers named John, Owen, and Vincent, whose father was named John Lloyd. Most importantly, though, they were in the same age order as the eighteenth century brothers from Rhuddlan, Wales. I had established that Vincent was a rare name thus making these nineteenth century brothers most likely related. Owen Lloyd's brother, Vincent, became a prime suspect in the hypothetical link. But everyone was born in Wales, not England. And this John Lloyd was still in Wales in 1861 disqualifying him. I was convinced, however, that this family had connections to the family of Owen and John. I contacted Gill Winstanley of Abergavenny, Wales, to pick up the trail. She was able to trace the family back to a John and Catherine Lloyd at Llandeilo Talybont, Glamorgan, in the early 1800s but these Lloyds were still in Wales in an area distant from Rhuddlan. I believe that, not only were these three brothers in the family tree of Owen Lloyd, but the legend of his deeds had survived into the nineteenth century, at least in the Lloyd family. Outside of the Lloyd family, the 1851 England census documents thousands of entries for people born in Flintshire, Wales, the home of the Lloyd brothers, but were living in England when John Lloyd was thirteen years old. A number of these were born in the eighteenth century. With this great migration, it is certain that the story of revenge and buried treasure was carried not only by some of those named Lloyd but others as well. At this same time On May 23, 1947, Lloyd Osbourne died in California. The headlines around

there had been worked since the Romans occupied the area 2,000 years ago. Owen Lloyd's father owned a lead mine for a time.was also a large migration of Welsh miners to America. Some worked the coal mines in the east while others risked it all after news of the discovery in 1859 of the Comstock Lode, the largest deposit of silver ever found in the United States. It was the following year that John Lloyd arrived in America. In either case, the miners were escaping the slave conditions under which they were forced to work in Wales. Flintshire, the home of Owen Lloyd, was noted for its lead mines

When the same search was done in the census for 1841, only thirty-eight entries were found for people living in England and born in Flintshire. Comparing this to the 1851 census proves that there were many people omitted from the 1841 census. If John Lloyd's family was one of those omitted, any further research would be fruitless.

The historical record leaves us little on this man named John Lloyd who had influenced the lives of the wife and step-children of Robert Louis Stevenson. We will never know what John Lloyd may have said to Stevenson when they met in San Francisco. Belle Osbourne retained the memory of John Lloyd's quest of his two brothers who went to sea. Her little brother, Lloyd, would later draw a map of an island and asked for a story about it. That story is known today as *Treasure Island*.

Owen Lloyd was not forgotten at St. Kitts either. Nearly a century and a half later, Lloyd was still remembered more as a folk hero than a criminal. In an internet search for descendants of the Caines clan, I found an Yvette Caines who had this to say:

> I do not know my family history back to the 1700s, my grandparents were born late in 1800s. I have never heard of a Christian Caines in our family but the names Charles, Lloyd, and Owen, are names in our family. We have family who immigrated to Bermuda, Santo Domingo and I think some also went to Trinidad. There are Caines in the Bronx and up state NY who are our relatives.

THE INVESTIGATORS

In Spain

LEFT: The Archivo General de Indias in Seville, Spain. It is in this archive that most of the documents related to Spain's trade with the New World since the time of Christopher Columbus are stored. Photo courtesy of Wikimedia Commons.

LEFT: Victoria Stapells has worked with the author since 1980 at various archives in Spain. She is standing at the entrance to the Archivo Provincial in Cádiz, Spain, where she found the will of Juan Manuel Bonilla. Victoria spent hundreds of hours at the Archivo General de Indias studying various documents of the 1750 fleet. Her research travels also took her to the Naval Museum in Madrid, the National Archives in Madrid, and the Archivo General de Simancas. Photo by the author.

In England

LEFT: Tim Hughes of Tim Hughes and Associates in London in front of the National Archives of England, formerly the British Public Record Office. Tim provided a great deal of help in the colonial records as well as work in the British Library. BELOW: Dianne Strang of btmrgeneology.com dogged the Lloyd brothers in the British Admiralty records, which included the records for the Royal Navy Hospital at Greenwich, England, outside of London. She appears here at the former hospital, now a museum. Not shown, Simon Niziol and Peter Galagher who also rendered assistance.

In Denmark

ABOVE: The Statens Arkiver Rigsarkavit, the Danish National Archives, courtesy of the archive. BELOW LEFT: Peter Phister of Copenhagen who unearthed a cache of documents about the stolen treasure and its aftermath. BELOW RIGHT: Dr. Birgit Christensen of Copenhagen, who discovered additional records and provided valuable translations on the documents related to the end of Owen Lloyd.

The Investigators

In The Netherlands

ABOVE: The Nationaal Archief, the National archives of The Netherlands in The Hague. Photo courtesy of Wikimedia Commons. Not shown are Nicole Brandt and Victor van den Bergh, who worked for the archives and located the documents related to Owen Lloyd and his captor, Governor Johanes Heyliger at St. Eustatius. LEFT: Anne Lee of europeantranslations.net in London, who translated the old Dutch documents as well as the French documents found in Denmark.

In California

LEFT: John Flora of ancestryexperts.com handled the California connection between Robert Louis Stevenson and John Lloyd. His travels took him to San Francisco, Monterey, and Carmel, California. He is pictured here next to the Robert Louis Stevenson Memorial at Portsmouth Square in San Francisco.

In The Isle of Man

Carole Carine, using her experience in genealogy, concluded that there was no record of John Lloyd's family at the Isle of Man. His cremation record in California said he was born there but the stepdaughter of Robert Louis Stevenson described him as a Welshman. But this mysterious John Lloyd did not show up in Wales or England either.

In Scotland

LEFT: Alan McLeod of Edinburgh probed the archives in Edinburgh and Glasgow in pursuit of Robert Louis Stevenson, his great grandfather, Alan Stevenson, and the family's connections to St. Kitts, the epicenter of the treasure event of 1750. He is standing in front of the Robert Louis Stevenson House at 17 Heriot Row in Edinburgh. Stevenson's family moved here in 1857. The house was still owned by the family when *Treasure Island* was written. Photo by Laurence Harvey.

In Wales

Maggi Blythin of The Family Business in Rhuddlan, Wales, the home town of the Lloyd brothers, located important wills and land documents in Wales and made the connection between Bodryddan and St. Kitts, which proved to the author that the family of Owen Lloyd had been found. Not shown is Llona Jones of the National Library of Wales, who made the initial connection. Valuable contributions were also made by Gill Winstanley, Bronwyn Curnow, Catherine Richards. and Jennifer Lewis. The ruins of Bodryddan Castle are in the background.

In St. Kitts

ABOVE: The former Treasury Building, which houses the St. Kitts National Trust, formerly the St. Kitts Heritage Society. Lindon Williams (not shown), formerly of the Society, provided valuable research into the Caines Plaintation. Also not shown, Victoria O'Flaherty, Director of the National Archives, who provided the first clue in the hunt for Owen Lloyd. She also was always available for questions during the entire project.

Pam Coronado
Psychic Investigator

The author turned to Pam Coronado when the hunt for Owen Lloyd came to and end. She was featured in eleven episodes of Sensing Murder on the Discovery Channel and a special on A&E called We See Dead People. Because of her insistence and vivid descriptions of how and when Owen Lloyd met his end, the author was able to document that Owen Lloyd most likely was buried on St. Croix. She also provided fascinating insights into the appearance and personalities of many of the forgotten characters of this story.

the country read: "Lloyd Osbourne Taken By Death, 'Treasure Island' Inspiration, Dead," and "Boy Who Inspired Treasure Island, Dies." Lloyd Osbourne had lived to be seventy-nine years old.

Lloyd had been preceded in death by his father, Sam Osbourne, who disappeared in 1886 and was believed dead when a bag of clothes that resembled his had washed ashore in San Francisco Bay. Fanny Stevenson, with the royalties earned by her husband, would bestow a pension on Sam's widow as she was left a pauper. Robert Louis Stevenson died of a brain hemorrhage at American Samoa at his estate called Vailima on December 3, 1894, the eve of the feast of St. Barbara. With Stevenson at the end was his mother, Margaret, Fanny, his step-daughter Belle, and Lloyd. He was buried on the top of Mount Vaea overlooking the sea. An elaborate monument was erected at the site. His mother moved back to Scotland and passed away in 1897.

Fanny moved to San Francisco a few years later. She built a house on the hill at the corner of Hyde & Lombard Streets to capture the ocean view but she happened to also be near the home of John Lloyd. Fanny would deposit the substantial royalties earned from Stevenson's works in the bank run by John Lloyd. He died of a stroke on August 25, 1910, leaving his wife Christina. In his will drafted in 1895, he named Christina as his sole heir. Christina died on July 23, 1913. The cause of death was cirrhosis of the liver. She never hid the fact that she did not like Fanny Stevenson.

In 1906, Fanny wrote a letter to her friend Dora Williams and said this about John Lloyd and his wife: "They have, I imagine, a fancied grievance against me." This statement was made twenty-three years after *Treasure Island* was published and Fanny was cashing the royalty checks. Before *Treasure Island* was written, she said, "The more one knows him and how reliable and straightforward he is the more you like him." She named her first son after him, giving Sam Jr. the middle name of "Lloyd." John Lloyd's devotion to her is well documented. Late in his life he confessed to Fanny's daughter, Belle, that his quest of looking for his two brothers who went off to sea was only a fantasy. What changed and why? That secret was taken to his grave.

Fanny moved to Santa Barbara, California, in 1908, an idyllic spot described by her sister Nellie as "perhaps the loveliest spot on the peaceful shore of the sunset sea, under the patronage of the noble lady, Saint Barbara." Santa Barbara was blessed by Father Junípero Serra in 1782 and was to be his tenth mission, succeeding the last one credited to him at San Buenaventura. A special place for sure as he never forgot his miraculous deliverance on board the *Nuestra Señora de Guadalupe* by Saint Barbara in 1749. Fanny Stevenson died here February 18, 1914, at the age of seventy-four. Her ashes were carried to Mount Vaea in Samoa where she joined her husband.

Lloyd Osbourne lived large with his inheritance and his share of Stevenson's royalties. He not only saw two world wars but lived to see *Treasure Island* made into numerous movies, plays, and illustrated versions of the book. In total there have been more than fifty movie and TV adaptations of *Treasure Island*.

Most of the pirate characterizations in popular culture today can be traced to *Treasure Island*. Long John Silver may be the best known pirate in the world. America's largest fast food seafood chain is called "Long John Silver's."

In 1950, Walt Disney made a color version of *Treasure Island*. Inspired in part by the success of that movie, a Pirates of the Caribbean ride was built at Disney World in 1967. This in turn grew into a multibillion dollar franchise everyone knows as *Pirates of the Caribbean* which includes movies, video games, and a theme park. The fourth movie will be released in May of 2011. Without *Treasure Island* there probably would be no *Pirates of the Caribbean*. Jack Sparrow may well owe his existence to the long forgotten Owen Lloyd. Stevenson unknowingly made this prophetic statement on August 25, 1881, when he began *Treasure Island*: "I am now on another lay for the moment, purely owing to Lloyd, this one." He was talking about his stepson who first drew the map. Regardless of how you interpret his credit, his debt is to Owen Lloyd.

Owen Lloyd never got to enjoy the treasure he stole. In fact, it cost him his life. But millions of wannabe pirates and treasure hunters owe him for their imaginative and romantic adventures. He has waited patiently for centuries for his story to be faithfully told. The first installment, a story about returning to a deserted Caribbean Island to recover a treasure buried in 1750, was delivered by Robert Louis Stevenson who was born November 13, 1850, one hundred years to the day that Owen Lloyd buried his loot on Norman Island.

POST SCRIPT

From the narrow streets of Hampton, Virginia, to the sandy shores of Ocracoke, to the secret coves of Norman Island, to the tropical beaches of St. Kitts, St. Thomas, and St. Croix, Owen Lloyd led me on a great adventure. And without knowing it, when I visited Navy Island at Port Antonio, Jamaica, made famous as a retreat of Errol Flynn, the Hollywood pirate, that it was here that John Lloyd and his uncle James disembarked from HMS *Happy* in February 1730. My researchers pursued him in England, Wales, Spain, Denmark, and The Netherlands. And in my travels, I also came to know Juan Manuel Bonilla. I visited Veracruz, Mexico, where the journey of the treasure began. I walked inside the fort of San Juan de Ulúa and held a bronze mooring ring that may have secured the *Guadalupe*. I slept in the former Franciscan convent where Father Junipero Serra would have stayed and probably Bonilla. Across the Atlantic, I visited Seville and Cádiz, Spain, where I saw his burial place and entered the church where his funeral had been held. It was an adventure of a lifetime and a privilege to bring to life a story that certainly influenced one of the most famous adventure stories of all time.

Epilogue
And Last

On August 18, 1750, six Spanish ships and one Portuguese cleared Havana harbor for Cadiz, Spain. This little fleet had been assembled from ships that had been delayed in their arrival at Havana after having missed the treasure convoy which had departed earlier that year. The fleet's sailing day was met with additional fateful delays because of weather, cargos, crews, and administrative decisions that would synchronize the fleet's ultimate departure with the approach of a West Indian hurricane. That cyclone was aimed at their intended course up the Straits of Florida. A change in departure by only hours would have totally changed the projected outcome. Unlike other treasure fleets before and after them that had met their end at the hand of Mother Nature, impaled on tropical reefs to be salvaged later by modern man, two of these ships were carrying a cargo of not only doubloons and pieces of eight but history that only now can be weighed and understood.

From this fateful encounter with the hurricane at the precise intersection needed to effect the intended outcome, two classics in children's literature owe their existence to this incredible rendezvous. The first, *Misty of Chincoteague*, is a story for girls about a wild horse which legend says descended from those that swam ashore from the shipwreck of *La Galga*, the warship that was acting as escort for the fleet. *Misty* was written in 1947 by Marguerite Henry and was made into a movie in 1961. Millions of people visit Assateague Island each year to see the horses which still run wild there today.

Treasure Island, a story for boys, owes its genesis to the fate of the *Nuestra Señora de Guadalupe*, a ship that should have perished the year before her historic voyage. She survived and arrived the following year at Ocracoke Inlet, North Carolina, her appointed destination. Days later, a sloop left Hampton, Virginia, bound for the Caribbean on a course that would take her well off the coast of

Epilogue

North Carolina. As if on cue, the sloop sprung a leak and diverted for Ocracoke. On board was a man named Owen Lloyd whose own vicissitudes had prepared him for the fateful meeting that was about to take place. Then, a fabulous treasure was stolen and buried on a deserted Caribbean island.

The rest is history.

Bibliography

Note to the reader: Everything in this book is based on documented facts. However, the author took license in some cases to create dialogue and some scenes for the sake of illustration. Dates in the narrative have been adjusted from the Julian Calendar to the Gregorian Calendar which did not go into effect in England until 1752. Spain used the Gregorian Calendar since 1582. The Gregorian Calendar was eleven days later in 1750. Dates in the notes and bibliography are not adjusted. This is most common when referring to English newspapers prior to September, 1752.

Spanish Primary Sources

AGB	Archivo General de Marina Álvaro Bazán, Viso del Marquès, Cuidad Real
AGI	Archivo General de Indias, Sevilla
AGS	Archivo General de Simancas, Simancas
AHC	Archivo Histórico Provincial de Cádiz
ACH	Archivo Catedralicio Histórico de Cádiz
AHN	Archivo Histórico Nacional, Madrid
MN	Museo Naval, Madrid

Archivo General de Indias, Sevilla (AGI)

Contratación

2017-18. Registros de venida de Nueva España, 1749.
2476. Registos de venida de la Habana. N.2, R.1 – *La Galga*, maestre Tomás Velando, 1751.
2526. Registros de venida de Veracruz y San Juan de Ulúa. N.1 – *N. S. de los Godos*, Francisco Ortiz, maestre. 1751.
2527. Registros de venida de Veracruz y San Juan de Ulúa. N.4 – *N.S. Guadalupe*, Juan Manuel Bonilla, maestre, 1751; N.5 – *Nuestra Señora de la Soledad,* José Ventura de Respaldiza, 1751.
2625 Registros de venida de Cartagena. N.4 - *El Salvador*, maestre Juan Cruañas, 1749.
2626 Registros de venida de Cartagena. N.2, R.2 – *San Pedro*, maestre Manuel Martínez Aguiar, 1751.
2902A. Libros de registros, 1739-83.
4729. Cartas Cuentas de los oficiales reales de Veracruz, años 1690-1766.
4759. Expedientes pidiendo certificaciones, 1750-57.
4927. Relaciones de oro, plata y efectos, 1701-55.
4935. Relaciones de pertrechos de guerra y mercaderías, 1747-59.
5078 - 5079. Reales Cédulas y Órdenes a la Casa de Contratación, 1750- 1751.
5157 - 5161. Cartas al Tribunal de la Contratación, 1750- 1754.
5546 Twenty religiosos sacerdotes en el navío nombrado *N.S. Guadalupe*, maestre don Juan Manuel de Bonilla que salio a navegar a la Veracruz, en 31 de agosto de 1749.
5800. Relaciones sobre derechos de Toneladas, 1671-1778.

Bibliography

Audiencia de Santo Domingo

292. Cartas y Expedientes de los oficiales reales, 1748-1753.
297. Cartas y Expedientes de personas seculares, 1737-1758.
326. Consultas y Decretos, isla de Cuba, 1731 – 1766.
345- 348. Minutas de consultas y despachos, isla de Cuba, 1746-1754.
366 Cartas y Expedientes del Gobernador de Santiago, 1747-1749.
368. Cartas y Expedientes del Gobernador de Santiago, 1751.
387 - 392. Cartas y Expedientes del Gobernador de la Habana, 1744-1752.
412. Cartas y Expedientes de los oficiales reales de la Habana, 1728-57.
427 – 432. Cartas y Expedientes de personas seculares, 1744 – 61.
433. Cartas y Expedientes de Sevilla, Cádiz y otros lugares que tratan de asuntos dedicha isla de Cuba, 1687-1759.
500. Expedientes y Papeles de la Compañía de la Habana, 1741-65.
548 - 549. Cartas y Expedientes del Gobernador de Puerto Rico, 1746-1759.
554. Cartas y Expedientes de personas seculares de Puerto Rico, 1730-59.
574. Puerto Rico. Expedientes sobre varias presas de embarcaciones extranjeras hechas en la isla, 1751-1761.
942. Cartas y Expedientes del Gobernador de Santo Domingo, 1744-1752.
1009 - 1010. Santo Domingo. Expedientes e instancias, 1729 -1758.
1072. Presas hechas a los ingleses: Santo Domingo, 1745-1753
1098. Presas, represalias, corsos, armadores de la isla de Santo Domingo, 1728-1774.
1130 - 1131. Consultas, Decretos y órdenes: Cuba, 1741-1753.
1194. Correspondencia oficial con los Gobernadores de la Habana, 1730 – 67.
1197. Correspondencia oficial con sus Gobernadores. 1771-1851.
1204 - 1205. Correspondencia del Gobernador de la Habana, 1743-1761.
1207. Correspondencia del Gobernador de la Habana, 1742-1746.
1219. Cartas y expedientes de Gobernadores de Cuba, 1720-1749.
1318 - 1319. Cartas y Expedientes del Gobernador de la Habana, 1747 – 1755.
1322. Duplicados del Gobernador de Santiago de Cuba, 1734- 1749.
1501 - 1502. Cuba: Expedientes, instancias de partes, 1748 – 1754.
1571 - 1572. Duplicados de cartas y expedientes de personas seculares, 1716-1759.
1812 - 1813. Cartas y Expedientes de los oficiales reales de Cuba, 1730 – 1757.
1827. Duplicados de cartas y expedientes de los oficiales reales de Cuba, 1715- 1749.
2005- 2006. Expediente de tabaco, azúcar, y otros frutos: Cuba, 1746-1748.
2009 - 2010. Expedientes de tabaco, azúcar, y otros frutos: Cuba, 1750 – 1752.
2065. Expedientes de comisos, 1747 – 1763.
2168 - 2170. Expedientes de presas, represalias, corsos y armadores, 1745 – 1751.
2197. Licencias de embarques: Cuba, 1726-68.
2208. Expedientes sobre asientos de negros, 1739-1751.
2298. Cartas y Expedientes del Gobernador de Puerto Rico, 1737-1754.
2470. Cartas y Expedientes de los oficiales reales de Puerto Rico, 1730-1776.
2513. Puerto Rico. Expedientes de presas, represalias, corsos y armadores, 1729-1771.

Audiencia de México

384. Consultas y reales decretos, 1743-1749.
385. Consultas y reales decretos, 1750-1759.
512 - 515. Cartas y Expedientes del Virrey, 1748 – 1751.
542 - 543. Cartas y Expedientes de la Audiencia, 1747-1754.
569. Cartas y Expedientes de personas seculares, 1746-51.
746. Cartas y Expedientes de los oficiales reales de México, 1730-1760.
853. Cartas y Expedientes del gobernador de Veracruz, 1742-1761.
862. Cartas y Expedientes de oficiales reales de Veracruz, 1740-1759.

1346. Duplicados de cartas del Virrey de Nueva España, 1749-1750
1689. Cartas y Expedientes, 1742-1762.
1850. Expedientes e instancias de parte, 1749-1751.
1922 - 1923. Duplicados de cartas y documentos particulares,1747-9, 1750-3.
2501. Expedientes del Consulado y Comercio, 1709-1754.
2914. Cartas y Expedientes de oficiales reales de Veracruz, 1743-1751.
2970. Registros de barcos, permisos para navegar y construir barcos, licencias de embarque etc. 1747-49
2971. Registros de navíos y licencias de embarque, 1749-1752.
2979. Expedientes de flotas y incidencias, 1740-1749.
2980. Expedientes de flotas y incidencias, 1750-1756.
2998. Expedientes sobre presas, represalias, corso y armadores, 1742-1763.

Indiferente General

8. Consultas, Reales Decretos y Órdenes: Nueva España, 1737-1758.
59. Cartas y Expedientes de personas seculares y Eclesiásticas, 1743-1759
800. Consultas Indiferente General, 1708- 1860.
1201. Cartas remitidas al Consejo, 1698-1832.
1299 - 1300. Órdenes generales, expedientes e instancias, 1749-1753
1501. Peticiones y Memoriales, 1735-1779.
1989 - 1991. Correspondencia con el Presidente de la Casa de la Contratación. 1745 – 1747 – 1755.
2023 - 2027. Cartas y Expedientes de la Casa de la Contratación, 1741-1753.
2044. Cartas y Expedientes del Consulado de Sevilla y Cádiz, 1748-1754.
2209. Entradas y registros de las embarcaciones de América, 1700-1784.
2304. Expedientes del Consulado Comercio y dependencias de Cádiz, 1748-1753.
2345. Correspondencia y expedientes, Consulado de Sevilla, 1708-1768.
2525. Reales Cédulas sobre asuntos de Armadas y Flotas, 1583-1800.
2724. Expedientes de varios papeles sobre flotas, 1718-1772.

Escribanía de Cámara

62. Pleitos de la Habana, 1744-1745.
70 A. Pleitos de la Habana, 1749-1750.
99B. Residencia de Francisco Cagigal de la Vega, Gobernador de la Habana. 1754 –1760.
1128C. Pleitos de la Casa de la Contratación, 1748-1749.

Arribadas

17. Oficios de José Patiño a Francisco de Varas Valdés, 1731-1733.
29 - 32. Oficios del marqués de la Ensenada a Francisco de Varas, 1747-1751.
136. Órdenes desde el Consejo de Indias, 1743-1759.
172. Cartas particulares y oficio, 1721-1753.
178B. Instrucciones y otros papeles pertenecientes a las flotas, 1730-82.
181. Reconocimiento y arqueo de navíos, 1739-1767.
325B. Correspondencia de oficio con Nueva España, 1735-1765.

Ultramar (Isla de Cuba)

1002. Tabacos. Compañía de la Habana, 1749-1762.

Consulados

78. (Libro) Correspondencia del Consulado de cargadores a Indias, 1750-3.
88. Correspondencia del Consulado de cargadores a Indias, 1681-1812.

Bibliography

204 - 205. Correspondencia del Consulado de cargadores a Indias, 1750 – 1751.
295 - 296. Correspondencia del Consulado de cargadores a Indias. Secretaría, 1748-1754.
325 - 326. Correspondencia del Consulado de cargadores a Indias. Secretaría, 1749-1756.
347-348. Correspondencia del Consulado de cargadores a Indias. Secretaría, 1733-67.
796. Cartas cuentas representaciones de los Diputados de Comercio en México, Veracruz y la Habana, 1745-1754.
861. Prorrateo de la plata y frutos salvados del navío *N.S. Guadalupe* que naufragó en la costa de Virginia, 1750.

Archivo General de Simancas, Simancas, Spain (AGS)

Secretaría de Estado

806-846, 2511-2604, 3955-3979, 6820-7040. Negociaciones de Inglaterra, 1480-1780.
5266-5351. Secretaría de Estado, correspondencia con ministros y embajadores, 1724-88.
6340, 6341, 6342. Diplomatic Correspondence from Amsterdam, 1757-1769.
6928, 6929, 6931, 6932, 6934. Diplomatic Correspondence from London, 1755-1756.
6727, 6728, 6734. Diplomatic Correspondence from Copenhagen, 1751-1763.
6309, 6323. Diplomatic Correspondence from The Hague, 1753-1763.
6915, 6916, 6917, 6919, 6920, 6928, 6929, 6931, 6933, 6934. Negociaciones de Inglaterra, 1749-1756.
8133-8333. Embajada de Inglaterra, 1764-1833.

Secretaría de Marina

15-1, 15- 2. Oficiales de Guerra de Marina, 1751-1752.
16.1, 16-2. Oficiales de Guerra de Marina, 1753-1754.
145. Ministerio de Marina, 1750-1751.
251, 256, 258, 259, 276. Negociado de Matriculas, 1742-1752.
392-428. Expediciones a Indias, 1711-1783.
434- 438. Expediciones de Europa, 1740 – 1753.
493-523. Navegación de particulares. Españoles y extranjeros, 1718-1783.
524-551. Corsos, presas, prisioneros, 1726-83
727. Canje y conducción de prisioneros, años 1740-1749.
96. Memoriales y Expedientes de Marina, años 1751-1753.

América
6952-7050. Nueva España. Correspondencia con virreyes y gobernadores, 1748-1805.

Archivo Histórico Nacional, Madrid. (AHN)

Secretaría de Estado

2320. Consejo de Indias, 1746-1754.
4263, 4264 A-B, 4265 A-B, 4270, 4273, 4277, 4294, Correspondencia Diplomatica con Inglaterra, 1750-1763.
3854, 4719, 3845, 4743, 2888, 2988. Dinamarca Expedientes, cuentas 1708 – 1800.

Sección Consejos Suprimidos – Consejo de Indias.

20197-99. Consejo de Indias. Sala de Justicia. Escribanía de Cámara. Casa de la Contratación,
21729. Consejo de Indias. Memoriales. 1744-1779.
21796. Consejo de Indias. Expedientes eclesiásticos y papeles varios, 1739-1769.

Sección Consejos Suprimidos – Consejo de Hacienda.

34902. Escribanía de la Junta de Hacienda.
34127-133. Escribanía de la Junta de Haciendas.
38.519-28. Escribanía de la Junta de Haciendas.
Archivo General de Marina Álvaro de Bazan, Viso del Marqués (Ciudad Real) (AGB)
Cádiz – Contaduría 8118 – 113.
Reales Órdenes 6518

Archivo Histórico Provincial de Cádiz (AHPC)
Sección de Protocolos: Cádiz y San Fernando, 1738-1772.
Tomo 39. (fols. 202-220).
Tomo 1.006 (fols 19-20).
Tomo 3.645 (fols 374-376).
Tomo 3.649 (fols. 337-399).

Archivo Catedralicio Histórico de Cádiz (ACHC)
Tomo 16, 23, 54. Libros de Funerales, Matrimonios y Bautismos.

Archivo Municipal de Sevilla (AMS)
Gaceta de Madrid. Nos. 8-10, 13-14 (Años 1750-1752, 1759-1760).

National Archives of England (NAE)
ADM 67/86. Records of Royal Greenwich Hospital.
ADM 1/2583. Captains Letters.
ADM 1/2659. Captains Letters.
ADM 1/305-6. Letters from Commanders-in-Chief, Leeward Islands. 1745-1759.
ADM 1/2659. Captains Letters "W."
ADM 36/3428. Muster log of *Shark* March 7 to August 31, 1751.
ADM 33/410. Pay Books, HMS *Chichester*.
ADM 6/224. Register of candidates for admission to Greenwich Hospital. 1752-1763.
ADM 73/36. General Entry Book of Officers and Pensioners (2 parts) 1704-1803.
ADM 73/51. Rough Entry Book of Pensioners 1704-1756.
ADM 73/36. General Entry Book for Officers and Pensioners 1707-1803.
ADM33/334. Ships Muster for the HMS *Lyon*, Jun 1727-Dec 1728.
ADM36/1441. Ships Muster for the *Happy* Sloop, January 1727 – July 1735.
ADM6/427. List of ships with succession of warrants to Midshipmen Extra, Volunteers, Chaplains, Schoolmasters & Masters at Arms.
ADM33/322. Ships Muster HMS *Northumberland.*
ADM51/625. Captains Log, HMS *Northumberland* 1723-1727.
ADM36/1194. Royal Navy Ships' Musters, HMS Fox – November 1727 – October 1728.
ADM 36/3428. Muster log of HMS *Shark.*

Ships Logs:
HMS *Bedford*, ADM 51/135.
HMS *Chichester*, ADM 51/198 ADM 52/452.
HMS *Hector*, ADM 51/425; ADM 52/615.
HMS *Otter*, ADM 51/662.
HMS *Scorpion*, ADM 51/886; 51/4335.
HMS *Shark*, ADM 51/894; ADM 52/708.
HMS *Swan*, ADM 51/958.
HMS *Sybil*, ADM 51/2563-4.
HMS *Triton*, ADM 51/1012; ADM 52/734-5.

Colonial Office
CO 5/1446. Naval Office Port of Hampton 1735-1756.

Bibliography

CO 7. Colonial Office Correspondence Antigua and Montserrat.
CO 152/13. Leeward Islands Correspondence with Board of Trade.
CO 152/22-23. Leeward Islands Correspondence with Board of Trade.
CO 152/27. Leeward Islands Original Correspondence.
CO 152/41. Leeward Islands Original Correspondence, Secretary of State.
CO 152/45. Original Correspondence Secretary of State. There are a number of Spanish documents here.
CO 5/297. Board of Trade Correspondence with North Carolina.
CO 5/849. Shipping Returns Massachusetts, 1752-56.
CO 5/1327. Original correspondence Board of Trade, 1748-1753.
CO 5/1338. Original Correspondence Secretary of State, 1746-1753.
CO 41/6-7. Bermuda Shipping Records 1738-1751.
CO 142/15. Jamaica Shipping Records 1727-1753.
CO 33/16. Barbados Shipping Records, 1708-1753.
CO 5/1035-6. New Jersey Shipping Records 1722-1751, 1743-1764.
CO 27/12. Bahamas Shipping Returns 1721-1751.
CO 5/510. South Carolina Shipping Returns 1736-1763.

SP 94/ 138-144. Secretary of State: State Papers Foreign, Spain.
TI 489. St. Christopher's (St. Kitts) Naval Office.

Statens Arkiver Rigsarkavit Denmark (DNA)
Chamber of Customs 1760-1848. Generaltoldkammeret - ældre del, Vestindisk-Guineisk renteskriverkontor. 1760-70. Indkomne Europiæske (og Guineiske) breve. 1762 A. 1763 A. 706-936.
General Chamber of Customs (GCC) Older part, Westindian-Guinean "Renteskriverkontor" Royal Resolutions Box #4, 1760-1763.

Royal Resolutions concerning the West Indies and Guinea Files, 1760-1771, Box #4-6.
Extracts of royal resolutions concerning the West Indies and Guinea, 1760-1771, Box #7.
Copies of Proposals and pertaining royal resolutions concerning West Indian and Guinean cases, Box #8.

Nationaal Archief, The Netherlands (NAN)
Staten General inv. nr. 3509, 3512, 3514, 5785, 7146.
West Indische Compagnie
WIC inv.nr. 251.
WIC inv.nr. 1188.
VEL inv.nrs. 1426-1431.
MIKO inv.nrs 310, 339.

List of repositories and their abbreviations
LOC   Library of Congress.
NAE   National Archives of England (formerly the British Public Record Office).
NAN   National Archief, The Netherlands.
DNA   National Archives of Denmark.
SK   National Archives of St. Kitts.
AB   National Archives of Antigua and Barbuda.
VSL   Virginia State Library, Richmond, Virginia.
KM   Kirn memorial Library, Norfolk, Virginia.
EC   Pasquotank County Courthouse, Elizabeth City, North Carolina.
JRW   John D. Rockfeller, Jr. Library, Williamsburg, Virginia.
NARA   National Archives, Washington, DC and College Park, Maryland.
MM   Mariner's Museum, Newport News, Virginia.

Published Sources
Alison, Robert. The Anecdotage of Glasgow. Thomas D. Morison, Glasgow, 1892.

317

Allen, William. *A Decade of Addresses Delivered to the Senior Classes at Bowdoin College* 1830, n.p.
———. *A Book of Christian Sonnets Northampton*, Bridgman & Childs, 1860.

Abercromby, James. The Letter Book of James Abercromby, Colonial Agent, 1751-1773. Ed. John C. Van Horne and George Reese. Virginia State Library, Richmond.

Amrhein, John Jr. *The Hidden Galleon: The true story of a lost Spanish ship and the wild horses of Assateague Island.* New Maritima Press, Kitty Hawk, NC, 2007.

Anderson, William. *A biographical History of the People of Scotland.* Fullarton, Edinburgh. [1859] -63.

Baker, John. *The diary of John Baker, barrister of the Middle Temple, solicitor-general of the Leeward Islands: being extracts therefrom.* London: Hutchinson & Co., 1931.

Baker, Samuel, Lt. RN. *A new and exact Map of the Island of St Christopher in America, according to an actual and accurate Survey made in 1753.* CO 700, NAE.

Balfour, Graham. *The Life of Robert Louis Stevenson.* Vols. 1-2. Charles Scribner's Sons, New York, 1901.

Ballantyne, Robert. *Coral Island; a tale of the Pacific Ocean.* Cornhill Publishing Company, Boston, 1923. First edition 1858.

Bancroft, Hubert Howe. *The Works of Hubert How Bancroft, Vol. XI, History of Mexico: 1600-1803*, A.L. Bancroft & Co., Publishers, San Francisco, 1883.

Bay, Christian J., ed. *The Manuscripts of Robert Louis Stevenson's Records of a Family of Engineers. The Unfinished Chapters.* Chicago, Walter M. Hill, 1929.

Belcher, Jonathan. *Jonathan Belcher Letterbooks*, Vol. IX. Massachusetts Historical Society.

Berthier, Louis-Alexandre. *Plan d'Hampton pour servir a l'Etablissement du Quartier d'hiver de la Legion de L'auzun, le 1 Novembre, 1781.*

Booker, Jackie, R. *Veracruz Merchants, 1770-1829: A Mercantile Elite in the Late Bourbon and Early Independent Mexico.* Westview Press, Boulder, CO, 1993.

Byrd, William. *Histories of the Dividing Line Betwixt Virginia and North Carolina.* Dover Publications, 1987.

Calendar of State Papers, America and West Indies, London H.M.S.O. 1994.

Calder, Jenni. *R.L.S.: Life Study of Robert Louis Stevenson.* Oxford University Press, New York, 1980.

Clark, Frances Watson. *Suffolk and Nansemond County*, Arcadia Publishing, Charleston, SC, 2002.

Coke, Thomas. *History of the West Indies…*3 Vols. Nuttall, Fisher, and Dixon, 1808-11. Volume III.

Colonial Records of North Carolina, Second Series Vol. IV, Department of Cultural Resources, Division of Archives and History, Raleigh, North Carolina. 1988. http://docsouth.unc.edu/csr/index.html/volumes/volume_04 (Disregard 'The' in alphebetizing. This should appear in the 'Cs')

Defoe, Daniel. *The Life and Strange Surprizing Adventures of Robinson Crusoe of York, Mariner.* W. Taylor, London, 1719.

Bibliography

Dobson, David. *The Original Scots Colonists* 1612-1783. Genealogical Pub Co, Inc., Baltimore, Maryland, 1999.

―――――. *Scots in the West Indies 1707-1857*. Clearfield, 2009.

Douie, Robert. *Chronicles of the Maltmen Craft, Aird & Coghill*, Printers, Glasgow, 1879.

Duffus, Kevin P. *The Last Days of Blackbeard the Pirate*, Looking Glass Productions, Inc., Raleigh, NC, 2008.

Dyde, Brian. *A History of Antigua, The Unsuspected Isle*, MacMillan Education, Ltd., London, 2000.

―――――. *Out of Crowded Vagueness, A history of the islands of St. Kitts, Nevis, & Anguilla*. MacMillan Caribbean, Oxford, England, 2005.

Earle, Peter. *The Treasure of the Concepción, The Wreck of the Almiranta*. Viking Press, New York, 1980.

Emory, Frederic. *Queen Anne's County Maryland, Its Early History and Development*, Centreville Observer, 1886-1887, reprinted by the Maryland Historical Society, 1950.

Ekirch, Roger A. *Birthright: The True Story That Inspired Kidnapped*, W. W. Norton & Company, London, 2010.

Evans, Hamilton H. *Lost Landmarks of Old Hampton, Revolutionary Port Town*. The Woman's Club of Hampton, Inc., 1985.

Executive Journals of the Council of Colonial Virginia, Virginia State Library, D. Bottom, Supt. of public printing, Richmond, VA 1925-1966.

Field, Isobel. *This Life I've Loved*. Longmans, Green and Co., New York and Toronto, 1937.

Fisher, Anne B. *No More a Stranger, Monterey and Robert Louis Stevenson*. Stanford University Press, Stanford, CA, 1946.

Flint, James. *Letters from America, containing observations on the climate and agriculture of the western states, the manners of the people, the prospects of emigrants, etc.,* W. & C. Tait, Edinburgh, 1822.

Geiger, Maynard., O.F.M. "The Franciscan 'Mission' to San Fernando College," Mexico, 1749. *The Americas*, Vol 5, 1, July, 1948.

Graham, Eric J. *Burns & the Sugar Plantocracy of Ayrshire*. Ayrshire Monographs 36, Ayrshire Archaeological and Natural History Society, Ayr, 2009.

Grimes, John Bryan. *Abstracts of North Carolina Wills*. Raleigh, NC, North Carolina Department of State, 1910.

Gwynn, Stephen. *Robert Louis Stevenson*, Macmillan and Co. Limited, London, 1939.

Hamilton, Douglas, J. *Scotland, the Caribbean and the Atlantic world, 1750-1820*. Manchester University Press, Manchester and New York, 2005.

Hancock, Ralph and Julian Wesson. *The Lost Treasure of Cocos Island*. Thomas Nelson and Sons, 1960.

Harman, Claire. *Myself & the Other Fellow: A life of Robert Louis Stevenson*. Harper Perennial, New York, 2006.

Hennessy, John Pope. *Robert Louis Stevenson*. Simon and Schuster, 1974.

Howe, Walter. *The Mining Guild of New Spain and its Tribunal, 1770-1821*. Harvard University Press, Cambridge, MA, 1949.

Hubbard, Vincent K. *A History of St. Kitts, A Sweet Trade*. McMillan Caribbean, Oxford, 2002.

Howe, Walter. *The Mining Guild of New Spain and its Tribunal General, 1770-1821*. Harvard University Press, Cambridge, 1949. P. 456.

Irving, Washington. [Geoffrey Crayon] *Tales of a Traveler*. Twayne Publishers, Boston, 1987 [1824].

Issler, Anne Roller. *Happier for His Presence*, Stanford University Press, Stanford, CA, 1949.

————. *Stevenson at Silverado, The Life and Writing of Robert Louis Stevenson in the Napa Valley, California, 1880*. Valley Publishers, Fresno, CA, 1974.

Jameson, J. Franklin. *Privateering and Piracy in the Colonial Period*. The MacMillan Company, New York, 1923.

Johnson, Captain Charles [Daniel Defoe]. illus., Alexina Ogilvie, *A General History of the Robberies & Murders of the Most Famous Pirates*, Printed & sold by Philip Saintsbury at the Cayme Press, Kensington, 1925-1927.

Journal of the Commissioners for Trade and Plantations, H. M. Stationery off., 1920-38; Nendeln, Kraus Reprint, 1969-70.

Journal of the Governor and Council of New Jersey., J. L. Murphy Publishing Co., Trenton, N.J., 1890-93.

Kingsley, Charles. *At Last: A Christmas in the West Indies*, Macmillan & Co., London, 1874.

Lapierre, Alexandra. *Fanny Stevenson, A Romance of Destiny*. Carroll & Graf Publishers, Inc., New York, 1995.

Letters from Virgin Islands. J. Van Voorst, London, 1843.

Lewisohn, Florence. *Tales of Tortola and the British Virgin Islands: Five Centuries of Lore, Legend, and History of Las Virgines*, [n.p., 1966].

Lloyd's List London. Available at Mariners Museum, Newport News, VA.

Lloyd's Register of Shipping, Mariners Museum, Newport News, VA.

Mackay, Margaret. *The Violent Friend, The Story of Mrs. Robert Louis Stevenson 1840-1914*, J. M. Dent and Sons Limited, London, 1969.

Mackintosh, John. *The History of Civilization in Scotland*, Volume IV, Alexander Gardner, 1896.

McCabe, Gille C. *The Story of an Old Town, Hampton, Virginia*. Old Dominion Press, Richmond, VA, 1929.

Maixner, Paul, ed. *Robert Louis Stevenson, The Critical Heritage*, ed. London: Routledge & Kegan Paul. 1981.

Marley, David F., *Pirates of the America*s, ABC-CLIO, Santa Barbara, CA, 1994

———— *Sack of Veracruz: The Great Pirate Raid of 1683*, Netherlandic Press, Windsor, Ontario, Canada, 1993.

Marx, Robert F. *The Treasure Fleets of the Spanish Main*, World Publishing Co., Cleveland, OH, 1968.

Bibliography

Mather, Cotton. *Instructions to the living from the condition of the dead...*, Printed by John Allen, for Nicholas Boone, at the sign of the Bible in Cornhill, 1717.

Nickerson, Roy. *Robert Louis Stevenson in California, A Remarkable Courtship*. Chronicle Books, San Francisco, 1982.

Nisbet, Stuart M. "Early Glasgow Sugar Plantations," *Scottish Archaeological Journal*, Edinburgh University Press, 31, 1-2 (2009).

Oliver, Vere Langford. *Caribbeana*. Mitchell, Hughes and Clark, London, 1910-1919.

Order Book and Related Papers of the Common Hall of Norfolk, Virginia, Brent Tarter Editor, Virginia State Library, Richmond, VA, 1979.

Osbourne, Lloyd. *An Intimate Portrait of RLS*, Charles Scribner's Sons, New York, 1924.

Osbourne, Katherine Durham. *Robert Louis Stevenson in California*, A. C. McClurg & Co. Chicago, 1911.

Padgett, Dora Adele. *William Howard, the last Colonial Owner of Ocracoke Island, North Carolina: His family and Descendants*. Padgett, 1974.

Palou, Francisco. *Relacion historica de la vida y apostolicas tareas del venerable padre fray Junipero Serra, y de las misiones que fundo en la California Septentrional, y nuevos establecimientos de Monterey.* Mexico, Don Felipe de Zuniga y Ontiveros, 1787. English translation, George Wharton James, Pasadena California, 1913.

Phipps, Pownoll W, MA. *The Life of Colonel Pownoll Phipps with Family Records*, Richard Bentley and Son, London, 1894.

Poe, Edgar Allen. *The Gold Bug*, contained in, *Tales*. Wiley and Putnam, New York, 1845.

Prescott, William Hickling. *The Conquest of Mexico*, Hooper, Clarke & Co., Chicago, 1843.

Records of the Executive Council, 1735-1754, Robert J. Cain, ed, Department of Cultural Resources, Division of Archives and History, Raleigh, North Carolina, (Date is missing. Also, disregard 'The' in alphebetizing. This should appear in the 'Rs')

Sanchez, Nellie Van de Grift. *The Life of Mrs. Robert Louis Stevenson*. James Stevenson Publisher, Fairfield, CA, 2001.

Scots Magazine, Volume 34, January 1772. A. Murray and J. Cochran, Edinburgh.

Sheridan, Richard B. *Sugar and Slavery: an economic history of the British West Indies, 1623-1775*, Johns Hopkins University Press, 1974.

Smollet, Tobias. *The Adventures of Roderick Random, London*, 1748.

Starkey, Marian. *History of Hampton The First Plantation, a history of Hampton and Elizabeth City County, Virginia, 1607 -1887*, Houston Printing and Publishing House, Hampton, VA, c1936.

Steuart, John A. *Robert Louis Stevenson. A Man and a Writer: A Critical Biography*. 2 Vols., Ryerson Press, Toronto, 1924.

Stevenson, Robert Louis. *My First Book – Treasure Island*. S.S. McClure, New York, 1894.

———. *Records of a Family of Engineers*, Chatto & Windus, London, 1912.

———. *The Works of Robert Louis Stevenson*, W. Heinemann, London, 1924.

———. "The English Admirals." *Cornhill Magazine*, London, July, 1878.

Southey, Captain Thomas. *Chronological History of the West Indies*, 3 Vols. Longman, Rees, Orme, Brown, & Green, London, 1827.

Stockton, Frank R. *Buccaneers and Pirates of Our Coasts*, The MacMillan Company, Ltd., London, 1919.

Suckling, George. *An historical account of the Virgin Islands, in the West Indies*. London: printed for Benjamin White, 1780.

Temple, Sydney. The Carmel Mission, Western Tanager Press, Santa Cruz, California, 1980.

Tormey, James. *How Firm a Foundation, The 400-Year History of Hampton Virginia's St. John's Episcopal Church The Oldest Anglican Parish in the Americas*, The Dietz Press, Richmond, VA, 2009.

Tyler, Lyon G., MA, LLD. *History of Hampton and Elizabeth City*. County Board of Supervisors E.C. County, Hampton, VA, 1922.

Walker, George. *The Voyage and Cruises of Commodore Walker*, Cassell and Co., Ltd, London, 1928, First published, 1760. pp. xxxix, 128-36.

Watson, Alan D. *Wilmington: Port of North Carolina*, Columbia S. C., 1992.

Watson, Harold F. *Coasts of Treasure Island; a study of the backgrounds and sources for Robert Louis Stevenson's romance of the seas*. Naylor Co., San Antonio, 1969.

Wilkins, Harold T. *Pirate Treasure*, E. P. Dutton & Co., Inc., New York, c1937.

William and Mary Quarterly. Institute of Early American History and Culture, Williamsburg, VA.

Woodard, Colin. *The Republic of Pirates: Being the True and Surprising Story of the Caribbean Pirates and the Man Who Brought Them Down*, Houghton Mifflin Harcourt, 2007.

Yarsinske, Amy Waters. *The Elizabeth River*, History Press, Charleston, SC, 2007.

Commonly used newspapers

BNL *Boston Weekly News Letter*
MG *Maryland Gazette*
SCG *South Carolina Gazette*
NYG *New York Gazette*
VG *Virginia Gazette*

Endnotes

Chapter One
Owen Lloyd, Privateer

Page 1. The marriage of Owen Lloyd. Parish records for St. John's Cabosterre, St. Kitts, do not record the marriage of Owen Lloyd and Christian Caines. In the deed books of Norfolk County, Virginia, the court records of 1746 record a sale of slaves from Mrs. Christian Malone, spinstress, of St. Kitts to Owen Lloyd. This deed of sale was witnessed by John Lloyd and Charles Caines. Caines' presence in Norfolk suggests not only the wedding but that Christian Caines had been married before (Malone). Norfolk County Deeds May 1, 1746. The Marriage Bonds for that year seem to be incomplete. Reverend Charles Smith, Pastor 1742-1760, would have performed the ceremony. Yarsinke, op. cit. See Chapter Thirteen for more on Christiana Malone.

Page 1. King George's War. http://www.usahistory.info/colonial-wars/King-Georges-War.html

Page 1. The *Elizabeth*. CO 5/1445-1446, Naval Office Lists Port of Hampton 1735-1756, NAE. The movements of the *Elizabeth* are recorded here. November 30, 1745, entered into Hampton, from St. Kitts, registered at St. Kitts to Owen Lloyd & Co. Cargo: rum, molasses, claret, salt, prize goods. January 25, 1746, Lloyd entered out for St. Kitts. Cargo: pitch, turpentine, pork, corn, candles, tallow, staves, heads, shingles, oats. June 25, 1746, entered in from St. Kitts. Cargo: rum, molasses, sugar, 24 negroes. February 19, 1747, entered out under John Lloyd, no guns and 12 men. Lloyd captures French Guineaman, *St. James Evening Post*, London, July 27, 1745, Lloyd is working for Gibbons. Similar account in *Virginia Gazette* June 20, 1745, p. 3 and *BNL* June 6, 1745.

Page 2. Gibbons' Plantation. Samuel Baker, op. cit., the map shows plantation of Nicholas Gibbons at the north end of St. Kitts on west side of the town of Dieppe Bay. Charles Caines is on east side. Nicholas Gibbons married Janet Caines. Probably the daughter of Thomas Caines.

Page 2. Charles Caines. CO 152/13, NAE, April 12, 1721. Account of number of acres in French part of St. Kitts. Charles Caines had 178 acres. Ravell's Survey, Oliver, op. cit., August 15, 1726, Charles Caines, Sr. submitted proposal for plantation based on survey for 152 acres. Thirty acres planted in sugar cane. Dwelling house was thirty-six feet long with two rooms, a kitchen, stewards room, with a chamber joining and a little house, a wooden boiling house with four coppers, two houses below the path thirty-two feet each with outhouse all boarded and shingled. He proposes to give £5 per acre. He ended up with 128 acres. February 21, 1728, he bought a 4,000 sq. ft. lot in Dieppe Bay Town for £5. His will was recorded in Book F #1 at St. Kitts National Archives covering the year 1737 which is now missing. Thomas Caines was coroner in 1735, St. Kitts Council Minutes. Also mentioned, Charles Caines member of council 1731-1735. Charles Caines, brother of Christian, died June 9, 1799, age 74.

Page 2. Caines family. Council Minutes St. Kitts, 1747. Thomas Caines Jr., Field Marshall, Thomas Sr. Deputy Provost Marshall. Council minutes for 1782-3, Charles Sr., Charles Jr. and Thomas on council.

Page 2. Lloyd trading with Boston. *BNL*, Lloyd enters from North Carolina, June 9, 1743; June 30, 1743, Lloyd clears for North Carolina; Lloyd arrives at Boston, July 26, 1744; Lloyd leaves for St. Kitts, September 20, 1744. Issue of June 26, 1744, gives account of St. Kitts engaging in the war.

Notes from pages 2 to 5

Page 2. Proclamation from Antigua. *BNL,* June 29, 1744. As soon as St. Kitts knew of war with France, two privateers set off for St. Martin and plundered the inhabitants.

Page 3. In 1746, privateer sloop belonging to St. Kitts took Spanish snow with 36,000 pesos, *West India Monthly Packet of Intelligence,* February 22, 1746. Ibid., March 31, 1746, HMS *Woolwich* took a large Spanish Galleon. Also in the *London Daily Advertiser,* April 28, 1746. Captain's Letters ADM 1/305. *London Daily Times,* May 13, 1746, says she captured a thirty-six gun French man of war from Havana ballasted with pieces of eight, said to be very rich.

Page 3. Owen and John Lloyd born in Rhuddlan Wales to Vincent and Alice Lloyd. The family of Vincent Lloyd and Alice from Cefn du and Rhydorddwy. John born January 18, baptized January 26, 1709, family described as of Rhydorddwy; Vincent, born November 18, baptized November 24, buried December 1713, family described as of Perthkinsey; Elizabeth born January 7, baptized January 11, 1714; Oedenus (Owen) born May 28, baptized, May 29, 1715; Vincent born March 15, baptized March 23, 1716, family described as of Cefn du. Philip born April 21, baptized April 22, buried May 2, 1717. Rhuddlan Parish Records, National Library of Wales, Bangor. Episcopal Records (3) D / DL 214 - 215 dated 1711 are leases in which Vincent and Alice are described as of the parish of Rhuddlan. Vincent Lloyd's will was proved in Chester (C 1724 / 9). http://hdl.handle.net/10107/965041

Page 3. John Lloyd joins HMS *Adventure* 1720. ADM33/303, Pay books. Sailed to Jamaica, discharged January 28, 1723. In 1726, he joined HMS *Northumberland* at Revel Bay in Denmark, ADM6/427. James Lloyd joined navy in 1706. Testified he had been thirty-nine years in the navy in 1747 when he was court martialed, ADM1/5282. James came from HMS *Royal Oak* as 2$^{nd.}$ lieutenant and later promoted to 1$^{st.}$ lieutenant. Capt James Lloyd was admitted to Greenwich in 1747 and died early in 1761. June 23, 1729, John and James on board HMS *Lyon* together, ADM33/224, Ship's Muster for *Lyon.* John serves on HMS *Royal Oak,* ADM33/341, Muster List for *Royal Oak.* John was discharged from *Royal Oak* November 18, 1729, and transferred to HMS *Seaford,* ADM36/3496-7. John and James at Port Royal on board HMS *Happy.* February 8, 1730, James and John joined the *Happy* from HMS *Anglesea,* ADM8/17 – 1729; ADM 36/1437-8, John discharged March 13, 1731. John Lloyd minuted December 29, 1752, ADM6/224/6; said at Greenwich hospital that he was a privateer who served on *Happy,* ADM 73/36: John Lloyd entered Greenwich Hospital April 11, 1753, discharged dead, June 26, 1761, ADM 73/51, John Lloyd aged 45 born in Wales, last served on *Happy,* snow, lost left leg, privateer. Owen Lloyd, midshipman, joined *Happy,* June 2, 1732, at Townsend Creek (probably Shipyard Creek), Charleston, discharged at Deptford, July 4, 1735 to HMS *Alborough.* ADM36/1446; ADM51/27, Captain's log *Alborough.* Sailed up and down coast of England and he requested discharge October 25, 1735.

Page 4. Lloyd's slaves. January 18, 1749, Court Orders Norfolk, Hutchings v. Owen Lloyd, in chancery. The slaves were ordered appraised as well as their annual profits.

Page 5. Blackbeard, Duffus; Black Sam Bellamy, Woodard, op. cit.

Page 5. Captain John Hutchings three-time mayor and councilman. *Order Book of the Common Hall of Norfolk.* His will described his real estate holdings. Will dated October 3, 1760, proved May 19, 1768. Norfolk County Deeds & Wills.

Page 5. John Lloyd takes the *Elizabeth.* Contract with MacKenzie, *William and Mary Quarterly* Vol. XX, Series 1, p. 170, contains the shipping contact between John Lloyd and MacKenzie. Elizabeth City County Deeds & Wills p.124. Guns removed, clearance Port Hampton records, CO 5/1446, NAE.

Page 5. John Lloyd captured by Pedro Garaicochea. Captain Lloyd from Madeira to Virginia taken with 42 sail between April 1 and June 2, 1747, *MG,* January 27, 1748, via Philadelphia, Dec 22, 1747; *BNL,* January 7, 1748, list of vessels taken into Havana April-November, 1747. In a letter to the Marqués de Ensenada on July 20, 1747, the Governor of Havana wrote: "On the 20th of this month, the *teniente de navío* don Pedro de Garicochea y Ursúa arrived in this port aboard his frigate *La Galga* (alias *N.S. del Carmen*) which is outfitted as a corsair. In the space of three months and ten days, he has captured fourteen prizes..." In the list, "A sloop with 100 pipes of wine from Madeira having set sail from this island for Virginia," Santo Domingo 2170,

Notes from pages 5 to 7

AGI. If Garaicochea was not patrolling the Caribbean he would be found along the American coast up to the Delaware Capes. He captured many vessels going in and out the Chesapeake and the British Navy wanted him bad enough that they had warships out on patrol looking specifically for him. In the summer of 1745, Don Pedro and other Spanish privateers were credited with nearly sixty captures of English vessels between South Carolina and Virginia. Lloyd, along with a number of other hapless vessels, was taken to Havana. Don Pedro Garaicochea y Ursúa, Escribania de Camara 62 and 70A, AGI; *SCG*, December19, 1743. This *La Galga* should not be confused with the fifty-six gun frigate of Daniel Huony. México 2971, AGI, June 29, 1750. The *Nuestra Señora del Carmen* was most often called by her alias *La Galga*. To avoid confusion with the subject of this book the former name is used. For activities of Don Pedro, see *MG*, July 26, 1745; October 18, 1745; *BNL*, August 22, 1745; *West India Monthly Packet of Intelligence*, February 2, 1746; *PG*, June 6, 1745; *PG*, April 3, April 19, July 31, August 21, October 30, November 6, and November 20, 1746.

Page 6. The *Rawleigh,* Jamaica Shipping Returns, CO 142/5: 180 tons, 10 guns, 16 men, built in Norfolk, VA, in 1746. Entered in Jamaica, September 5, 1747, with corn, pork, and shingles from VA. November 4, 1747, left Kingston, owned by John Hutchings, in ballast to VA. At Hampton, VA, arrived February 27, 1748, *Rawleigh* from Barbados, Edward Bishop, CO 33/16, NAE. Owen Lloyd to Virginia, May 22, 1747. The *Rawleigh* entered on May 5 with a different captain, Joseph Peat.

Page 6. Lloyd informs Virginia of Garaicochea's intentions. *The Virginia Gazette* was not in publication at the time. The *Maryland Gazette* published the news as a letter from Virginia, February 24, 1748.

Page 6. Lloyd needed money, mortgages slaves. Norfolk County Deeds, July 23, 1747, p. 70. April 2, 1748, p. 236, he names Arabella. Mentions slaves and furniture. Witnessed by Christiana Malone. Lloyd to Hutchings, May 9, 1750 p. 485, Norfolk County Deeds, Lloyd quitclaims to Hutchings slaves and furniture. Lloyd to Maisterson, May 9, 1750 p. 242, received slave Marianna and her four children from Hutchings, formerly mortgaged in full recompense for all damages done Lloyd by Maisterson p. 485-6, Hutchings representing Maisterson. P. 487 Selden witnesses Lloyd's release and Lloyd received slaves. Robert Armistead swore that Hutchings came to him to discharge Lloyd who was under arrest for suit brought by Mary Brodie. Lloyd was discharged from Hutchings suit before Lloyd signed the release, doing so willingly. Witness said Lloyd was told not to sign release to Hutchings or Maisterson if he was not willing. Hutchings bound unto Lloyd for £250 which payment will be made, May 10, 1750, Norfolk County Deeds, p. 488. If Hutchings delivers five slaves to Lloyd the above obligation will be allowed to remain. Lloyd's letter from jail. May 11, 1750, Norfolk County Deeds. Lloyd did receive the slaves, bond was satisfied.

Page 6. Christian Lloyd's fortunes dwindle, she mortgages mahogany furniture. Norfolk County Deeds, November 2, 1747, recorded April 21, 1748. She is described as a spinstress in a deed from Christiana Malone to Owen Lloyd for slaves in 1746. Christian Lloyd and Christiana Malone are believed to be same person. See Chapter Thirteen.

Page 7. It is assumed that Owen Lloyd was still working for Hutchings. The port records for Hampton do not cover this period. The port records for Barbados are missing for this time period as well as at St. Kitts. Jamaica does not show him going there. He most likely went to St. Kitts or Barbados. The *MG* of August 10, 1748, describes two vessels of Hutchings being captured near Cape Henry. The log of HMS *Hector*, ADM 51/662, suggests an intervention. Recaptured prizes transferred Spanish prisoners to *Hector*. Log of HMS *Otter*. ADM 51/662, July 20, 1748; *SCG*, July 20, 1748. Records do not state that Lloyd was on board Hutchings sloops. It has been inferred because Owen Lloyd signed a release of his mortgage slaves to John Hutchings whereupon five were given to Captain Maisterson. Lloyd to Hutchings, May 9, 1750, Norfolk County Deed Books "the said Samuel Maisterson having me apprehended brought back and confined on board his Majesties Ship *Hector* by way of Hue and Cry or any other matter Cause or thing Whatsoever from the beginning of the World then to the day of this said presents."

Page 7. Owen takes John to St. Kitts. This is assumed as John Lloyd soon afterwards was captain of a sloop from St. Eustatius to Philadelphia per *PG*, October 20, 1748. The *MG* of February 24, 1748, describes Owen Lloyd's return to Norfolk.

Notes from pages 7 to 9

Page 7. *Hector* captures Spanish privateers. *BNL*, July 21, 1748. Log, ADM 51/425; ADM 51/662, NAE.

Page 7. Cessation of Hostilities. *BNL*, October 6, 1748.

Page 7. Description of Hampton. Starkey, op. cit. and various deeds in Elizabeth County Court House.

Page 7. Lloyd transfers to Hampton. Elizabeth City County Deeds 1737-1749, p. 341, August 1,1749, Charles and Ann White sell 1/2 lott or ¼ acre on north side of Queen St. to Owen Lloyd for £130. Bound by Judith Bailey, John White and the Town Ditch. Lot originally granted to Thomas Faulkner in 1706, p. 292. He was the owner of the church property. The size of the lot and relation to the Town Ditch indicates the location of the lot.

Page 8. Reverend Fyfe. Tomey, p. 51, op. cit.

Page 8. Hurricane of October 7-8, *MG*, November 8, 1749, Hampton had four feet of water in the street; There was eight feet of water in Mother Hawkins' Tavern, a yawl was paddled through the passage.

Page 8. Owen Lloyd goes to jail, Norfolk County deeds pp. 498-9. Built by Merritt Sweeny in 1744-45. Three rooms, 30x18, 10 ft high, walls three bricks thick. Lined with pine and oak plank. July 3, 1750, Sheriff Robert Armistead protested that prison was insufficient and it was ordered repaired. March 6, 1750, prison location described "…up North Street to the Town Ditch then up ditch to prison." However, Tyler, op. cit., says prison is on south side of Queen St.

Page 8. Christian Lloyd left Hampton sometime between May and August. It is assumed she traveled on the *Peggy* as she was the only vessel going to St. Kitts. Port of Hampton Naval Office, CO 5/1446. Arabella was named in Norfolk County Deed Book and in St. Kitts.

Page 8. Pending lawsuits. Elizabeth City County, Order Book 1747-1755. A lease from Bertrand Servant to Owen Lloyd, p. 122. Indenture of lease and release between Owen and Christian Lloyd and Archibald Campbell, March 7, 1750, p. 156. Case of Owen Lloyd v John Brodie in trespass and battery, dismissed, August 7, 1750, p. 182. In Norfolk, John Hutchings v Owen Lloyd dismissed, p. 183. John Holden v John Lloyd dismissed, April 19, 1750. Hutchings v Lloyd dismissed, May 17, 1750. Lloyd v Fitzgerald, August 21, 1746, returned not to be found dismissed. Norfolk County, Brodie v. Lloyd, November 7, 1750, p. 199. Lloyd did not show. Judgment will enter unless he shows at next court. John Holden v. John Lloyd dismissed, p.183. Mary Brodie v Owen Lloyd: Conditional judgment, confirmed £78, 17 shillings, 6 pence, the defendant ruled to give special bail, failed to do so, April 3, 1751, p. 224. Owen Lloyd vs John Brodie in trespass and battery dismissed. September 4, 1750 p. 182.

Page 9. The marriage of John Lloyd, Marriage Bonds Norfolk County. John Lloyd owns tenement, Norfolk County Deed Book, February 1, 1751, John Lloyd to William Freeman 1/2 lot on west side of Church St. between William Nimmo and Francis Dyson.

Page 9. John Lloyd buys land in Pasquotank County. Elizabeth City, NC, Pasquotank Deeds, Book B, p. 92, May 2, 1750, Joshua Nash to John Lloyd of Norfolk, Virginia, 150 acres on north side of Pasquotank River and west side of Arenuse Creek at mouth of creek. Then on August 18, 1752, James Montier of Pasquotank buys the 150 acres from John Lloyd. Recorded November 29, 1752. Book C, p.147.

Page 9. *Peggy* returns to Hampton. Port of Hampton Naval Office, CO 5/1446, NAE.

Page 9. The approaching storm. Weather observation from the Log of HMS *Triton*.

Notes from pages 12 to 14

Chapter Two
Pieces of Eight

Page 12. Veracruz background, see generally, Booker, Bancroft and Prescott, op. cit.

Page 12. Italian, French, Irish in Mexico. October 23, 1754, letter from Juan Manuel Bonilla to the Merchant Guild (Consulado) of Cádiz. Consulados 796, AGI.

Page 12. The Acapulco Galleon, Marx, op. cit.

Page 12. Lorencillo. Marley, op. cit.

Page 13. Bonilla at Cádiz 1749. Contratación 2902 A, AGI.

Page 14. In 1733, three azogue (mercury) ships were sent to Mexico under the Conde de Vena. These were the *San Antonio* as Capitana and the *Lanfranco* as Almiranta. The third ship was Bonilla's ship, *N.S. Remedios* alias *La Ninfa*. This ship belonged to the "widows of Utrera": doña Manuela de Cifuentes and doña Angela de Prado. (Their husbands were don Luis and don Agustin de Utrera) The master of the *Remedios* for the trip was Juan Manuel Bonilla. Arribadas 17 and 134A, Mexico 2979, AGI. In 1749, Angela de Prado was the wife of Francisco Antonio de Villasota, *Administrador de Millones* de Cádiz. Although it does not say so outright, it appears that doña Angela held a greater share in the ship than Bonilla himself. Contratación 1522, AGI. She was Bonilla's mother-in-law: "In Cádiz on Sunday the 10th of October 1734, I Dr. don Pedro Francisco de Alcantara González…officiated and joined in legitimate matrimony according to the ordinances of the church of our Holy mother, don Juan Manuel de Bonilla, legitimate son of don Pedro Bonilla and doña Maria Antonia de Esquivel with doña María Agustina de Utrera y Prado, legitimate daughter of don Luis Francisco de Utrera and doña Angela de Prado y Sarmiento. The couple are both from Sevilla and residents of this city (Cádiz). Witnesses were residents of this city, the priest, don Cristóbal Muñóz and don Tomas Miconi and don Francisco Cagigal. Signed: Dr. Don Pedro Francisco de Alcalá González. Tomo 23: f. 57, ACHC.

Page 14. Repairs to the ship and outbound manifest, Contratación 1522, AGI.

Page 14. Taxes, Contratación 5546, AGI.

Page 14. On August 21, Ciprian Autran and his two assistants, Nicolas Pinzon and Bernardo Isassi, went on the *Guadalupe* for a final inspection before she set sail. These officials found that the ship was overloaded and the following items were taken off and put on small boats and taken back to Cádiz: 4 casks of wine - registered by Juan Mauricio Ortega; 3 casks of vinegar – registered by Julian Bautista López; 7 casks of wine – registered by Gaspar Hue and 330 iron bars loaded on Bonilla´s account. Ciprian Autran, caballero del orden de San Luis and Capitan de Navio de la Real Armada, crown official of the "Maestranzas of the Real Armada." Autran was responsible for overseeing the inspection and confirming the sizes and state of all the ships sailing to and from the Indies. The inspection of the *Guadalupe* was carried out in the presence of two others, the Fiscal Judge, Alsedo, and the notary, Pedro Sanchez Bernal. The ship was measured: 311 and 2/8 toneladas. (Autran added a further 31 for the steerage), length: 54 codos (1 codo = 41.8 cm); keel, 46 codos; beam, 14 codos, 14 pulgadas; floor, 10 codos; depth of hold, 6 codos, 6 pulgadas; steerage, 2 codos, 16 pulgadas. Contratación 1522, AGI.

Page 14. 1747 voyage of *Nuestra Señora de los Remedios*, Contratación 1513; Contratación 2902A; Contratación 5155, AGI. Records show that Bonilla had made earlier trips to Veracruz, Contratación 2499; Contratación 1504, AGI. Angela de Prado and Manuela de Cifuentes request permission for their ship, *N.S. de los Remedios* alias *La Ninfa Americana* to be included in the next fleet to sail to the Indies. The ship is twenty two years old but in good condition and is presently anchored in Cádiz. She was built in the shipyard of Rio de Tacotalpa in Tabasco, Mexico. When the fleet under Rodrigo de Torres arrived damaged in 1730, part of the fittings of the *Ninfa* were removed to outfit the king's ships. It took a year to find replacements for it to be able to sail to Spain. Once in Cádiz, further repairs were necessary. Mexico 2979, AGI, undated document, c.1737. One tradition held that Nympha (Ninfa) was a virgin martyr from Palermo who was put to death for her faith at the beginning of the fouth century

Notes from pages 15 to 20

Page 15. Walker, pp. xxxix, 128-36, op. cit.

Page 15. Ortuño had been responsible for the *Leon* and *Lanfranco* which sailed to Mexico in 1737 with azoque. See: AGI Mexico 2970. Memorial of Ortuño in a letter from Rubalcava to Ensenada dated Cádiz, August 1, 1747. The log for the *Jorge* is in Mexico 2970, AGI. The convoy of five ships sailed from Cádiz on February 14, 1747. The other ships were: *San Vicente, La Perla, La Ninfa,* and the *San Cayetano.*

Page 15. Commodore Walker. *MG*, June 16, 1747, via London March 24 captured *Nympha* with 180,000 pesos; Walker, op. cit.

Page 16. The *Remedios* is lost. Mexico 2970; Indiferente General 1989, AGI; Log of HMS *Bedford* ADM 51/135, Oct. 21 – Dec. 7, 1747; ADM1/2583, Captains Letters, "Townsend," November 25, 1747, NAE.

Page 16. 1749 Voyage of the *Nuestra Señora de Guadalupe*. Owned half by his mother-in-law, Mexico 2980, AGI.

Page 17. Bonilla's children. Little Juan Manuel Bonilla, born May 23, 1748, in Cádiz: On the 28th of May, I don Juan Fragela priest in this city with the license of the señor provisor, baptized Juan Manuel Antonio Marias Pascual Bonilla (who was born on the 23rd of this month), the son of don Juan Manuel de Bonilla and doña Maria Agustina de Utrera y Prado, his legitimate wife, who were married in this city in the year of 1734. The child's god father is don Francisco Antonio de Villasota, who was advised of his obligations. Witnesses were a priest, don Manuel de la Llave and don Juan Marán, all of these being residents of this city. Signed: don Juan Fragella Source: Tomo 54: Fol. 50, ACHC.

Page 17. Franciscan priests and Father Junipero Serra. Contratación 5546, AGI, Mission de San Francisco para Collegio de San Fernando de Mexico 1749. Number 17 on the list: Padre Fray Junipero de Serra, a priest from the town of Petra in Mallorca, age 35, medium build, not much beard, dark-skinned, black eyes and hair. He was a reader in Theology., ff. 13, 55, AGI.

Page 18 -19. Palou, op. cit. pp. 12-16. Father Palou describes Father Serra's recognition of the miracle: "As soon as the two bands, ours and that of the Dominican Fathers, had safely landed, a solemn celebration was held by them both in honor of our glorious Protectoress, Santa Bárbara, in proof of our gratitude and in order to fulfill the vows which we had made in the moment of great affliction. At this service our Venerable Fr. Junipero preached, giving a complete narrative of even the smallest circumstances and the little incidents which had happened during the long voyage of ninety-nine days. This he did with perfection and eloquence that he produced wonderment in them all, and on top of his reputation as most exemplary, which he already had, he acquired the other title of being very wise and very humble, for up to this time scarcely the least of his talents had been recognized."

Page 19. Veracruz hospitals. The Governor and the Treasury Official to the Marqués de Ensenada. Veracruz, October 23, 1749, Mexico 1850, AGI.

Page 19. Governor Diego de Peñalosa. Mexico 853. Veracruz, October 19, 1749; Mexico 1923, AGI.

Page 20. *La Galga* and *La Reyna*. November 24, 1749, Mexico 2971, 1850. *La Reyna, La Galga,* and *El Fuerte,* Mapa de las Caudeles, Contratación 5156, AGI.

Page 20. Sailed from Havana with Andres de Reggio. *La Galga* was held back. Marina 400-1, f. 139, AGS.

Page 20. Mexico's mint output. *The Mining Guild of New Spain*. In 1750, the production was 13,228,030 pesos in silver and 476,294 pesos in gold.

Page 20. *La Reyna* sails. Letter from the Conde de Gomera, Cádiz, April 24, 1750, Mexico 2971, AGI.

Notes from pages 20 to 24

Page 20. *Nuestra Señora de los Godos*. Left Cádiz, October 21, 1749, Contratación 2902 A; Mexico, 2980; Arribadas 30, AGI. The warship *La Reyna* in December sighted *Los Godos* thirty leagues from Veracruz. Letter from the Conde de Gomera, Cádiz April 24, 1750, Mexico 2971, AGI. Manifest, Contratación 2526, AGI. *N.S. Godos* alias *El Arenton* (the *Harrington*). Owner Pedro Pumarejo, Master Francisco Ortiz. Leaves Veracruz May 18, 1750, Mexico 1346, AGI.

Page 20. *Los Godos* and *Guadalupe* still in Veracruz in April 1750. Mexico 2971, AGI. Letter from the President of the Casa de Contratación to the Marqués de Ensenada, Cádiz, July 30, 1750, Mexico 2971, AGI.

Page 20. Don Joseph Ventura de Respaldiza sailed from Spain to Veracruz in the *San Antonio*, September 1749. Indiferente General 1988, 1989, AGI. He was shipwrecked near Veracruz then purchased the *Nuestra Señora de Soledad y San Francisco Javier*, México 2971, Cádiz, September 15, 1750, AGI.

Page 21. Bonilla fell ill. Contratación 2527, AGI.

Page 21. *El Salvador*. Sets sail from Cádiz for Cartagena. Alias *El Enrique*, owner is Salvador Arizon, Master Juan Cruañas, Arribidas 30, AGI.

Page 21. *San Pedro*. A Portugese register ship licensed to sail with Spanish ships. August 23, 1749, Contratación 2626, AGI.

Page 22. *Guadalupe* leaves Veracruz, July 12, 1750, the manifest is closed. July 24, 1750, takes on cargo at Havana. Contratación 2527, AGI.

Page 22. Bonilla's relationship with the governor of Havana. Bonilla was married Sunday, October 10, 1734, in Cádiz. One of the witnesses was Don Francisco Cagigal. Tomo 23: f. 57 Cádiz, ACHC. Francisco Cagigal de la Vega was the Governor and Captain General of Havana. Contratación 2527. Cádiz, 3773, ff. 140-148, AGI.

Page 22. Bonilla requests escort. Testimony of Daniel Huony, Secretaría de Marina 15 – 1. Expediente 184, AGS.

Page 22. *La Galga's* departure delayed, Secretaría de Marina 313, 318, 401-2 ff. 695-7; It was anticipated that *La Galga* would be ready sometime in June, Montalvo to Huony, May 29, 1750. Secretaría de Marina 15 – 1 Expediente 184, AGS.

Page 22. Astilla. Stems and fragments of tobacco. A total of 214,283 pounds of tobacco products were loaded on board *La Galga*. Contratación 2527, AGI.

Page 22. Repairs in Havana 1750. *Report Of The Carpentry And Caulking Repairs Carried Out In The Port Of Havana During The Careening Of H.M. Frigate Named La Galga*. Havana, August 4, 1750. Secretaría de Marina 401-2. f. 699, AGS. *La Galga's* register, Contratación 2476, AGI.

Page 23. Thomas Wright, prisoner. Traded with the Spanish. His sloop, *Pretty Betsey*, entered Charleston, SC, July 7, 1748, from Spanish Coast. SCG, July 7, 1748.

Page 24. Description of the storm. Contratación 5157, 2527; Indiferente General 1990, AGI; HMS *Triton* at Norfolk, Virginia, *Triton* log. HMS *Scorpion* at Charleston, South Carolina, ADM 51/1012, ADM 52/734-735, NAE; Secretaría de Marina 15-1, Oficiales de Guerra, 1751-2 Expediente 184, f. 599-600, AGS. Those officers from *La Galga* who testified were: Daniel Huony, Joseph de la Cuesta y Velasco, Vicente Marcenaro, Manuel de Echaniz, Diego Guiral y Concha, Juan Bernardo Mayonde, Francisco Izaguirre, and Gabriel Muñoz. Captain Pumarejo of *Los Godos* filed his report at México 2971, AGI; Estado 4263A, AHN; Respaldiza's account, Respaldiza submits expenses April 1, 1751. He arrived at Cádiz on the *Fanny* March 11, 1751, Contratación 2527, AGI.

Notes from pages 27 to 28

Chapter Three
Ocracoke, Pirates Lair

Page 27. Mother Hawkins' Tavern. The record says that Ann Hawkins took over the administration of her brother-in-law, Sam Hawkins' estate. He ran a tavern in Hampton and was granted an ordinary license as early as 1736, perhaps sooner. Orders 1731-1747, p. 112. By 1742, she was granted license to run the ordinary. It appears that she inherited the house or was leasing it. The inventory taken in 1741 of Sam Hawkins estate shows a backgammon table, a dozen leather chairs, 30 old pewter, a dozen plates, 7 gallons of rum, 1 gallon French brandy, 32 of Arrac, 5 gallons of Madeira, Order Book p. 108. Reference to her tavern can be found in the *Maryland Gazette* of November 8, 1749 and the *Pennsylvania Gazette* of October 26, 1749. "At Hampton, there is likewise much damage done; a noted tavern there, kept by Mrs. Hawkins (who gave the name to Mother Hawkins' Hole) was eight feet in water, and a yawl was paddled thro' her passage." Mrs. Hawkins ran the tavern until the end of 1751. Her last license was granted in April 1750, Order Book p. 159. And record shows she was still operating in August 1751. John Watson and Juan Manuel Bonilla visited this tavern which was documented in expense account of John Watson, see Chapter Nine. Her house was mentioned, *VG*, December 15, 1752, and not associated with a tavern. Her tavern was located at the intersection of King St. and Rudd Lane, site #44HT38, Virginia Department of Historic Resources, Richmond, VA. *VG* of September 5, 1755, p. 4 describes the building now owned by Alexander Kennedy: "A large Brick House with six fire rooms and Closets, two kitchens, a Smoak House, and a Stable, with a large lot and Garden pail'd in, situate on the main Street, opposite to the George Tavern." This tavern may have been run by Janet Wheeler in 1751. Kennedy later leased it to Francis Riddlehurst for £25 annually for seven years, p.46, Wills and Deeds, June 16, 1758. Riddlehust is "now living" there. He had been granted an ordinary license in 1756. Riddlehurst reopened as the Bunch of Grapes Tavern. In the *VG* of June 13, 1766, there is a description of an elegant celebration at the Bunch of Grapes Tavern celebrating the repeal of the Stamp Act on the king's birthday. In 1767, Nathaniel Elby is now owner of the building and was offering the property for lease as Riddlehurst was going to England, *VG*, April 16, 1767. Riddlehurst resumed the tavern but was living in James City County and it was noted in 1780 that he declined to renew his license but would take in lodgers, *VG*, February 19, 1780. This was without a doubt a legendary tavern as the 1902 U.S. Coast Pilot by the U.S. Coast and Geoditic Survey describes an anchorage inside Hampton Bar and near the wharves of Old Point Comfort with a depth of eighteen to twenty-five feet of water and was locally known as "Mother Hawkins' Hole." This author's guess is that she serviced vessels from her tavern that were anchored here and couldn't enter Hampton River.

Page 27. Ann Hawkins seemed more interested in running the tavern than tending to her family. When her husband died in 1742 he referred to her as his loving wife and named her executrix and gave her the annual profits of his estate as long as she remained unmarried. She refused both. There were five children: Thomas was the oldest who inherited all of his real estate. Then son John and three daughters, Sarah, Ann, and Elizabeth. Wills, p. 146. She did, however, administer Samuel Hawkins' estate, Orders, March 18, 1740, p. 247. Son John referred to as an orphan of John Hawkins June 4, 1754 Court Orders p. 433. December 4, 1750, Thomas Hawkins chose Anthony Tucker as his guardian. Owen Daily was summoned to court on complaint of Thomas Hawkins that he was misusing John Hawkins, orphan. Elizabeth City County Deeds and Wills, 1737-1756.

Page 28. Major Wilson Cary Naval Officer. The Customs Collector was Cary Mitchell in 1750. Liverpool Plantation Registers 1744-1773, M1373, JRW.

Page 28. Spanish ships at Hampton. *Los Godos* into the Cheapeake Bay, Pumarejo, México 2971, AGI.

Page 28. *Executive Journals*, Council of Colonial Virginia. p. 333. Council meeting of September 27, 1750, Pumarejo petitions council, Bonilla petitions p. 335, October 12, 1750; p. 338, *San Pedro*, Manuel Martines Aguiar.

Page 28. CO 5/1338 NAE records the events of August 30, 1750, Thomas Lee to Duke of Bedford, f. 85. Council meeting September 27, 1750, f. 89.

Page 28. *Los Godos*. CO 5/1327, NAE, August 30, 1750 to the Board of Trade. *Los Godos* has made no application

Notes from pages 28 to 33

yet. *Los Godos* condemned October 20, 1750.

Page 28. The *Harrington* entered Hampton, VA, July 10, 1745 from Jamaica registered to Jonathan Hanbury and Co. of London in 1744: 400 tons, 20 guns, 90 men, Captain John Hunter. Built on the River Thames in 1734. CO 5/1446, NAE. Later captured by Huony on the *Fuerte*. Santo Domingo 1501, AGI; Secretaría de Marina, 400 – 2, AGS. The *Harrington* was often referred to by the Spanish as the *Arenton* (Arribadas, 30, AGI) including when she was in Norfolk in 1750 but more commonly know by her religious name the *Nuestra Señora de los Godos*. The *SCG* of February 23, 1747, gave this account: "Captain Edward Lightwood came in from Havana in Flag of Truce, the brigantine *Foesby*, with 18 English prisoners. [Taken] the *Harrington*, William James, Master, from Jamaica to London, on December 9, nine leagues to windward of Morro Castle by a Spanish Man of War of 60 guns commanded by Capt. Daniel O'Honie…" Santo Domingo 1572, Havana, March 18, 1747, AGI. CO 142/15, NAE, Shipping Returns Jamaica: The *Harrington*, 26 guns, 75 men, loaded with sugar, rum, cotton, mahogany, and pimiento bound for London, November 20, 1746. Apparently she was captured on return to Jamaica. Pedro Pumarejo paid 34,109 pesos for her in 1749. Santo Domingo 1501, AGI.

Page 28. *La Galga* For the complete story of *La Galga* see Amrhein, *The Hidden Galleon*.

Page 28. Thomas Lee, President of the Council and acting governor of Virginia. *Executive Journals*, op. cit.

Page 28. Sherriff Robert Armistead. Elizabeth City County Court documents.

Page 29. George Ware. Convicted as a common drunkard, p. 194, November 6, 1750, Elizabeth City County Court Orders. Ware is mentioned in other documents as being owed money or buying items in estate sales.

Page 29. Benjamin Tucker and the *Hannah*. Last vessel for St. Kitts in the Hampton Port Records was the schooner *Samuel*, Joseph Calcole, 35 tons. Cleared July 3, 1750. The sloop *Hannah*, 25 tons, 4 men, registered to Alexander MacKenzie, April, 1737, cleared August 29, 1750 (OS) for Montserrat. She had entered into Hampton on August 14, 1750, from Barbados. Sloop named after his wife, Hannah. He was Clerk of the Court in 1731 and Deputy Surveyor of His Majesties Customs, November 20, 1745, Orders, p. 461, Elizabeth City County.

Page 30. Money due Owen Lloyd. Power of attorney from Lloyd to Thomas Caines, Book R #1, pp.184-90, St. Kitts National Archives.

Page 30. *Hannah* sinks. Per *PG*, Sept 6, 1750, a Gentleman from Hampton reported that two ships and a schooner from Barbados was lost at Ocracoke. The *Hannah* springing a leak: Testimony of James McMahon at St. Eustatius. November 30, 1750. WIC inv.nr.251 p. 107. He said the sloop sank after springing a leak. The port records for Hampton do not show her return.

Page 30. The house of John Oliver, Ocracoke pilot. November 11, 1750, Bonilla to the House of Trade, says there was only one house in the area. Contratación 5157, AGI; CO 152/45 f. 84-90, NAE; John Oliver, pilot at Ocracoke, 1740, *The Records of the Executive Council 1735 – 1754*, 373. Expense account of Juan Manuel Bonilla names him. GCC Box #4, DNA.

Pages 31-33. Blackbeard at Ocracoke. Duffus, op. cit.; Johnson, op. cit.

Page 31. Ocracoke Island. John Lovick patented 2,110 acres between Hatteras and Ocracoke inlets, Patent Book 1, page 295. Lovick owned 1000s of acres along Nuese River.

Page 33. Israel Hands. Johnson, op. cit.

Notes from pages 35 to 38

Chapter Four
Blackbeard's Last Prize

Page 35. *Nuestra Señora de Guadalupe*. Cádiz. Testimony by the Second Pilot, Domingo Luis de Mora, of Cádiz,

Page 35, May 27, 1751. Other declarants at the end of May were: Antonio Moreno of Cádiz, pastrycook of the ship, age 26; Juan Jimenez, of Cádiz and caulker on the ship, age 40. Both these men arrived on the *Scorpion* on January 27, 1751. Their testimonies were repetitions of that of the second pilot, Contratación 2527, AGI. Pilot, Pedro Garcia on return to Spain, Contratación 5158, AGI. Letter from J. M. Bonilla, Ocracoke, Indiferente General 2305, AGI.

Page 35-39. Letter from Bonilla to the Marques de Ensenada, November 11, 1750, CO 152/45 f. 84-90, NAE; Consulados 861, ff. 88-9, AGI. *Soledad*: Testimony of Respaldiza, Contratación 2527, AGI.

Page 36. *El Salvador*: "that the Cartagena snow (which had 200,000 dollars on board upon register, besides private money, etc) was ashore upon Cape Lookout, only three men and a boy sav'd; but that most of the money was supposed to be on board Ephriam & Robert Gilbert's sloop, (a Bermudian that had been drove ashore upon the same Cape, but had the good fortune to be got off again…"), *SCG*, November 5, 1750. Shipping Returns for Bermuda, CO 41/6-7: The *Relief*, 15 tons, 4 men and 4 guns registered to Ephriam and Benjamin Gilbert cleared Bermuda for North Carolina loaded with 300 bushels of salt on July 21, 1750. *El Salvador* drove ashore the night of August 29th. The *Relief* did not return to Bermuda until December 16th where she registered fifty barrels of beef, a quantity of wrecked cocoa, old junk, and a hundred feet of cedar timber. Gilbert paid dues on the wrecked goods. The cocoa no doubt came from *El Salvador*. On April 2, 1751, the *Southampton*, owned by Thomas Gilbert and others, shipped "42 casks of foreign cocoa imported from North Carolina being saved from a Spanish wreck, 1 barrel of balsam, 10 dry hides, 1 small bunch of copper, 2 bundles of seats for chairs, 120 tons of foreign logwood to London." (Note dates NS). Respaldiza, owner of the *Nuestra Señora de Soledad* which wrecked at Drum Inlet just up the coast from *El Salvador*, wrote a letter to Gabriel Johnston which was forwarded to Spanish Ambassador Wall in London. He forwarded on December 16, 1750, to José Carvajal y Lancaster, Spain's Secretary of State, Secretaría de Estado, E6917-6, AGS. Respaldiza declared that the captain of a frigate from Bermuda had made off with the sails and part of the rigging from the *Salvador* which had come into shore. Respaldiza also believed that the same captain also took some chests of silver and the governor dispatched an order to arrest the sloop. Note that the Spanish records say that the four survivors from *El Salvador* were taken to Respaldiza at Drum Inlet. Pedro Pumarejo writes to the Marqués de Ensenada from Norfolk on October 15, 1750: "…The packetboat *Salvador* of don Jacinto de Arizon went onto a bank and came apart, the people all drowned except for three sailors and a boy and the cargo of cacao, 16 chests of silver and four of gold. I have been told with certainty that on the same night, an English sloop ran ashore right beside it, it managed to get out and save some of the silver. Respaldiza is involved in the investigation as this misfortune was next to his [ship] and those that survived sought his protection," Mexico 2971, AGI. If the Gilbert's did in fact recover some money would they bring it back and declare it or would they hide it somewhere? It seems they had plenty of time to do the latter and a motive for not declaring any money that they allegedly stole.

Page 37. Samuel Dalling. *VG*, February 21, 1751, describes auction of a snow as she now lies on shore near Ocracoke Inlet. The description matches that of Sam Dalling's packet boat. A later *Roanoke* was registered to Dalling, a sloop built on Roanoke in 1753, registered in Edenton 1754. CO 5/849.

Page 37. Bonilla ferries treasure ashore. Bonilla Expenses, June 15, 1753, Consulados 861, ff. 49 -59, AGI; Bonilla to House of Trade, November 11, 1750. CO 152/45 f. 84-90, NAE; Consulados 861, ff. 88-9, AGI.

Page 38. Sam Dalling of the *Roanoke*. Lloyd may have known Dalling previously as both captains travelled between Boston and Ocracoke in 1740s see *BNL*. Description of his involvement p.1304, *Colonial Records of North Carolina*, letter to Johnston, September 18, 1750. He is referred to here as "Captain Darling."

Page 38. Rodriguez declares voyage over, ibid. Payment of 100 pesos each, Bonilla's expenses, Consulados 861,

Notes from pages 38 to 41

ff. 49-59, AGI.

Page 38. Owen Lloyd hired. Contratación. 5157, AGI; Bonilla to the House of Trade, November 11, 1750, CO 152/45, f. 84-90, NAE; Consulados 861, ff. 88-9, AGI. Expense account of Bonilla, GCC Box #4, DNA.

Page 39. Towing the *Guadalupe*. Ibid.

Page 40. Bonilla's report of September 17, 1750, Indiferente General, 2305; Contratación. 5157, AGI.

Page 40. *El Salvador* and the *Soledad*. SCG, November 5, 1750; *Colonial Records of North Carolina*, p. 1305; Pumarejo to Ensenada, Mexico 2971, AGI. April 12 at Cádiz, arrived English frigate *Fanny*, Captain John Green from Carolina with part of the cargo saved from the frigate *N.S. Soledad y San Francisco Javier*, Master Joseph Ventura Respaldiza. Respaldiza had originally sailed from Spain on the *San Antonio de Padua y N.S. del Rosario* alias *La Bella Sahara* but this ship wrecked in the port of Veracruz and was substituted by the *N.S. Soledad*. Contratación 2527; Ships returning from the Indies to Spain, AGI. Ship *Fanny*, J. Green, cleared for departure for Gibralter, *NYG*, February 11, 1751. The *Fanny* arrived at Hampton in from North Carolina, March 17, 1751, CO 5/1446, NAE.

Page 40. Bonilla fears *Los Godos* is lost, Bodies seen washed up: Paris, December 2, 1750, Pimartely to the Marqués de Ensenada, Secretaría de Marina 15-1, Expediente 184, AGS: Contratcíon, 5157, AGI.

Page 41. Spanish privateers at Ocracoke, *The Records of the Executive Council 1735 – 1754*, p. lix.

Page 41. John Oliver, pilot at Ocracoke, 1740, ibid, 373. Expense account of Juan Manuel Bonilla names him. GCC Box #4, DNA.

Page 41. *"Outlaws and Vagabonds." Colonial Records of North Carolina*, p. 1303.

Page 41. Summer 1747, *Records of Executive Council*. p.lix. Spaniards at Ocracoke 1741. *BNL* October 1, 1741. Cape Fear, July 7, 1741, Estrada at Ocracoke, *BNL* October 1, 1741, and Santo Domingo 428 and 1194, AGI. In the summer of 1747, Spaniards came from St. Augustine and burned ships, killed several people and slaughtered a vast number of black cattle and hogs. Pedro Estrada, a noted privateer from Havana, was equipped by the governor of St. Augustine, Florida, Don Manuel de Montiano, to raid English shipping along the southern coast. One hundred and twenty men set sail from St. Augustine on the sloop *La Nueva España* and after having captured five frigates, seven sloops and six bongos and canoes, arrived at Ocracoke Inlet where they set up tents and burned some houses on the beach and captured the cattle belonging to the Bankers. On Sunday, July 5, 1741, they sent a long boat thirty miles up Pamlico Sound and intercepted a sloop bound to the West Indies, much terrifying the English inhabitants. Estrada remained there for eight days having fortified the shore, taking four pedreros, a barrel of gunpowder, a chest of weapons and a flag. Estrada's crew found various jewels which the locals had hidden there. Besides these valuables, there was a large stash of naval stores which he ordered burned. When this news reached Charleston, a privateer was fitted out to go after them. While at Ocracoke, Estrada, who probably was trying to impress Governor Montiano, began issuing passports signing them as originating at *"Nuevo San Agustin de la Florida."* These passports were given to various Englishmen who had served him against their own nation, rewarding them for their service with boats and other items that had been captured. Estrada then returned to St Augustine. He made quite the public impression as he was observed by everyone in the garrison and as a consequence Don Pedro was highly acclaimed. He was also duly honored for having supplied the port with more than 1000 barrels of rice which he sold to them and especially the 670 barrels which he provided the Royal Treasury, all of which had been plundered from the English along the Carolinas. *Records of Executive Council*, pp. 376-8. Estrada was granted Spanish nationality in a document dated Aranjuez, June 30, 1750, Santo Domingo 346, AGI. See also, *Records of the Executive Council* 1735-54, p. 922; *BNL*, October 1, 1741.

Page 41. 1748 Brunswick. *MG*, November 9, 1748, and for Cape Fear, November 23, 1748. *Records of Executive Council* pp. lix, 481; Brunswick, *BNL*, October 20, 1748; Estado 6, AGS; *Colonial Records of North Carolina*,

333

Notes from pages 42 to 47

Volume IV, p. 922,1306. Indiferente General 2305, AGI. November 20, 1750, report of Governor Johnston. The people near the location of the ship "are lawless and desperate individuals who planned to sack the ship with the pretext that it was legitimate. This was in revenge for the great losses endured by their neighbors at Brunswick of the same province who have been attacked by Spaniards."

Page 41. PEACE. *MG*, May 3, 1749.

Page 42. Editor of *NYG* suggests all Spaniards be seized. This statement was made in the *NYG*, November 19, 1750, after describing the number of English prisoners on *La Galga*.

Page 42. Crew demands wages. Bonilla's expense account, June 15, 1753. Consulados 861, ff. 49-59, AGI.

Page 43. Thomas Wright as a prisoner, Contratación 5157, AGI. Bonilla requests his help; Bonilla to Ensenada, November 11, 1750. CO 152/45 f. 84-90, NAE: Consulados 861, ff. 88-9, AGI; p. 1304, *Colonial Records of North Carolina*. Wright arrived at Charleston from Cape Fear, *SCG*, October 29, 1750. His description of events, November 5, 1750, *SCG*.

Page 43. Oliver's house is attacked by Bankers. Bonilla to Ensenada, November 11, 1750. *Guadalupe's* remaining cannon: Later when the ship was towed to Hampton Roads she was recorded to have seventeen cannon, Port of Hampton Naval Office. Bonilla had said fifteen. With regard to the *Guadalupe* and of interest is "the ship was attacked one night while the crew was on shore with most of the cargo by an English sloop whose men robbed some of the cargo and opened boxes of documents. Another group of Englishmen tried to enter the house where the treasure was being safeguarded in case of theft or the ship sinking. Source: Indiferente General 2305, AGI.

Page 43. Zebulon Wade. Wade enters Boston. His age given in his deposition at St. Eustatius, WIC inv.nr. 251, p. 93, NAN. *BNL*, August 15, 1750; Wade is ready to sail, *BNL*, August 22, 1750; Wade clears out, August 29, 1750. Wade in Boston with Lloyd, See *BNL*; Lloyd was in Boston from most of June 1743, June 9, 1744, June 30, 1744, and May 3, 1744. Wade leaves for North Carolina, May 17, 1744, Wade for North Carolina, September 13, 1744. Lloyd left the following week for St. Kitts, September 20, 1744; Wade marries Mercy Norton of Edgartown, Martha's Vineyard, October 24, 1744, Familysearch.org.

Page 44. Wade's Crew. Jonathan Deacon, Isaac Raye, Abraham Pritchett, and Thomas Hobson were identified in Dutch documents, testimony at St. Eustatius. WIC inv.nr. 251, pp. 93-124, NAN.

Page 44. Wade said he was a one third owner of the *Seaflower* in his testimony at St. Eustatius. Court of Common Pleas, Plymouth County, Massachusetts: Wade was sued by Thomas Mann and Benjamin Briggs over a charter contract. He had been delayed December 28, 1749 in the sloop *White Oak*. Wade left for North Carolina, *BNL*, January 4, 1750. May 23, 1750, Wade in from North Carolina. Court says sloop returned on May 22, 1750, and had been out four months twenty-four days. Wade didn't pay all of money due. Wade forfeited £200 which he is being sued for. Wade sold ½ acre to Thomas Mann in Scituate, bound west on the Way, NE and South on Turner's land together with buildings and fences, July 3, 1752. Parents Joseph and Ruth lived north of Meeting House in Scituate. Zebulon Wade appellant v. Benjamin Briggs, Jr. of Scituate. Briggs to recover from Wade £1 16s 9p. p. 219. P. 231, December 12, 1751, Wade v William Duells failed on note to Wade £2 13s 4p, damages 31s 4p cost of court, p.230, March court, 1753. Will of Joseph Wade, January 13, 1762, says Zebulon is deceased. Wade cleared for Ocracoke the last time, August 15, 1750, (NS 8-26-1750), *BNL*.

Page 45. Teach's Hole. Blackbeard killed here November 22, 1718. Duffus, op. cit; Johnson, op. cit.

Page 46. Felipe García arrived at Norfolk on October 5, with Bonilla's letter of September 20. October 3, 1750, to Bonilla while on road to Virginia, Consulados 861, f. 171, AGI.

Page 46. Lloyd and Wade. It seems most likely that Owen Lloyd and Zebulon Wade already knew each other. They both traded between Boston and Ocracoke in previous years. The roasting pan was listed in the auction of the *Seaflower* at St. Thomas. GCC Box #4, DNA.

Notes from pages 47 to 51

Page 47. Huony wrote Bonilla at the end of September. Consulados 861, October 16, 1750, ff.176 -7, AGI. Huony writes on October 16, appoints men to go to Ocracoke, letter not sent, he adds that two vessels have been hired and are ready to leave. He is supposed to meet with the governor of Virginia on October 20, ff. 181-2. October 23, Garcia is ill and in bed. Huony sent Father Martin, chaplain, to Williamsburg, declaration of Daniel Huony, Secretaría de Marina 15 – 1. Expediente 184, ff. 599-600, AGS; Contratación 5157, AGI. Martin named as chaplain, AAB Cádiz – Contaduría 8118 – 113 – f. 3v. The two vessels are the brig *Letitia*, Matthew Delany and schooner, *Molly*, Jonathan Pitton. They came in from Ocracoke with Spanish goods, CO 5/1446, NAE. Also sloop, *Harry*, Jonathan Loyall, in from Ocracoke, registered to Durham Hall, mayor of Norfolk, with Spanish goods and schooner *Amelia*, fifty tons, five crewmen, Captain John Abraham, registered to John Hunter, cargo mahogany, sugar, hides, and tobacco. Back to Ocracoke October 12. Had cleared in ballast to Ocracoke, October 5, 1750. *Molly*, in November 22, owned by John Hutchings. She had cleared Norfolk, October 8, 1750, CO 5/1446, NAE. For more on Spaniards at Norfolk, see *Executive Journals of the Council of Colonial Virginia*, op. cit. *Order Book, Norfolk*. op. cit.

Page 47. Blackbeard, see Chapter Three.

Page 47. Gabriel Johnston at Edenton. Governor Johnston, CO 5/297, NAE. Board of Trade Correspondence with North Carolina. http://www.far http://www.famousamericans.net/gabrieljohnston/

Page 48. The Gilberts and *El Salvador*. Pedro Pumarejo writes to the Marqués de Esquilache from Norfolk on October 15, 1750, Mexico 2971, AGI. He reports that *El Salvador* was close by and was carrying sixteen chests of silver and four of gold. An English sloop managed to get away with some. Letter from Ambassador Wall in London to Carvajal y Lancaster Estado 6917 – 7, December 16, 1750, AGS.

Page 48. Johnston's letters to Duke of Bedford and James Abercromby, *Colonial Records of North Carolina*, p.1304; February 11, 1751, Indiferente General 2305, AGI. Johnston was in contempt of king's orders for not filing reports or passing any bills, *Records of Executive Council of North Carolina*, p. 931.

Page 49. "A wickedness only observed among the Spaniards." Letter from Respaldiza, September 30, 1750, Consulados 861, f. 169-170, AGI.

Page 49. "Villainous confederacy." *Colonial Records of North Carolina*, p.1300.

Page 49. Customs officers ask permission to seize. Peter Randolph was Surveyor General of the Customs. In 1746, Robert Dinwiddie appointed Peter Randolph of Virginia as Surveyor General to replace him. http://www.lib.udel.edu/ud/spec/findaids/dinwidie.htm *Colonial Records of North Carolina*, p.1309.

Page 49. Respaldiza to Bonilla. Letter from New Bern, September 30, 1750, Consulados 861, f. 169-170, AGI.

Page 49. Johnston hears of plot. *Colonial Records of North Carolina*, p. 1300.

Page 50. Colonel Innes sent to Ocracoke. Ibid, p. 1305.

Page 50. Johnston sends expresses to HMS *Scorpion*. Ibid, p. 1306.

Page 50. Weather at Ocracoke deduced from logs of HMS *Triton* at Norfolk, VA, ADM 51/1012, and ADM 52/735; and HMS *Scorpion* at Charleston, SC, and later at Cape Fear, NC, ADM 51/4335. *Guadalupe* pounding bottom, Bonilla to House of Trade, November 11, 1750, CO 152/45 f. 84-90, NAE; Contratación 5157, AGI.

Page 50. William Blackstock enters Ocracoke. Blackstock deposition, CO152/45 ff. 169-172, NAE.

Page 50. Sloop *Mary* enters Ocracoke, Captain Samuel Fitz-Randolph. *Mary* "six"(60?) tons, three crewmen built in New Jersey, 1745, registered at Perth Amboy, August 25,1746, to Sam Jr. bound for North Carolina with

335

Notes from pages 50 to 55

beer, rum, cider, July 26, 1746. New Jersey Shipping Returns, Perth Amboy, CO 5/1035-6, NAE.
Page 50. James McMahon and Enoch Collins hire on the *Seaflower*, testimony of Abraham Pritchett, WIC inv. nr., 251, f. 118, NAN.

Page 51. Bonilla offers 570 pesos. Expense Account of Bonilla with Watson & Cairns, GCC Box #4, DNA.

Page 51. Waller's testimony, *Journal of the Governor and Council of New Jersey*.

Page 52. Hanging for piracy. Mather, op. cit.

Page 52. William Dames. Owen Lloyd identified him as Thomas Dames, a merchant living in Annapolis, Maryland, in his deposition at St. Eustatius, WIC inv.nr. 251, p. 99, NAN. He actually lived on the Eastern Shore of Maryland in Kent and Queen Anne Counties, Maryland. Queen Ann's County Deeds RTC p. 330, February 18, 1747, says he is from Chestertown. P. 255 says he is a merchant of Chestertown. Resident of Queen Anne's County, 1768 Book H p. 155. Rent Roll Abstracts 1736-1798 by Leslie and Neil Keddie describe Dames as church warden in 1756, p. 120. Involved in construction of church, pp. 167, 172. Another reference places a William Dames at Newtown, Maryland, which is present day Pocomoke in Worcester County, Maryland also on the Eastern Shore. *PG*, February 3, 1747: Captain Dames salt rum, molasses, & other goods bound for Maryland is lost among the ice near Newtown, part of cargo saved. See *VG*, September 4, 1746, says he is from Chestertown, MD. Elizabeth City County (Hampton, VA) Deeds, Will, Bonds, p. 240, John Brodie of Hampton sold slaves to William Dames of Newtown, March 12, 1746. Hampton records show his son John and his grandson George as residents of Elizabeth City County, Virginia, in the late eighteenth century. *MG*, August 9, 1749 an ad says he is from Queenstown but he had an Irish servant run away from him at Nanticoke River while working for him. There is an area called Dames Quarter at mouth of Nanticoke in Somerset County, Maryland. Thomas Hobson referred to him as "Captain Dames" in his deposition at St. Eustatius, WIC inv. nr.251 p. 107, NAN. McMahon referred to him as an "Irishman." If there are two William Dames then the one in Queen Anne's County who recorded a deed RTC p. 437 January 3, 1750(1) to Sam Massey of Chestertown was probably not on board the *Seaflower*. See William Dames at end of notes to Chapter Ten.

Page 52. Charles McLair. Referred as Charles Livingston in William Blackstock's deposition. He is properly identified by Owen Lloyd and Abraham Pritchett in their depositions at St. Eustatius, WIC inv.nr.251, pp. 99 – 118, NAN.

Page 52. John Lloyd judgment against William Dames. Norfolk County Court Orders, July 18, 1749. Eighty-four pounds, seventeen shillings, judgment granted. Attachment levied on a parcel of iron in Robert Todd's store. Sheriff ordered the iron sold for cash.

Page 53. Innes arrives at Ocracoke, *Colonial Records of North Carolina*, p. 1307. Bonilla to House of Trade, November 11, 1750, CO 152/45 f. 84-90, NAE; Consulados 861, ff. 88-9, AGI.

Page 53. Movements of HMS *Scorpion*, log, ADM 51/4335, NAE. This detour probably cost Bonilla his treasure. If they had headed directly for Ocracoke the *Scorpion* would probably have arrived before 2 p.m., October 20th. *Scorpion* was at Brunswick on October 23 NS and celebrated the King's Coronation with a fifteen gun salute. Previous to her leaving Charleston, large amounts of beer were loaded aboard almost every other day. *Scorpions* arrival was further delayed by a headwind.

Page 53. Bonilla's orders. *Colonial Records of North Carolina*, p.1307; Consulados 861, ff. 88-9, AGI.

Page 53. Bonilla leaves for New Bern. *Colonial Records of North Carolina*, p.1305-6; Bonilla to House of Trade, November 11, 1750, CO 152/45 f. 84-90, NAE; Consulados 861, ff. 88-9, AGI.

Page 55. Captain Huony sends vessels. Letter to Bonilla from Huony, Norfolk, Va., October 16, 1750, f. 176-177, Consulados 861, AGI. This letter was appended on the October 18 letter when García was ready to leave. Felipe García to Bonilla, October 18, 1750, Consulados 861, f. 175, AGI.

Notes from pages 56 to 67

Page 56. García takes ill, Huony sends Echanis. Letter from Felipe García to Bonilla. Norfolk, October 23,1750, Consulados 861, f. 181–2, AGI.

Page 56. Thomas Wright announces his departure. Carriedo to Bonilla, October 21, 1750. Consulados 861, f. 179-80, AGI.

Page 56. HMS *Scorpion* enters Cape Fear River. Log.

Page 57. The events of October 20, 1750. Deposition of William Blackstock CO152/45 ff. 169-172, NAE; Owen Lloyd, Zebulon Wade, Abraham Pritchett, Thomas Hobson depositions at St. Eustatius, WIC inv.nr.251, pp. 93-124, NAN; Tomás Carriedo to Bonilla October 21, 1750. Consulados 861, f. 179-80, AGI; Letter to the House of Trade from Bonilla dated November 11, 1750, at Ocracoke, CO 152/45 f. 84-90, NAE. The record seems to show that a duplicate was sent to the Marqués de Ensenada; Expense statement by Bonilla in Cádiz, June 15, 1753, Consulados, 861, ff. 49-59, AGI; *Colonial Records of North Carolina*, page 1304.

Chapter Five
The Voyage

Page 61. St. Bartholomew's. Blackstock is the only one to mention this island. He may have been unfamiliar with the West Indies. His deposition. CO152/45 ff. 169-172, NAE.

Page 62. Movements of the *Scorpion*. Scorpion log.

Page 62. Blackstock suggests paltry share. Owen Lloyd fetches Zebulon Wade from his cabin. Depositions Wade, Lloyd, Hobson, Pritchard, McMahon. WIC inv.nr.251, pp. 93-124, NAN.

Page 62. Express rider. *Colonial Records of North Carolina*, p. 1300, 1306.

Page 62. Weather at Cape Fear from the log of HMS *Scorpion*.

Page 63. Wade remains in cabin. WIC inv.nr.251, pp. 93-124, NAN.

Page 63. *Seaflower's* name changed. The auction documents of St. Thomas found in GCC Box #4, DNA.

Page 63. Blackstock and Pritchett at helm, Depositions WIC inv.nr. 251, pp. 93-124, NAN.

Page 63. Description of Virgin Islands. July 11, 1751, Report of James Purcell regarding the state of the Virgin Islands. Upwards of 400 families and about 8,000 slaves living at Tortola. Chief products cotton, wool, and sugar. CO 152/27, NAE.

Page 64. Spanish Galleon wrecks in 1734. William Matthew to Board of Trade, June 17, 1734, CO152/21 ff. 86-87, NAE.

Page 64. Coral Bay was described as Crawl Bay on contemporary maps.

Page 65. Moorehouse stays with Lloyd. WIC inv.nr.251, pp. 99- 103, NAN.

Chapter Six
Treasure Island

Page 67. *Seaflower* arrives at Norman's Island on November 12. Governor of Puerto Rico to the Marqués de

337

Notes from pages 68 to 69

Ensenada included a letter from Stephen Debroses of St. Thomas: "Around November 12, an English ship arrived at Norman island headed by a man named Owen Lloyd," Santo Domingo, 2298, AGI. Depositions, WIC inv.nr. 251, pp. 93-124, NAN; CO 152/45 f. 152, NAE, says that Blackstock left Norman's Island on the "3rd of November." This would be November 14, 1750, NS.

Page 68. Inventory of treasure based on Bonilla's claim. However Carriedo had stated fifty-five chests. Consulados 861, ff. 49-59, AGI. Consulados 861, ff. 179-180 and attached list, f. 37-8. AGI. Coins = 165,000 in 55 chests @ 3,000 per chest.

Page 68. November 13. Lloyd would have been the last to bury his loot.

Page 68. McMahon remains on board and refuses to go with Blackstock. His deposition, WIC inv.nr. 251, pp. 111-118, NAN.

Page 69. Thomas Wallis. Blackstock deposition. CO152/45 ff. 169-172, NAE.

Page 69. William Blackstock discovered. Ibid.

Page 69. Abraham Chalwell. Ibid.

Page 69. James Purcell, Lt. Governor of Tortola. One of the most daring engagements in which a British privateersman demonstrated his valor and the inferiority of the Spanish, took place on December 27, 1742, just off Europa Point within site of the British garrison at Gibraltar. Captain James Purcell, of the privateer brigantine *Pulteney*, was outmanned and outgunned and defeated two Spanish xebeques. The governor of Gibraltar and officers presented Captain Purcell with a silver plate inscribed to commemorate the event. Purcell was made Lt. Governor of the Virgin Islands a few years later and moved to Tortola while maintaining a plantation at St. Kitt's. *SCG*, June 6, 1743; *BNL*, March 21, 1743; April 28, 1743.

Page 69. "*old man if you have any money.*" Blackstock deposition, CO152/45 ff. 169-172, NAE.

Page 69. Captain Purser. Ibid.

Page 69. Dames convinces Tortolans to pay him some of the money. At four in the afternoon a small boat called the *Dove* belonging to Foster Cauleff Esq. and Co. of Liverpool, brought over John Collins, Dr. Thomas Young, Christopher Hodge, and James Webb, all of Tortola, and John Stewart and William Bayron, mariners, to search for treasure. On the way they met up with John Haynes in his sloop the *Tryall* going there as well. The word of the treasure had not only spread quickly around the island of Tortola, but the neighboring islands as well. When they arrived, Haynes suggested that the others join in his gang but Collins and the others objected to this idea until Haynes found three bags of coins and Collins' gang had only found one. It was decided that the two gangs would join in together with some others who were at the spot and form one company and they agreed that every man and boy would share alike and each vessel would share one eighth for carrying the loot back to Tortola. The *Tryall* returned to Tortola with Collins and Haynes with the four bags of dollars and deposited it at Haynes's house. They immediately sailed again for Norman's as the others were still there searching. On the way, they met up with a coble belonging to Thomas Stephens and Christopher Hodge from Tortola which had a large quantity of money on board. Collins and Haynes felt they had a right in a share of Stephens' find so they took it back to Haynes' house and stored it separately, and then returned to Norman's to pick up the others and the additional treasure they had found. On the return to Tortola a dispute arose between them and Stephens and Hodge over the division of the money but it was decided that Stephens and Hodge could keep what they had brought over in the coble. At Tortola the treasure was divided: The first bag found by Collins contained 883 dollars which one quarter, 220 dollars, went to the boat, the remainder was divided seven ways with three shares being retained by Collins totaling 282 dollars. After this the total amount shared was 6,701 dollars out of which Collins took 837 which was the boats part, Haynes got the same for his sloop. There were now twenty two shares equaling 228½ dollars. Collins total equaled 1,567½ dollars. He then paid William Dames 100 dollars which Dames said was rightfully his. Examination of John Collins by James Purcell, July 3, 1751. GCC Box #4, DNA.

Notes from pages 70 to 73

Page 70. "rob the robbers." Letter from Gilbert Fleming the Board of Trade. CO 152/41, f. 22, NAE.

Page 70. *Seaflower* anchors at West India Company harbor. Tutein to West India Company, June 21, 1762; Gert Sprewart de Wint discovers *Seaflower*, letter December, 1752; Suhm December 4, 1752, GCC Box #4, DNA.

Page 71. Lloyd leaves *Seaflower* with Abraham Pritchett. Depositions, WIC inv.nr. 251, pp. 93-124, NAN.

Page 71. Pritchett and McMahon go to St. Kitts. Depositions, WIC inv.nr. 251, pp. 93-124, NAN.

Page 71. Sheriff Ditlev Wilhem Wildhagens. Lit. D, GCC Box #4, DNA.

Page 71. Jan Watts sells sloop. Lloyd deposition, WIC inv.nr. 251, pp. 99-107, NAN. Augustin Pareja to Gilbert Fleming, December 25, 1750, says the vessel was sold by Peter Heyliger, CO. 142/45, f. 209, NAE.

Page 71. Bonilla dispatched one of his officers. A Spanish gentleman from *Guadalupe* went to Boston looking for his money. *MG*, December 12, 1750, via Boston, November 12. Two vessels had come from North Carolina, *BNL*, November 8, 1750.

Page 72. Haynes, Collins, Hodge, and Stephens. CO 152/41, f. 22, NAE.

Page 72. Wallis takes Blackstock back to Norman's. Blackstock deposition, CO152/45 ff. 169-172, NAE.

Page 72. Rebecca Purcell. Ralph Payne to Fleming, November 19, 1750, CO 152/45 ff. 102-3, NAE.

Page 72. Council meeting of November 21, 1750. CO 152/45 f. 139, NAE. Council voted to let Blackstock, Dames, and McClair keep the money.

Page 73. Money divided among Blackstock and others. Blackstock deposition, CO152/45 ff. 169-172, NAE.

Page 73. They gave two bags to Chalwell as a present, one bag to the Collector of Tortola, Walter Gray, one to Thomas Wallis, and one bag to Captain Purser for use of his shallop. Blackstock, Dames and McClair, each kept five bags. Needing cash, McClair and Dames sold their cochineal to Thomas Pickering, Esq., for one hundred pounds (£100) a bag. Blackstock kept a bag of indigo for himself and Dames sold his to Walter Gray. President Chalwell permitted them to keep all of the money as well which was divided equally amongst the three of them which totaled close to nine thousand five hundred dollars. Chalwell, besides getting the cochineal as a present, was given five pieces of silver plate weighing one hundred and four ounces from William Dames as a present for his wife. Dames now had Chalwell's cooperation. When John Downing, Will Ronan, Thomas Stephens, Christopher Hodge and John Collins returned from Norman's with treasure, Dames signed a release to them as if the money was rightfully his and in return received from them eleven hundred eighty Spanish dollars. GCC Box #4, DNA.

Page 73. Dames and Blackstock buy Purser's shallop. Blackstock, ibid.

Page 73. William Dames purchases *Rebecca* built in Christiansted in 1748. Dames then sold the sloop to Robert Brown and George Forbes who returned in the sloop to Bermuda where the Bermuda shipping records say it was registered at Tortola, November 20, 1749. William Dames proceeded on to Ireland. William Dames back dated registration. George Nibbs replaced Walter Gray as Collector of Customs as he had been caught selling blank customs clearance forms with the forged signatures. Bermuda Naval Office, January 30, 1751, entered *Rebecca*, schooner, 40 tons, 4 guns, 4 men, built Christiansted, 1748, registered at Tortola November 20, 1749 (this of course is 1750) to William Dames in ballast from Tortola. Cleared Feb 2, 1751, sloop *True Blue*, George Rankin, captain, registered to William Dames, built Christiansted 1748, 16 tons, 4 guns. *True Blue* came in April 22 from New Providence now owned by Robert Brown & George Forbes carrying 3000 ft. of Madeira plank, January 30, 1751. Entered *Rebecca*, George Rankin, sloop, 16 tons, 4 men, May 2, 1751.

339

Notes from pages 73 to 78

Page 73. McClair marries. CO 152/45 f. 160, NAE. Chalwell said McClair (Livingston) married a young woman from his family, Fleming to Duke of Bedford, December 12, 1750, CO 5 152/45 f. 159-63, NAE.

Page 74. Hogsties Reef. This reef provides a safe anchorage for vessels trading at Dieppe Bay and the Caines plantation. Samuel Baker, op. cit.

Page 74. Blackstock leaves for St. Eustatius. Blackstock, CO152/45 ff. 169-172, NAE.

Page 74. Charles Caines informs Owen Lloyd. Deposition Owen Lloyd, WIC inv.nr. 251, pp. 99-107, NAN. Charles had inherited the estate from his father, Charles senior, who had died in 1737.

Page 74. Lt. Governor Burt. Gilbert Fleming and Payne. Fleming to Duke of Bedford, November 22, 1750, CO 152/45 ff. 104-5, 159-63. NAE.

Page 75. Lloyd gives Charles Caines treasure. His deposition WIC inv.nr. 251, pp. 99-107, NAN; and Payne to Fleming, November 19, 1750, CO 152/45 f. 102. Payne said that two barrels of dollars were sent to his wife at St. Kitts. *Record of the effects recovered by John Watson in the Windward Islands*, Consulados 861, f. 56, AGI.

Page 75. Moorehouse, Deacon, Raye go ashore. Lloyd deposition. WIC inv.nr. 251, pp. 99-107, NAN.

Page 75. Governor Johannes Heyliger gets notice of Lloyd, letter of February 27, 1751. WIC inv. nr. 1188, No. 23, NAN.

Page 75. Treasure seized by Heyliger. ibid.

Page 76. Moorehouse, Deacon, and Raye, flee St. Eustatius. The record shows that they were with Lloyd when he arrived at St. Kitts. Lloyd's deposition, WIC inv.nr. 251, pp. 99-107, NAN. They would have gone with them to St. Eustatius. They were ashore when Heyliger sent soldiers to Lloyd's sloop.

Page 76. Benjamin Gumbs. CO 152/45, ff. 151-2, NAE.

Page 76. Fleming departs for Antigua, Log of HMS *Shark*. CO 152/41 and CO 152/27, St. Christopher's, December 22, 1750, Fleming to the Board of Trade, CO 152/45; *SCG*, January 1, 1750. At the end of October 1749, a great celebration was held at the "New Courthouse" honoring King George II's birthday. Many important citizens from Antigua and St. Kitts were present. That night a ball was held at the Free Masons Lodge. Original story from November 3, 1749, *Antigua Gazette* which is no longer extant.

Page 76. Fleming appoints Ralph Payne deputy governor. Fleming to Duke of Bedford, November 22 (written day he addressed council). CO 152/45 f. 100 and 104-5 NAE.

Page 76. William Burt. Ibid. Fleming addresses Burt's conduct, CO 152/45, f. 63, 101, NAE.

Page 77. Governor Suhm, Hyldloft, Desbroses. His wife was Maria Malleville, daughter of John Malleville of St. Thomas, Her brother, Thomas Malleville, was later governor. Suhm died 1759, age forty at Copenhagen. Christian Suhm's younger brother Anker Suhm, was a distinguished judge in Copenhagen. Allen, op. cit.

Page 77. Greeting from Governor Suhm. GCC Box #4, DNA.

Page 77. Desbroses files report. Santo Domingo 2298, AGI. Letter from Stephen Desbroses, dated December 3, 1750, Puerto Rico, to Governor Augustin Pareja. GCC Box #4, DNA.

Page 77. Governor Pareja to Suhm. Ibid.

Page 78. Interrogation of Lloyd and others at St. Eustatius. WIC inv.nrs. 251, pp. 93-124, NAN. John Baker,

Solicitor General of St. Kitts, Baker *Diary*, op. cit. In Contratacíon 2527, Thomas Carreido testified that the crew of the *Seaflower* had surprised them with "various weapons." *BNL*, November 8, 1750, a passenger from *Guadalupe* who had arrived at Newport, RI, said that the Spanish were threatened with small arms.

Page 79. Lloyd convinces Heyliger to go to Norman's Island. WIC inv.nrs., 251, pp. 93-124, NAN.

Page 80. Jan Farrow, the *Don Phillip*, and Commandant Ravene. WIC inv.nrs. 251, pp. 104-106, NAN.

Page 80. Payne to Fleming, November 30, 1750. November 19, 1750, OS, from St. Christopher's, CO 152/45 f. 102 NAE, says Lloyd in a cistern, John Hynde had 40,000, Robert Hack had 30,000, Mrs. Purcell 20,000 and Mrs. Jeff two canoe loads of jewels and plate. Lloyd sent two barrels of dollars to St. Kitts. Payne applied to Judge Wilson to issue a warrant, CO 152/45, ff. 102-3, NAE.

Page 81. Fleming as Commissioner of Land. http://www.historicbasseterre.com/hs_summation.asp?HSID=7

Page 81. Judge Richard Wilson. His name is mentioned as judge in John Watson's power of attorney. GCC Box #4, DNA; CO 152/45, ff. 102-3, NAE.

Page 81. HMS *Shark* arrives at Antigua. Fleming readies shallop, *Christian*. The *Christian* was owned by David Warner & Co. GCC Box #4, DNA. Fleming assembles armed guard: Fleming to Duke of Bedford, from Antigua, November 22, 1750, CO 152/45 ff. 100-101; *SCG*, January 28, 1751. Soldiers boarded were a captain, a lieutenant, an ensign, two sergeants, four corporals, two drummers, and sixty private men.

Page 81. Fleming to the Duke of Bedford, CO 152/45 ff. 62-63; CO 152/41 ff. 19-24; CO 152/27 ff. 22-23, NAE.

Page 82. Fleming's reception at Antigua courthouse: *SCG* of January 28, 1751, repeats *Antigua Gazette*.

Page 82. Fleming stops at St. Kitts with proclamation November 24, 1750, CO 152/45 f. 165 and f. 133, NAE. Also, Fleming to Duke of Bedford, December 12, 1750, CO 152/45 ff. 159-63 "only a regard for the truth" relates details of Blackstock's deposition. Says he landed at Tortola November 25, 1750, OS. Blackstock said there was one named Trevet on board. He probably was referring to Abraham Pritchett, who was from North Carolina. This indicates that Blackstock was not in allegiance with some of the *Seaflower* crew. Charles McLair must have been in company with William Dames.

Page 83. Smith was "*so hardened in his villainy*, Fleming to Suhm, Antigua, February 15, 1751, Lit. F, GCC Box #4, DNA.

Page 83. Fleming relates his findings to the Duke of Bedford, December 12, 1750, CO 152/45 ff. 159-63 NAE.

Page 83. "Only a regard for the truth," CO 152/45, ff. 136-9, NAE.

Page 84. *Don Phillip* stops at Saba then to Norman's Island, WIC inv.nrs. 251, pp. 125-8, NAN.

Page 85. Fleming arrives at Tortola December 6, 1750. Letter of November 30, 1750, CO 152/45, f. 145, NAE.

Page 85. Fleming to Duke of Bedford, December 12, 1750. CO 152/45 f. 151-9, NAE, describes trip from Antigua to St. Kitts and to Anguilla and Tortola. Says Purcell has gone a great way in civilizing these people. Reports on Heyliger sending soldiers to Norman Island.

Page 86. Fleming calls council meeting. CO 152/45, ff. 139-141, NAE.

Notes from pages 86 to 94

Page 86. Fleming issues new proclamation December 8, 1750. CO 152/45 f. 166-7. NAE.

Page 86. December 19, 1750 council meeting. CO 152/45, ff. 139-141, NAE.

Page 86. Phipps, op. cit. Captain James Phipps, born 1653, settled at St. Kitts. Although uninhabited, Norman Island was owned by the Phipps family of St. Kitts, who were cousins to Sir William Phipps who in 1687 had discovered and salvaged the *Nuestra Señora de la Concepción* lost on a reef north of Santo Domingo in 1641. This reef was known as the "Silver Shoals" from that day on.

Page 86. Fleming wants church. Council Minutes Tortola, December 8, 1750, CO 152/45, ff. 139-141, NAE.

Page 87. Fleming dispatches Captain Fraser to St. Thomas. CO 145/45 f. 145, NAE. Gilbert Fleming to Governor of St. Thomas, Tortola, November 30, 1750. A vessel "commanded by one Lloyd" committed an Act of Piracy at North Carolina. Asks that if the pirates are apprehended in his jurisdiction they be turned over. Wants *Seaflower* and effects.

Page 87. CO 152/45 f. 145, Fleming to Suhm, November 30, 1750, from Tortola sends Blackstock's deposition. Nov 10, 1750, Fleming at St. Kitts to Duke of Bedford.

Page 87. Captain Fraser goes to St. John's. CO 152/45, f. 90, NAE. Enoch Collins was not captured. Zebulon Wade said in his testimony at St. Eustatius that he was a prisoner. No verification of that has been found.

Page 87. News at Scituate, Massachusetts. *BNL*, November 8, December 20, 1750; *NYG* of November 19, 1750, refers to a letter from Boston, November 12, 1750. News of theft, and December 20, 1750, Wade captured. Also *MG*, December 19, 1750.

Page 88. Interrogation of Pritchett and McMahon. WIC inv.nr. 251, pp. 111-124, NAN.

Page 88. Council meeting of December 9, 1750, at St. Eustatius. WIC inv.nr. 251, pp.125-128, NAN.

Page 89. Re-examination of Owen Lloyd. WIC inv.nr. 251, pp 104-6, NAN.

Page 90. The council issues sentence. WIC inv.nr. 251, pp 140-156, NAN.

Chapter Seven
The Unfortunate Spaniard

Page 93. Spaniards pursue Owen Lloyd. Carriedo to Bonilla, October 21, 1750. Consulados 861, f. 179-80, AGI.

Page 93. Prisoners locked in hold of *Guadalupe*. Carriedo to Bonilla, ibid.

Page 93. Treasure theft on *Mary* discovered. Carreido to Bonilla, October 21, 1750.

Page 94. John Lloyd tries to escape, ibid. Escape in canoe mentioned in Bonilla's expense account June 15, 1753, Consulados 861 f. 49-59, AGI.

Page 94. Carreido questions prisoners Carriedo to Bonilla, October 21, 1750, Consulados 861, f. 179-80, AGI.

Page 94. Contract between Bonilla and Governor Johnston to hire HMS *Scorpion*. It appears that before the cargo was loaded on the *Scorpion* it was agreed with the Governor of Carolina that payment would be made "...

as was custom for the trip from there to Europe..." With that in mind, the difference paid by the Spanish should be returned. Estado 4263A, AHN.

Page 95. Letter from Bonilla to Tomás Carriedo, New Bern, October 23, 1750. Consulados 861 f. 183 -184, AGI.

Page 95. "the English aboard be separated from each other." Ibid.

Page 95. Carriedo's letter to Bonilla, October 21, 1750, Consulados 861 f. 179-80, AGI.

Page 95. "*your old friend Thomas Wright*," *Colonial Records of North Carolina*, p. 1304.

Page 95. John Lloyd referred to as "peg-leg," Carriedo to Bonilla, October 21, 1750, Consulados 861, f. 179-80, AGI. In Carriedo's report John Lloyd is referred to as Owen's father, but the later deposition of William Blackstock who sailed with Owen on the *Seaflower* said they were brothers. It is clear however that John was Owen's older brother by more than a few years.

Page 95. "Men of the devil." Bonilla to Carriedo, October 23,1750, Consulados 861, f. 183-4 AGI.

Page 95. "Hands of Death." Bonilla to House of Trade, November 11, 1750, CO 152/45 f. 84-90, NAE; Consulados 861, ff. 88-9, AGI.

Page 96. Sloop from Edenton. Bonilla paid 346 pesos for a sloop from Edenton to carry the prisoners to New Bern. Bonillas expenses, Cádiz, June 15, 1753, Consulados 861 f. 49-59, AGI. Bonilla reported that "The night they reported for duty, they were "tricked" by the English official who took away their guns and gave them to the prisoners for their escape plan. The reference to "English official" seems to indicate Oliver. Carriedo to Bonilla: "And to ensure that everything will go on the sloop with the prisoners, the pilot is to sail with them. He will be a witness as he was aboard and can give his testimony to the Governor."

Page 96. Willam Waller. *Journal of the Governor and Council of New Jersey*, pp. 277-283; Jonathan Belcher, *Letterbooks*, June 1, 1751, Belcher to the Duke of Bedford. *NYG*, April 8, 1751, men apprehended in New Jersey taken to Pert Amboy. Waller escaped and recaptured, *BNL*, April 18, 1751.

Page 96. When Governor Johnston heard of Lloyd's escape with the treasure he sent express messages to the West Indies and impressed two sloops to go after him. One was owned by a Revell Monroe and the other by a Captain Freeman. Watson & Cairnes Expenses, GCC Box #4, DNA.

Page 97. HMS *Scorpion* arrives at Ocracoke Inlet, North Carolina. *Scorpion* log.

Page 97. To Ocracoke to help with the unloading of the *Guadalupe* in October. From *La Galga*: Antonio Fernández, Bartolomé García, Bernardo Iglesias, Fernando Rivera, Diego López, Domingo Martínez, Antonio Felix, Francisco Aguin, Contaduría 8118 – 113, AGB.

Page 97. Actions of HMS *Scorpion*. Log.

Page 97. Customs Collector attempts seizure of *Guadalupe*. *Colonial Records of North Carolina*, p. 1309.

Page 98. Description of cargo transferred October 31, 1750. Consulados 861, f.168, AGI.

Page 98. Receipt for treasure. Consulados 861 f. 168 AGI.

Page 98. Bonilla to Ensenada, November 11, 1750, CO 152/45 f. 84-90, NAE; Consulados 861, ff. 88-9, AGI.

Notes from pages 98 to 102

Page 98. Pedro Rodriguez put on sloop to Virginia. "The boatswain has been arrested," Bonilla to House of Trade, November 11, 1750. Log of *Scorpion*.

Page 98. Captain Randall ordered to stop at Brunswick, on Cape Fear River. *Scorpion* log.

Page 99. *"it was not in the power of man"* Gabriel Johnston to the Duke of Bedford, November 18, 1750. *Colonial Records of North Carolina*, p. 1308.

Page 99. Colonel Innes and Thomas Child at Brunswick. Bonilla to Ensenada, Wilmington, December 15, 1750. CO 152/45 f. 116-7, NAE and Consulados 861, f. 78-9 AGI.
Page 99. Negotiations between Bonilla and Innes. Ibid.

Page 100. Governor of South Carolina makes demands for treasure. Ibid.

Page 100. Governor Glenn warned. Duke of Bedford to Glen, March 12, 1751, SP94/139 f. 112, NAE. Should the King get wind of it, he "will no longer suffer you to remain in your Government." February 8, 1751, Keene to the Duke of Bedford, f. 50.

Page 100. Five English captains make demand for treasure. Bonilla to Ensenada, Wilmington, December 15, 1750. CO 152/45, f. 116-7, NAE and Consulados 861 f. 78-9, AGI. It should be noted that the editor of the *NYG* stated in December 17, 1750, issue that the Spaniards should be seized until restitution be made for their illegal depredations.

Page 100. Captain Pumarejo is warned. Ibid.

Page 100. March 2 at Cádiz. Arrived English ship the *Dorothy* from Norfolk, Virginia, with the cargo saved from the *N.S. Godos*, master Francisco Ortiz, owner Pedro Pumarejo. Contatación 2526, AGI. Also, March 2 at Cádiz. arrived English ship *Alerton*, James Wales from Norfolk with the cargo from the Portuguese ship, *San Pedro*, master Manuel Martínez de Aguiar, which wrecked off the coast of Virginia as she sailed from Cartagena. This ship had originally left for Cartagena from Lisbon. The *Alerton* was also carrying the register of the frigate *La Galga*, Captain Daniel Huony, this ship having wrecked off the coast of Virginia. Mexico 2971; Secretaría de Marina 401 –2. f. 708; Secretaría de Marina 15 –2, Expediente 208, f. 732 – 737, AGS; Reales Órdenes, 6518, AGB; GM-9, AMS.

Page 100. Four chests of treasure taken from *Scorpion*. Ibid.

Page 101. HMS *Scorpion* departs, log. *Scorpion* arrives at Cádiz. January 28, 1751. English paquebot *Scorpion*, Captain Randall from Ocrecock with part of the cargo from the *N.S. Guadalupe*, whose master is Juan Manuel de Bonilla and *apoderado,* Thomas Carriedo. Consulado 861 f. 77, AGI.

Page 101 Carriedo writes the House of Trade, Brunswick, December 16, 1750, CO 152/45 f. 106, NAE.

Page 101. Description of early Wilmington. Watson. Op. cit.

Page 101. Bonilla to Ensenada. Wilmington, December 15, 1750. CO 152/45 f. 116-7, NAE and Consulados 861, f. 78-9, AGI. The Consulado to the Marques de Ensenada, January 29, 1751. CO 152/45 f. 123-5, NAE.

Page 101. Bonilla goes to New Bern, Indiferente General 2304, AGI.

Page 101. Bonilla says Johnston is liable for sloops. Consulados 861, ff. 49-59, AGI; Revell Monroe and Captain Freeman, Expenses of Bonilla, GCC Box#4, DNA

Page 102. *"There is no place in the World…"* Byrd, *Histories*, op. cit.

Page 102. Bonilla goes to New Bern jail. Bonilla's expenses, Cádiz, June 15, 1753, Consulados 861 f. 49-59, AGI.

Chapter Eight
The Empty Gallows

Page 105. Thomas Hobson was let go. After he was interrogated there is no more record of him at St. Eustatius. He was not sentenced.

Page 105. Owen Lloyd as prisoner. WIC inv.nr. 251, pp 99-106, NAN.

Page 106. Commandant Ravene. W.IC inv.nr. 251, pp 134-153, NAN

Page 106. Jan Schraders. Ibid.

Page 106. Jan Jansen and Jan Fredericks. Ibid.

Page 106. The escape plan. It is assumed that Charles Caines and his sister were allowed to visit Owen Lloyd while in prison.

Page 107-8. The escape. The record is clear that the escape was well organized and that the guards were bribed.

Page 108. Schraeders and Charles Caines aid in escape. WIC inv.nr. 251, pp 134-153, NAN.

Page 108. Corporal Praat. Ibid.

Page 108. Governor Heyliger convenes inquiry. WIC inv.nr. 251, pp 134-153, NAN.

Page 109. Owen Lloyd's power of attorney. Lloyd to Thomas Caines, Book R #1 pp.184-90, St. Kitts National Archives.

Page 109. St. Thomas. http://virgin-island-history.dk/eng/high.asp http://www.sa.dk/media(467,1030)/RAFolder35_Danish_West_Indies.pdf

Page 109. William Stapleton, Volume 11, 1682, #777, "What a bad neighbor is the governor of St. Thomas." In 1684, #1537, Thomas Hill Deputy Governor of St. Kitts "Pray remind my lords of the nest of thieves that resorts to St. Thomas." Calendar of State Papers.

Page 109. Ibid, #1546 "The Governor of St. Thomas has been a protector to runaway debtors, servants, and negroes and to pirates, which is a great prejudice to us."

Page 109. John Hamlin. Calendar of State Papers.

Page 109. Captain Kidd. The *Flying Post* of London, August 12, 1699, reported that Captain Kidd had been at St. Thomas where he offered the governor 45,000 pieces of eight in gold for one month's protection which he refused. French Pirate Trompeuse was "received and entertained" by Governor Esmit, himself a privateer. Calendar of State Papers, #1313, #1190, #1216.

Notes from pages 111 to 114

Chapter Nine
The Governors' Greed

Page 111. "*You very well know Sir that Pirates are of no Nation*" Gilbert Fleming to Governor of Puerto Rico, December 8, 1750, CO 152/45, f. 149, NAE.

Page 111. Puerto Rico is a "Pirate's Island," William Matthew to Duke of Bedford from Antigua, March 31, 1749, CO 152/45 f. 27. Spaniards are sending armed vessels out of Puerto Rico to cruise the Virgin Islands and "Insult with Violence His Majesty's Subjects" refers to PR as the "chief nest of pirates" and inhabited by "lawless wretches."

Page 111. Fleming to Pareja, December 8, 1750, CO 152/45 f. 183-4, NAE, says he will do what he can to recover the money.

Page 112. Pareja to Fleming, December 25, 1750, CO 152/45, f. 209, NAE. Says he received Fleming's letter of December 10.

Page 112. Pareja's response to Fleming, December 29, 1750, CO 152/45 f. 193, NAE.

Page 112. Commodore Francis Holburne, Log of HMS *Tavistock*.

Page 112. Orders HMS *Shark* and HMS *Otter* to go after the *Seaflower*. ADM 1/306. Log of *HMS* Shark.

Page 112. HMS *Otter*. Log of *Otter*.

Page 112. December 24, 1750 Fleming reports to the Duke of Bedford his recoveries of treasure. CO152/45 ff. 143-4, NAE.

Page 113. Hynde, Hack, Purcell, and Jeff. Ralph Payne's letter of November 30, 1750. CO 152/45, ff. 102-3, NAE.

Page 113. "*Besides the difficulty of bringing ignorant and wantious people,*" Fleming to the Board of Trade, from St. Christopher's, December 22, 1750. CO 152/41 ff. 21-24, NAE.

Page 113. Governor Benjamin Gumbs and the Smith brothers. Fleming to Suhm, Antigua, February 15, 1751, Lit. F, GCC Box #4, DNA.

Page 113. Antigua, February 14, 1751, Fleming to Suhm from St. Kitts describes Smith brothers. March 30, 1751, St. Kitts, Fleming to Suhm, sent by James Young from Fleming at Antigua sends other letter and asks prosecution of the two Smiths. Lit F, GCC Box #4, DNA.

Page 113. John and Daniel Smith. Ibid.

Page 113. When he wrote the Governor of Puerto Rico in December 17 he commented on the "sickness which rages here" and on January 2, 1751 while at St. Kitts he wrote to the Duke of Bedford that "I laboured there under all sorts of inconveniences, some of them painful, nor was [I] discouraged by the sickness which usually visits the Island at this season, which had seized my secretary, the acting Marshall, the Constables, and several inhabitants of the island." CO 152/27, f.24, NAE.

Page 113. Fleming to Duke of Bedford from Antigua January 25, 1751, CO 152/45 f. 185-8. Transmits correspondence.

Page 114. Gumbs goes after nephews. GCC Box #4, DNA.

Page 114. Governor Suhm to Fleming December 15, 1750. CO152/45 f. 147, NAE.

Page 114. Manuel Franco dispatched to St. Thomas and Tortola. Pareja to Fleming, December 30, 1750, CO 152/45 f. 201, NAE.

Notes from pages 115 to 119

Page 115. Suhm responds to Pareja, January 16, 1751, re: Hyldloft and Desbroses. GCC Box #4, DNA.

Page 115. Ricardo Wall to José Carvajal y Lancaster, December 31, 1750. E6917-7, AGS.

Page 115. December 30, 1750, steps are being taken "to find the criminals and hang them." Wall is confident that His Majesty will take measures "...in those ports to search for these criminals and the stolen cargo although it is feared that this may be an act of piracy..." Estado 6917-7, 6919, AGS.

Page 115. Pareja to Fleming December 25, December 29, and 30, CO152/45 ff. 193, 201. Debroses went to Porto Rico and advised the Governor on December 3, Santo Domingo 2298, AGI. December 26, 1750, Pareja wrote to Governor Suhm and demanded return of the sloop and its contents. Suhm to Pareja, January 16, 1751, GCC Box #4, DNA.

Page 116. *SCG*, February 18, 1751, St. Johns, *Antigua Gazette*, December 28, 1750, Fleming returns from Tortola, says that the "negroes" were the first discoverers of the money. Minutes of Council December 8, 1750, CO 152/45, f. 141, NAE.

Page 116. Consules asks Ensenada for warships. CO 145/52 f. 123-5, NAE.

Page 116. Consules characterized Owen Lloyd and Gabriel Johnston. Ibid.

Page 116. Fleming's letter to *Antigua Gazette*. *SCG*, January 28, and February 18, 1751.

Page 116. Franco presents demand to Fleming February 5, 1751, CO 152/45 f. 191, NAE.

Page 116. Pareja questions Fleming January 25, 1751, CO 152/45, f. 209, NAE.

Page 117. Pareja writes Suhm. GCC Box #4, DNA.

Page 117. Ocracoke, Letter from Pedro de Ortega to Juan Manuel de Bonilla, Ocracoke, January 8, 1751. Consulados 861, f. 185-186, AGI.

Page 117. John Oliver assists. Ibid.

Page 117. Bonilla hires John Watson and Alexander Cairnes. Consulados 861, f.188-190, AGI.

Page 118. Bonilla sends James Campbell. Letter from James Campbell. New Bern, January 22, 1751, addressed to Captain Juan Manuel de Bonilla at Edenton. Consulados 861, f. 159, AGI.

Page 118. Joseph Balch paid 385 pesos. Bonilla's expenses June 15, 1753, Craven County Minutes 1747-52, Raleigh, NC, John Foster licensed to keep tavern at New Bern. Balch was recommended to be sheriff in 1750.

Page 118. Bonilla is released from jail. Bonillas expenses, June 15, 1753. Consulados 861, f. 49 -59, AGI.

Page 118. Governor Suhm advertises auction of *Seaflower*. GCC Box #4, DNA.

Page 118. Gert Sprewart de Wint buys *Seaflower*, wants third of proceeds. Auction details and letter, June 21, 1762, Tutein to West India Company. Ibid.

Page 119. *Nuestra Señora de Guadalupe* (*Nympha*) auctioned. *VG*, February 2, 1751.

Page 119. Bonilla arrives at Suffolk, Va. Letters from David Meade and John Watson to Messrs. Mauman and Macé in Lisbon, from Suffolk, VA, February–March 1751, f.188-190, Consulados 861, AGI. David Meade was a prominent Virginia merchant. His portrait is found in *Virginia Magazine of History*, Vol. 32, p. 140, his biography at *William and Mary Quarterly*, Vol. 13W(i) pp.73-102.

Notes from pages 119 to 124

Page 119. 1749 *Virginia Almanac* describes roads from Charleston to Williamsburg. Description of New Bern by Christopher Von Graffenreid, founder of New Bern. *N.C. Historical Review*, 1945-46. http://docsouth.unc.edu/nc/graffenried/bio.html

Page 120. Bonilla and Watson travel to Williamsburg, VA. Consulados 861, ff. 192-3, AGI; Samuel Ormes named in Bonillas expenses, GCC Box #4, DNA. Ormes was a noted apothecary and a neighbor and friend of Governor Johnston.

Page 120. Benjamin Waller draws up power of attorney. GCC Box #4, DNA.

Page 120. The *Scorpion* arrived in Cádiz, Spain, the afternoon of January 28, 1751. The Madrid newspaper reported the event: "The *Consulado* received the news of the events which it seems were passed on to the His Grace, the Marqués de la Ensenada. A General Meeting in the names of the interests of those involved was held in order to request compensation and apologies from the English crown. Acting with condemnation, zeal and concern they resolved that the most prompt action in the benefit of the interests of the said Don Juan de Bonilla in the said occurrences be taken. They agreed that the distribution of the remaining silver and other cargo according to the arrangement signed with the English captain be left in the charge of the same *Consulado* " In Cádiz, an inventory of her cargo was taken. Besides the sacks of red dye and tobacco, there were 133,724 pesos and 4 reales in silver, 4 chests of jewels and silverware. Felipe Garcia who returned with the *Scorpion* had his own chest with 2500 pesos of which only half were his. The other half belonged to other sailors and officials and, there were some small sacks addressed to the wives of the sailors who had drowned during the hurricane. Contracíon 2527. *Scorpion* cargo printed in the *London Gazette*, June 4, 1751.

Page 120. Fleming to Suhm February 25, 1751. GCC Box #4, DNA.

Page 121. Suhm gives Fraser inventory. GCC Box #4, DNA.

Page 121. Louisa of Hanover. http://www.cracroftspeerage.co.uk/online/content/Hanover.htm

Page 121. Major James Young, arrived at St. Thomas in March 1751. GCC Box #4, DNA. Page 121. Suhm says he would turn over any English bandit. GCC Box #4, DNA.

Page 121. Young arrives at Antigua then goes to St. Kitts. GCC Box #4, DNA.

Page 122. Fleming to Suhm. March 30, 1751. Lit. F, GCC Box #4, DNA.

Page 122. Bonilla writes Mauman and Macé. Consulados 861, f. 161, 188-90, AGI

Page 122. David Meade's cover letter. Ibid.

Page 123. Bonilla learns of Lloyd's escape. Ibid.

Page 123. Governor Johnston issued an order of apprehension at Cape Hatteras. *VG*, March 7, 1751.

Page 123. *True Patriot* arrived at Yorktown, Virginia, *VG*, March 7, 1751.

Page 123. *Jubilee*. *VG*, March 7, 1751; *MG*, March 13, 1751; *NYG*, April 8, 1751. No record was found for the fate of Pedro Rodriguez. He obviously had a lot to lose by arriving in Spain for his trial. It is logically assumed that any innocent Spaniards traveling home on the *Jubilee* would not need to mutiny. The mutiny was probably instigated by Rodriguez.

Page 124. Meade sends John Stallings to Norfolk, VA. Bonilla expenses, GCC Box #4, DNA.

Page 124. *Guadalupe* registered to David Meade. CO 5/1446, NAE.

Notes from pages 124 to 128

Page 124. The expense accounts of Watson, Cairnes, Meade, Bonilla. GCC Box #4, DNA.

Page 125. Thomas Gibson, son of James Gibson. Will of John Lidderdale names John Watson and James Gibson to be joint attorneys, p. 189, Norfolk, Wills. October 26, 1758, James Gibson vestryman of Nansemond County.

Page 125. The *Caesar*. March 18, 1751, OS. Ship *Caesar* 230 tons, 2 guns, 18 men, Captain James Sword to St. Kitts owned by John King & Co. of Bristol carrying oats, hoops, tar, turpentine, pork, corn, tallow, staves, heads, and shingles. Arrived St. Kitts April 9, 1751, *Lloyd's List*, June 7, 1751; Expenses, GCC Box #4, DNA.

Page 125. David Meade to the Consules March 29, 1751. Re *Scorpion*. Consuldos 861, f. 188-90, AGI.

Page 126. Watson hires John Baker, Expenses, GCC Box #4, DNA.

Page 126. Power of attorney recorded, Lit. T, ibid.

Page 126. Watson makes demand on Charles Caines, ibid.

Page 126. Robert Nichol's Tavern, expenses, GCC Box #4, DNA.

Page 126. Watson arrives at Antigua, ibid.

Page 127. Power of attorney recorded, Lit T, ibid.

Page 127. Watson presents petitions, Expenses, ibid.

Page 127. Duke of Bedford consults with solicitors and Ambassador Wall. SP 94/139, ff. 110-11, 189, 204-210; SP 42/138, ff. 496-99, NAE.

Page 127. Fleming gets £1,000. His accounting ,May 21, 1751, certified by John Watson in London, February, 1752. GCC Box #4, DNA.

Page 127. For the Spaniards at St. Kitts see *SCG*, September 5, 1743.

Page 127. Fleming goes with Watson to St. Kitts. GCC Box #4, DNA.

Page 127. Fleming's expenses. Ibid.

Page 127. Governor Gumbs reimbursed. Ibid.

Page 128. Vessel from Cumaná. Letter from John Watson to Bonilla. Antigua, May 12, 1751. Consulados 861, ff. 210-11, AGI.

Page 128. Watson writes "…it is my opinion that the action of the Governor of St. Thomas…is such a wicked thing for having made him (Lloyd) a resident of that island and announcing publicly that he (Lloyd) was under his protection …" Consulados 861 f. 210-1, AGI.

Page 128. Watson to Bonilla, May 12, 1751. Letter from John Watson to Bonilla, Antigua, Consulados 861, f. 210- 211, AGI.

Page 128. Hunter's warehouse. Letter from Pumarejo to Bonilla or in his absence, Pedro M. de Ortega. Norfolk, December 1, 1750, Consulados 861, f. 212- 213, AGI.

Page 128. *Polly* in from North Carolina April 1, 1751, Captain Crawford. *Polly* cleared April 30. CO 5/1446, NAE. The ship was owned by Thomas Lamden of Maryland and rated at one hundred and eighty tons. The

Notes from pages 128 to 135

Polly had come in from London on April 12 NS, sent by the Lidderdale Company, Meade's correspondents and Bonilla's insurers. The contract also allowed for a freight guarantee for Crawford when he left Cádiz for London. Each party was then bound to a £1000 penalty for breach of contract. Contract for the outfitting of the 180 ton *Polly*, anchored in the James River, Virginia. Williamsburg. April 23, 1751. Consulados 861, f.192-193, AGI.

Page 128. *VG*, April 15, 1751, from Boston account of stolen money and Spanish depredations, also *NYG* account February 4, 1751, about Waller.

Page 129. The *Polly* sails. CO 5/1446, NAE.

Page 129. Meade to Consules, May 15, 1751. Letter from David Meade to the Prior and Consules del Comercio de España (Cádiz), Suffolk, Virgina, May 4, 1751, Consulado 861 f. 203-4, AGI.

Page 129. Bonilla at Mother Hawkins'. Expenses, GCC Box #4, DNA. While in Hampton, they stayed at the inn of Mrs. Jane Wheeler, ibid. Robert Wheeler died 1748. Will dated June 18, heirs are wife Jannett and son, estate was sold, she was executor, Elizabeth City County Deeds and Wills, p. 288.

Page 130. *Polly* boarded by two Algerian men-of-war. Hugh Crawford wrote that about 70 leagues from Cape St. Vincent, his ship came across two Algerian ships which followed them for two days until reaching the cape. There, the *Polly* met two Spanish warships and a tartana and these pursued the Moorish ships at once. México 2971 – Cádiz June 22, 1751; *VG*, October 11, 1751.

Page 130. Perth Amboy, Waller apprehended. *BNL*, April 18, 1751. *Jonathan Belcher Letterbooks*, op. cit.

Page 130. Watson leaves Antigua. Consulados 861, ff. 210-11, AGI. He arrived at St. Eustatius on June 9, 1751. Estado 4263B, AHN.

Page 130. Watson gets six bags cochineal found on Blackstock. GCC Box #4, DNA.

Page 131. Watson leaves for St. Eustatius, purchase broadsword. Expenses, GCC Box #4, DNA.

Page 131. Watson's demand. GCC Box #4, DNA.

Page 131. Heyliger convenes council. SG 5787, NAN.

Page 131. Watson goes to St. Thomas. GCC Box #4, DNA.

Page 132. Watson demands custody of Owen Lloyd, GCC Box #4, DNA. There is no doubt Owen Lloyd would have been hung by the English government. A Captain White was hung at Antigua for robbing a Spanish advice boat in 1757, CO 152/46.

Page 133. Governor Suhm responds. Suhm to Watson, June 30, 1751, GCC Box #4, DNA.

Page 134. Watson files protest. Expenses, GCC Box #4, DNA.

Page 134. Fleming sends HMS *Shark*. Log.

Page 134. Movements of *Shark*, ADM 36/3428, NAE, muster log of *Shark*, March 7 to August 31, 1751.

Page 134. Fleming to Pareja, May 21, 1751. CO 152/45 f. 255, from St. Christopher's. Fleming responds to Pareja's of April 13 and December 29, 1750 which was an answer to Fleming's of December 10. Fleming sends Captain Falkingham of the *Shark*. He has orders to go to St. Thomas "to repeat and enforce my demand of Lloyd the pirate who is protected there."

Notes from pages 134 to 139

Page 134. *Guadalupe* arrives at Suffolk, VA. Suffolk was built around Constant's Wharf, the center of town and the landing place for ships. Clark, op. cit., p. 7.

Page 135. Mathias Jones, Bonilla expenses, GCC Box #4, DNA.

Page 135. Governor Purcell holds examinations. GCC Box #4, DNA.

Page 135. Gilbert Fleming reinforces treaty with Spain, Fleming to Pareja, May 21, 1751. CO 152/45 f. 255, NAE. Fleming to the Duke of Bedford, June 26, 1751, from St. Christopher's. CO 152/45 f. 229, delivers money to Watson deducting expenses. Gives Watson letters for Heyliger and Suhm. Made a second demand for Lloyd where he "has found protection and is admitted a Burgher." Commodore Holburne has sent the *Shark* to enforce it. Says he furnished Franco with account of dollars.

Page 135. Watson petitions for release of cochineal. GCC Box #4, DNA. Six bags of cochineal quarantined at St. Kitts were being forwarded to London on the ship *Howstown*, Captain George Douglas, which arrived that August and the cochineal was sold. Magens received £1,000. London, August 1752, Consulados 861, f. 304; GCC Box #4, DNA.

Page 135. Chavera. Expenses of Watson at St. Kitts and Antigua, GCC Box #4, DNA.

Page 136. James Doig and John Halliday. Well known merchants of Antigua of Scottish descent employed by Bonilla. Doig and Halliday to Bonilla, July 27, 1751, wrote to Bonilla and reported on Watson's success. They told him that the treasure deposited with them was on its way to London in the *Prince Frederick*, Captain John Burton, and was being delivered to the Lidderdales. Letter to Bonilla from James Doig and John Halliday. Antigua, July 16, 1751, (OS), Consulados 861, f. 206, AGI. Owen Lloyd makes overtures through friends. Letter from Bonilla to the Prior y Consules del Comercio de Cádiz, London, December 2, 1751. Consulados 861 f. 221-2, AGI.

Page 136. Watson returns to St. Kitts. Expenses, GCC Box #4, DNA.

Page 137. The *Caesar* returns to Hampton, VA, August 13, 1751, with sugar, 7,000 gallons of rum, 1,000 gallons of molasses. CO 5/1446, NAE.

Page 137. Bonilla leaves Suffolk. GCC Box #4, DNA.

Page 137. John Blair entertains Watson. *William and Mary Quarterly*, VIII, Series 1, p. 11.

Page 137. Watson makes final accounting. GCC Box #4, DNA.

Page 137. Watson and Bonilla leave for Spain and England. He may have gone via Lisbon. Bonilla was in Cádiz by October 13, 1751. He was able to check on cochineal that had been carried on the *Polly*. Cádiz, October 13, 1751, Contratación 4759.

Chapter Ten
Silver and the Embassies

Page 139. Bonilla arrives in London. Letter from Bonilla at London to the Prior y Consules del Comercio de Cádiz,December 2, 1751, Consulado 861, f. 221-2, AGI.

Page 139. *Guadalupe* was insured in London. Mexico, October 23, 1754, Consulados 796, AGI.

Page 139. Robert and John Lidderdale. Scottish merchants who had interests in Virginia and London. Consulados 861, f. 161, AGI. http://www.lidderdale.com/gen070.html

Notes from pages 140 to 144

Page 140. Ricardo Wall visits the Duke of Bedford. Wall communicated all of this to the Spanish crown and "...I have the most strict orders from H.M. the King to contest not only the excessive amount charged for the saving of the cargo but also that...it is not acceptable that benefits should be made from the hospitality granted to those who arrive by shipwreck along the coasts of Your Majesty's dominions and require repairs, provisions, and other things..." Wall cites the examples of a 1726 French ship which wrecked off Murcia (Spain) and an English ship off Gibraltar both of which received assistance from the Spanish. Estado 4263A, AHN.

Page 140. Coded messages. Wall to Carvajal, London, January 28,1751; Wall to Carvajal London, March 4, 1751; Wall to Carvajal London, March 11,1751; Wall to Carvajal, London, March 24, 1751. Estado 6919, AGS.

Page 140. King Ferdinand at Aranjuez, May 3, 1751. Estado 4263B, AHN.
Carvajal y Lancaster to Wall. Ibid.

Page 141. Wall reports on President Lee in Virginia. Estado 4263A, AHN. August 7, 1751, f. 103, Duke acknowledges approval by the king of Lee's treatment of Spanish. He is concerned that Johnston took £12,000, f. 91. Account of shipwrecks, September 28, 1750, NS.

Page 141. Solicitors general, Messrs. Paul, Ryder, and Murray. SP 42/138, NAE, June 4, 1751, to the Duke of Bedford. They are of the opinion that all money recovered at Norman and Tortola should be returned to Bonilla. See also SP 94/139 f. 208, NAE.

Page 142. Johnston and freight charges. Letters from the Marqués de Ensenada to Varas y Valdés, February 6, July 12, July 27, 1751. Arribidas 32, AGI.

Page 142. Benjamin Keene, England's ambassador to Spain. London, June 24, 1751, Wall to Carvajal y Lancaster and the Marqués de Ensenada, Estado 4263 A, AHN.

Page 142. Marqués del Puerto, Spain's ambassador to The Netherlands. Madrid, November 22, 1751, Arribadas 32, AGI.

Page 142. The Marques relates efforts of John Watson. October 14, 1751, SG 3514, ff. 332-335, NAN.

Page 143. The States General. Presentation by the Marquis del Puerto, October, 12, 1751, SG 3509, ff. 367-9, NAN.

Page 143. Governor Heyliger's letter of August 23, 1751, WIC 251, f. 192, NAN.

Page 143. *"punish the authors of such a horrible crime."* October 14, 1751, SG 3509, ff. 367-9, NAN.

Page 143. Marqués de Puerto demands treasure. SG 3512, f. 238, NAN.

Page 144. Copies sent to West India Company and Dutch ambassador. Ibid.

Page 144. Wall appoints Felix José Abreu y Bertodano, to carry on his duties. London, August 30, 1751. Letter from Wall to Carvajal y Lancaster, Estado 6920, AGS.

Page 144. Lord Holderness. Robert Darcy, 4th Earl of Holderness, was a British diplomatist and politician. From 1744 to 1746 he was ambassador at Venice and from 1749 to 1751 he represented his country at The Hague. In 1751, he became Secretary of State for the Southern Department. http://www.cracroftspeerage.co.uk/online/content/Holderness1682.com

Page 144. James Doig and John Halliday. Magens to Fabritius, Consulados, 861, ff. 239-40, AGI.

Notes from pages 144 to 146

Page 144. Deposit of £20,000. London, August 27, 1751, Wall to the Marqués de Ensenada, Estado 4263B, AHN.

Page 144. Bonilla reports to Consules about treasure recoveries. Record of the effects recovered by John Watson in the Windward Islands, Consulado 861 f. 56, AGI.

Page 144. Bonilla calculates the total amount to be 107,265 ½ pesos, Consulados 861, f. 56, AGI, broken down as follows:

       39,629 ½ pesos de a 8 reales
       55,900 pesos mexicanos (44,720 1/10 hacen de a 8)
       6,986 pesos (1,945 libras, 17 chelines, 9 pesos)
       1,000 pesos in silverware
       3,750 pesos for 1,200 libras of grana at 12 chelines y 6 peniques

Page 144. Bonilla conveys list of auctioned cargo to House of Trade Camara de Indias, Customs. April 2, 1763, Consulados 861, f. 135v, AGI.

Page 145. James Abercromby writes to Governor Johnston. *Abercromby Letterbook*, the 5,500 pesos was retained by Johnston, the rest was for actual expenses "as gratification for those generous, important, good offices." Abercromby, op. cit. July 13, 1751.

Page 145. Letter to Gabriel Johnston, December 9, 1751, p. 21. Bonilla is with Watson in London "has already applied to the Spanish minister for restitution from you. Mr. Watson is your friend in this matter, yet he is concerned for the Spaniards." Ibid.

Page 145. Abercromby's special salary, xxiii, ibid.

Page 145. Abercromby to Johnston. P. 18, "Child is determined to keep what he has got and so has Innes," ibid.

Page 145. John Watson reporting to Abercromby, ibid, p. 41.

Page 145. December 16, 1751, Bonilla receives money. Letter from Bonilla to the House of Trade. London, December 16, 1751 Consulados 861, f. 216, AGI.

Page 145. By March 2, 1752. Letter from Bonilla to the House of Trade. London, March 2, 1751. Consulado 861 f. 225 – 6 AGI.

Page 145. Bonilla purchases *York*. London, July 14, 1752, Contratación 1548, AGI. The *York* is renamed the *Peregrina*. The *Peregrina* was of English construction.

Page 145. Watson is complaining, recommends Magens. Letter from Bonilla to the House of Trade. London, March 2, 1751, Consulados 861 f. 225 – 6, AGI. When Watson gave up power of attorney, he acknowledged the sum of £576 pounds 18 shillings, and 6 pence by a bond dated February 20. In this bond, Bonilla and Nicolas Magens were bound jointly under penalty of £1,000 pounds to Watson for payment of the said £576. In consideration of the money paid, Watson quitclaimed to Bonilla all claims against him for his services. Watson then exempted Bonilla from suit by David Meade and Alexander Cairnes in another bond with Meade in the amount of £748, and all other powers of attorney were cancelled. Soon afterwards Magens left for Antigua. GCC Box #4, DNA.

Page 146. Bonilla hires Nicolas Magens. Bonilla to the Consules de Cádiz, London, April 1752, Consulados 861 f. 223 – 224, AGI. Magens is coming back from Antigua.

Page 146. Bonilla to House of Trade. London, March 2, 1751, Consulados 861 f. 225 – 6, AGI.

353

Notes from pages 146 to 150

Page 146. Magens identifies William Dames. Letter from Bonilla to the House of Trade. London, March 2, 1751 Consulados 861 f. 227, AGI.

Page 146. Magens appoints William Gideon Deutz and Justus Fabritius. Magens to Consules, October 2, 1752, Consulados 861, ff. 237-8, AGI.

Page 146. Watson writes Governor Suhm on March 3, 1752. GCC, Box #4, DNA.

Page 147. Bonilla receives word he can return home. Bonilla to Consules of Cádiz. London, April 1752. Consulados 861, f. 223-4, AGI.

Page 147. Watson receives letters from home. Abercromby, op. cit.

Page 147. *"although these are rich men"* Bonilla to Consules of Cádiz. London, April 1752, Consulados 861, f. 223-4, AGI.

Page 147. "the governor of North Carolina as Governor ought not to Demand any Duty or Gratification whatsoever to himself upon that Acco^t." Paul, Ryder and Murray, June 4, 1751, f. 204-5, SP 94/139, NAE.

Page 147. Gabriel Johnston dies at Eden House. *VG*, July 24, 1752.

Page 147. Salary in arrears £13,000. Abercromby continued to prosecute his salary arrears. Abercromby, op. cit.

Page 147. Johnston's widow remarries. http://files.usgwarchives.net/nc/wayne/heritage/johnston.txt

Page 147. Bonilla's losses not insured. Mexico, October 23, 1754, Consulados 796, AGI. His losses for the *Guadalupe* were mentioned in his case of the loss of the *Peregrina* cargo, Contratación 5161, AGI.

Page 148. West India Company investigates Heyliger. SG 3514, NAN.

Page 148. *"the proof and the evidence are bright like the sunshine."* SG 5785, NAN. In a letter from St. Kitts, October 16, 1747, William Mathew to Board of Trade, CO 152/25, NAE, he reports that 90% of all trade at St. Eustatius goes through Heyliger's hands and also there was an illicit trade from St. Kitts to St. Eustatius.

Page 148. Marques del Puerto alleges auction rigged. SG 5785, NAN.

Page 148. Heyliger tries to discredit Watson and Fleming. Ibid.

Page 149. The council backs Heyliger. Ibid.

Page 149. Meeting of the Board of Ten of the West India Company. SG 5785, NAN.

Page 149. Heyliger dies. John Baker *Diary*, p. 69, op. cit.

Page 149. Halliday forwards effects. Consulados 861, f. 57, 61, AGI.

Page 149. Halliday and James Doig had been to St. Thomas. Letter from Nicolás Magens to Juan Manuel de Bonilla. London, July 30, 1752. Consulados 861 f. 232, AGI.

Page 150. Magens reports successes to Bonilla. Ibid.

Page 150. Reports on Danish court. Letter from Nicolas Magens to Juan Manuel de Bonilla. London, December 7, 1752. Consulados 861 f. 245, AGI.

Page 150. "because a pirate is everywhere deemed a common enemy." Geronimo de Ariscum to Magens

Notes from pages 150 to 156

translated out of Spanish, September 12, 1752, GCC Box #4 DNA.

Page 150. *Guadalupe* prepares to return. July 19, 1751, came in *Nympha*, Cornelius Campbell, 430 tons, 17 guns, 12 men, registered to David Meade. *Nansemond* came in same day. May 31, 1751, NS, cleared for Ocracoke in ballast John Hews. *Nansemond* described as former French prize of 1748. Another entry December 11 says she was a Spanish prize. CO 5/1446, NAE.

Page 150. HMS *Triton* ordered to escort. Log of *Triton*.

Page 151. *Guadalupe* in distress. Ibid; Reports. ADM 1/2659, NAE.

Page 152. Thomas Child in London. Letter from Bonilla to the House of Trade. London, December 9, 1751 Consulado 861 f. 219-20, AGI.

Page 152. Three thousand pesos and the silverware sent to Amsterdam aboard the ship *Zorg & Rust*, Captain Carl Frederic Brandt. Letter from Nicolas Magens to the Consules of Cádiz, London, August 8, 1754, Consulados 861, f. 140 –1,147, AGI. Copies of the memos were ordered sent to representatives of the King and to Sir Huyninck and the other administrators of the General Chartered West-Indian Company at the Presidial. WIC 251, NAN.

Page 152. May 17, 1753, Magens reports. Consulados 861, ff. 140-7, AGI.

Page 152. *"...so much time is wasted in writing letters."* Magens to Fabritius in Copenhagen, Consulados 861, ff. 239-40, AGI.

Page 152. John Boydell publishes some engravings. Found in Walker, op cit.and Greenwich Maritime Museum. See page 92.

Page 152. Bonilla's expense reports. Filed June 15, 1753, Consulados 861, ff. 49-59, AGI.

Page 153. West India Company sends ruling to Suhm.GCC Box #4, DNA.

Page 153. Bonilla boards the *Peregrina*. Contratación 5161, AGI.

Page 153. *Peregrina* is overloaded. Consulados 796, AGI.

Page 154. Description of voyage. Ibid. Contración 5156, AGI.

Page 154. Arrives at Bay of San Antonio. Ibid.

Page 155. Langara arrives. Ibid.

Page 155. Carreido dies at sea. Ibid: March 19 at Cádiz from Veracruz, *La Reina de los Angeles* alias *La Peregrina*. Master Manuel Prieto replacing Tomas Carriedo who died on the outgoing trip. This ship arrived with the *Oriente*, *N.S. de la Rosa* and *N.S. Ariarte*. Contratación 2555, AGI.

Page 155. Viceroy of Mexico calls hearing. Ibid.

Page 156. Authorities in Puerto Rico ask that Bonilla be charged. Ibid.

Page 156. October 23, 1753 Bonilla writes merchant guild. Ibid.

Page 156. *Peregrina* returns to Cádiz, 1756. Contratación 2555; Contratación 1548 - Registro de ida de la *Peregrina*. AGI.

Notes from pages 157 to 161

Page 157. June 1754 meeting of Consules. Consulados 861, ff. 308-9, AGI.

Page 157. August 8, 1754 Nicolas Magens reports to the Consules. Consulados 861 f. 140-1, AGI.

Page 157. April of 1755, he wrote to Don Gerónimo Ariscum. Letter from Nicolas Magens to D. Gerónimo Ariscum in Cádiz. London, April 8, 1755. Consulados 861 f. 157- 8, AGI.

Page 157. Queen Barbara dies. http://www.answers.com/topic/ferdinand-vi-of-spain

Page 158. Juan Domingo Pignatelli, was now Bonilla's representative. Estado 6734, AGS.

Page 158. Governor Christian Suhm dies. www.vifamilies.org/images/Suhm.doc

Page 158. King Ferdinand dies. http://www.nndb.com/people/932/000097641

Page 158. Governor of Jamaica stakes claim. Letter from Julian de Arriaga to Estebán Joseph de Abaria. Madrid, January 26, 1759. Consulados 861 f. 251, AGI.

Page 158. Copenhagen demands new claim. September 15, 1761, Pignateli to Wall, Estado 4734, AHN.

Page 158. Bonilla prepares his will. Tomo 5754 f. 132-7, APC.

Page 159. List of shippers marks. *Rateo del liquido producido por 100 tercios de grana, 6 de añil, 3 caxones de vanilla y 82 cueros curtidos que habiendo sido robados por un pirata inglés del registro español nombrada* La Guadalupe… *Cádiz 19 de junio de 1764*. Consulados 861 f. 136, AGI.

Page 160. Bonilla was buried at the Convento de los Descalzos, Tomo 16: f. 56, ACHC.

Page 160. Magens still employed. Letter from Nicolas Magens to the Consules of Cádiz, London, September 12, 1760, Consulados 861,f. 249-50, AGI.

Page 160. On January 7, 1760, the Chamber of Customs replaced the Chamber of Revenue.

Page 160. Don Joseph Cadalso arrived in Copenhagen. Paris, July 15, 1761. Letter from Joseph Cadalso to Lorenzo de Aristegui, diputado de Comercio de Andalucia, Consulados 861 f. 256, AGI.

Page 160. Pignatelli notifies Baron von Bernstorff. September 15, 1761, Pignateli to Wall, Estado 4743, AHN. Johann Hartwig Ernst Bernstorff, 1712-72, Danish politician, of German (Hanoverian) origin. As minister of foreign affairs (1751-70) under Frederick V and Christian VII, he successfully kept Denmark at peace. http://wwwencyclopedia.com/doc/1E1-BernstorJHE.htm

Page 160. Cadalso arrives at Copenhagen, September 15, 1761, Estado 4743, AHN.

Page 161. Pignatelli advised Ricardo Wall in Madrid 1761. Estado 4743, AHN.

Page 161. Juan Domingo Pignateli to Ricardo Wall, Copenhagen. February 22, 1763. The Spanish ambassador Juan Domingo Pignatelli to Ricardo Wall, Estado 6734, AGS.

Page 161. Cadalso comes down with a fever. Copenhagen, October 6, 1761, Juan Domingo Pignateli to Ricardo Wall. Estado 4743, AHN.

Page 161. Spain and the Seven Years War. http://www.historyworld.net/wrldhis/PlainTextHistories.asp?historyid=aa66 On February 10, the Treaty of Paris was signed officially ending the bloody conflict known in the future as the Seven Years War. England became the world's superpower.

Notes from pages 161 to 162

Page 161. Bernstorff to Pignatelli. February 21, 1763, Copenhagen, Letter in French from Monsieur Bernstorff to the Spanish ambassador Pignatelli. Cadalso was the owner of the some of *Guadalupe* cargo. The Spaniards are to be reimbursed. Estado 6734, AGS.

Page 161. Constant receives 27,623 pesos. February 22, 1763, Copenhagen. The Spanish ambassador, Juan Domingo Pignatelli, to Ricardo Wall. Constant granted power of attorney from Cadalso. March 29, 1763, Copenhagen Pignateli to Wall Estado 6734, AGS.

Page 162. The treasure is disbursed. Letras remitidas by Joseph Constant from Copenhagen procedentes del valor de efectos robados del navío *Guadalupe* de D. Juan Manuel Bonilla. June 21 – July 20, 1763. Consulados 861 ff. 134, 255, 258, 262, 280, 288 AGI. Camara de Indias, April 2, 1763.

Page 162. Bonilla's children. Tomo 913, ff.174-198; Tomo 117, ff. 489-90; Tomo 133, Protocolos de San Fernando (Cádiz), ff. 212-216; TOMO 54, f. 50. ACHC.

Page 162. William Howard acquires Ocracoke. http://www.ocracokepreservation.org/mullet/fall02pg01.pdf

Page 162. The outcome of the crews of the *Seaflower* and the *Mary*:

Abraham Pritchett – First Mate. Born in New Bern, North Carolina. His Father, Abraham owned land on the west side of South Dividing Creek, on the south side of the Pamlico River. He obviously survived as he had a son named Abraham, Jr. born July, 7, 1756 in Rowan County, North Carolina. Abraham's Father died in 1749. He had been Justice of the Peace for Beaufort County in 1734 and 1739. Pritchett escaped with Lloyd from St. Eustatius and witnessed the power of attorney signed at St. Kitts. He was noted as a mariner of Boston in deed from him to Philip Pritchett, October 1, 1759, Beaufort County Wills and Deeds #3, p. 540. In 1772, there was a deed to" Zebulon Pritchett," Book #4 p. 441. He later married Mary and had a son Abraham, July 7, 1756.

Thomas Hobson – Ship's Boy on the *Seaflower*. Testified that he was fourteen years old and born in North Carolina. The name Francis Hobson appears in North Carolina documents, probably his father. On March 6, 1769, will recorded for Thomas Hobson: five children, Mary Ann, Elizabeth, Thomas, Thebe, Adcock. Beaufort County Wills, Raleigh, NC.

James McMahan – Approximately twenty six years old as he stated in his deposition. He said he was born "on the island." This probably meant at St. Eustatius, but it might refer to Ocracoke. He described himself as only a passenger on the *Seaflower* and came aboard with Enoch Collins as hired hands. He said that he was at Ocracoke because his vessel had been lost in the hurricane. There was a James McMahan born in Rowan County, North Carolina in about 1724 per familysearch.org. He had a son named James born in Rowan in 1747. In his deposition he called himself James Matthews but admitted that "some say that in fact his family call him James McMahon." He had been left at St. Thomas by Lloyd and Wade and was later captured at Saba and taken to St. Eustatius. He then escaped with Lloyd and Wade from there.

James Moorehouse – William Blackstock identified him as being part of his original crew when he sailed from Rhode Island. Blackstock said he was from Connecticut and may be his son-in-law or brother-in-law. A James Moorehouse was born in Fairfield, Connecticut in 1719, christened November 11, 1719, married about 1743, died after 1753. Another James Moorehouse born about 1731 Stratfield, CT. Married October 2, 1756 to Lavinia. Familysearch.org. Lloyd said he was with him at St.Eustatius. He gave no recorded testimony, however, and was not listed as an escapee. He, Isaac Ray, and Jonathan Deacon escaped capture at St. Eustatius as they had been ashore when Lloyd, Wade, and Hobson were apprehended on board their schooner at St. Eustatius.

Isaac Raye – He appears to be one of the original *Seaflower* crew from Wade's deposition. Owen Lloyd testified that he was with him at St. Eustatius. He gave no recorded testimony however, and was not listed as an escapee. He, James Moorehouse, and Jonathan Deacon escaped capture at St. Eustatius as they had been ashore when Lloyd, Wade, and Hobson were apprehended on board their schooner at St. Eustatius. An Isaac Ray was born in Haddam, Middlesex, Connecticut in 1723, and died in 1802. Familysearch.org

Notes from pages 161 to 166

Jonathan Deacon - He appears to be one of the original *Seaflower* crew from Wade's deposition. Owen Lloyd testified that he was with him at St. Eustatius. He gave no recorded testimony, however, and was not listed as an escapee. He, Isaac Ray, and James Moorehouse escaped capture at St. Eustatius as they had been ashore when Lloyd, Wade, and Hobson were apprehended on board their schooner at St. Eustatius. There was a Jonathan Deacon christened in Marblehead, Massachusetts in1757. His father was listed as Jonathan Deacon, with no birth date given. Jonathan Deacon born June 14, 1729, Boston, Suffolk, Massachusetts, married to Eleanor, had a son named Jonathan Deacon born July 3, 1757, at Marblehead, Essex, Massachusetts. Familysearch.org

Enoch Collins – Came aboard the *Seaflower* with James McMahan at Ocracoke. He was left at St. Thomas with Abraham Pritchett and James McMahan by Wade and Lloyd. He was not with Pritchett and McMahan when they were captured at Saba. Wade testified that he was an Irishman and "a prisoner." This would have to be at St. Thomas. In GCC Box #4, Lit. D, DNA, this statement seems to refer to Collins:" keeping watch by the English sailor from the barque for 5 days and nights, sitting at the court, two questionings of the English sailor in the house where he was lodging, being on board the barque Elisabeth during the unloading." It is believed that he escaped since no further mention is made of him at St. Thomas. An Enoch Collins was born in December of 1731 in Chatham, Barnstable, Massachusetts, no death date recorded. Familysearch.org

Charles McClair – Came on board the *Seaflower* with William Blackstock and William Dames. He used the alias of Charles Livingston at Tortola. Referred to as an "old man" and was left at Norman Island by Lloyd and Wade. The records from Tortola say he remained there and married woman from President Chalwell's family

William Dames – Came on board the *Seaflower* with William Blackstock. Lloyd testified he was from Annapolis. Blackstock said he was from Virginia. Wade and McMahan described him as an "Irishman." Records in Hampton, Virginia, 1746, describe him as being from Newtown (Pocomoke), Maryland. The *Pennsylvania Gazette* of February 3, 1747, gives an account of the loss of a vessel owned by Mr. Dames of Newtown having been cut to pieces by ice there. The vessel was carrying salt, rum, and molasses, which indicated he traded in the West Indies. The port records of Bermuda record a sloop named *Rebecca*, Captain George Rankin, registered to a William Dames came in to Bermuda in ballast from Tortola January 30, 1751. Other articles in the *Gazette* mention a William Dames from Queen Ann County, Maryland. This is directly across the Chesapeake Bay from Annapolis. A search of the Anne Arundel County records (Annapolis), produced nothing on a William Dames. In 1745, the *Gazette* described him as being from Cecil County, Maryland at the top of the bay and in 1746 as being from Chestertown. A search of land records verified this: He was an early lot owner in the little town called Kingstown directly across the Chester River from Chestertown. A search for Dames in Worcester, County (Pocomoke) and neighboring Somerset County yielded no one named Dames. It is uncertain if the William Dames who was with Lloyd is the same one who resided on the Eastern Shore of Maryland until he died in the 1770s. Most likely it is. An ad placed in the *Maryland Gazette* of August 9, 1749, for a runaway Irish convict servant belonging to William Dames, merchant of Queen Ann's County said the servant had been working for Mr. Dames in Somerset County. Assuming it is the one and the same William Dames it opens the door to a great deal more on our "one time pirate." The records in Queen Anne's County go on to describe him as a prominent citizen and church warden. In 1769, he gave one hundred thousand bricks to the building of the new St. Paul's Church in Centreville, Maryland. This contribution indicates that he had money. The next year he was paid to pull down the old church. See Emory, op. cit.

William Blackstock – Said he was born in Dumfries, Scotland. Wade described him as a Scotsman by birth but the captain of a vessel from North Carolina. Lloyd said he was a former captain of a North Carolina vessel who ran away to go on board the *Seaflower*. Described by all as a "one eyed Scotsman." Gilbert Fleming failed to describe this feature but did say that he "seemed as ingenuous as if he had only a regard for truth," CO 152/45 f. 136-139, NAE. Familysearch.org lists a William Blackstock christened January 22, 1738 at Dumfries, Scotland born to John and Mary Blackstock. No birth date given. This of course makes him too young. North Carolina Early Census on Ancestry.com places him in Pasquotank County, NC in 1754. Pasquotank County Deeds Book C, p. 408 1763 John Davis to Blackstock 255 acres at head of Indian Creek running into Great Flatty Creek., DRE p. 35, Grant F&G pp. 157, Trader, 307, referred to as planter, lives at Turkey Buzzard Ridge, 324, 316, 459. Court Orders p. 239 January Court 1761, granted license to keep at tavern at his house.

Zebulon Wade – Captain and part owner of the *Seaflower*. Born in Scituate, Massachusetts, March 3, 1716. He married Mercy Norton October 24, 1744. It appears he had a son named Zebulon, born in 1749. Son Barney, daughter Nanny, His father Joseph left will January 13, 1762, names two brothers of Zebulon, Jacob and Simeon. Zebulon had previously died. Plymouth County Wills. Wade routinely traded between Boston and Ocracoke. He returned to Scituate and died prior to 1759. It seems from the records he never returned to sea, at least as a vessel owner or captain.

And on the *Mary* in company with John Lloyd:

Samuel Fitz-Randolph, Sr. – Captain and owner of the *Mary*, born in 1711, at Woodbridge, New Jersey. Married Joanna Kinsey. The *Mary* was built in 1745 and registered to Fitz-Randolph at Perth Amboy August 25, 1746. He made previous trips to Ocracoke. His will proved August 5, 1754, Archives of New Jersey, Vol. XXXII.

Samuel Fitz-Randolph, Jr. – Born April 17, 1734, Woodbridge, New Jersey. He was married in Virginia, no death date found. Familysearch.org.

Kinsey Fitz-Randolph – Mate aboard the *Mary*. Born November 11, 1732, Woodbridge, New Jersey. In 1755, he made several trips as captain in the *Flying Fish* to and from Virginia and New Jersey. The *Flying Fish* was registered in Virginia in 1752 to Samuel Fitz-Randolph. No death date found. Familysearch.org.

Benjamin Moore – Born October 10, 1705 at Elizabethtown, New Jersey. Died November 22, 1758. Familysearch.org.

Silas Walker – Born about 1730 at Woodbridge, New Jersey. No death date noted. Familysearch.org.

Joseph Jackson – Apparently from Woodbridge, New Jersey as his father James was from there. His mother was Mary Fitz-Randolph.

Thomas Edwards – Born in 1735 at Manalapan, New Jersey. Died May 9, 1816, no location given. Familysearch.org.

William Waller – Actually not there when John Lloyd came aboard. He had left for New Jersey only days before. The only note found was that he married Margaret Fitz-Randolph in September, 1750. He resided in the home of Robert Fitz-Randolph in Woodbridge. He was apprehended in New Jersey and later escaped by bribing the jailor.

Chapter Eleven
Return to Treasure Island

Page 167. *Antiquity*. http://www.sailantiquity.com

Page 168. *La Galga* and the 1750 fleet. Amrhein, *The Hidden Galleon*.

Page 169. Columbus names the Virgin Islands. http:aglobalworld.com/holidays-around-the-world/virgin-island-st-ursulas-day

Page 170. The *William Thornton*. Named after Dr. William Thornton. http://www.aoc.gov/aoc/architects/thornton.cfm

Page 173. *The Money Diggers*. From *Tales of a Traveler*, Vol. II, Part IV. Irving, op. cit.

Page 173. Captain Kidd. Don Mitchell, *The Buccaneers and Anguilla*. http://www.aahsanguilla.com/

Notes from pages 173 to 202

Selected%20Readings/8.%20Buccaneers.pdf

Page 191. Dutch pirate named Norman. *Letters from the Virgin Islands*, p. 242-3. There was an English pirate with Henry Morgan named Richard Norman, Marley, pp. 292-3.

Page 191. Wilkins, *Pirate Treasure*, op. cit.

Page 191. The Phipps Family. The will of Francis Phipps. Vol. H Series One, p. 123, The St. Kitts Register, Basseterre. William Phipps and the *Nuestra Señora de Concepcion*. See Earle, op. cit.

Page 193. Log of HMS *Sybil*. ADM 51/2563-4.

Page 194. RMS *Rhone*. http://www.divebvi.com/dive-sites/rms-rhone

Page 196. "Any pirate for a small matter of money." *Calendar of State Papers* 1706-1708, p. 24.

Page 196. "According to rumor." HMS *Scorpion* arrives at Cádiz, observation of House of Trade. Consulados 861, f. 73 and 218, AGI. Inventory of treasure at North Carolina. Letter from Carriedo to Bonilla, October 21, 1750, Consulados 861, ff. 179-180 and attached list, f. 37-8. AGI. Coins – 165,000 pesos; Silverware – 2 chests; Grana (cochineal) – 128 sacks; Añil (indigo) – 7 sacks; Vanilla – 3 chests; Hides – 457; Tobacco – 140 packets.

Page 197. Lloyd told Heyliger. Deposition of Owen Lloyd. WIC inv.nr. 251, f. 99, NAN.

Page 197. Lloyd wanted to negotiate. Letter from Bonilla to the Consules in Cádiz. London, December 2, 1751, Consulados 861, f. 221-2, AGI.

Page 197. Fleming's account of treasure. CO 152/45 f. 143. NAE.

Page 198. Dames in Ireland. Letter from Bonilla to the House of Trade. London, March 2, 1751, Consulados 861, f. 225 – 7, AGI.

Page 198. John and Rebecca Purcell. Will of John Purcell, Prerogative Court, April 6, 1771, ff. 285-6.PROB 11/966, NAE.

Page 198. "Is there any money left?" Letter from John Watson at Antigua to Bonilla, May 12, 1751. Consulados 861, f. 210-211. Explains that Lloyd was at St. Thomas outfitting a small sloop which he had used previously for his trips to San Juan, St. Croix and St. Martins "and that it has been thought that he went to the said islands with the intention of picking up the treasure which he had buried there." He mentions that Lloyd had given 30,000 pesos as a gift to the Governor of St. Thomas to guarantee his personal safety and freedom and that Lloyd had bought two "haciendas" on St. Thomas. Fleming to Duke of Bedford, from Antigua November 22 says that Payne had informed him that Lloyd had stopped at St. Croix and disposed of some of the money before going to Norman. CO 152/45 ff. 100-102.

Page 198. Blackstock, Dames, and Mclair. See Chapter Six.

Page 200. Abraham Pritchett testifies. WIC inv.nr. 251, f. 118, NAN.

Page 200. "A writer from Tortola", *Letters from the Virgin Islands*, p. 12. Prospectus, p. 242, refers to Norman Island Treasure Company voluminous folios of a prospectus. Also Lewisohn, op. cit.

Page 200. Captain Thomas Southey. Southey, op. cit.

Page 202. "another part of the bay." Blackstock deposition CO 152/45 f. 171. NAE.

Chapter Twelve
Stevenson's First Book

Page 205. Quotation from Stevenson's first book, *My First Book*, p. xxi

Pages 205. Early days of RLS. Frank Mclynn, p. 24, op. cit.

Page 205. Allison Cunningham, "Stevenson's Nurse Dead," *New York Times*, August 10, 1913. It should be noted that a Robert Cunningham was a prosperous Scottish merchant who owned plantations on St. Kitts. No connection was attempted.

Page 206-8. Grez-Sur-Loing. LaPierre, pp. 144-190; Harman, pp. 139-159.

Page 208-9. Fanny in Monterey. LaPierre, pp. 248-281; Harman, pp. 177-189

Page 209. Stevenson in ill health. LaPierre, p. 265.

Page 209. Stevenson falls from horse. LaPierre, p. 273.

Page 209. French Hotel. Harman, p. 183.

Page 210. "I want to tell you something." LaPierre, p. 279.

Page 210. *The Monterey Californian.* LaPierre, pp. 281-287; Balfour, Vol. 1, p. 201.

Page 211. "There you may here God served." Stevenson, *The Old and New Pacific Capitals*, "Monterey." Stevenson had tears in his eyes, Fisher, p. 250, op. cit.

Page 212. Mission church of San Carlos Borroméo. Temple, op. cit; http://www.carmelmission.org/

Page 212. Stevenson makes appeal for preservation of the mission. Nickerson, op. cit., pp. 50-52. *Monterey Californian.*

Page 213. Stevenson moves to San Francisco. LaPierre, p. 289-93; Harman, pp. 191-195.

Page 214. Stevenson's marriage. LaPierre, p. 312; Harman, pp. 194-5.

Page 214. Stevenson and Silverado. Issler, *Stevenson at Silverado;* Harman, pp. 196-200.

Page 214. Stevenson arrives in England. LaPierre, pp. 319-337.

Page 214. The date of the first chapter was given by Edmund Gosse, English poet, author and critic, who was at Braemar with Stevenson when he wrote the early chapters. Stevenson wrote fifteen chapters in fifteen days. Mehew, pp. 190-1, op. cit.

Page 215. Lloyd Osbourne recalls the map. *My First Book*, p. x.

Page 216. Edward Hawke. http://www.nndb.com/people/164/000101858/

Page 216. Battle of Fontenoy. http://www.britishbattles.com/battle_fontenoy.htm

Page 216. Stevenson to Henley, gets Johnson's book on pirates. Mehew, 191-2, op. cit.

Page 217. Stevenson admits to using *Robinson Crusoe. My First Book*, xxiv.

Notes from pages 217 to 224

Page 218. Flint kills six crewman. *Treasure Island*, Chapter Fifteen.

Page 219. Map sent to Cassel & Co. *My First Book*, xxix.

Page 219. Lloyd Osbourne attests to the labeling of the map. Ibid., ix, x.

Page 220. More on the Cocos Island treasure. Hancock, op. cit.

Page 220. Stevenson describes his father's influence. *My First Book*, xxv, xxix.

Page 220. The *Walrus*. In all of the author's research covering thousands of names of vessels, the name *Walrus* was never encountered until 1879. *Walrus*, 870 tons, built at Glasgow, 1878, owned by J. Burns of Glasgow, *Lloyd's Register* of Shipping 1879. *Record of American and Foreign Shipping* 1880, shows another *Walrus* built 1860 in Deptford England owner J. & W. Stewart.

Page 220. W.G.H. Kingston (1814-1880), wrote many sea stories that would have interested Stevenson in his youth; R. M. Ballantyne (1824-1894) wrote *Coral Island* in 1857; James Fenimore Cooper (1789-1851) wrote *The Sea Lions* in 1849. For more on literary influences on Stevenson see, *Coasts of Treasure Island*, op.cit.

Page 221. Stevenson relates the story of Alan and Hugh Stevenson. *A Family of Engineers*, pp. 206-8. http://www.electricscotland.com/webclans/mcphail/stevenson.htm

Page 221. Oil painting of a ship. It should be noted here that on April 20, 1773, the brig, *Lilly*, from Greenock, owned by Alexander Houstoun & Co. arrived at St. Kitts with herring. Her captain was James Lyon, she was 100 tons burthen, built in 1766 at Massachusetts Bay, and registered in 1770 to Houstoun. "Lilly" was the maiden name of Alan Stevenson's wife. T1 489, Naval Office of St. Kitts, NAE.

Page 222. Stevenson's family tree. Scottish Genealogy Society, cabinet FC9.

Page 222. Scottish newspapers. *Glasgow Courant*, November 10, 1750. The *London Gazette* of December 1, 1750, gave an account of the loss of the 1750 fleet and though it made no reference to stolen treasure, it did mention the stolen treasure in the issue dated May 24, 1751. Furthermore, in Scotland, the *Edinburgh Evening Courant* of November 13, 1750, first reported the news of the Spanish losses at Virginia. The November 19 issue repeated the news from the *Philadelphia Gazette* of September 6. On December 6, the *Edinburgh Courant* gave a full account on the front page including an account of the *Guadalupe's* treasure being unloaded at Ocracoke. It appeared that the editor of the *Courant* had a great interest in the story as compared to other publications. But issues after December 31, which could have given more details, are not available today. It was possible that later news of Lloyd's theft would have been carried in some early 1751 issues as it had been in the *South Carolina Gazette* of November 5, 1750. This issue gave a detailed account of the theft but at that time it was not known where Lloyd was headed with the treasure.

Page 222. Merchant firm of Dunlop & Peter. Letters from David Meade and Watson to Messrs. Mauman and Macé in Lisbon. Suffolk, Virginia, February 27, 1750, Consulados 861, f. 161, AGI. See page 123.

Page 223. Milliken and McDowell. Hamilton, op. cit.; Alison p. 99, op. cit. Nisbet, p. op. cit, p. 116.

Page 224. Alan Stevenson as a store clerk. Register of Edinburgh Apprentices, August 18, 1788, NAS. "Stevenson, Robert, son of late Allan, storekeeper in St. Christopher." Hugh owned tenement. Alan and Hugh not ship owners, T1/489 Naval Office of St. Christopher's, Feb 3, 1772 to August 31, 1773; Greenock Import and Export Books, Scottish Record Office E 504/15/21-25 Vols. 22-25. Scottish Record Office Customs Records Vols. 19-23, Port Import and Export Books, Port Glasgow 1771-74, NAE. Also, At Edinburgh, Mr. Robert Stevenson, Tinsmith, married miss Jean Smith, eldest daughter of Mr. Thomas Smith, Tinsmith in Edinburgh. June 3, 1798 P. 479, *The Edinburgh Magazine, or Literary Miscellany.*

Notes from pages 225 to 230

Page 225. Alan and Hugh owned an island. Stevenson, *A Family of Engineers*, p. 206, op. cit.

Page 225. Suckling, op. cit.

Page 225. Ralph Payne 1773. Suckling, op. cit.

Page 226. Alexander Brown. The Stevenson family tree records his marriage to Elizabeth Stevenson, sister of Robert Stevenson, in 1744. States he is a sugar refiner in Glasgow. St. Kitts records an Alexander Brown ca 1732, Book F, Series 1, Doc No.1389 (fragile cannot be viewed). The will of Alexander Brown of Quarter Merchant married to Elizabeth Stevenson died in 1769 or before. His will p. 235, 1769, names one son named Alexander. This may be Alexander Brown, resident of Old Craig, Daviot, Aberdeenshire settled at St. Kitts pre 1756, ABR Deeds 1757, NAS. Hugh and Allan Stevenson may have been working with their cousin Alexander Brown. See, Mackintosh op. cit., p. 394. Sugar works were first established in Scotland in 1667. In 1715 sugar refining was carried on in Glasgow. Malting, or the production of malt, was big business as it was used in brewing and distillation of spirits. See also, http://www.nndb.com/people/111/000097817/ and http://www.electricscotland.com/webclans/mcphail/stevenson.htm

Page 226. "From a few scraps of paper." *A Family of Engineers*, p. 208, op. cit.

Page 227. Letter to Sidney Colvin in 1884. Mehew, p. 262, op. cit.

Page 227. Stevenson adds to his confession. Stevenson, *My First Book*, xxiv-v, op. cit.

Page 228. Stevenson to Purcell. Mehew, p. 308 op. cit.

Page 228. Stevenson credits Henley with character of Long John Silver. Hennessey, p. 180, op. cit.

Page 228. Scenery for *Treasure Island*. *Coasts of Treasure Island*, p. 159-60, op. cit.

Page 229. Edward Trelawny Governor of Jamaica, 1738-1751. http://www.britannica.com/EBchecked/topic/1336176/Edward-Trelawny.

Page 229. Tobias Smollet. Sent as surgeon aboard HMS *Chichister*, ADM51/198, ADM 52/452. Pay book ADM 33/410. His first literary contribution was an account of Cartagena, *The Adventures of Roderick Random*.

Page 229. James Flint. Flint, op. cit.

Page 229. Don Daniel Huony. Amrhein, op. cit.

Page 229. Frank Gywn, op. cit.

Page 229. A writer a century ago. John Blake, *Nebraska State Journal*, August 5, 1921.

Page 230. "I might say it was the whole." Stevenson, *My First Book*, xxix-xxxi.

Page 230. "I am now on another lay for the moment." Stevenson to Henley [August 24, 1881] about Lloyd. Maixner, op. cit., p. 124, uses "Lloyd." Mehew, p. 191 says "Sam." By this time he was starting to be called "Lloyd." Stevenson to Lloyd Osbourne, February 1880.

Chapter Thirteen
The Hunt for Lloyd

Page 233. Documents from PRO now NAE were from CO 152/45 microfilm found in the Manuscript Reading

363

Notes from page 233 to 245

Room, LOC.

Page 234-7. The Reese River days and early San Francisco. *This life I've loved,* Isobel Fields, pp. 8-23. P. 17. John Lloyd described as a Welshman. LaPierre, pp. 44-56.

Page 235. Virginia City, ibid, p. 56-71.

Page 237. Sam Osbourne returns. Harman, p. 133.

Page 237. "The more one knows him." LaPierre, p. 84.

Page 238. Lloyd Osbourne is born. Harman, p. 133.

Page 238. Virgil Williams. Harman, p. 135; Lapierre, p. 101.

Page 238. Bohemian Club. Harman, p. 134.

Page 238. John Lloyd gets married. The U.S. Census of 1900 said that he had been married since 1873.

Page 238. Fanny announces she wants to leave for Europe. Lapierre, pp. 116-120.

Page 238. Reaction at the Bohemian Club. Ibid.

Page 239. Stevenson at Monterey. Mackay, pp. 64-69; Harman, pp. 177-120; LaPierre, pp. 256-269.

Page 239. Rearden meets Stevenson. Mackay, p. 68.

Page 239. Fanny and Stevenson are married. Ibid., p. 77.

Page 239. Stevenson at the Bohemian Club. Harman, pp. 134-5; Katherine Osbourne, p. 73.

Page 239. John Lloyd and Henry Hyde. San Francisco City Directories.

Page 239. John Lloyd expresses jealous feelings. Harman, pp. 134-5.

Page 239. Fanny to Dora Williams. Mackay, p. 345.

Page 240. *The Monterey Californian.* On December 16, 1879, there was an article, "Hidden Treasure," which has been attributed to Stevenson.

Page 240. The book containing Owen Lloyd's power of attorney: Lloyd to Caines, Book R #1 pp.184-90, St. Kitts National Archives. The *London Chronicle and Universal Evening Post of* July 28, 1759, records a letter from Montserrat, June 12, 1759, noticing the death of Thomas Caines, "a very considerable planter of St. Kitts."

Page 242. Baker map. *A new and exact Map of the Island of St Christopher in America, according to an actual and accurate Survey* made in 1753 by Samuel Baker, Lt. RN., 1753, CO 700.

Page 244. Fleming is bitten by monkey. Baker, *Diary,* op. cit.

Page 245. John Lloyd's death record. San Francisco Odd Fellows Crematorium.

Page 245. John Lloyd Greenwich hospital. ADM 6/224 f.6, Register of candidates for admission to Greenwich Hospital. 1752-1763; ADM 73/36, 5,1 General Entry Book of Officers and Pensioners (2 parts) 1704-1803 and Rough Entry Book of Pensioners 1704-1756 ADM 73/51, ADM 6/224, NAE.

Notes from pages 247 to 258

Page 247. Depositions of Owen Lloyd, Zebulon Wade, Abraham Pritchet, Thomas Hobson, James McMahon. WIC inv.nr. 251, pp. 93-124, NAN.

Page 249. Port records of Hampton, VA. CO 5/1446, NAE.

Page 250. *Rawleigh*, Port records of Hampton, VA. CO 5/1446; Jamaica Shipping Records, CO 142/15, NAE.

Page 250. Norfolk County. Deeds and Wills, 1742-1746, 1746-1750, pp. 109, 118, 242-244.

Page 250. Lloyd's letter, May 11, 1750, Deeds, p. 488. John Hutchings (1691-1768), a son of Daniel Hutchings, a mariner, and a grandson of John Hutchings of Bermuda, succeeded George Newton as mayor and was again mayor in 1743 and 1755. He is buried near the south gate of St. Paul's Churchyard. "Norfolk Highlights 1584 – 1881," George Holbert Tucker, Norfolk Historical Society; 1st edition (1972).

Page 252. Owen Lloyd buys house on Queen St., Hampton, VA. Elizabeth City County Deeds 1737-1749, p. 341, August 1,1749, Charles and Ann White sell 1/2 lott or ¼ acre on north side of Queen St. to Owen Lloyd for £130. Bound by Judith Bailey, John White and the Town Ditch. Lot originally granted to Thomas Faulkner in 1706, p. 292. He was the owner of the church property. The size of the lot and relation to the Town Ditch indicates the location of the lot.

Page 252. Lloyd v. Rodriguez, Court Orders Norfolk, January 17, 1751. John Lloyd served on jury, Court Orders Norfolk, August 17, 1751.

Page 253. John Lloyd sells tenement. John Lloyd witnesses deathbed will of John Drury in Norfolk, February 19, 1751, p. 212, Wills and Deeds I. 1736-1753. February 21, 1751 John Lloyd leases one half lot on West side of Church St. (now St. Paul's Blvd.) lying between William Nimmo and Francis Dyson for five shillings for the term of one year. Deed of sale for 30 pounds ten shillings. Elizabeth leaves her mark "X."

Page 253. John Lloyd captured. *MG*, January 27, 1748; John Lloyd in Spanish document, Santo Domingo 2170, AGI. One of the sloops captured by Garaicochea: "A sloop with 100 pipes of wine from Madeira having set sail from this island for Virginia." This was John Lloyd.

Page 253. Shipping contract with MacKenzie. *William and Mary Quarterly*, Vol. XX Series 1 p. 170. Swem's Index has John Lloyd listed as "Loyd."

Page 254. The *Hannah*. Port of Hampton. CO 5/1446, NAE.

Page 254. Owen Lloyd leaves Jamaica. Jamaica Shipping Records, CO 142/15, NAE.

Page 255. Owen Lloyd found in land lists. The West India and Guinea Company 1671-1754, Land Lists for St. Thomas 1748-54, #749, DNA.

Page 257. Peter Phister finds documents. GCC Box #4, DNA.

Page 257. Shipwreck of *Princesse Wilhelmine Caroline*. Lit C. GCC Box #4, DNA. A collection of copies of letters in English. One has note on the bottom of the page saying that it was sent "here" on the wrecked ship *Princesse Wilhelmine Caroline* and delivered by the captain Nicolai Hoyer December 28, 1752.

Page 257. Outcome of Lloyd's crew, see notes end of Chapter Ten,

Page 258. Blackstock in Pasquotank County. Pasquotank County Deeds, Book C, p. 408. John Davis to William Blackstock of Pasquotank 25 acres at head of Indian Creek making out of Great Flatty Creek. John Davis 30 acres to Blackstock at Turkey Buzzard Ridge June 11, 1761, F&G p. 157. William Blackstock, trader of Pasquotank, to Patrick Pool, 150 acres known as Halfway Tree Old Field Land granted 1757 to Blackstock, p.

Notes from pages 258 to 289

307; June 26, 1759, William Blackstock, planter to John Davis 60 acres Turkey Buzzard Ridge where Blackstock lives. P. 314; October 27, 1757, William Blackstock, planter, paid 18 shillings to John Earl Granville for land in St. John's parish, Pasquotank, adj., Poole, Reed, Hezekiah, Cartwright, Pritchard, p. 361; April 11, 1759, Granville to Blackstock for 10 shillings, 287 acres at Turkey Buzzard Ridge, St. Johns Parish. p. 459; Joseph Keaton to Blackstock, 15 acres adjoining Blackstock and Keaton, July 8, 1761; Blackstock petitioned to keep a tavern where he lived, granted January 1761, p. 239, Order Book. Administration of Blackstock's estate to his son John Blackstock, orphan. January 12, 1762, p. 285, 301,

Page 258. John Lloyd in Pasquotank County. May 2, 1750, Book B, p. 92. Sells land Book C p. 147. Pasquotank County Deed Books.

Page 259. "Treasure Point." Book 27, p. 536, June 13, 1746, Surlie R. Stevens and M.D. Stevens to Merritt A. Hooper and Goldie B. Hooper. Pasquotank County Deed Books.

Page 259. Plan of fort. Vel. 1427, WIC, NAN.

Page 261. Power of attorney St. Kitts and Antigua. GCC Box #4, Lit. C, DNA.

Page 280. The Lloyd family in Rhuddlan. Bodryhddan, Flintshire. Archives of Wales. Will of a Vincent Lloyd of Cefn du, Rhuddlan proved in Chester (C 1724 / 9). http://www.archiveswales.org.uk/anw/get_collection. php?inst_id=39&coll_id=10986&expand

Page 283. St. Thomas Church Record. Kirkbøger, Copulerede 1691-1795 v. 1-2, Transcription in *Landsarkivet for Sjælland*, Provincial Archives of Zeeland.

Page 285. Conspiracy. The *Diary* of John Baker. Op. cit.

Page 288. Rebhun, West Indies Chancery, 1746- 1771, 1771-1773, Vol. 641, FHL #0426768, item 2; Vol. 429, FHL #0410350, Mormon Church microfilm records.

Page 289. Church records for St. John's St. Kitts British Library S. Transcripts (typewritten) of Parish Registers of St. Kitts in the West Indies by Lt.-Col. H. R. Phipps from copies made by John Bromley, viz.:-(a) Christ Church, Nichola Town: Baptisms (1730-1751), f. 142, and Burials (1730-1755), f. 146; (b) St. Anne, Sandy Point: Baptisms (1771-1799), f. 149, Marriages (1724-1798), f. 153, and Burials (1763-1793), f. 159;-(c) St. George, Basseterre Marriages (1747-1820), f. 162;-(d) St. John, Capisterre: Baptisms and Burials (1731-1756), f. 177, and Marriages (1738-1806), f. 182. Prefaced (f. 139) by an explanatory letter of H. R. Phipps. See also Add. MS. 41178N. Presented in 1925 and 1930 by John Bromley, Esq., and Lt.-Col. H. R. Phipps, D.S.O.MS 41295. Church records of St. George's, British Library, Add 43866. Entries Relating To Baptisms and Burials, 1747-1800, in the parish registers of St George, Basseterre, St. Kitts in the West Indies. Type- written copy made by Lt.Col. H. R. Phipps from a transcript by John Bromley and his wife.

Page 289. Owen Lloyd's marriage. See Chapter One.

Page 289. Lloyd buys six slaves from Christian Malone. Norfolk County Deeds, Norfolk, VA.

Page 289. Power of attorney from Christian Malone. August 7, 1753, Hampton, VA, Court Orders, p. 383, power of Attorney from Christian Malone to John Riddle proved by oath of John Loyall. On April 3, 1763, the estate of John Loyall received £170 10s from David Wilson Curle for house and lot where Roscoe Sweeney lives on north side of Queen St. It appears that Loyall may have been the purchaser of Owen Lloyd's house. Deeds, p. 414, Elizabeth City County Deeds.

Page 289. Susanna Caines in Williamsburg. Christiana Malone buried at St. Kitts December 13, 1765, St. John's; Peter Malone, sailor, age 37 buried St. John June 7, 1779. In a letter from Susanna Riddell in Williamsburg to William Innes in London, October 5, 1781, she discloses that her brother is Charles Caines of St. Kitts. This is

Notes from pages 290 to 308

the nephew of Owen Lloyd. M281 MS 24322, JRW; St. Kitts Book I, p. 98, George Riddell to Charles Caines; Hampton, VA, Court Orders 1755-57, p. 57, notes a suit of George and John Riddell v John Hunter.

Page 290. The will of Christiana Malone. St. Kitts Register, December 13, 1765.

Page 290. Rebhun's will. Danish Chancery, Vestindiske Sager, 1746-1771. Confirmation of last will, Christiansborg, April 27, 1770. Mormon Church microfilm 0410350.

Page 291. Elizabeth Lloyd was buried at Basseterre, October 9, 1759. ADD 43866, Baptisms and burials of St George and St Peter Basseterre, 1747-1800, British Library.

Page 294. For the *Happy* and the Lloyd's, see notes Chapter One.

Page 294. The will of James Lloyd. Prerogative Court of Canterbury, PROB 11/863.

Page 296. Belle reflects on John Lloyd, Field, p.16, op. cit.

Page 307. News of Lloyd Osbourne's death. "Lloyd Osbourne Taken By Death," *San Mateo Times*, May 23, 1947; "Treasure Island" Inspiration, Dead," *Indiana Evening Gazette*, Indiana, Pennsylvania, May 24,1947; "Boy Who Inspired Treasure Island, Dies," *Racine Journal Times*, Racine Wisconsin May 24, 1947.

Page 307. Sam Osbourne is missing. Mackey, p. 332; Lapierre, p. 313, op. cit.

Page 307. Stevenson dies at Samoa. Hamlin, pp. 455-7., op. cit.

Page 307. Fanny moves to San Francisco. Mackey, p. 332, op. cit.

Page 307. Christine Lloyd died of cirrhosis of the liver and chronic myocarditis. Death certificate of "Christiana" Lloyd, #4238, City of San Francisco. *San Francisco Chronicle* July 26, 1913.

Page 307. Fanny to Dora Williams. Mackay, p. 345, op. cit.

Page 307. Fanny moves to Santa Barbara. Sanchez, p. 297, op. cit.

Page 308. Lloyd Osbourne draws map. Stevenson's *My First Book,* pp. x-xi, op. cit.

Index

Abaco, 64
Abaria, Estebán, 356
Abercromby, James, 48, 145, 147, 335, 353-4
Aberdeenshire, Scotland, 363
Abraham, Captain John, 335
Abreu y Bertodano, Don Felix José, 144, 146, 150, 352
Acapulco, Mexico, 12
Admiral Benbow Inn, 169
Adventure, HMS, 3, 324
Agatha, ship, 16
Aguiar, Manuel Martines, 330, 344
Aguin, Francisco, 343
Aix-La-Chapelle, Peace Treaty of, 7
Albemarle Sound, 45, 48,
Alborough, HMS, 4, 324
Alexander Houstoun & Co, 223, 362
almirantazgo tax, 14
Alsedo, Fiscal Judge, 327
American Samoa, 307-8, 367
American Yacht Harbor, St. Thomas, 168
Amrhein, Delphine, xi, 167-9, 176, 180, 194, 203, 240, 243-4, 262
Amrhein, Madeline, xi, 176, 179, 180, 182, 183, 186, 192, 193, 194,
An Inland Voyage, 214
Anegada, 64, 169, 191, 192, 194, 195,
Anglesea, HMS, 324
Angola, 2
Anguilla, xii, 64, 83, 342, 360; William Blackstock at, 76 130; Gilbert Fleming at, 113-4, 120, 127, 130
Annapolis, Maryland, 336, 358
Antigua, Gilbert Fleming at, 76-7, 80-3, 112, 116, 120-2, 340-2, 347; HMS Otter at, 112; John Watson at, 126-7, 130, 136, 144, 257, 261-2, 349-51, 360; mentioned, xi, 2, 63, 87, 131-2, 136, 142, 144-7, 149, 191, 197, 224, 240, 262, 276, 279-80, 324, 346, 348, 350, 353-4, 366
Antigua and Barbuda National Archives, xi, 276, 279
Antigua Gazette, 82, 116, 340-1, 347
Antiquity, ketch, xii, 192, 194; at Norman Island, 167-9, 171-2, 175, 182, 184-5, 202-3
Antwerp, Belgium, 238
Apostle of California, 212

368

Index

Arabella, slave, 9, 251, 290, 325-6
Aranjuez, Spain, 141, 333; King Ferdinand at, 352
Archivo General de Indias, 244, 300
Archivo General de Simancas, 300
Archivo Histórico Nacional, 300
Archivo Histórico Provincial, 300
Arenuse Creek, North Carolina, 258-9, 326
Ariscum, Don Geronimo de, 157, 355-6
Aristegui, Joseph de Lorenzo de, 356
Arizon, Don Jacinto de, 332
Arizon, Salvador, 329
Armistead, Sheriff Robert, 8, 27-8, 250-1, 325-6, 331
Arriaga, Julian de, 356
Asia, ship, 153-4
Assateague Island, 25, 28, 47, 168, 234, 281 310
Astaphan, Carla, xi, 270
At Last: A Christmas in the West Indies, 194, 227
Austin, Nevada, 234-5, 291
Autran, Ciprian, 14, 270, 327
Aztec, 12
Back to My Roots Geneaology Services, 294
Bailey, Judith, 326, 365
Baker, John, Solicitor General of the Leeward Islands, 79, 122, 125-6, 149, 270, 285-6, 349; diary of, 341, 354, 365-6
Baker, Lt. Samuel, RN, 242-3, 323, 340, 365
Balch, Joseph, 118, 347
Bald Head, Cape Fear, North Carolina, 56
Ballantyne, Robert M., 205,
Bankers, (Outer), 37, 40-3, 45, 49-51, 55-6, 58, 94, 96-7, 333-4
Banks, Pam, xii
Basseterre, St. Kitts, 83, 240, 260, 291, 341, 360, 366-7; picture of, 110; ship, *Caesar,* at, 125; HMS *Otter* at, 113; tavern at, 126; sloop, *Christian,* at, 83; John Watson at, 126
Bath, North Carolina, 32-3, 97
Bay of Cádiz, 17, 156
Beachy Head, England, 16
Beaufort County, North Carolina, 357
Bedford, Duke of, 48, 76, 81, 83, 85, 99, 100, 111-3, 127, 130, 135, 140-1, 330, 335, 340-4, 346, 349, 351-2, 360
Bedford, HMS, 16, 328
Belcher, Governor Jonathan, of New Jersey, 130, 343, 350
Bell, Adrienne, xii
Bellamy, Sam, 5, 324
Benbow, Admiral John, 228
Benures Bay, Norman Island, 184-5, 199

369

Bermuda, 73, 253, 298, 332, 339-40, 358, 365
Bernal, Pedro Sanchez, 327
Bernstorff, Johann Hartwig Ernst, Baron von, 158, 160, 161, 356-7
Bethlemites, 19
Big Thatch Island, BVI, 194
Billy Bones, bar, 169-72, 174, 176, 180, 191. *See also* Bones, Billy
Bishop, Captain Edward, 325
Blackbeard Point, 29
Blackbeard, Edward Teach, 5, 31-35, 45, 47, 59, 324, 331, 332, 334-5
Blackstock, John, 258
Blackstock, William, (alias William Davidson), deposition of, 83, 85, 87, 171, 191. 202, 233, 247, 249, 337-8, 341, 343; at Ocracoke, 50-2, 56, 146, 335, boards the *Seaflower*, 57-8, 61; voyage to Norman Island, 62-3, 65, 171, 198, 200, 202, at Norman Island, 68-9, 72, 338-9; at Tortola, 69, 71, 73-4; at Anguilla, 76, 83, 113-4, 128, 130, 340; at St. Eustatius, 76, 340; lives in Pasquotank, NC, 162, 257-8, 366; mentioned, 51-2, 56-8, 61-3, 65, 68-74, 76, 78-83, 88-90, 113-4, 128, 130, 146, 162, 171, 186, 191, 195, 198, 200, 247, 257-8, 342, 350, 357-9, 361
Blair, Dr. Marian, xi,
Blair, John, 137, 351
Blake, John, 363
Blythin, Maggi, xi,
Board of Ten of the West India Company, 149, 354
Board of Trade, England, 64, 69, 152
Boca Chica, 50
Bodrhyddan, 280
Bohemian Club, San Francisco, 238-240, 364
Bones, Billy, 216, 218, 219-20, 228
Bonilla, Antonio, 162
Bonilla, Francisco, 162
Bonilla, Juan Manuel, at Cadiz, 13-17, 137, 147, 150; at Edenton, North Carolina, 118-9; at Havana, 21-23; at Hampton, Virginia, 124-5, 129, 137; at London, 139, 142, 144-7; at New Bern, North Carolina, 54-5, 94-6, 101-2, 117-9, 197; at Ocracoke, 35-40, 42-3, 46-51, 53-4, 71, 98, 254; at Puerto Rico, 18, 154-155; at Suffolk, Virginia, 118-9, 122-4, 129-130, 134-5, 140; at Veracruz, 13, 18-20, 155-6; at Williamsburg, Virginia 120; at Wilmington, North Carolina, 99-101; captured by English, 15-16; contract with Governor Johnston, 97-8, 141; described, 13; expenses of, 126, 128, 135, 136, 137, 152, 256; married, 22; hires Owen Lloyd, 38; his power of attorney, 126-7, 132-3, 261; will of, 158-160; mentioned, xv, 14, 16, 18, 24-5, 67-8, 75, 97, 99, 115, 131, 134, 140, 142, 144, 146, 147-153, 157-8, 161-2, 196-7, 211, 222, 233-5, 252, 255, 257
Bonilla, Juan Manuel (Jr.), 162, 328
Bonilla, Juana, 17
Bonilla, Maria, 17, 22, 95, 160, 162, 327
Borough Church (Norfolk, VA), 1, 9, 266
Boston, MA, news from, 71, 88, 246, 249, 342, 350, mentioned, 2, 41, 43-4, 46, 51-2, 56, 59, 162, 332, 339; 357-9
Boston News Letter, 44, 71, 246, 249, 323

Index

Boydell, John, viii, 152, 355
Braemar, Scotland, 214, 362
Brandt, Captain Carl Frederic, 355
Brandt, Nicole, xi, 247, 303
Brandylane Publishers, xii
Breashears, Jim, xii
Briggs, Benjamin, 334
Brimstone Hill, 243, 269
Bristol, England, 123, 125, 216, 292, 349
Brodie, John, 8, 326, 336
Brodie, Mary, 8, 250, 325
Brookings, John, 152
Brouncker, Henry, 131, 135-6
Brown, Alexander, 222, 226, 363
Brown, Robert, 339-40
Brunswick Town, NC, 41, 62, 98-101, 333-4, 336, 344
Buchanan, Connie, xii
Bunch of Grapes, tavern, 330
Burt Pt., Tortola, 198
Burt, William, Lt. Governor of St. Kitts, 74-6, 82, 340
Burwell, Lewis, 120
Bush Street, San Francisco, 213, 239
Buskirk, Ann, xii
Butler, Anthony, 15
Byrd, William, Governor of Virginia, 102, 345
Byron, Lord, 229
Cabildo, 19
Cadalso, Don Joseph, 160-1, 356-7
Cádiz, Spain, Juan Manuel Bonilla at, 13-17, 20, 22, 124, 139, 147, 150, 153, 158-160, 162, 343, 345; mentioned, 95, 97, 99, 100-1, 115, 117, 120, 122-3, 125, 129, 137, 144, 151-2, 155, 156, 157, 161, 266, 278, 300, 309-10, 327-9, 332-3, 337, 344, 348, 350, 351, 354-7, 360
Caesar, ship, 124-5, 136-7, 349, 351
Cagigal de la Vega, Francisco, Governor of Havana, 6, 22, 327, 329
Caicos, 64
Caines Car Rentals, 240
Caines Plaintation, pictures of, 271-2; treasure at, 81, 126; mentioned, 2, 3, 7, 74, 75-6, 223, 243, 260, 288-9, 291, 306, 340
Caines, Charles, aids Owen Lloyd's escape, 106, 108; death of, 289, 323; at Norfolk, Virginia, 1, 289; goes to St. Eustatius, 106; mentioned, 2, 79, 81,108-9, 126, 191, 223, 241-2, 270, 279-80, 288, 323, 340, 345, 349, 364, 367
Caines, Christian, 1, 81, 283, 290, 298, 323. *See also* Christian Lloyd
Caines, Col. Charles, 1, 223, 240, 243
Caines, Frances, 3
Caines, Janet, 323

Caines, Susanna, 367
Caines, Thomas, 109, 191, 242-3, 286, 331, 364
Caines, Yvette, xi, 298
Cairnes, Alexander, 117-9, 123-4, 129-131, 137, 257, 347, 349, 353. *See also* Watson & Cairnes
Calcole, Joseph, 331
California, xii, 19, 207-9, 211-2, 214, 228, 230, 235, 239, 244-5, 278, 282, 296-7, 304, 307, 361
California Market, 239
California Street, 239
Calle de Comedias, Cádiz, Spain, 159
Calle de la Palma, Cádiz, Spain, 159
Calle del Veedor, Cádiz, Spain, 160
Camara de Indias, 161, 353, 357
Cambbell, Archiblad, 326
Campbell, Cornelius, 134, 355
Campbell, James, 118, 347
Campeche, Mexico, 18
Canary Islands, 17, 153
Cape Cantin, 17
Cape Charles, Virginia, 25
Cape Fear, NC, 41, 46, 62, 99, 101, 333-5, 337
Cape Fear River, NC, 41, 49-50, 57, 62, 97-8, 99, 337, 344
Cape Hatteras, NC, 24-5, 30, 36, 123
Cape Henry, VA, 7, 25, 29, 325
Cape St. Vincent, 350
Carine, Carole, xii, 245, 304
Carkett, Captain, 41
Carmel, California, 210-12, 278, 304
Caribbean, xv, 1, 3, 25, 29, 31, 63, 74-6, 97, 109, 117-8, 123, 126, 128, 135-7, 140, 142, 152, 167, 169-70, 172, 211, 216, 218, 222, 229, 244, 247, 256, 325
Carriedo, Tomas, at Cadiz, 16-7, 153; at Ocracoke, 25, 36, 53, 57, 94-96, 337; at Puerto Rico, 154; at Veracruz, 13-4; boards HMS *Scorpion*, 98; dies at sea, 155, 355; mentioned, 101, 145, 337-8, 342-4, 360
Cartagena, Columbia, 22, 50, 229, 329, 332, 344, 363
Carvajal y Lancaster, José, 115, 140-1, 332, 335, 347, 352
Carvel, the, 186
Cary, Major Wilson, 27-29, 55, 254, 330
Casa Bonifacio, 208
Casa de Contratación, *see* House of Trade
Casanova, Fr. Angelo Delfino, 210-11
Castilla, ship, 157
Cefn du, Wales, 324
Centreville, Maryland, 162, 358
Chalwell, Abraham, 69-70, 73, 81, 83, 85-6, 113, 197, 202, 226, 338-40, 358
Chalwell, Abraham, Jr, 72.197, 226
Chalwell, Tortola, 198

Index

Chamber of Customs, Denmark, 160, 356
Chamber of Revenue, Denmark, 160, 356
Charlotte Amalie, St. Thomas, USVI, 70, 195, 277
Chavera, Diego, 101,102, 119, 124-6, 131, 135-6, 279, 351
Chesapeake Bay, 1, 6, 9, 25, 29, 40, 325, 358
Chester, England, 324, 366
Chester River, Maryland, 358
Chestertown, Maryland, 336, 358
Child, Thomas, 99-101, 120, 140, 144-5, 150, 152, 344, 353, 355
Chowan River, 47
Christian, shallop, 81-83, 127, 341
Christiansted, St. Croix, 224, 282, 284, 339-40
ChuChu, 214
Church Street, Norfolk, Virginia, now St. Paul's Blvd. 9, 253, 365
Cifuentes, Manuela de, 327
Civil War, 235-6, 259
Clayton, Indiana, 237-8
Cochineal, 12, 2, 38-8, 51, 53, 67-9, 70, 72, 73, 76-8, 83, 90, 98, 116, 118, 128, 130, 133, 135-6, 143-5, 148-9, 159, 161, 202, 339, 350-1, 360
Cocos Island, 220, 362
Collegio de San Fernando de Mexico, 328
Collins, Enoch, 50-2, 56-7, 71, 80, 87, 162, 336, 338-9, 342, 357-8
Collins, John, 70, 7, 338-9
Columbine, Lt. E.H., RN, 193-4,
Columbus, Christopher, 169, 300, 360
Colvin, Sidney, 227, 363
Comstock Lode, 235, 298
Conde de la Gomera, 20, 329
Connecticut, 50, 357-8
Constant, Joseph, 161, 357
Consulados 861, 244, 327
Consulado, (Merchant Guild), 16, 159-160, 162, 327, 348
Convent of San Francisco, 18-19, 264, 309
Convento de los Descalzos, 160, 278, 356
Cook, Liv, xi
Cook, Shane, xi, 176, 180, 182, 183, 188, 190, 192, 194-5, 202, 274
Cooper, James Fenimore, 220, 362
Copenhagen, Denmark, researchers at, 246, 302; mentioned, 144, 146, 149, 152-3, 158, 160-1, 283-4, 340, 355-7
Coral Bay (Crawl Bay), 64-5, 195, 337
Coral Island, 205, 362
Core Banks, North Carolina, 24, 42, 45, 119
Cornhill Magazine, 220
Coronado, Pam, xii, 282, 284-6, 288, 290; helps author discover document, 283; picture of, 287, 306

Corso Castle, 217, 220
Crawford, Captain Hugh, 128-130, 350
Crawl Bay, *see* Coral Bay
Creque, Henry, 191, 225
Crispen, Mrs., 126
Cruañes, Captain Don Juan, 21, 36
Crusoe, Robinson, 201, 217, 227, 362
Cuesta y Velasco, Joseph de la, 329
Cunningham, Alison, 205, 361
Curaçoa, 121
Curnow, Bronwyn, xi
Curtis, Gray, xii
Daily Light, The, 172
Daily, Owen, 330
Dalling, Captain Samuel, 37-8, 46, 332
Dames, William, blamed by James McMahon, 8; blamed by Owen Lloyd, 79, 90; church warden, 162; history of, 358; in Ireland, 146, 198; at Norman Island, 65, 68-9, 83, 198, 200; at Ocracoke, 52, 56; at Tortola, 70, 73, 338-9; purchases sloop, 73, 339-40; sued by John Lloyd, 52; mentioned, 78-9, 89-90, 146, 162, 171, 198, 200, 285, 336, 338-41, 354, 358, 360-1
Danish National Maritime Museum, xi, 284
Danish National Archives,(Statens Arkiver Rigsarkavit), xi, 255, 290, 302
Darcy, Robert, *see* Lord Holderness
David Warner & Co., 341
Davidson, William, *see* William Blackstock
Davos, Switzerland, 214
Day, Captain, 41
de Graf, Johan, 131
de Wint, Gert Sprewart, 71, 153, 339, 347
de Wint, Peter, 118-9
de Wint, Lucas, 284, 288
Deacon, Jonathan, 44, 57, 61, 71, 74-6, 90, 162, 274, 285, 334, 340, 358
Dead Chest Island (The Deadman's Chest), Virgin Islands, 190, 194, 200, 227
Deadman's Bay, Virgin Islands, 227
Dean, Captain, 127
DeCuir, Captain David, xii, 168-9, 174, 176, 178, 180, 183-6, 190, 192-4, 199, 202, 240, 259, 277; picture of 203
DeCuir, Claudia, picture of, 203
Deep, The, 190, 194
del Alamo, Bernardo, 15
Delany, Capt. Matthew, 55, 335
de Mora, Domingo Luis, 332
Denmark, xi, 109, 114, 119, 121, 132, 137, 140, 142, 146, 148-9, 150, 153, 157-161, 195, 246-7, 255-7, 261-2, 279, 283-4, 302-3, 309, 324, 356. *See also* Frederick V, King of
Desbroses, Stephen, 77, 115, 131-2, 340-1, 347

Index

Deutz, William Gideon, 146, 152, 354
Deutz, John, 152
Devonia, ship, 209
Dewitte, Private Pieter, 107
Dieppe Bay, St. Kitts, 7, 41, 126, 233, 242, 291, 323, 340
Dinwiddie, Robert, 335
Discovery Channel, 282, 306
Dismal Swamp, 119
Dock Street, Wilmington, North Carolina, 101
Dog the Wind, dinghy, 90
Doig, James, 136, 144-6, 149, 351, 353-4
Don Phillip, bark, 84, 341
Don Quixote, 229
Dorothy, ship, 100, 344
Douglas, Captain George, 351
Dove, vessel, 338
Downing, John, 197
Drakes Channel, 192
Drum Inlet, 35, 153, 332
Dublin, Ireland, 146
Duells, William, 334
Duke of Bedford, *see* Bedford, Duke of
Dumfries, Scotland, 359
Dunlop & Peter, Scottish merchants, 123, 222, 363
Duque, Joseph del, 98
Dyer, Matthew, 130,
Dyson, Francis, 253, 326, 365
Earl of Wilmington, 47
East Oakland, California, 213, 238
Eastern Shore of Maryland, 48, 52, 336, 358
Echanis, Lt. Manuel, 56, 97, 337
Eden House, 47, 147, 354
Eden, Governor Charles, 31-2
Eden, Penelope, 47
Edenton, North Carolina, Gabriel Johnston at, 47, 96, 119; Juan Manuel Bonilla at, 118-19, 124, 129; Guadalupe auctioned at, 119, 134; mentioned, 134, 332, 335, 343, 347
Edgartown, Massachusetts, 334
Edinburgh Evening Courant, 222, 362
Edinburgh Magazine, 363
Edinburgh University, 205
Edinburgh, Scotland, 205, 207, 221, 223-24, 305, 363
Edwards, Thomas, 51, 54, 359
El Salvador, snow, 21, 24, 35-6, 40, 48-9, 61, 329, 332-3, 335
Elby, Nathaniel, 330

Elizabeth City County, Virginia, 250, 252, 324, 326, 330, 331, 336, 350, 365, 367
Elizabeth City, North Carolina, 258-9, 326
Elizabeth River, Norfolk, Virginia, 28, 40
Elizabeth, sloop, 1-6, 46, 249, 253-4, 280, 323-4; *Seaflower* renamed as, 63, 65, 118, 255, 280
Elizabethtown, New Jersey, 359
Elliot, Captain Charles, 150-1
Eluethra, Bahamas, 164
England, Captain Edward, 217
Eques, Admiral Don Juan de, 20, 327
Esmit, Adolph, Governor of St. Thomas, 109, 345
Estrada, Pedro, 41, 333
Etherington Conservation Services, xii
Europa, ship, 157
Europa Point, Gibralter, 338
Fairfield, Connecticut, 357
Falkingham, Captain, RN, 351
Fanny, ship, 329, 333
Farrow, Captain Jan, 80, 84, 341
Faulkner, Thomas, 326, 365
Felchenhauer, Governor Harrien, of St. Thomas, 158
Felix, Antonio, 343
Ferdinand VI, King of Spain, 11, 22, 29, 36, 62, 116, 141, 157-8, 352, 356
Fernández, Antonio, 343
Fifth Street, San Francisco, 237
Finch, Isaac John, 242
First Horizon Home Loans, Inc., 167
Fitz-Randolph, Captain. Samuel, 50-1, 54-7, 93-6, 102, 194, 244, 335, 359
Fitz-Randolph, Kinsey, 51, 54, 97, 359
Fitz-Randolph, Robert, 97
Fitz-Randolph, Sam, Jr., 50, 97, 359
Fleming, Gilbert, Lt. General of the Leeward Islands, at Anguilla, 113; at Antigua, 80-2, 116, 120, 126-7, 130, 276, 279; at St. Kitts, 75-6, 83, 114, 121, 135, 244, 286, 365; at Tortola, 85-7, 111-3, 197; on board HMS *Shark,* 81; on board sloop, *Christian,* 82-3, 113; home of, 270; proclamation of, 82; mentioned, 74, 80-1, 111, 121-2, 127-8, 132, 134, 141, 144, 148, 195, 226, 233, 257, 285, 339-42, 346-51, 354, 359, 360
Fleming Street, Tortola, 198
Flint County (Flintshire), Wales, 3, 229, 296-8, 366
Flint, Captain James, 169, 217-20, 228-9, 362
Flint, James, author, 219, 363
Flora, John, xii, 245, picture of 304
Flying Fish, sloop, 359
Flying Post, newspaper, 345
Fontenoy, Battle of, 224, 362
Forbes, George, 339-40

Index

Fort Oranje, St. Eustatius, 105, 247, 260, 273-5
Fort Purcel, Tortola, 198
Foster Cauleff Esq. and Co., 338
Fragela, Fr. Juan, 328
Franciscan(s), 17, 19, 24, 162, 328; churches of, 160; convent of, 278, 309
Fraser, Captain, 87, 121, 342, 348
Frederick V, King of Denmark, 121, 148, 160-1, 356
Fredricks, Jan, 106, 345
Free Masons Lodge, Antigua, 340
Freeman, Captain, 343
Freeman, William, 253, 326
French Guineaman, 2, 3, 5, 31, 46, 74, 323
French Hotel, Monterey, California, 209-10, 361
French Riviera, 206
Frenchman's Reef Hotel, St. Thomas, USVI, 168
Fuerte, ship, 20, 153-4, 328, 331
Fyfe, Rev. William, 8, 326
Galagher, Peter, xi, 301
Gallega, La, 12
Garay, Don Juan de, 161
García, Bartolomé, 343
García, Felipe Pedro, 46-7, 55-7, 98, 101, 145, 332-5, 337
García, Juan Andrés, 128
Garraicochea, Don Pedro de, 5-6, 63, 253-4
General History of the Robberies and Murders of the Most Notorious Pirates, A, 216
George Tavern, Hampton, Virginia, 330
Gerard, Jacob, see Wade, Zebulon
Gibbons, Nicholas, 1-2, 242, 323
Gibson, James, 125, 349
Gibson, Thomas, 125-6, 131, 135-6, 279, 349
Gideon, William, 146, 152, 354
Gilbert, Benjamin, 332
Gilbert, Ephraim, 48, 332, 335
Gilbert, Thomas, 48, 332, 335
Glasgow Courant, 362
Glasgow, HMS, 81, 245
Glasgow, Scotland, 123, 222-4, 226, 305, 362, 363
Glenn, Governor, of South Carolina, 100, 344
Gøbel, Erik, xi
Gold Rush, 235
Gonzáles, Esther, xi
Gonzáles, Isidro, alias Churribillu, 56-7
Gonzáles, Dr Pedro Francisco de Alcantara, 327
Graffenreid, Christopher Von, 348

Granville, John Earl, 366
Gray, Curtis, xii
Gray, Walter, 339
Grear Flatty Creek, North Carolina, 359
Greenwich Hospital, 245-6, 253, 258-9, 281, 285, 293-4, 301, 324, 365
Greenwich Maritime Museum, xii, 245-6, 249, 293-4, 355
Grez-Sur-Loing, France, 206-9, 361
Guarnsey, sloop, 41
Guiral y Concha, Diego, 329
Gumbs, Benjamin, Governor of Anguilla, 76, 83, 113-4, 127-8, 130, 340, 346, 349
Gwyn, Frank, 229
Hack, Robert, 112-3, 341, 346
Haddam, Connecticut, 358
Hague, The, 142, 144, 246, 353
Hall, Durham, 9, 335
Hall, Elizabeth, *see* Elizabeth Lloyd
Halliday, John, 136, 144, 145-6, 149, 351, 353-4
Hampton Bar, 330
Hampton courthouse, 252, 289-90, 367
Hampton jail, 8, 250-1, 325-6
Hampton River (Hampton Creek), 7, 25, 28-9, 33, 128, 330
Hampton Roads, Virginia, 7, 27-8, 129, 134-5, 256, 266, 334
Hampton, Virginia, 3, 5-9, 25, 27-30, 32-3, 37, 51, 55, 100, 124-5, 128-30, 136-7, 222, 246, 249-51, 253-5, 266, 281, 287-9, 309, 323-6, 330-1, 333, 336, 350-1, 358, 365
Hands, Israel, 31, 33, 217-8, 331
Hannah, sloop, 29-30, 254, 331, 365
Happy, HMS, ship, 4, 246, 294-5, 309, 324, 367
Happy, merchant snow, 249
Harman, Claire, 296, 361, 364
Harry, sloop, 335
Havana, Cuba, English prisoners at, 23, 100, 141; John Lloyd in prison at, 6-7, 46, 253-4, 265; Juan Manuel Bonilla at, 13, 21-2, 120, 154, 329; Owen Lloyd goes to, 254; Spanish privateers from, 5-6, 41, 324, 333; mentioned, 36, 46, 117, 120, 141, 154, 157, 159, 258, 265, 310, 328-9, 331
Hawke, Admiral Edward, 216, 219, 245, 292, 294, 362
Hawkins, (Mother) Ann, 350; tavern of, 27-9, 39, 129, 222, 256, 287, 326, 330
Hawkins, Elizabeth, 330
Hawkins, Jim, 166, 169, 174, 177, 182, 185, 187-8, 190, 216-8, 292
Hawkins, John, 27, 330
Hawkins, Sam, 27, 330
Hawkins, Sarah, 330
Hawkins, Thomas, 330
Haynes, John, 70, 72, 112, 197, 338-9
Hector, HMS, 6-7, 250
Hedges, Captain, 131, 136

Index

Henley, William E., 216, 228, 230, 362-3, 364

Hews, Captain John, 134, 355

Heyliger, Johannes, Governor of St. Eustatius, arrests Owen Lloyd, 6, 261, 340; convenes inquiry, 108, 345; death of, 149, 354; goes to St. Croix, 286; hears of piracy, 75, 340; holds the treasure, 88, 152, 196-7; interrogates prisoners, 78-80, 88, 360; investigated, 148-9, 247, 354; meets John Watson, 131, 142, 350; needs permission for death sentence, 105; rigs auction, 143, 145, 148; sends Owen Lloyd back to Norman Island, 80, 85, 195, 341-2; sentences prisoners, 90; suspected conspiracy to kill Owen Lloyd, 285-6; mentioned, 85, 90, 128, 142, 157, 261, 270, 303, 345, 351-2, 354

Heyliger, Peter, 339

Higgs, Lewis, 197

Hispaniola, 64

Hispaniola, vessel, 216, 219, 229

Hobson, Adcock, 357

Hobson, Elizabeth, 357

Hobson, Francis, 357

Hobson, Mary Ann, 357

Hobson, Thebe, 357

Hobson, Thomas, at Boston, 44; at Ocracoke, 44-6, 59; at St. Croix, 71, 285; at St. Eustatius, 75, 334; at St.Kitts, 74-5, 105-6; at Norman Island, 68; captured, 76; released, 80, 345; interrogated, 247, 337; mentioned, 63, 108, 162, 336, 357

Hodge Estate, Tortola, 198

Hodge, Christopher, 70, 73, 197

Hodge, Peter, 197

Hogsties Reef, 74, 340

Holburne, Commodore Francis, RN, 112, 134, 346, 351

Holden, John, 326

Holderness, Lord, 144, 352-3

Hollenberg, Johan George, 134

Hooper, Merritt and Goldie, 249, 366

Hornigold, Captain Benjamin, 31

Hotel Chevillon, France, 206-7

House of Burgesses, Virginia, 251

House of Trade, Spain, 14, 40, 97, 99, 144, 146, 196, 331-3, 335-7, 343-4, 353-5, 360

Houstoun, Alexander, 223, 362

Howard, William, 31, 45, 162, 357

Howstown, (Houston) ship, 351

Hughes, Tim, xi, 301

Hullet, Buddy, xii

Hunter, John, 28, 100, 128-9, 331, 335, 350, 367

Huony, Captain Don Daniel, Bonilla requests escort by, 22; captures Harrington, 28; sends help to Ocracoke, 46-7, 55-7; mentioned, 20, 23, 40, 46-7, 98, 168, 229, 325, 329, 331, 335-7, 344, 363

Hutchings, Captain John, 58, 47, 250-1, 289-90, 324-6, 335, 365

Hyde Street, San Francisco, 307

Hyde, Henry, 239, 364

379

Hyldloft, Mathias, 77, 115, 340, 347

Ibáñez, Francisco Vaso, 159

Iglesias, Bernardo, 343

Indian Creek, North Carolina, 359

Indiana, 235, 237

Indiana Evening Gazette, 367

Indians, The, Norman Island, 167, 169, 171

Innes, Colonel. James, 49-50, 53, 54, 94-5, 99-101, 118, 145, 335-6, 344, 353

Innes, William, 367

Irving, Washington, 173, 200, 228, 360

Isassi, Bernardo, 327

Isle of Man, xii, 245, 291, 304

Izaguirre, Francisco, 329

Jackson, James, 96-7, 359

Jackson, Joseph, 51, 96, 359

Jackson, Mary, 97, 359

Jakobsen, Henriette Gavnholdt, xi

Jamaica, 4-6, 158, 222, 229, 246, 249-50, 254, 295, 309, 324-5, 331, 356, 363, 365

James City County, Virginia, 330

James Fort, Antigua, 81

James Young, Tortola, 198

Jansen, Corporal Jan, 106-8, 345

Jarecki, Dr. Henry, 191

Jeff, Adrianna, 72, 113, 197, 341

Jimenez, Juan, 332

John D. Rockefeller Library, Williamsburg, Virginia, 249

Johns, Sarah, 256

Johnson, Captain Charles, 216-7, 334

Johnson, Claude, & Son, 149

Johnston, Frances, 147, 354

Johnston, Governor Gabriel, at Edenton, 96, 118-9; at New Bern, 101-2; and Bonilla's treasure, 99-101, 75-6, 96-7, 102, 142, 145, 157, 352; death of, 147, 354; issues orders, 48, 57, 96, 98-9, 123, 348; learns of Spanish shipwrecks, 47-9, 332; meets with Juan Manuel Bonilla, 53, 94, 101, 141, 343; proclamation of, 76; 96, 123, 343; reports to the council, 49; salary of, 48, 99, 142, 147, 352; sends Col. James Innes to Ocracoke, 50; advises the Duke of Bedford, 99, 335, 344; mentioned, 116-120, 123, 127, 137, 140-2, 145, 147, 150-1, 157, 217, 279, 332-3, 343-5, 347-8, 353

Johnston's Fort, 57, 62, 99

Johnston, Richard, 265

Jonathan Hanbury and Co., 331

Jones, Llona, xi, 280, 305

Jones, Mathias, innkeeper, 135, 256, 266, 351

Jorge, ship, 328

Jost Van Dyke, British Virgin Islands, 192

Journey Across the Plains, 214

Index

Joyner Library, East Carolina University, xii
Jimenez, Juan, 332
Jubilee, ship, 123, 252, 348
Keene, Ambassador Benjamin, 142, 344, 352
Keith, George, 258
Kelly, Betty, 236
Kelly, Captain John, 21
Kidd, Captain, 59, 109, 139, 173-4, 195, 345, 360
King Carlos III, 158
King George II, 53, 57, 62, 81-2, 98, 100, 114, 121, 127, 147, 157, 340
King George's War, xv, 1, 265, 323
King Street, Hampton, Virginia, 8-9, 27, 29, 266
King, John, & Co., 125, 349
Kingsley, Charles, 194, 227
Kingston, Jamaica, 6, 325
Kingston, W. G. H., 220, 362
Kinsey, Joanna, 359
Kirn Memorial Library, 249, 293
La Bella Sara, ship, 20
La Galga, ship, 20, 22-5, 28, 40, 42, 46-8, 56, 97, 100, 168, 229, 233-4, 244, 28, 310, 324-5, 328-9, 331, 334, 343-4, 360
La Marianna, ship, 25, 28
La Ninfa, ship, see *Nuestra Señora de Guadalupe* and *Nuestra Señora de los Remedios*
La Perla, ship, 328
La Reina de los Angeles, see the *Peregrina*
La Reyna, ship, 18, 20-1, 328-9
Lamden, Thomas, 350
Lanfranco, ship, 327-8
Langara, Don Juan de, 153-55, 355
LaPierre, Alexandra, 296, 361, 364, 367
Lee, Anne, xii, 247, 303
Lee, Thomas, President of the Virginia Council, 28, 47, 120, 141, 330-1, 352
Leeward Islands, 2, 29, 63-4, 74, 76, 81-2, 86, 109, 126, 224-5, 233, 244, 257, 270, 285-6
Leinster Bay, St. John, U.S. Virgin Islands, 169
Leon, ship, 328
Lesser Antilles, 63, 227
Letters from America, 229
Leverworst, Corporal Johan Casper, 107
Library of Congress. 191, 193, 201, 233
Lidderdale, John, 117, 122-3, 128, 130, 135-6, 140, 148, 152, 222, 349-52
Lidderdale, Robert, 117, 122-3, 128, 130, 135-6, 140, 148, 152, 222, 350-2
Lindsay, John, tavern of, 126, 136
Lisbon, Portugal, 15-6, 122, 344, 348, 351, 363
Little Thatch Island, British Virgin Islands, 194

Livesey, Dr, 183, 216, 292

Livingston, Charles, *see* McClair, Charles

Lloyd, Alice, mother of Owen Lloyd, 324

Lloyd, Captain James, RN, 3-4, 294; will of, 295

Lloyd, Christian(a), (Caines), (Malone), (Rebhun), as Christian Malone, 289-90, 323, 325, 367; at Hampton, VA, 8, 266; at St. Kitts, 74-5, 105-6, 108-9; goes to St. Thomas, 109; leaves for St. Kitts, 8-9, 326; marries Christian Cornelius Rebhun, 283-6, 288; marries Owen Lloyd, 1-2, 46; mortgages furniture, 6, 250; goes to St. Thomas, 109; will of, 290-1; mentioned, 3, 4, 6, 8-9, 30, 63, 74-5, 77, 81, 242-4, 249, 266, 281, 289-91, 298, 325-6

Lloyd, Christine, (Christina), (Christiana), wife of John Lloyd, 238-9, 245, 307, 367

Lloyd, Cornelius, 295

Lloyd, Elizabeth (Hall), sister of Owen, 3; wife of John, 9, 252-3, 269; at St. Kitts, 291, 367

Lloyd, John, at Greenwich Hospital, 245-6, 253, 258-9, 280-1, 292-4, 301, 324, 365; at Havana, 265; at Mrs. Hawkins, in Virginia, 29, 52, 254, 336; at Norfolk VA, 252-3, 253, 365; at Ocracoke, 30, 37-8, 40, 46, 51-2, 55-8, 93-6, 244, 342-3; at *St. Eustatius*, 7; at St Kitts, 7, 325-6; buys 150 acres in North Carolina, 258-9, 326, 258; captured by Spanish privateer, 5-6, 253, 324-5, 365; marriage of, 266; of Rhuddlan, Wales, 280, 296, 298, 305, 324, 366; serves in British navy, 3, 4, 324; mentioned, xv, 1, 3-5, 88-9, 102, 142, 196, 233, 249, 289, 301

Lloyd, John (2), acquaintance of Robert Louis Stevenson, 230, 233-240, 244-5, 288, 291, 294-8, 304, 307, 364-5

Lloyd, Captain John, RN, 245

Lloyd, John, of Ormskirk, 295

Lloyd, Owen, as a privateer, 2-3, 5; as a merchant, 3, 6-7, 323, 325; at Boston, 334; at Jamaica, 6, 246, 254, 365; at Mrs. Hawkins', 29; at Ocracoke, NC, 30, 37-8, 40, 42-3, 46, 51-2, 54-9, 267-8, 332-3, 342; at Norman Island, 68, 200, 202-3; at Saba, 84; at St. Eustatius, 75-6, 78-80, 89-90, 105-8, 113, 116, 123, 141, 197, 223, 253, 259-60, 262, 270, 275-5, 303, 360; at St. Kitts, 74-6, 81, 241-2, 249, 271-2, 279-80, 296, 298, 301, 306, 326, 364; at St. Thomas, 71, 77, 87, 112, 121, 128, 132, 135, 144, 149-50, 153, 196, 247, 255-7, 277, 282, 285-6, 302, 349-51, 360, 365; at St. Croix, 71, 198, 277, 282-5, 287, 306, 360; at Virginia, 7, 47, 249-50, 290, 326; buries treasure, 68; buys home in Hampton, Virginia, 8-9, 252, 266, 326, 365; death of, 283-6; escapes prison, 108, 123, 126, 345, 348; in Hampton jail, 8, 250-1, 365; interrogation of, 79-80, 89-90, 248-9, 257, 336-7, 339-41; marriage of, 266, 289, 323; on board the *Don Phillip*, 84-5; on board the *Seaflower*, 58-9, 61-5, 67-70, 83, 255; returns to Norman Island, 85, 198; sentenced to death, 91, 342; of Rhuddlan, Wales, 280, 296, 298, 305, 324, 366; serves in British Navy, 4, 292, 324; mentioned, xv, 1, 81, 83, 100-1, 111-2, 114-8, 120, 125, 127-30, 134, 136-7, 139-142, 144, 146, 152, 158, 162, 167-8, 170-2, 174, 186, 191,195-6, 199, 219, 222, 226, 229, 233-4, 240, 244, 246-9, 252, 254, 258, 270, 276, 279, 291, 308, 338, 351, 357-9, 362

Lloyd, Philip, 297, 366

Lloyd, Thomas, 291

Lloyd, Vincent, 3, 288, 366

Lloyd Vincent, father of Owen, 298, 366

Lloyd's Coffee House, 152

Lombard Street, London, 152

London, England, 47-8, 95, 99, 115, 117, 120, 122-3, 125, 128-30, 135-7, 139

London Bridge, 139

Index

London Magazine, 223
López, Diego, 343
López, Julian Bautista, 327
López, Vicente, 41
Lorenson, Governor Johan, 109
Louisa of Hanover, 121, 348
Lovick, John, 331
Loyall, Captain Jonathan, 335
Loyall, John, 367
MacDonald, Captain, RN, 112-4
Macé, Mr., 122, 348, 363
Macias, Genoveva Enriquez, 11
MacKenzie, Alexander, 5, 254, 324, 331, 365
MacKenzie, Hannah, 254
Madagascar, 109, 217
Madeira, Portugal, 4-5, 73, 151, 253, 324, 340
Madeira wine, 5, 115, 253, 325, 330, 365
Madrid, Spain, 20, 115, 140-2, 149, 161, 300
Magens, Nicolas, 145-6, 149-50, 152, 157, 160, 351, 353-6
Mahew, Catherine and Donald, xii
Maisterson, Captain Samuel, RN, 7, 250, 325
Malabar, 217
Malleville, Jean (John), 255-6, 340
Malleville, Maria (Suhm), 256, 340
Malleville, Thomas, 340
Malone, Christian(a), *see* Christian Caines
Malone, John, 290
Malone, Peter, 291
Manalapan, New Jersey, 359
Mann, Charles Wager, 126, 136
Mann, Thomas, 334
Man-of-War Bay, Norman Island, map of, 170, 193; pictures of, 178-81, 187; mentioned, 167, 169, 176, 192, 194, 199-200, 202-3
Maracaibo, Venezuela, 20
Marblehead, Essex, Massachusetts, 358
Marcenaro, Vicente, 329
Mardenbrough, Captain Christopher, 130
María Agustina de Utrera, 160
Marqués de Ensenada, 16, 40, 96, 98, 101, 115-6, 324, 328-9, 332-4, 337-8, 344, 347-8, 352-3
Marqués del Puerto, 142, 148-9, 352, 354
Marianna, slave, 325
Martin, Colonel Samuel, 82
Martin, Fr. Juan, 47
Martínez, Domingo, 343

Martinique, 2, 46
Mary, sloop, 50-1, 53-5, 57-8, 93-4, 96-7, 102, 130, 335, 342, 357, 359
Mason, George, 235
Massey, Sam, 336
Masterman Ready, 227
Matthew, Captain General William, 64, 76, 81, 337, 346
Matthews, James, *see* McMahon, James
Mauman, William, 15, 122, 348, 363
Maynard, Lt. Robert, RN, 32-3, 45
Mayonde, Juan Bernardo, 329
McClair, Charles, (alias Livingston), at Norman Island, 65, 68-70, 83, 198, 200; at Ocracoke, 52, 56; at Tortola, 73; marries, 73, 340; marooned 68-9; mentioned, 78, 88, 90, 171, 181, 339-40, 358
McDowell, William, 223, 225-6, 363
McGregor, Mrs., 215
MacLeod, Alan, xi,
Mclynn, Frank, 361
McMahon, James, at Ocracoke, 50-2; at St. Eustatius, 85, 88, 275; at St. Thomas, 71, 80; escapes, 107-8; captured at Saba, 84; interrogated, 88, 331, 342; on the *Seaflower*, 57, 336, 338; sentenced to death, 91; mentioned, 142, 162, 336-9, 357, 365
Meade, David, 119-20, 122-5, 128-31, 134, 266, 348-50, 353, 355, 363
Merchant's Hall in Glasgow, 222
Mexico, 11-2, 14, 16-17, 20-2, 31, 72, 159, 162, 263, 309, 327-9; viceroy of, 156, 223, 355
Mexico City, 11, 19
Middlesex, Connecticut, 358
Milliken, James, 223, 225-6, 363
Mitchell, Don, Anguilla, xii
Mitchell, Cary, Hampton, VA, 330
Mold, Wales, 297
Moll, Verna Penn, xii
Molly Molone's, 168, 192
Molly, schooner, 55, 335
Money Bay, 188-9, 202-3
Money Diggers, The, 173, 200, 360
Monimia, slave, 73
Monroe, Captain Revell, 343
Montalvo, Lorenzo, 22, 329
Monterey, California, 208-12, 239, 304
Monterey Californian, The, 210, 212, 220, 240, 361
Montiano, Don Manuel de, 333
Montier, James, 258, 326
Montserrat, 29, 64, 76, 82, 128, 130, 254, 257, 331, 364
Moore, Benjamin, 51, 359
Moorehouse, James, at Norman Island, 65, 69, 89, 200; 50, 90; at Ocracoke, 50; at St. Kitts, 74; at St. Eustatius, 75-6, 274, 340; at St. Thomas, 71; mentioned, 78, 162, 274, 285, 337, 357-8

Index

Morales, Don Lope de, 159
Moreno, Antonio, 332
Morente, Guadalupe Fernández, xi
Mormon Church, xii, 282-3, 366
Morro Castle, Havana, 23, 265, 331
Mother Hawkins' Hole, 330
Mount Vaea, 307-8
Mountfort, ship, 16
Mt. Mazinga, St. Eustatius, 75, 105, 244
Mt. Misery, St. Kitts, 74
Muñoz, Cristóbal, 327
Muñoz, Gabriel, 329
Muñoz, Joseph León, 41
Museum of London, xii
My First Book, 205, 215, 219-20, 227, 361
Nansemond River, Virginia, 119, 129, 266
Nansemond, brig, 134, 355
Nanticoke River, Maryland, 336
Nationaal Archief, 247-8, 259, 303
National Archives of Antigua and Barbuda, 279
National Archives of England, 242, 301
National Archives of St. Kitts, 233, 241
National Library of Wales, 280, 305, 324
National Maritime Museum, Greenwich, 245, 259, 293, 355
Navy Chronicle, 201
Nebraska State Journal, 363
Nelson, Admiral Horatio, 262
Netherlands, The, xii, 7, 105, 108, 137, 140, 142, 146, 148, 246-8, 257, 259, 303, 309, 352
Nevis, 82, 226, 244, 269
New Bern, North Carolina, Governor Gabriel Johnston at, 48, 50, 94, 100-1; jail at, 102, 117, 119, 244; Spaniards at, 49, 53-4, 94, 96, 101, 117, 119, 197, 335; mentioned, 35, 44, 96, 118, 197, 244, 335-6, 343, 345
New Hanover County, North Carolina, 147
New York Gazette, 42, 72, 246
New York Times, 229
New York, New York, 118, 209, 214, 235, 238, 245-6
Newport, Rhode Island, 87
Newtown, Maryland, (Pocomoke), 336
Nibbs, George, 228, 339
Nibbs, Tortola, 198
Nichols, Robert, 126
Nimmo, William, 253, 326
Nisbet, Stuart M., 226
Niziol, Simon, xi, 245

Norfolk, Virginia, Lloyd brothers at, 1, 3, 5-7, 52, 252-3, 258, 266, 281, 289, 336; mayor of, 5, 9, 251, 335; records of, 249-52, 293, 323, 324-6, 365, 367; Spaniards at, 28, 40, 47-8, 57, 137, 331-2, 334-7, 350; mentioned, 1, 3, 5-9, 27-8, 40, 43, 47-8, 50-2, 54, 57, 119, 124, 137, 150, 197, 249-53, 258, 266, 281, 289, 293, 325, 344, 349

Norman Island Treasure Company, 200-1, 361

Norman(s) Island, British Virgin Islands, map of, 170, 193; Owen Lloyd at, 67, 79, 84-5, 89, 132, 141, 149; owner's of, 86, 191, 225, 270, 286; restaurant at, 169-171, 174, 176, 178, 180, 187, 199; treasure buried at, 68-9, 78, 80, 88-9, 106, 195, 202, 223, 308; treasure recovered at, 69, 72-3, 77, 80, 82, 86-7, 112, 116, 120, 135, 197, 226, 279, 285; mentioned, 65, 70-1, 83, 111, 134, 146, 167-203, 227, 234, 240, 259, 262, 276

Northumberland, HMS, 324

Neuse River, 48-9, 331

Nuestra Señora de Ariarte, 355

Nuestra Señora de Concepción, 191, 342, 360

Nuestra Señora de Guadalupe, auction of, 119-20, 124, 347; at Cádiz, Spain, 13-4, 16-7, 327; at Havana, 21-3, 265; at Ocracoke, North Carolina, 35-59, 93-6, 99, 117-8, 124, 254, 267-8, 333-5, 342-3, 362; at Suffolk, Virginia, 129, 134-5, 137, 156, 266, 349, 351; at Veracruz, 13, 18-21, 263-4, 309, 329; travels to Veracruz, 17, 211, 278, 328; in storms, 18, 24-5; treasure shipped on HMS *Scorpion*, 98, 344; treasure stolen from, 57-59, 93-4, 97, 140, 156, 158, 191; returns to Spain, 151, 278, 355; mentioned, 125, 129, 147, 150, 153, 155-6, 159-160, 162, 168, 233, 308, 310, 332, 339, 341, 352, 354, 356-7

Nuestra Señora de la Rosa, 355

Nuestra Señora de los Godos, at Cadiz,, Spain, 329; at Veracruz, 20; at Havana, 22-3; at Norfolk, Virginia, 25, 28, 40, 330; mentioned, 24, 100, 331, 333, 344

Nuestra Señora de los Remedios, 14, 24, 95, 139, 152, 327, 328

Nuestra Señora de Soledad y San Francisco Javier, 20, 24, 35-6, 40, 47-9, 61, 153, 329, 332-3

Nuestra Señora de Mercedes, 22, 24, 25

Oaxaca, Mexico, 12

Ocean Terrace Inn, St. Kitts, 240, 262

Ocracoke Inlet, North Carolina, Blackbeard at, 31, 45, 217; Blackbeard killed at, 29; *Guadalupe* anchored near, 24, 35-40, 42; *Guadalupe* at, 39-40, 43, 48-59, 71, 93, 117-8, 135, 196; John Lloyd captured at, 93-4, he escapes, 96, 252; Owen Lloyd trades with, 30; Owen Lloyd shipwrecked at, 30; pilot of, 30, 36-8, 41-3, 50, 96, 117, 267-8, 331, 333-4, 343, 347; HMS *Scorpion* at, 97, 343; *Seaflower* arrives at, 44-5, leaves with treasure, 57-59, 247; Spanish privateers at, 41, 333; mentioned, 61-2, 64, 70, 74-5, 90, 105, 107, 112, 115, 124, 128, 130, 132, 146-7, 152-3, 158, 162, 222, 233, 244, 254, 259, 266-68, 295, 309, 310-1, 331-2, 334-7, 347, 355, 357-9, 362

O'Flaherty, Victoria, xi, 240, 243-4, 279, 306

Old and New Pacific Capitals, 214

Oliver, Jeanie, xi

Oliver, John, 30, 36-8, 41-3, 50, 96, 117, 267-8, 331, 333-4, 343, 347

Oliver, Spencer, xi

Oriente, ship, 355

Ormes, Samuel, 120, 147, 348

Ormskirk, England, 295

Ortega, Don Pedro Manuel de, 25, 117-8, 129, 137, 156, 347, 350

Index

Ortega, Juan Muricio, 327
Osbourne, Fanny, *see* Stevenson, Fanny
Osbourne, Hervey, 206, 238
Osbourne, (Field) Isobel, 206-7, 209, 234-8, 291, 294, 296, 298, 307, 367
Osbourne, Sam, 207-10, 213, 233-6, 237-9
Osbourne, Samuel Lloyd, 206-7, 209-10, 214, 237-8, 288; picture of, 232; inspiration for *Treasure Island*, 219, 230, 298, 307-8, 367; death of, 307
Otter, HMS, 6-7, 112-4, 276, 325, 346
Our Lady of Guadalupe, portrait of, 20; shrine of, 19
Palou, Fr. Francisco, 211, 328
Pamlico River, North Carolina, 45, 357
Pamlico Sound, North Carolina, 32, 48, 333
Panama, 235, 238, 245
Pareja, Agustin de, Governor of Puerto Rico, 77, 111-2, 114-7, 132, 338-9, 341, 346-7, 351
Paris, France, 206-7
Parladorio, Antonio
Pasea Estate, Tortola, 198
Pasea, James, 197
Pasquotank County, North Carolina, 50, 162, 258; courthouse, 258-9
Pasquotank River, 9, 258
Paul, Ryder, and Murray, Solicitors General, 141, 352, 354
Payne, Ralph, Deputy Governor of St. Kitts, Gilbert Fleming appoints, 75-6, 340; Governor Gumbs visits, 7-6; plantation of, 83; reports to Fleming, 80-1, 112, 339, 341, 346; mentioned, 123, 225-6, 233, 340-1, 360; Ralph Payne, Jr, 225, 363
Pearl, HMS, 32
Peat, Captain Joseph, 325
Peggy, schooner, 8-9, 326
Peñalosa, Governor Don Diego de, of Veracruz, 19-21, 328
Pentland Rising, A, 205
Peregrina, ship, formerly the *York*, 145, 147, 150, 152, 153-56, 197, 353-6
Pérez, Esther Gonzáles, xi
Perth Amboy, New Jersey, 50, 97, 130, 335-6, 350
Peter Island, British Virgin Islands, 185, 190, 194, 199-201, 227
Petra, Mallorca, 328
Philippines, 12
Philips, Lt. General, 81
Phipps, Francis, 191, 270, 360
Phipps, Robert, 86, 191, 270
Phipps, William, 191, 342
Phister, Peter, xi, 246-7, 255-6, 262, 283, 302
Pickering, Thomas, 339
Pickering, Tortola, 198
Pickering, William, 197
Pignatelli, Juan Domingo, 157, 160-1, 356-7

Pine Street, San Francisco, 239
Pinzon, Nicolas, 327
Pirate Treasure, 191
Pirates Bar, 180, 187, 191, 199
Pirates of the Caribbean, 308
Pitlochry, Scotland, 214
Pitton, Capt. John, 55, 335
Plymouth County, Massachusetts, 334, 359
Poe, Edgar Alan, 229
Polly, snow, 7
Polly, ship, 128-130, 350-1
Porto Bello, 217
Portsmouth, England, 4, 16
Portsmouth Square, San Francisco, 304
Praat, Corporal Christian, 107-8, 345
Prado y Sarmiento, Angela de, 14-6, 95, 150-3, 327-8
Prasca y Arbore, 159
Presidial Chamber of Amsterdam, 144
Prince Edward, privateer, 15
Princesse Wilhelmine Caroline, ship, 257, 366
Pritchett, Abraham, at St. Eustatius, 85, 88, 275; at St. Kitts, 242; captured, 84; escapes, 107-8; interrogated, 89, 200, 247, 336-7, 342, 361; sentenced to death, 91; mentioned, 44-6, 61, 63, 70-1, 80, 142, 162, 196-7, 334, 339, 341, 357-8
Privateer Bay, 186, 200, 202-3
Pruett, Robert, xii
Public Record Office, *see* National Archives of England
Puerto de Santa Maria, 17, 159, 162
Puerto Rico, 18, 64, 77, 80, 113, 115-6, 130, 134, 149, 154-6, 355; governor of, *see* Pareja, Agustin de
Pulteney, brigantine, 338
Pumarejo, Captain Pedro, 20, 28, 40, 100, 329-33, 335, 344, 350
Purcell, Edward, 228, 363
Purcell, James Lt. Gov, 69, 72, 81, 135, 198, 270, 337, 339, 342, 346, 351; as a privateer, 338
Purcell, Captain John, 85, 127, 148, 198, 270, 286; will of 360
Purcell, Rebecca, 72, 112, 197-8, 339, 341
Purser, Captain, 69-70, 73-4, 338-9
Quarter Merchant, Scotland, 363
Queen Anne's Revenge, ship, 31-2, 61
Queen Anne's County, Maryland, 319, 336, 358
Queen Barbara of Spain, 157, 356
Queen Street, Hampton, Virginia, 7-8, 29, 252, 266, 288-9
Quiberon Bay, Battle of, 219
Raapzaet, Sergeant Jacob, 107-8
Racine Journal Times, 367
Randall, Capt. Thomas, RN, 57, 62, 97-8, 125, 129, 344

Index

Randolph, Peter, 48-49, 53, 335

Rankin, George, 340

Rat Island, Antigua, 81

Ravene, Commandant Andres, 80, 84, 85, 106, 108, 149, 341, 345

Rawleigh, ship, 5-6, 250, 254, 325, 365

Raye, Isaac, 71, 74-6, 90, 162, 274, 285, 334, 340, 358

Real Armada, 14, 327

Real Compañia, 22-3

Rearden, Timothy, 238-9, 364

Rebecca, sloop, 73, 339-40, 358

Rebhun, Christian Cornelius, 283-4, 288, 290, 366; his will, 367

Red Hook, St. Thomas, 168

Reese River, Nevada, 234, 364

Reggio, Andrés, 328

Relief, sloop, 332

Respaldiza, Don Joseph de, 20, 35, 40, 47-9, 102, 153, 329, 332, 333, 335

Revel Bay, Denmark, 324

Revenge, sloop, 31-3

Rhode Island, 50, 71, 87, 357

Rhone, RMS, 190, 194, 360

Rhuddlan, Wales, 3, 280, 295, 297, 305, 324, 366

Rhydorddwy, Wales, 324

Richards, Catherine, xi

Richardson, Addison, xii

Riddell, George, 289, 367

Riddell, John, 289, 367

Riddell, Susanna, 289, 367

Riddlehurst, Francis, 330

Rivera, Fernando, 343

Road Town, Tortola, 67, 172

Roanoke Inlet, North Carolina, 32

Roanoke, snow, 37-9, 332

Robinson Crusoe, 201, 217, 227, 362

Rodríguez, Julián, 98

Rodriguez, Pedro, at Ocracoke, 35-6, 38-9, 51, 97; at Veracruz, 13, 18; confined on HMS *Scorpion*, 97-8; in the storm, 24; takes charge of the *Seaflower*, 53-6; 123, 332, 344, 365; shot returning to Spain, 124, 348

Ronan, William, 197, 339

Rose, HMS, 81

Rowan County, North Carolina, 357

Royal Family, 15

Royal Fuerza, 6,

Royal Oak, HMS, 4, 324

Royal West India Company, 160

Rudd Lane, Hampton, 330

Rum Cay, 64
Rutherford, John, 147
Saba, 80, 84-5, 88, 341, 357-8
Salt Island, British Virgin Islands, 194
Salt River, St. Croix, 294, 282
Salter, Edward, 31
Samuel, schooner, 331
San Antonio Bay, Puerto Rico, 154, 156
San Antonio de Padua y Nuestra Señora del Rosario, ship, 20
San Antonio, ship, 327
San Carlos Borroméo, 210, 361
San Cayetano, ship, 328
San Diego, California, 19
San Francisco, California, 19, 206-10, 212-4, 220, 235-9, 245, 288, 291, 296-8, 304, 361, 364-5, 367
San Francisco Bay, California, 307
San Francisco, Puerto Rico, 154
San Hipolito, 19
San Juan de Dios, 19
San Juan de Montesclaros, hospital, 19
San Juan de Ulúa, 12, 18, 263, 309
San Mateo Times, 367
San Pedro, ship, 21, 24-5, 28, 40, 329-30, 344
San Vicente, ship, 328
Sanchez, Adolpho, 210
Santa Barbara, California, 307-8, 367
Santiago, Juan Bernardo, 128
Santo Domingo, 25, 191; galleon wrecked, 298, 342
Savage Garden, London, 145
Schraeders, Jan, assistant constable, 106, 108, 345
Scituate Historical Society, xii
Scituate, Massachusetts, 43, 56, 78, 87, 136, 162, 334, 342, 359
Scorpion, HMS, at Brunswick, 99-100; at Cape Fear, 56-7, 62, 336-7; at Charleston, 49, 62, 329; ordered to Ocracoke, 49-50, 53, 55, 62, 97-8, 335, 343-4; Bonilla contracts with, 94, 97, 129, 141, 343; carries treasure to Spain, 98, 100-01; arrives in Spain, 120, 124-5, 196, 332, 344, 348, 360; treasure removed from, 101, 142, 145-6, 344; mentioned, 349
Scotland, xi, 47, 207-8, 213-4, 221-4, 229, 239, 305, 307, 359, 362-3
Sea Cook or Treasure Island; A Story for Boys, The, see Treasure Island
Sea Cow Bay, Tortola, 73
Seaflower, sloop, auction of, 118-9, 255, 257, 284, 334, 347; arrives at Norman Island, 65, 68-9, 186, 195, 198-200, 202, 338; arrives at St. John, 65, 196-7; abandoned at St. Thomas, 70-71, 77, 116, 121, 153, 198; at Boston; 43-44: at Ocracoke, 45, 51, 55-6, 268; Blackstock comes aboard, 58; crew of, 45, 51-2, 63, 88, 203, 247, 257, 280, 285, 336, 341, 357-9; Gilbert Fleming demands possession of, 87, 114, 342; livestock aboard, 77; Owen Lloyd goes aboard, 46, 53-4, 57, takes command of, 63; treasure loaded on, 51, 53, 196; takes off with treasure, 58-9, 61-2, 112, 196; proclamation to apprehend, 75-6; renamed the *Elizabeth,* 63,

Index

280, 337; Zebulon Wade, part owner of, 44, 334; mentioned, 71, 80, 93, 96, 162, 195, 343, 346

Seaford, HMS, 4, 324

Sea Lions: The Lost Sealers, The, 221, 362

Sensing Murder, 306

Serra, Fr. Junípero, the Apostle of California, 212; at Carmel, California, 210, 212; at the Convent of San Francisco, 264, 309; blesses mission of Santa Barbara, 308; celebrates the miraculous deliverance of the galleon by St. Barbara, 19; establishes missions, 19; image of, 211; on board the Guadalupe, 18, 211; statues of, 213, 279; travels to the shrine of Our Lady of Guadalupe, 19; mentioned, 328

Servant, Bertrand, 326

Seville, Spain, 14, 40, 244, 300, 309

Shadwell, St. Kitts, xi, 83, 270

Shark, HMS, 76, 81, 112, 134, 340-1, 346, 350-1

Shelly, Percy, 229

Shropshire, England, 296

Silver Shoals, 342

Silver, Long John, 33, 175, 178, 195, 216-20, 228, 223, 245, 292, 294, 308, 363

Silverado, 214

Silverado Squatters, 214

Simoneau, Jules, 210

Sims, Valerie, 171, 191

Skeleton Island, 188, 215

Slave Path, 260, 262, 274

Smith, Daniel, 76, 83, 113-4, 120-2, 341, 346

Smith, Jean, 363

Smith, John, 113-4, 120-2, 346

Smith, Rev. Charles, 1, 323

Smith, Thomas, 221, 363

Smollet, Captain Alexander, 229

Smollet, Tobias, RN, 229, 363

Soldier Bay, 182-3, 192, 195, 199

Somerset County, Maryland, 336, 358

Soper's Hole, West End, Tortola, 169

Soutar, Captain, 221

South Carolina Gazette, 246

South Dividing Creek, North Carolina, 357

Southey, Captain Thomas, 200-01

Southampton, sloop, 332

Spanish Town, 64, 149, 195, 286. *See also* Virgin Gorda

Sparrow, Jack, 308

Spotswood, Governor Alexander, 32-3, 45

Sproul, Andrew, 119

Spyglass Hill, 186-9, 195, 203

St. Andrews, Scotland, 47

St. Anne's, Sandy Point, St. Kitts, 291

391

St. Augustine, Florida, 41, 333

St. Barbara, 19, 307-8, saves the *Nuestra Señora de Guadalupe*, xii, 18, 24, 211, 264, 278, 328

St. Bartholomew's, 2, 61, 337

St. Christopher's, *see* St. Kitts

St. Christopher's Gazette, 224

St. Christopher's Heritage Society, xi, 243, 260

St. Croix, U.S. Virgin Islands, Owen Lloyd at, 71, 77, 80, 149, 197-8, 202, 282, died at, 277, 282-4, 306; treasure buried at, 128, 199, 285, 287, 360; mentioned, xi, 64, 84, 113-4, 118, 120-1, 134-5, 148, 224, 246, 257, 259, 285 -6, 288, 309

St. Eustatius, Owen Lloyd at, 75-6, 78, 105, 113, 116-7, 141, 196, 223, 242, 244, 248, 257, 341, 342, 357-8, sentenced to death at, 90-91, 106, 115, 253, escapes from, 106-8, 123, 126, 144, 162, 198, 240-1, 244, 285, 357; pictures of, 273-5; treasure at, 112, 142-3, 148, 152, 196-8; plans of fort at, 247, 259; view of, 269, 272; mentioned, 7, 71, 74, 76, 80, 84-5, 88, 114, 118, 128, 131, 134, 148, 195, 224, 246-7, 259, 260, 270, 303, 326, 331, 334, 337, 340, 345, 350, 354, 357-8

St. Francis, 21, 24, 160

St. George's Church, Basseterre, St. Kitts, Alan Stevenson buried at, 269, 291; 336

St. James Evening Post, 323

St. John(s), U.S. Virgin Islands, 64-5, 71, 79, 87,128, 167, 169, 178, 194-6, 200, 246, 342

St. John's Cabosterre, St. Kitts, 272, 289, 291; 323, 366-7

St. John's Episcopal Church, Hampton, Virginia, 252, 266

St. John's, Antigua, 76, 81, 126, 279; courthouse at, 82, 276, 279, 347

St. John's Parish, Pasquotank County North Carolina, 366

St. Kitts (also known as St. Christopher's), Alan and Hugh Stevenson at, 221-2, 224-6, 288-9, 291; archives of, 240-1, 251, 261, 279, 290-1, 305-6, 323-5, 339, 341, 345, 360, 364; assembly and council of, 191, 223; Christian Lloyd buried at St. Kitts, 290-1, 367, returns to, 8-9, 109, 251, 290-1, 326; courthouse at, 81, 240, 262; Gilbert Fleming at, 76, 81-3, 113, 121, 127, 270, 285-6, 341-2, 346; governors of, 76, 82, 225, 270, 285, 345; John Lloyd at, 6-7, 325; John Watson goes to, 124-8, 134-6, 257, 349, 351; map of, 242; Owen Lloyd brings treasure to, 61, 70-1, 74-5, 80, 126, 142, 198, 223, 340-1, leaves, 76-7, trades with, 1-4, 246, 249-50, 334, plans to return to, 9, 29-30, 38, 46, 63, 105, 195, 280, 331, remembered at, 298; pictures of, 269-72, engraving of, 110; Scottish merchants at, 221-6, 361-3; tavern at, 126, 349; mentioned, xi, 1-4, 46, 63, 69, 74-6, 80-1, 86, 106-8, 112-4, 116, 130, 144, 149, 191, 197, 203, 223, 227, 233, 240, 242, 244, 252, 254, 259, 262, 280-1, 285, 288-9, 305, 309, 348, 351, 354, 357, 361, 366

St. Martin's, 2, 260

St. Ursula, 169

Stallings, John, 124, 349

Stamp Act, 330

Stapells, Victoria, xi, 244, 253, 300

Stapleton, William, Governor of Leeward Islands, 109, 345

Statens Arkiver Rigsarkavit, 255-6, 261, 302

Statuary Hall, Washington, DC, 212-3

Stephens, Thomas, 70, 86, 197, 338-9

Stevenson, Alan, death of at St. Kitts, 203, 269, 291; 214-5, 223, 225-6, 288-9, 363

Stevenson, Elizabeth, 222

Stevenson, Fanny, biographies of, 296; in California, 208, 212-13, 235-8; in Indiana, 235, 238; in Nevada,

Index

234-6; in Paris, 206-8, 233; death of at Santa Barbara, 308; and John Lloyd, 233- 239, 288, 291, 295-6, 307, 364; marries Robert Louis Stevenson, 214, 220; mentioned, 209-10, 239, 245, 295-6, 307-8

Stevenson, Hugh, 214-5, 223, 225-6, 288-9, 363

Stevenson, Jean (Lilly), 224, 226

Stevenson, Margaret Balfour, 205-6, 209

Stevenson, Robert, 224, 226, 363

Stevenson, Robert Alan Mowbry

Stevenson, Robert Louis, goes to California, 209, 238, at Carmel, 210, in Monterey, 209-10, 239, 296, 364, at San Francisco, 213, 239, 304, 364; in Paris, 206-7; in Scotland, 205-6, 214, 305; death of 230, 307; family of, 221-2, 291, 298 and *A Family of Engineers,* 224; inspired by Father Junípero Serra, 210-12; meets Fanny Osbourne, 207; goes to London, 208; gets married, 214, 236; and the *Monterey Californian,* 210, 212, 240; and *My First Book,* 205, 215, 219-20, 227; picture of, 204; stepdaughter of, *see* Isobel Osbourne; stepson of, *see* Samuel Lloyd Osbourne; writes *Treasure Island,* 214-221, 226-30, and *Treasure Island,* 33, 169-70, 190, 192, 194, 233; mentioned, xi-xii, xv, 288, 361-4

Stevenson, Thomas, 205, 209, 213-4, 226; influences *Treasure Island,* 219-21, 226, 362

Strang, Dianne, xi, 293-4, 296, 301

Stratfield, Connecticut, 357

Strong, Joe, 209

Suckling, George, 225, 363

Suffolk, Massachusetts, 358

Suffolk, (Nansemond) Virginia, 117, 119, 122-4, 129-31, 134-5, 137, 140, 348, 350, 363; Nuestra Señora de Guadalupe at, 135-7, 266, 351; inn at, 256

Suhm, Christian, Governor of St. Thomas, daughter of, 288; death of, 158, 356; gives protection to Owen Lloyd, 121, 128, 133-4, 144, 150, 198, 257, 282, 286; marriage of, 256; seizes *Seaflower,* 77, 114, auctions *Seaflower,* 118, 143, 148-9, 153, 255, 347; witnesses marriage of Christian Lloyd, 284; mentioned, 70-1, 77, 87, 112, 115-122, 128, 131-5, 143, 146, 257, 277, 285, 339-42, 346-8, 350-1, 354-5

Sweeney, Roscoe, 367

Sweny, Merritt, 326

Swem's Index, 365

Sword, Captain James, 125, 349

Sybil, HMS, 193-4, 360

Sykesvilledesign.com, xii

Tales of a Traveler, 228

Tavistock, HMS, 81, 346

Teach's Hole, 33, 39, 45, 124, 268, 334

Thames, River, 139, 293, 331

Thornton, William, 360. *See also* the vessel, *William Thornton*

Tobias Knight, 32

Todd, Robert, 336

Topsail Inlet, Blackbeard at, 32. *See also* Cape Lookout

Tortola, British Virgin Islands, xii, 64, 67, 69, 71, 74, 82, 83, 111, 116, 127, 134-5, 142, 169, 171-2, 182, 186-7, 192, 194, 198-202, 225, 279, 337-42; treasure recovered from residents of, 70, 72, 79, 81, 112-3, 116, 127, 135-6, 141, 144, 198, 223, 257; council meetings at, 73, 85-7, 181, 226, 233

Toulon, Battle of, 216, 294

Tower of London, 139
Town Ditch, Hampton, Virginia, 326, 365
Townsend's Creek, 295, 324
Townsend, Captain, 16
Treasure Island, 169-70, 174-5, 177, 178, 182-3, 185, 187, 188, 190-2, 194-5, 205, 211, 233, 245, 278, 294, 296, 305, 307; the genesis of, 214-221, 226-30; inspiration for, 215, 232 , 298, 307-8; the movie, 308
Treasure Island, *see* Norman Island
Treasure Point, Norman Island, 171; caves at, 174, 177, 186, 191
Treasure Point, North Carolina, 259
Treasure Seekers, 228
Trelawney, Squire, 229, 292
Trelawny, Edward, 229, 363
Trippel, Corporal Adolf, 107
Triton, HMS, at Norfolk, Virginia, 50, 326, 329, 335; escorts *Nuestra Señora de Guadalupe* back to Spain, 150-1, 266, 355
Trompeuse, 345
True Blue, sloop, 73, 340
True Patriot, sloop, 123, 348
Tryall, sloop, 338
Tucker, Anthony, 330
Tucker, Captain Benjamin, 29-30
Turkey Buzzard Ridge, North Carolina, 359, 366
Turtle Beach Bar, 244
Union Army, 235
Vailima, 307
Valdes, Don Francisco de Varas y, 40, 352
Valenciano, Carlos, 14
Van de Grift, Fanny, *see* Fanny Stevenson
Van de Grift, (Sanchez) Nellie, 209-10, 307
Van den Bergh, Victor, xi, 247
Vargas, Joseph Perez de, 162
Vega, Francisco Cagigal de la, governor of Havana, 6, 22, 329
Venice, 352
Veracruz, (Vera Cruz), Father Junípero Serra at,18-19; governor of, 19-21; hospitals at, 19; pictures of, 263-4; Juan Manuel Bonilla at, 11-14, 18-21, 155-6, 197; plan of, 10; treasure shipments from, 12, 17, 20, 22, 157, 159; mentioned, 14-16, 18, 23-4, 43, 147, 150, 152, 154, 159, 162, 309. *See also* San Juan Ulúa
Viceroy of Mexico, 156, 223, 355
Villasota, Francisco, 327-8
Virgin Gorda, *see also* Spanish Town, 64, 72, 134, 169, 192, 194, 195, 198, 200
Virgin Islands chart of, 170; mentioned, 64, 83, 112, 120, 127, 149, 167, 169, 171-2, 191-2, 196, 198, 201, 203, 225, 240, 270, 277, 285-6, 337-8, 346, 360-1. *See also* St. Thomas, St. John, St. Croix, Tortola, Anegada, Norman Island, Peter Island, Salt Island, Jost Van Dyke, Virgin Gorda, Spanish Town
Virgin Mary, 24
Virginia Almanac, 348

Index

Virginia Capes, 6, 7, 25, 28-9, 254, 325
Virginia City, Nevada, 235-6, 364
Virginia Gazette, 119, 128, 150, 246, 249, 254
Wade, Anna, 44
Wade, Barney, 44
Wade, Joseph, 59, 72, 87, 334
Wade, Mercy (Norton), 43, 56, 72, 87-8, 105; marries Zebulon Wade, 334
Wade, Ruth, 59, 72, 87
Wade, Zeb, (Jr.), 44
Wade, Zebulon, at Boston, 43-4, 334; at Norman Island, 68-70; at Ocracoke, 45-6, 51-2, 54-8, 268; at Scituate, Massachusetts, 43-4, 136, 162; at St. Eustatius, 76, 78-80, 105-8, 116, 274-5, interrogation of, 78-9; at St. Kitts, 74-5; at St. Thomas,70; blamed for theft, 132, 136; on way to West Indies, 61-63, 65; sentenced to death, 90-1, escapes, 108; death of, 162; part owner of *Seaflower,* 44, 334; mentioned, 142, 197, 200, 247, 255, 257, 262, 285, 334, 337, 342, 357-9
Walker, Commodore George, 15, 139, 328, 355
Walker, Silas, 51
Wall, Ricardo, Spain's Ambassador to England, 115, 127, 140-1, 144-5, 161, 332, 335, 347, 349, 352, 353, 356-7
Waller, Benjamin, 120, 348, 350
Waller, William, 51, 96-7, 130, 336, 343, 359
Wallis, Thomas, 69, 72, 198, 202, 338-9
Walrus, ship, 169, 220, 228, 362
Walt Disney Studios, 308
Ware, George, 29, 331
Warner, Ashton, 127
Washington, DC, 212, 282
Wassenaar, Mr. van, 144
Wats, Jan, 71
Watson & Cairnes, 118-9, 123, 129, 131, 343. *See also* John Watson and Alexander Cairnes
Watson, John, at Antigua, 126, 130, 136, 349-50; at Hampton, 124, 137, 330; at St. Croix, 135; at St. Eustatius,131, 142, 144, 148, 350; at St. Kitts,125-8, 130, 136, 349, demands treasure held by Charles Caines, 126; at St. Thomas, 131-4, 144, 255, 350; at Suffolk, 117, 157; at Tortola, 127, 135, 144, 198; at Williamsburg, Virginia, 120, 136, 348; collects treasure, 128, 130, 144, 282, 340, 351, 353; expense account of, 124, 126, 135, 349; hired by Bonilla, 117, 347; in London,137, 139-40, 144-6, 353; power of attorney from Bonilla, 120, 125, 127, 133, 146, 261-2, 279, 341; mentioned, 119, 123, 130-1, 150, 152, 159, 161, 257, 348, 352, 354, 360, 363. *See also,* Watson & Cairnes
Wattling Street, London, 122
West India and Guinea Company, 160, 354, 365
West India Company, 70, 119, 146, 148-9, 153, 60, 290, 339, 347, 352, 355; replaced by Chamber of Revenue, 160
West India Monthly Packet of Intelligence, 324-5
West Indies, 5, 7-8, 25, 29-30, 37, 51, 64, 70, 75, 96 , 120, 124, 129-30, 195, 221-3, 225, 257, 333, 337, 358, 366
Westerman, Jacob, 13

Westminster, England, 152
Wheeler, Janet, 256, 330, 350
Wheeler, Robert, 350
White Oak, sloop, 334
White, Andrea, xii
White, Ann, 326, 365
White, Captain, 350
White, Charles, 252, 326, 365
White, John, 326
White, Mrs., 85-6
Whitehaven, England, 249
Whitwell, Captain Matthew, 150-1
Wickham, George, 197
Wildhagens, Sheriff Ditlev Wilhem, of St. Thomas, 71, 339
Wilkins, Harold T., 191, 360
William and Mary Quarterly, 254, 324, 348, 351
William Thornton, vessel and bar, 171, 176
Williams, Dora, 239, 307, 364, 367
Williams, Lindon, xi, 243, 260, 306
Williams, Virgil, 238-9, 364
Williamsburg, Virginia, 28, 47, 119-20, 137, 249, 254, 289, 335, 348, 350, 367
Willie T., see vessel *William Thornton*
Wilmington, North Carolina, 47, 101, 145, 344
Wilson, Judge Richard, 81, 126
Windward Islands, 63, 353
Winstanley, Gill, xi
Woodbridge, New Jersey, 50, 96-7, 359
Woolwich, HMS, 3, 324
Wright, Thomas, 23, 36-7, 43, 49, 51, 56, 95, 329, 334, 337, 343
Wynne, Beth, xii
Wynne, Ken, xii
Wyscarver, Marylyn, xi
York, ship, *see Peregrina*
Young Folks, 219
Young, Dr. Thomas, 74
Young, Major James, 73, 111, 114, 121. *See also* James Young, Tortola
Zegers, Absolom, 197
Zorg & Rust, ship, 152, 355